THE 'END TO END' STORY

A CENTURY OF CYCLE RECORD BREAKING

JOHN TA

FIRST PUBLISHED 2005

WRITTEN AS A TRIBUTE TO THE BRAVE HEROIC RIDERS WHO HAVE EMBARKED UPON THIS PUNISHING JOURNEY FROM LANDS END TO JOHN O' GROATS ON A CYCLE, HOPING TO GET THERE IN RECORD TIME. ALL RECORDS ARE TIMED, OBSERVED AND AUTHENTICATED BY OFFICIALS OF THE ROAD RECORDS ASSOCIATION.

Published in the United Kingdom by
BtownBikes Ltd.
Unit 7, Lakeside Plaza
Bridgtown, Cannock, WS11 OXE
Tel: 01922 411180
www.btownbikes.com

A catalogue record for this book is available from
The British Library
ISBN 978-0-9562023-0-7

The author would like to say a special thank you to Robert Garbutt, Editor of the 'Cycling Weekly' for permission to use material from that source

DESIGNED AND PRINTED IN THE UNITED KINGDOM
BY
ADM IMAGING LTD
59-61 SUMMER LANE, BIRMINGHAM B19 3TH

CONTENTS

LIST OF ILLUSTRATIONS

The illustrations fall between pages 64-65 and pages 192-193

My thanks go to the following for allowing me the use of their photo's - Syd Parker, Les Brown, John Arnold, Harry Wilson, John Dalton, Phil O'Connor, Harold Harvey, Alasdair Washington, Bernard Thompson,'Cycling'.

SECTION ONE

INTRODUCTION

My book is dedicated to all of the riders who have been brave enough to start from one end of the country, hoping to reach the other end in record time.

Whether man or woman, whether on bicycle, tricycle, tandem or tandem tricycle, all but two of the rides were performed under the rules of the Road Records Association, so there is absolutely no doubt as to their authenticity.

Some of the riders have continued for the 1000 miles record at the end of a very long journey. Some have tackled the 1000 miles as a totally separate journey, on courses comprising of the counties of the 'Midlands' and the counties surrounding it. From Norwich and the Fens, to Bridgwater, to South Wales and as far north as Preston and Newcastle upon Tyne.

Not much has been written about records broken on tricycles, tandems and tandem tricycles so I hope to redress the situation. None of these records would be possible without the unselfishness of the teams of helpers and of course the RRA officials, so I have tried to profile not only the riders, but also some of the people surrounding the riders on these epic journeys.

I can only hope my book does them justice, and that I've not missed too many people out who have played a part in this unusual history. I'm thankful for the kind help I've received from some of the participants of these great records, who have delved back in time to remember interesting details from their journeys, and to members of the support teams and officials who have also helped me colour the picture. .

I've tried to be as accurate as possible about starting dates and times and interim mileages and times. I've tried to include comparisons of riders performances at certain landmarks but found quite conflicting reports from different sources of information.

If when you read the accounts of riders performances and towards the end of the ride, wonder how they can go from being 2.5 hours down on schedule in the Grampians, to breaking the record by over an hour or more, you must realise it was probably an ambitious and unrealistic schedule the rider was trying to keep to. Perhaps the schedule was made to have a slow last 120 miles for the severity of the hills and the tiredness of the rider. If the rider suddenly picked up a tailwind at Inverness as day was breaking and started to feel good and tackled the final miles at a higher speed than expected, then that is how these anomalies occur.

I must thank my wife Liz for typing out hundreds of pages and for putting up with me locking myself away from all distractions to create my 'labour of love', and to Lynne, my daughter, along with all the other End to End and 1000 milers for breaking the records. Sadly, quite a lot of the riders, officials and helpers have passed away, so I hope my book will save their 'epic deeds' from passing into obscurity.

I echo **Alan J Ray's** comments at the 'Introduction' in his book **"Cycling: Lands End to John O'Groats"** printed in 1971. **"There will be some who think it foolish for men and women to ride so rapidly over so great a distance. They will consider the lack of sleep, the hills,**

the cold and very possibly the wet, and they will point out that there are easier ways of getting there. I suppose it is foolish for the Masai warriors to hunt lions with spears, and certainly alternative methods offering greater ease and safety are to be found. But one cannot fail to see in both of these 'foolish' activities, a certain magnificence" It is with his words in mind that my story is written.

Alan in his book mentions riding his 'BSA' sports bike, a similar model to Opperman's, and confessed to a bit of hero-worship when he was a teenager. I too rode a 'BSA' Tour of Britain and followed Bob Maitland's exploits, mainly Continental ones, also those of Stan Jones 'Tiny-Thomas', and Arthur Ilsley, his team mates.

My first End to End hero was Dick Poole in 1965. I rode out to Bridgnorth to see him go round the last roundabout, and on into the dark night with drizzle falling. He had that fixed, stone-faced expression as he glided through, already down on schedule.

I rode home, some 30 miles creeping into the house at an unearthly hour. On waking for work next morning my first thought was 'I wonder if he's still going ?' Although I had ridden a few 24 hr time trials by that time and had seen Dick ride the same events with the Middlesex RC team, I still found it hard to grasp he had done his first 24 hours and was now continuing on for his second 24 hrs, going into his second night, riding on his own with no other riders to catch or talk to, and when I'd had a second nights sleep he would still be riding. It made me feel weary and inadequate just thinking about it.

Little did I know at the time just how big a part in my life "End to End" records would play.

When you try to explain to an 'outsider' to the sport what it means to ride a 24 hr race or an End to End record which takes two days, one sees looks of disbelief on their faces, usually followed by the question 'where do you stop to sleep ?' and when you answer 'there is no time to sleep as the men's record now stands at 1 day 20 hours, and the ladies at 2 days 4 hrs, they are even more unsure of what you are telling them. The usual reply is 'my uncle used to ride to Rhyl and back most Sundays when he was younger'. So you see, it is hard to believe !

Every long distance ride or record attempt can have its high, or more often its low, points, but an attempt on the Lands End to John o Groats on any form of cycle, whether it be solo bicycle, solo tricycle, tandem or tandem tricycle, there will no doubt be soul searching moments - not only for the riders, but also the helpers who are themselves tired, and trying to encourage their riders to push to their limits and beyond, with also some carrying on for the 1000 miles, nowadays an extra 160 miles is required plus 10 miles for safety margin. There are bound to be lots of drama's unfold.

Having read a lot of mountaineering books where the ultimate pursuit is the 'dash for the summit'. I liken this to the record breaker setting out to break a cycle record, telling their body and brain that its going to have the longest and hardest battering its ever had, and that they mustn't let anyone down. 'Its now or never' they must take that chance, even if it is a slim one! There have been some superb epic rides done that only those people closely connected to the riders know about. Having tried and failed to break the record myself on three occasions, I feel I'm well qualified to describe the scene's, having helped or officiated on Pat Kenny's trike End to End, Mick Coupe's bike etc, and my own daughter Lynne's mixed tandem with Andy Wilkinson (Wilko) and her two solo records in three consecutive years. I've studied the road records association RRA handbooks since the 1960's looking to see who held what records at what time.

My historical accounts start in 1929 after the RRA banned the use of ferries in Scotland in 1925 and set new standards. My predecessor Alan J Ray asks in his book in 1971 - 'What will become of records like the End to End and 1000 and indeed any RRA records with the demise of the pedal cycle as a form of transport'. Okay, so not many people are doing vast mileages any more, except in audaxes and 24 hrs, but there have been an encouraging number of rides on various machines since Dick Poole's in 1965; fifteen in fact, four solo ladies, five solo gents, one all male tandem, two mixed tandems and three male trikes; four of these records since the millenium year 2000. Paul Carbutt's solo victory in 1979 being the only true professional promotion for Viking Cycles, though I doubt whether hundreds went out and purchased 'Vikings' purely for that reason. John Woodburn's record was for a sponsored club and although he had his attempt sponsored and paid for, he was an amateur.

In the 30's, 40's and 50's there were a hard core of riders mainly ex time triallists who became professionals for such bicycle companies as 'Hercules', 'Raleigh' 'Sturmey-Archer' and 'BSA'. Names such as Lillian Dredge, Marguerite Wilson, and perhaps the greatest of them all, amassing no less than 28 road records, Eileen Sheridan, riding for Hercules. Jack Rossiter, Frank Southall, Sid Ferris, Cyril Hepplestone, Harry 'shake' Earnshaw, Bert James, Charlie Holland, Ken Joy, Bob Maitland, not forgetting the Australians, Ernie Milliken, 'Hefty' Stuart and Hubert Opperman.

In the mid 1930's and again in the mid 1950's cycle companies used the talents of these magnificent cyclists to break records to coincide with model launches and to tie in with cycle shows such as the Earls' Court show. Whereas in Alan Ray's day there were probably at any one time or any one year, five 24 hour riders who were capable of End to Ends, there is now probably only one every five years who has the pedigree and speed to tackle the daunting task and even less in the case of the women's title. There is now only one 24 hr race a year, the Mersey Roads, in which to test oneself . Time trialling is having to fight for its space on the road, such is the political strategy to get every man, woman and child into early obesity by eating rubbish convenience foods, sitting in a car, blocking the towns and cities and roads of our beloved country. Exercise, sport or competitiveness is now viewed as being politically incorrect in schools. The cycle is still seen as a poor mans transport, even if it has cost upwards of £ 1000, such is the stigma.

The nice thing about virtually all the End to Enders and 1000 Milers is that they are club cyclists. Even the professionals came up through club life and even when under contract to break a record, they were usually involved with a club, either socially or for training groups, or for help on their records.

Going back to the 50's, 60's, and 70's and before that , if you were a professional in any sport you weren't allowed to ride in amateur time trials unless it was an invitation event. The one unique thing about the RRA is that it has never differentiated between amateurs and professionals for the men's records, and I think the likes of Rossiter, Ferris, Opperman and Carbutt could have, and probably would have, broken the records without the lure of money at the end. I know of one professional rider from the Midlands who got double his money in the 1950's, which was £1 a mile in those days by breaking the Lands End to London in 1952, and after losing it to Ken Joy in 1953, he regained it in 1954, so earning enough money to buy a house virtually outright. But this same rider twenty years later could be seen riding a local 12 hr race and winning £10 for a veteran prize. So you see, at heart, he is just a dead keen cyclist who loves being out on his bike every day and is still riding to this day at 80 years of age. All but one of the male End to End riders on any machine since 1937 have been amateur status and half of the women riders have been amateur. Some have had help from a sponsor for petrol or vehicles or hotel bills; some have had equipment paid for. Quite a lot of well wishers and helpers have donated contributions and help, being almost as dedicated as the rider themselves to get the record. Club folks who have been out to see the rider through, and then have kept a constant vigil ringing HQ as to the riders progress, and not sleeping properly for thinking about them.

I was introduced to 24 hr riding and helping in 1960, and helped on my first record attempt in 1964. It being the successful Swinden and Withers tandem 1000 miles in 2 days 18 hrs 09 mins, having witnessed an heroic struggle by the riders to carry on into the third day after John Withers, a clubmate of mine, got terribly saddle sore due to a rain soaked leather saddle collapsing out of shape at about 36 hours. He was in a terrible state and having to have surgical spirit applied to the sore areas, which after two days of riding were open wounds. I witnessed heroism on a grand scale that day by both riders, as Pete Swinden had to find even more effort to secure the record. John wasn't to ride properly for nearly six months after this record.

By this time I was 21 years old and had already ridden a few 12 hr and 24 hr races, but luckily had never suffered badly in any of them. The only pain I'd experienced was stomach ache, leg cramp, and aching muscles, just general discomforts really. When Pete and John broke the tandem End to End I was working on a nightshift, unable to help them in any way, and sad that I had missed an epic piece of history with them putting up the biggest 24 hr mileage ever done on the End to End route at that time, and also getting within two hours of Dick Poole's time.

My next actual involvement on an End to End apart from three attempts with Pat Kenny on tandem trike, was in helping out on Pats North to South trike attempt which was abandoned in the Highlands, and then driving the following car on his successful south to north attempt in 1980. Pat had desperately wanted to break the End to End. He held various other records on the trike but felt that there was only a certain period of years in a man's life where the End to End is possible to get, and he was finding it difficult and frustrating to keep his level of fitness, speed, and enthusiasm going till he got a lucky break with good conditions. So with Pat's success, that is two End to End records for the Birmingham St Christophers CCC.
My next involvement was to be as Observer on Mick Coupe's record in 1982. Pat Kenny was timekeeper and I was in the feeding vehicle.

It made quite a change for me to just take notes of times of passing the rider, and making sure it was all done properly, although Mick's helpers did let me stretch my legs and help fetch the sponges or empty bottles, especially if Mick had carried them a long way or had thrown them into thick undergrowth.

It was worth all the sleepless effort to see Mick get beyond the border for the 24 hrs and get the record. I've got to admit to having a lump in my throat when I realised just how far he had got, and that I'd just seen history being made. Even though the records would only stand for a few weeks, until John Woodburn updated them.

Apart from seeing one or two unsuccessful attempts going through Gailey it would be another 18 years on before I got involved with an End to end again. The year 2000 started off a frenzy of End to End activity and I was directly involved with three out of four records. The first one in 2000 was the mixed tandem Lynne Taylor and Andy Wilkinson, taking the Groesbeck - Harris record. The second was in 2001, Lynne's solo bike in atrocious weather, taking Pauline Strong's record, and the third was in 2002, Lynne took her own End to End record down to 2 days 4 hrs 45 mins and also knocked over 9 hours off Eileen Sheridan's 1000 mile record put up nearly 50 years previously.

One everlasting memory of these rides is being at John o Groats in 2001 after Lynne had just broken the ladies record the previous day, and then seeing Gethin Butler finish his amazing ride and then to continue for the 1000. At that time there were four End to Enders present; Lynne, Andy Wilkinson, who had supported Lynne, Gethin, and John Arnold, who had also been on the team helping Lynne.

So nearly 40 years of involvement with this legendary journey. I even remember my sisters who are a tad older than me, talking about Eileen Sheridan's exploits. I must only have been about 10 or 11 at the time. My sisters Barbara and Margaret both rode dropped handlebar 'BSA's. In those days, bikes were one of the main forms of transport for anyone in the region. I lived near to large factories, the largest being 'Lucas Batteries and Lighting', and if you were unfortunate enough to be walking past the gates at dinnertime or home time you had to wait, as an 'army' of workers amassed and rode out of the gates on their bikes, possibly 200 or more, was no exaggeration. With just one or two cars at the back, probably the bosses ! How things have changed for the worse since then.

Having no television, the only three forms of media were newspapers, which to me were pretty boring, radio or cinema to where I went almost weekly. It was on the 'Pathe News' I remember seeing Roger Bannister, the first man under 4 minutes for the mile, and Eileen Sheridan dashing about on her bike and being interviewed in front of the camera. She always made it sound so much fun 'breaking records on a bike' and to this day at 80 years of age she's still as enthusiastic for the sport as ever.

The words at the end of **Alan Ray's** book in 1971 conclude **"I should have loved to have seen Beryl Burton in action against this stupendous challenge, but perhaps such a thought is unreasonable when one tots up the score of the vast achievements we have seen from her already".**

"But someone will come"

SECTION TWO

A BRIEF HISTORY OF THE END TO END AND 1000 MILES UP UNTIL 1929

The 1000 miles bicycle record was placed on the Road Records Associations books in 1897. Up until that time the longest road record was from Lands End to John o Groats, approximately 870 miles, using ferries in Scotland where there were no roads.

James Lennox was the first man to officially cover the End to End route in **1885** on an **'Ordinary Bicycle' (Penny Farthing)** in **6 days 16 hours 7 mins.** The following year **George Pilkington Mills - G.P.Mills** reduced the time by over 1 day 14 hrs to **5 days 1 hr 45 mins.** They were allowed to have followers, helpers and 'pacers' in those days, all on cycles. **G.P. Mills** went on to break the End to End record on six occasions on solo bicycle, tricycle and tandem. His last record over this journey being **1895** on a **tandem** with **T.A. Edge** in **3 days 4 hrs 46 mins.** Another three riders on **solo bicycle, T.A. Edge, L. Fletcher, and Robert H. Carlisle** all reduced the time using 'pacers' before **G.P. Mills** finally reduced the bicycle record to **3 days 5 hrs 49 mins** in **1894.**

T.R. Marriot in **1885** set figures for the **tricycle** of **6 days 15 hrs 22 mins** only for **G.P. Mills** to break them with **5 days 10 hrs** in **1886** and then finally break his own trike record in **1893** with **3 days 16 hrs 47 mins.**

What one must keep in perspective is the state of the road's or 'unmettled' cart tracks of the day. Don't forget the roads were now being neglected, as a lot of long distance travel was taken on by the 'Railways', having received 60 years of investment and growth into it. It is recalled in Alan Rays book that G.P. Mills struck trouble between Carrbridge and Inverness; the track for a branch line of the Highland Railway having been laid on top of the former road, thus making it necessary to follow cartwheel ruts through the heather on his tricycle taking four hours to cover one section of only twenty miles.

G.P. Mills had reduced his own trike record to **3 days 16 hours 47 mins** beating **Fletcher's** bicycle figures and all this with a gammy poisoned foot. Not bad for an invalid on a tricycle in **1893.**

In 1896 interest in record breaking was at its lowest ebb owing to police intervention. Only four records were passed. 1897 saw the introduction of the 1000 miles and Edinburgh to York records added to the list, also the recognition of **unpaced** records was decided upon as a separate category. Seventeen records were passed.

The first unpaced Lands End to John o Groats record was put up in **1903** by **C.J. Mather with 5 days 5 hrs 12 mins,** followed in **1904 by F.W. Wesley with 4 days 7 hrs 25 mins** and then **G.A. Olley in 1905** reduced it further **with 3 days 20 hrs 15 mins.**

GEORGE OLLEY - 3 DAYS 20 HRS 15 MINS - JULY 18 1905
SOLO BICYCLE END TO END

George Olley had a special bicycle made for his attempt by the New Hudson Cycle Company, but at the last minute felt that it was a bit too heavy and started on his lighter bike that he'd broken the Liverpool to Edinburgh record on. He also had his wrists bandaged and strapped just before the start at 8.00 am on the Tuesday, so as to strengthen them for his exploits, and should he fall off, the damage would be limited.

At Penzance the road surface was very rough but by Redruth in bright sunshine he was five minutes ahead of schedule. George Olley had a basket on his handlebars with tins fitted inside forming little separate divisions, one for sandwiches, one for rice pudding, and another for a bottle of either milk or soda water. He was riding to quite an ambitious schedule but reached Okehampton, Exeter, Taunton and Bristol all virtually on time, give or take a few minutes.

One small incident was mentioned when he encountered a large herd of Herefordshire cattle on a narrow bridge, and by some extraordinary good luck he managed to weave his way through the beasts, still astride his cycle, and not lose any time. He jokingly put this down to the fact that he was a vegetarian and for that the cows respected him, whereas his helpers following at a distance had to dismount and they were all meat eaters, being particularly fond of steaks and roast beef !

Later in the Exeter area he stopped for a meal at a 'rustic-ordinary', a simple type of hostelry on the roadside. I suppose it was a forerunner of today's transport café. When the Ostler took charge of the bicycles on their arrival, he remarked 'I suppose you want something to eat on a job like that'. "Yes" replied one of the helpers "six good square meals a day, besides a snack out of the basket occasionally" This evidently impressed the Ostler considerably, and while the party were at table, a procession from the different bars trooped past the dining room door and looked in admiration at the man who could eat that many full meals a day. He was even more admired by the commercial travelling representatives at the same table, who themselves were hearty eaters.

At Bristol a stop was called for at a famous masseur. He rubbed some life back into Olley's tired legs who was trying to ride for the first 36 hrs without sleep, but at 2 am Wednesday, Olley was feeling very drowsy. About this same time he picked up a front wheel puncture and he rested on the grass bank while his helpers tried to mend it. Just then one of the helpers turned up on his original 'New Hudson' John o Groats model onto which he clambered, and was away again.

He reached Gloucester just after 3 am Wednesday. After a bath, a rub down and a change of clothes, he resumed his journey as dawn was breaking. Gloucester, Worcester, Kidderminster, Tarporley, Warrington were all reached throughout the daylight of Wednesday, although he did take a 15 minute unofficial sleep. Against the wishes of his helpers, he lay down and slept amongst some horses in a field, and although some of the animals examined the sleeping rider curiously, they didn't disturb him.

He arrived at Kendal after 442 miles at 8.30 pm, for his first official sleep. He left fully refreshed at 2.50 am after being checked over by a local medical man who pronounced his condition as excellent and fit to continue. He proceeded through Carlisle, Gretna Green, Beattock, Abington, finally to arrive at the General Post Office at Edinburgh, some seven and a half hours ahead of the previous record holder, Dr F.W. Wesley, a G.P. from Nottingham, although Olley was only 10 mins inside his own very ambitious schedule.

On his way to Edinburgh, he had to take a short sleep on the roadside. After riding away from his helpers he'd built up a substantial lead on the road, when he came across a broken down car in the middle of the carriageway. The chauffeur was working under the bonnet and had spread his big thick coat down on the ground. When the rest of the helpers caught up they found Olley curled up asleep on the coat.

While waiting for the ferry steamer at Granton which crossed the Firth of Forth at 4.00 pm, he took a bath and put on clean clothes at the 'Ferry Hotel'. Once across the water the rider, followed by his helpers, resumed their ride through Perth, and onto the Grampians where a big storm struck them. It was a very dark mountainous road overhung by big pine trees. It was 11.30 pm by the time they made it to Blair Athol where everyone was dead beat. Just prior to Blair Athol, Olley had sprained the Achilles tendon in his heel which caused anxiety amongst his helpers. He took a light meal then was sponged, rubbed down and massaged while asleep. At 3 am he was awake and breakfasting to the sound of a kilted piper parading up and down playing wild music on an extra powerful set of bagpipes. By 3.45 am he was back in the saddle and pedalling strongly towards Inverness. It was a very rough journey over shocking roads.

He arrived at the Kessock Ferry crossing over the Beauly Firth just before midday. He was still 10 hours up on the record, but his ankle was troubling him. It was decided upon to engage a small sailing boat to make the crossing, so that with its shallow sides he could bathe his ankle in the water as they made the crossing. A gust of wind made the little craft keel over rather suddenly and threatened to upset the party, but she righted instantly and no harm came to anyone, while George Olley's ankle benefited greatly from this novel treatment.

After continuing the ride, a headwind sprung up and with it came 20 hours of continuous rain.. Hour after hour the rider struggled on, progress was extremely slow, the roads were now in a shocking state, his wheels were sinking deeply into the sand and loose stones, and the party of helpers were now becoming miserable. They took shelter in a roadside fisherman's cottage for an hour and tried to get dry, but within minutes of resuming their arduous task, they were soaked to the skin once again. Back on the road, they regularly had to stop and consult maps and route card and examine local landmarks to determine they were not lost. The one thing they were pleased about was the way George Olley's bike had performed over these treacherous surfaces.

The record breaker arrived at John o Groats at 4.15 am, so beating the previous record by 11 hours 10 mins, with a time of **3 days 20 hours and 15 minutes.**

I've used the episodes and articles written about G.A.Olley's End to End in 1905 and separate 1000 miles in 1907 because they are well documented and descriptive of what the rider had to expect and endure just after the turn of the century, when cars numbered just a few hundred as opposed to the millions of nowadays. In days when many folk never ventured far outside their village or town boundaries, let alone rode cycles from one end of the country to the other. So you will see that these men really were 'Pioneers'.

GEORGE OLLEY - 1000 MILES - SOLO BICYCLE - 1907

The first **1000 miles** attempt was in 1907 by **George A. Olley**. Starting at 4.00 pm he would soon be into darkness, there was no such thing as 'light pollution' in those days. The only lighting would be in big towns and then only for a mile or so provided by gas lamps lit by hand. He could only hope for a moon to light his way when his acetylene lamps ran out. It was done on roads mainly connected to the 'Great North Road' running from London to Scotland, now known as the 'A 1'. Starting at Hitchin, 34 miles from London, the farthest north he went on this route was Doncaster. This road was still in good condition being one of the old stagecoach routes from London.

Picture the scene, Hitchin High Street, the main London to York road, outside The Cock Hotel at the 34th milestone. A group of ten or more men are stood abreast on this quite wide road. All are either mounted on their straight handlebar roadsters of the day or stood leaning on their bikes. A stray dog stands in the road looking bemused at the spectacle. The men all wear a cap of some description, some are flat caps with a stiff peak that just perch on their heads, some are deep round caps with a raised button in the middle. F.T. Bidlake, the timekeeper, is also stood in the middle of the road. Its almost teatime, a few women are to be seen in Victorian costume, some have large flat bonnet type hats and dresses down to the ground with bustles at the back. We are still in the horse drawn age.

Why Bidlake sent him off at 2 minutes past four I don't know. Maybe it was something to do with local regional railway time compared to London time. Don't forget there wasn't a speaking clock on the telephone, or indeed telephone in those days, or BBC radio time signals or even radio. How wonderful ! How peaceful.

5,4,3,2,1 - Go - 'He's off' on a 1000 miles trip that would take him to Biggleswade, Girtford, Bedford, Stony Stratford, St Neots, Cambridge, Huntingdon, Alconbury, Peterborough, March, Wisbech, Kings Lynn, Spalding, Boston, Skegness, Sleaford, Grantham, Newark, Nottingham, Retford and finally Doncaster where he turned and retraced his journey.

The men who were with Olley at the start are his helpers who will follow him at an accepted distance . They carry his spare food, drink, tyres, clothes, and will go ahead at the direction of the timekeeper who is also following Olley on his bike, to arrange a meal, bath and bed at well known local inns. On his handlebars he has a small very useful basket attached where he keeps his food and drink. It's the month of March and its early evening with sleet showers lowering the temperature on this easterly sea board.

At Huntingdon with 75.5 miles covered he has gained 60 minutes on schedule and decides to take a break for food. Being a vegetarian he has toasted wheat flakes, bananas in custard, cheese and tomato paste sandwiches, ginger ale, milk, grapes and rice pudding. He fixes an acetylene lamp on his front fork bracket - it gives a brilliant light for the next two hours or so. At the 24 hr point he'd covered 280 miles.

Dotted about the course he had twelve or more cycles, all set with identical riding position. So was cycling at the turn of the century a 'Sport of Kings' ? Don't forget these men who were helping him, what sort of work did they do ? To be out on the road for a week in March; it wasn't even a bank holiday or annual holiday fortnight., and did they have such luxuries in those days for the masses ? It's a thought isn't it; in fact it isn't until the late thirties, forties and fifties, that bicycles could be afforded by the masses.

By the time 48 hours was up George Olley had completed 497 miles so averaging just over 10 mph so far. Whenever he stops for a drink of 'egg and milk' a crowd of local people amass to see him. They all spread out across the road. Old photos show the riders quite often riding in the middle of the road or even cornering on the wrong side which nowadays would bring certain death or injury. Of course the downside to this freedom from motorised traffic was the general state of the roads where heavy rain would wash the surface away or turn the surface into 6" of mud. The by products of horse drawn vehicles would also lie in mounds all waiting to mix with the mud and encase the poor cyclist with a thick coating of filth. So bad in fact that on certain record attempts, riders were turned away from hostelries for being too dirty.

Luckily, Olley only had the odd sleet, snow and drizzle to contend with on this journey which ended at 1.05 am Saturday, his **4 days 9 hrs 3 mins** had beaten the RRA standard by nearly nine hours. A truly magnificent performance in an age where it was thought that riding through 24 hours without sleep would knock 10 years off one's life. These were Victorian times of course, where most medical matters were looked upon with pessimism. G.P. Mills carried out twenty such rides.

Lieutenant-Colonel George Pilkington Mills, D.S.0. died in 1945 - he was 78 years old.

Tom Peck had just completed the End to End starting on June 24th 1907 and finishing after enduring over 700 miles of roads ravaged by rain. He suffered six hours of heavy rain in the Grampians, the roads had been turned into rivers of mud. At Golspie he had to have an ankle injury treated (which he sustained in Cornwall) for a bad swelling from the poisoning of the cut, filled with mud. Despite all this he'd taken some seven hours 22 minutes off Olley's 1905 record with **3 days 12 hrs 53 mins.**

W. Welsh took up cycling at 23 years of age and after riding for the New Hudson CC he joined the MC & AC - 'The Midlands Cycling and Athletic Club' based in the Birmingham area. It was Tom Pecks club and at the time had more aspiring record breakers than even the Anfield B.C. It was the same club that one, **Charles Moss** belonged to. He lived at Earlswood and was the Landlord of the 'Red Lion' Public House there, not far from Birmingham. The men he competed against at that time were **Peck, Olley, Monty Holbein, Welsh, Leon Meredith,** all respected road men or 'wheelers' at that time. Charles Moss won the Anfield 100 in 1910, 1911and 1912.

Charles Moss broke no less than 8 Midland Road Records between 1909 and 1922 ranging in distance and time from 50 miles to 12 hours. I think it was only finances that stopped him looking further afield at National road records where timekeepers and helpers fees would have to be afforded - also transport by train to and from locations was a costly business. I know he had to find his own expenses and passage when he rode in the Stockholm Olympics in 1912.

I worked with Charles Moss's grandson 'Inky' Moss as an apprenticed half-tone etcher, making printing plates on copper for the letterpress printing trade. Our direct boss and managing director at that time was one Charles Moss - the son of the MC and AC Charles Moss.

'Inky' Moss remembers hearing about his Grandad getting into trouble on his bike while training around the lanes with other members of the MC and AC and being stopped by the police for riding in a 'furious manner' and also for disturbing animals and incurring the wrath of pedestrians who were 'surprised' by the almost silence of a passing bicycle, compared to the horn and engine of a motor car and the hooves of a horse and the rattle of a cart. **Charles Moss** won the Bath Road Cup outright.

Inky is **Lynne Taylor's** uncle by marriage and my brother in law, and this is why he has taken such an interest in Lynne over the years. Christopher Moss, Inky's brother, with whom I also worked is an engraver, and remembers some years after his Grandad died, the family donated the Bath Road Cup to a local club to be used as an annual trophy. They have since lost contact with the club and the cup, so if anybody out there knows of its whereabouts, they, the family, would love to know its still in safe keeping and in annual use. It will have Charles Moss's performances for the 100 miles race inscribed upon it.

I digress, but felt it was so important to convey to you, the reader, how closely entwined our lives can be, so that this cycling history of ours isn't just facts and figures and names and times on paper. Its having links to the men and women who performed these deeds so many years ago, and to keeping that memory alive.

Back to the record breaking and history is made once again by **Welsh** in **1907** being the first man to break the End to End and retrace for the 1000 miles unpaced. **Welsh** made his start from Lands End at **6 am on Tuesday August 27th 1907.** He rode a 'New Hudson' bicycle with 3 speed 'Armstrong Triplex' gears and 'Le Paris' tyres. The weather was good, not much wind but a good temperature and dry. After a few breaks for food, Exeter was reached by 2.15 pm. Bristol at 14 hours put him well ahead of schedule, enough to stop for a bath and a change of clothes.

At Worcester, reached after midnight, he took a 40 minute stop for refreshments. He had a bad patch around the Hodnet area which slowed him down to arrive in Warrington with 349 miles done at 9.42 am. Although down on his schedule he was ahead of **Pecks** ride by an hour at this stage. He reached Kendal at 3.32 pm and took a bath and a meal there. He climbed Shap Fell using his 3 speed gear to good advantage. After a small break at Penrith he reached Carlisle at 7.17 pm on the second day.

After 500 miles was completed Welsh had another sleep at Moffat at the 'Allendale Arms'. He awoke refreshed to ride through to reach Edinburgh in just over 2 days at 7.05 am on Thursday. By 11.10 am he'd reached Perth some 600 miles, after being helped by a following wind these last few hours.

From Perth onwards the wind swung against him quite strongly. He had a short stop at Blair Atholl and at Kingussie a short 20 mins sleep refreshed him enough to get to Inverness. He cut his scheduled break there by over half the allotted time, stopping just 1.75 hours leaving at 2 am Friday. This put him exactly on schedule. By Tain at 750 miles he'd gained enough time to be up on Peck by 5 hours and felt that barring accidents or complete mechanical failure, that the record was almost his to take. Rather a rash presumption as at Helmsdale he took a nasty tumble. Luckily this didn't deter him and after another short break at Wick he reached his destination John o Groats in **3 days 8 hrs 4 mins** - 4 hrs 49 mins faster than **Tom Peck.** F.T. Bidlake timed him in at 2.04pm Friday August 30th but Welsh's efforts hadn't yet finished. There was the continuation for the 1000 miles with some 140 miles still to do.

After a nine hour sleep, Welsh rode out into the night, returning the way he had got there. F.T. Bidlake had gone back to Inverness by car to time him in. This last journey was completed in approximately 10 hours and the 'Midlander' was the new holder of both records. The **1000 miles** had taken a total of **4 days 7 hours 41 mins**, some 1 hr 22 mins faster than George Olley. The remaining miles for Welsh's 1000 had been ridden in atrocious weather, wind and rain over some of the hilliest roads in Scotland, as opposed to Olley's flat fenland course. Welsh had used only one bike and suffered no mechanical problems, not even a puncture. He had a medical check up at Inverness at the end of his ride and apart from slight swelling of the hands and wrists caused by road vibrations and a slight chaffing of the nether regions plus a small graze on his one knee, he was found to be, like his cycle, in perfect condition.

After an abortive attempt on the End to End by George Olley in 1907 which terminated at Wellington with severely cold weather and injuries sustained from a fall in Cornwall, both he and Peck decided to leave the assaults on this record until 1908 and what a dramatic year that was to be.

George Olley tried once more in 1908 to retain his 1000 miles record from **W. Welsh** but abandoned at 377 miles in the Fen district after hours of heavy rain had turned the roads into a quagmire. He was the first to break the End to End that year of 1908. He suffered his usual bad weather and after a few crashes due to having just a front brake with poor soft brake blocks, he completed the length of Great Britain in **3 days 5 hrs 20 mins,** but like his previous End to End record it wasn't to last long.

Harry Green nicknamed **'Goss'** - a new name in long distance records, made a fast start against George Olley's record which was only a few weeks old. By the time he'd covered 305 miles the wind had turned directly against him. Although he was the fastest rider ever to do this distance, he looked pale, drawn and very weary and retired soon after.

July 20th 1908 - Tom Peck himself attacked Olley's record and became the first man in history, like Dick Poole in more recent years breaking 2 days, Peck broke the 3 day barrier with **2 days 22 hrs 42 mins.** He had a hard ride to Bristol taking 13 hrs 49 mins and it wasn't until he crossed the borders into Scotland that conditions improved for him.

Harry 'Goss' Green left Lands end on his second attempt on **27th July 1908.** He took things slightly easier for his first 12 hrs or more, reaching Bristol in 13 hrs 32 mins. He'd suffered a fall and an upset stomach. He reached Preston and took a 90 minute break including a sleep and swapped onto a bike with oversized tyres fitted for the cobbles of Lancashire.

By Kendal he had dropped well behind Peck's figures and considered abandoning again. He was struggling to eat and was again showing signs of weariness. When you consider how Peck had struggled a week or two before this, to get to Carlisle and then gone like a rocket once over the border, it was going to be a tall order for Green to do the same.

F.T. Bidlake's advice at this time was for Green to continue to Carlisle where a railway station would provide transport home. At this time, Green was 1 hour 12 mins down on Pecks figures. It was a painful spectacle for his helpers to watch. Just on the approaches to Shap he stopped for a drink of water laced with brandy and swapped again to a very lightweight cycle with a 63" gear and from then on started to claw back time minute by minute. He now showed the speed that had been with him throughout his career so far.

G.H. Stancer who had looked after Green's career these last few years, caught a train to

Edinburgh hoping to get ahead of his rider and then trail him to Perth. When he got to the ferry at Granton, his man had already gone across the Firth. Don't forget, this is the man who in 1901 had raised the 24 hr record to 394 miles, so at last that drive, endurance and speed had returned to him. His diet and drinking habits were different to other riders. He took brandy and water to ease his stomach pains and drank freely of port and lemonade, port being a heavy sweet wine, offset by the lemonade which thinned it down to become a refreshing drink.

G.H. Stancer having missed his man at the ferry, caught another train to Perth where he learned that Green was already ahead of him and going strongly. G.H.S. went on ahead by train to Golspie on the north east coast where he had hoped to pick up the rider and follow him to the end, but heavy rain was now falling and Stancer continued on the train to Helmsdale, where he found a roadside inn, to wait for him.

A telegram had been sent to Helmsdale warning of his early arrival possibly as early as midnight. In fact, despite poor conditions, Green rode past the inn at 11.00pm just as G.H.S was stepping outside. By this time, Harry Green had ridden all of his helpers into the ground, so had no spare tyre or tube to fall back on. He turned and retraced to be met by a surprised Stancer.

Green's rear tyre was falling apart and had lost a lot of pressure. Luckily, one of the helpers arrived and Green took his bike and turned to the north once more, followed in hot pursuit by Stancer. The last remaining miles must have been exciting, as the night was pitch black and neither rider had a lamp. With the notoriously dangerous drop and climb at Berriedale to negotiate.

By Wick the dawn was rising and at 3.50 am Harry Green had reached his goal. **F.T. Bidlake** timed him over the line in **2 days 19 hrs 50 mins.**

Stancer's only regret was that Harry didn't carry on for the 1000 miles which had been improved by **T.A. Fisher** to **3 days 19 hrs** in May two months previously. This would have given Green 24 hours to complete the 140 miles or so.

Harry had taken a total of 15 RRA records in all. By the age of 33, Harry 'Goss' Green's record breaking career was all but over. He suffered debilitating rheumatism and finally succumbed to his illness in June 1950.

T.A. Fisher's 1000 miles route was virtually the same one used by George Olley the previous year, running from Hitchin to York on the A1 London Road and making deviations off to Lincoln, Spalding and Skegness.

He started at eight in the morning of Monday May 18th in Hitchin at the 34th milestone, the timekeeper again being Bidlake. It was a breezy but dry day which saw him gain on his schedule by the 100 mile point, passed in 5 hrs 58 mins. Unlike a lot of his predecessors he was a meat eater and he rode for the Unity CC. He was lean, very fit, and 'trained to the minute'. He rode a Rudge-Whitworth racer, geared at 74" with constrictor tyres on wooden rims.

At Grantham on the first day with 122 miles covered he was 56 mins up on schedule which allowed him plenty of time to walk the steep hill at Gonerby. His first 12 hrs of riding gained him 185 miles and three punctures in the process. After a 30 minute break for food and massage at Newark he was still some 20 mins up on schedule. Bright acetylene lamps had been fitted to his cycle and indeed to all of the helpers mounts. At Retford his second 100 miles was completed in 13 hrs 40 mins.

He reached York Tramway Terminus at 1.45 am on Tuesday. This was the farthest north he had to ride. A crowd of his club mates from the Unity CC gave him a rapturous welcome. He stopped for a meal of lamb chops, vegetables and finished off with a half dozen oranges. He turned and rode back south, but on the boring stretches between Selby and Doncaster he fell asleep and landed on the grass. His next scare was a young fox darting across in front of him.

Dawn broke on this second day. The 24 hrs was up just beyond Newark with 328 miles covered. Grantham saw a detour eastwards into the Fen district. Fisher's energy seemed inexhaustible. Being three quarters of an hour up on schedule, his helpers had a hard job keeping him in sight. He decided to delay his first decent sleep until 500 miles was reached. The second night was cold and he passed 'Tattershall Castle' with the deep red sun setting on its tower with 481 miles done in 36 hours.

At Sleaford 494 miles Fisher took his first decent sleep after 37 hours of riding. Two exciting incidents during the night made the 'rest' a memorable night for Bidlake who was also resting from his exertions of following and checking Fisher. Bidlake who was sleeping on a couch detected a smell of burning downstairs. He aroused Andrews who was Fisher's trainer and dashed downstairs to find the kitchen on fire. Between them they managed to quell the flames with a few buckets of water.

The next incident was the suspicious entry of a burly figure through a window some time later. Bidlake discovered the intruder to be none other than George Olley, looking for somewhere warm to sleep. He'd been following Fisher all of the previous evening.

Fisher, after a three hour sleep, a bath and massage, left Sleaford at 1.43 am. He was still, despite his long break, an hour up on schedule. After an 81miles circuit which brought him back to Sleaford at 8.12 am he took a 15 minutes break for food now that his 48 hours was completed. He turned at Stamford and rode east into the Fens. Through Market Deeping to turn at 'Bourn' level crossing 624 miles at 12.28. He was now over one and a half hours up on schedule.

At Peterborough he retraced to Stamford where he had a fruit and custard meal. His handlebars had to be padded with strips of bandage at this point as his hands had become very sore. After another 100 miles of very rough road he pushed himself to Wisbech, to take a sleep at 10.17 pm on this the third night. After a fish supper and a hot bath and sleep, Fisher left after three hours. He was hoping to push the 1000 miles record beyond the reach of riders hoping to just tag the extra mileage onto an End to End ride. In those days the rider had to prove he'd been turned at a predestined place on the road, by an independent witness, unless an RRA official was in place. At 'Eye Green' the turning point on the Peterborough road his checker hadn't turned out, although he'd got two helpers who witnessed him, he wanted an independent signature, so he aroused a cottage dweller to sign his form in the very early hours of the morning. Luckily, the man was enthusiastic with the venture and accepted the situation with good humour.

At 800 miles, Fisher was riding very strongly being some two hours or more up on schedule. He collided with a sheep and fell off, but even this didn't deter him. That last day and night were very cold and Fisher grew to twice his size with extra clothing to keep warm. At 8 o'clock on that last evening he took a good feed of raw eggs, boiled chicken, custard and bread and butter. He left at 8.18 and pushed onto 'Brampton Hut' against a stiff wind. Through Girtford Bridge and Biggleswade to finish his ride at one minute past 3am on Friday morning at the 37th milestone from London on this historic ride **3 days 19 hrs 1 min** gave a beating of Welsh's record by 12 hrs 40 mins. In the last 24 hrs Fisher had covered just 260 miles. His last 100 miles had taken 9 hrs 38 mins.

The next attack on the 1000 mile record was by our man from the MC and AC - **William Welsh** on **Monday 30th August 1909.** The course he was about to use was exactly the same one as Fisher had used in 1908. The only difference was that Welsh didn't really know the course having performed his previous 1000 miles on the End to End route in 1907. He wanted to use the same flat course as Fisher so that comparisons could be made after the ride. Don't forget in those days there was a tremendous pride and public interest taken in breaking a record and even more pride taken in regaining it.

Instead of teams of three helpers, Welsh could only muster three teams of two riders to do the job but they proved to be well up to the job. Welsh's bike was a 'Rover' and it was noticeable from photos the first to be used with dropped handlebars on a 1000 mile record. On virtually all of the photos Welsh is seen riding on the drops.

F.T. Bidlake was again the official RRA timekeeper who started Welsh at 5.00 am at Hitchin on Monday 30th August 1909. At 66 miles covered in 4 hrs a strong West North West wind had sprung up. Welsh had scheduled to beat Fishers record by 15 hours but after a hard run to Grantham at 122 miles, he was 50 mins down on Fishers actual time to here. The next part of the ride would take him to York, but it was to be done in very bad conditions, rain, wind and almost freezing temperatures saw him get to York some 1.75 hrs slower than Fisher. After the 'leg' through Boston to Skegness and back he reached Sleaford, so making good use of the last remaining daylight hours before taking a break. By taking a much shorter rest than Fisher here, he managed to level the time gap when he got back on the road. It was a bitterly cold night with a frost. He headed south to Spalding and he had now slowed considerably with the cold and had become despondent.

With the warmth that sunrise brings, he rode back to Stamford. He had dropped his gear from 78" to 73" and this had made a noticeable difference and at 8.50 am on Wednesday, he was only 37 mins behind Fishers time at this point, although well down on his own very ambitious schedule. On through Wisbech and Downham Market and back, by taking fewer rests and much shorter breaks than Fisher, Welsh had managed to get ahead of Fisher's time by Peterborough.

He left for Spalding at 4.15 on Thursday morning having covered 805 miles with a one hour 20 mins lead. He started his last 100 miles at 12.30 Thursday dinnertime with 108 minutes in hand over Fisher. Although he had missed out on hours of sleep, he showed no signs of slowing down and his final detours to Bedford and back through Biggleswade were done at 15mph.

He gained even more time over the closing miles to reach Bidlake at 8.57 pm, having taken 3 days 15 hrs 57 mins, an improvement of some 3 hrs 4 mins over Fisher's ride. Welsh had proved himself to be a 'stayer' of the very first class and a long distance rider of exceptional ability.

After this frenzy of record breaking over the last six or more years there was a silent halt to activities over these two journeys for some twenty years, during which time the 1914-18 'war' had taken its toll on our brave young men.

The End to End record resumes in 1929 with Jack Rossiter on solo bike, Tom Hughes on tricycle, followed in that same year by Les Meyers also on trike. The main difference now being the exclusion of ferries in Scotland.

This information courtesy of Cycling and the Road Records Association handbook with extra text from myself.

"YOU'RE NOT PUSHING VERY HARD."

SECTION THREE

A FULL LIST OF END TO END RECORDS
FROM 1929 USING AN ALL ROAD ROUTE WITH TOTAL OF RRA RECORDS
BROKEN BY EACH RIDER IN BRACKETS

1	1929	Tom Hughes	3 days 21hrs 55 mins	Tricycle	(6)
2	1929	L.J.Meyers	3 days 19 hrs 56 mins	Tricycle	(1)
3	1929	Jack Rossiter	2 days 13 hrs 22 mins	Bicycle Professional	(7)
4	1934	Hubert Opperman	2 days 9 hrs 01 mins	Bicycle Professional	(11)
5	1937	Sid Ferris	2 days 6 hrs 33 mins	Bicycle Professional	(5)
6	1938	Lilian Dredge	3 days 20 hrs 54 mins	Bicycle Professional Lady	(6)
7	1938	Innes & Thompson	2 days 14 hrs 48 mins	Tandem Bicycle	(4)
8	1939	Marguerite Wilson	2 days 22 hrs 52 mins	Bicycle Professional Lady	(22)
9	1947	Letts & Parker	2 days 22 hrs 41 mins	Tandem Tricycle: Letts	(4)
				Parker	(5)
10	1949	Bert Parkes	3 days 13 hrs 03 mins	Tricycle	(2)
11	1949	J.K. Letts	3 days 9 hrs 27 mins	Tricycle	(4)
12	1950	Bert Parkes	3 days 0 hrs 38 mins	Tricycle	(2)
13	1952	Cowsill & Denton	2 days 8 hrs 47 mins	Tandem Bicycle	(2)
14	1953*	Edith Atkins	2 days 18 hrs 04 mins	Bicycle Amateur* Lady	(12)
15	1954	Eileen Sheridan	2 days 11 hrs 07 mins	Bicycle Professional Lady	(28)
16	1954	Crimes & Arnold	2 days 4 hrs 26 mins	Tandem Tricycle: Crimes	(10)
				Arnold	(11)
17	1957	David Duffield	2 days 20 hrs 09 mins	Tricycle - **North to South**	(12)
18	1957	Albert Crimes	2 days 12 hrs 37 mins	Tricycle	(10)
19	1958	Dave Keeler	2 days 3 hrs 09 mins	Bicycle	(1)
20	1958	Reg Randall	2 days 1 hrs 58 mins	Bicycle	(2)
21	1960	David Duffield	2 days 10 hrs 58 mins	Tricycle	(12)
22	1960	Bailey & Forrest	2 days 4 hrs 48 mins	Tandem Bicycle	(2)
23	1965	Dick Poole	1 d 23 h 46 m 35 secs	Bicycle **(First inside 2 days)**	(1)
24	1966	Swinden & Withers	2 d 2 h 14 m 25 secs	Tandem Bicycle	(2)
25	1976*	Janet Tebbutt	2 d 15 h 24 m 20 secs	Bicycle Amateur* Lady	(2)
26	1979	Paul Carbutt	1 d 23 h 23 m 01secs	Bicycle Professional	(1)
27	1980	Pat Kenny	2 d 10 h 36 m 52 secs	Tricycle	(9)
28	1982	Mick Coupe	1 d 22 h 39 m 49 secs	Bicycle	(2)
29	1982	Eric Tremaine	2 d 6 h 18 m 35 secs	Tricycle	(1)
30	1982	John Woodburn	1 d 21 h 3 m 16 secs	Bicycle	(10)
31	1990	Pauline Strong	2 d 6 h 49 m 45 secs	Bicycle Lady	(7)
32	1990	Andy Wilkinson	1 d 21 h 2 m 18 secs	Bicycle	(3)
33	1992	Ralph Dadswell	2 d 5 h 29 m 01 secs	Tricycle	(35)
34	1998	Groesbeck & Harris	2 d 8 h 28 m 50 secs	Mixed Tandem Bicycle	(1)
35	2000	Wilkinson & Taylor	2 d 3 hr 19m 23 secs	Mixed Tandem Bicycle	
				Andy Wilkinson	(3)
				Lynne Taylor	(5)
36	2001	Lynne Taylor	2 d 5hr 48 m 21 secs	Bicycle Lady	(5)
37	2001	Gethin Butler	1 d 20 hr 4 m 20 secs	Bicycle	(4)
38	2002	Lynne Taylor	2 d 4 hr 45 m 11 secs	Bicycle Lady	
				(**Three** E to E Records)	(5)

1000 MILES RECORDS FROM 1907 INCLUDING LADIES

1907	G.A.Olley	4 days 9 hrs 3 mins	Separate Bicycle	
1907	W. Welsh	4 days 7 hrs 41 mins	Combined End to End Bicycle	
1908	T.A. Fisher	3 days 19 hrs 01 mins	Separate Bicycle	
1909	W. Welsh	3 days 15 hrs 57 mins	Separate Bicycle	
1930	J. Rossiter	3 days 11 hrs 58 mins	Separate Bicycle	
1934	H. Opperman	3 days 1 hr 52 mins	Combined End To End Bicycle	
1937	S. Ferris	2 days 22 hrs 40 mins	Combined End to End Bicycle	
1938	G. Lawrie	4 days 6 hrs 32 mins	Separate Tricycle	(7)
1938	Lilian Dredge	4 days 19 hrs 14 mins	Combined E to E Lady Bicycle	
1939	Marguerite Wilson	3 days 11 hrs 44 mins	Combined E to E Lady Bicycle	
1947	Letts & Parker	3 days 12 hrs 25 mins	Combined E to E Tandem Tricycle	
1952	Cowsill & Denton	3 days 7 hrs 41 mins	Combined End to End Tandem	
1953*	Wyn Wrightson	3 days 15 hrs 53 mins	Separate Lady Amateur* Bicycle	(1)
1954	Eileen Sheridan	3 days 1 hr 00 mins	Combined E to E Lady Bicycle	
1954	Crimes and Arnold	2 days 13 hrs 59 mins	Combined E To E Tandem Tricycle	
1956	David Duffield	3 days 12 hrs 15 mins	Separate Tricycle	
1956	Arthur Render	2 days 16 hrs 50 mins	Separate Bicycle	(1)
1958	Albert Crimes	2 days 21 hrs 37 mins	Separate Tricycle	
1960	Reg Randall	2 days 10 hrs 40 mins	Separate Bicycle	
1964	Swinden & Withers	2 days 18 hrs 09 mins	eparate Tandem	
1974	Janet Tebbutt*	3 days 9 hrs 29 mins	Separate Lady Amateur* Bicycle	
2001	Gethin Butler	2 days 7 hrs 59 mins	Combined End to End Bicycle	
2002	Lynne Taylor	2 days 16 hrs 38 mins	Combined E to E Lady Bicycle	

SECTION FOUR

THE START OF ALL END TO END RECORDS USING AN ALL LAND ROUTE

No 1 TOM HUGHES 21st JUNE 1929 SOLO TRICYCLE END TO END

Thirty six years after G.P.Mills rode a tricycle, paced by other riders and using ferries in Scotland, saw Tom Hughes of the Palatine CC break the new standard imposed by the RRA for an all-land route by 20 hrs 5mins.

"Young" Tom Hughes was the son of the veteran Wigan tricyclist, known affectionately as 'Owd Tom'. Friday morning 21st June at 8.00 am saw him start away into a slight northerly breeze. He made very good progress to Exeter and was 25 mins up on schedule. Not wanting to miss his marshalls and roadside help he waited a while to put himself back on time schedule. He had to use delaying tactics again between Exeter and Bristol as there was virtually no communication system or HQ the helpers could use to enquire of his progress. He was relying purely on roadside help for his food and drink.

With a slight drizzle and a wind now blowing from the south, 'young' Tom made very good progress to Worcester and Kidderminster. He stopped here to change his clothing and left still in good spirits after a short while. He passed through Shropshire to Cheshire where he punctured He reached his home in Wigan and took a 45 mins break, leaving on time at 4.15 pm on Saturday. He had now been riding for over 32 hours.

With good conditions, he gained enough time to take a 5.75 hrs sleep at Kendal, leaving in the small hours of next morning. There was now a strong westerly wind troubling him through Carlisle and over the Beattock Hills. From there on the route veered to the north east and Tom picked up speed to Dunkeld. He realised at this point that he could possibly beat G.P. Mills old tricycle 'paced' record of 3 days 16 hrs 47 mins.

He avoided a scheduled stop for sleep but by Blair Atholl he needed a break to prepare himself for the Grampians. He took a 90 mins sleep in a lightweight tent provided by his followers. He now had to battle against a nagging wind to reach Inverness where the road changes direction to go around the Beauly Firth.

After a break from the wind he was back out on the road to Aultnamain. From here on the road surfaces deteriorated rapidly and once he had begun that last 80 miles of coast road the wind troubled him enough to have to walk the major hills such as Helmsdale and Berriedale.

Tom pushed bravely on and was still ahead of schedule along here. In fact he was so far ahead he was reaching a lot of the schedule stops at hotels nearly 12 hrs ahead of time.

At Wick, drowsiness overcame him, but knowing he was so close to the end he fought bravely on. John Miller had followed him from Lanarkshire, and all through England and Scotland Tom had tremendous support from club cyclists.

He arrived at John o Groats hotel at five minutes to six on Tuesday morning. He had set a new record of **3 days 21 hrs 55 mins.** Although it was slower than G.P. Mills paced record it was a true reflection of one mans solo effort over this route.

This fine record was to stand for less than two months.

Young Tom Hughes, prior to the End to End, had finished his apprenticeship as a 'fitter' at 25 years of age and promptly got the 'sack', a common occurrence in those days, so he decided to repair cycles in his mother's back yard. He made such a success of it he built it into a business, eventually resulting in well known shops.

His father 'Owd Tom' had already become a tricycling legend, having founded the 'Autumn Tints Cycling Comrades' in June 1924, a cycling club for the 'over 50's'.

Young Tom became a cycle dealer and lightweight specialist with a ready-made catchment of clientele.

In the 1920's prior to his End to End, he'd broken many tandem and tandem trike road records, mainly with his two brothers. His End to End trike was presented to him by 'James', a well known make at that time. It had 7" cranks and a single freewheel gear of 60".

Information courtesy of The Cycling Magazine, John Arnold and Albert Winstanley.

No 2 L.J. MEYERS AUGUST 9th 1929 SOLO TRICYCLE END TO END

The previous tricycle End to Ender Tom Hughes had been presented with a shield from his club, The Palatine CC, commemorating his achievement, but within 46 days he had lost it to Les Meyers of the Southgate CC with a near two hour improvement on the record.

Les Meyers, nicknamed 'Uncle', left Lands End at 7 am on Tuesday August 9th. In these early years of record breaking the cycling world looked upon these riders as being 'fast tourists' - not a very apt description when one considers the enormous efforts they were making. I'm afraid this description was being used for all except the solo gents bicycle records until the 1950's whether it was tricycle, tandem or tandem tricycle. They were not looked upon seriously except by other record breakers or people involved with the RRA attempts.

Luckily the 'Cycling' magazine of the day gave them all at least a half page and usually a picture, otherwise these brave men would be just a name on a shield, but in those days, the 'cycling' press was run by management who were in touch with the English cycling club scene, whose members made up the majority of their readership, the same as today.

I digress but I wanted to show the readers of this book, just how much esteem us younger record breakers of today hold, for these earlier records and record breakers.

Les Meyers had a good start and by Bodmin he had two hours in hand over his schedule which was made out to give a six hour beating of Tom Hughes's record. He held this advantage in time until Bristol was reached that same evening.

It was time to put lights on but his following car had become stuck in traffic in the town and they had his lights. By the time he was reunited with his helpers he had lost nearly an hour. From Bristol onwards the wind dropped but Les managed to hold his time gain to reach Bridgnorth early on Wednesday morning.

From here onwards a north west breeze hampered his progress to Whitchurch. He maintained 14 mph through Warrington to Kendal where his first rest was taken.

He pressed on over Shap to Penrith where he was still 30 mins up on time. The north west wind slowed him even more along this stretch, becoming a headwind. By Stirling he had lost virtually all of his time gain, and 33 miles later at Perth he had dropped another 12 mins. At Pitlochry he was 35 mins down and at Blair Atholl, 40 mins down.

At Kingussie, he was 1 hr 22 mins adrift of his schedule and had to have a rest. He was in a terrible state and his helpers had to keep persuading him to go on. He was very saddle sore by this time.

Sid Collins, one of the helpers, who was an old clubmate of Syd Parker (the first tandem trike End to Ender) told Syd that he followed Les on a bike, and Les's wrists were so bad from the Grampians onwards he had to walk down the hills and walk up them. The deteriorating roads were not helping his dilemma at all.

Les bravely battled on losing time on his schedule to reach John o Groats, taking just a minute under two hours off Tom Hughes' record, with **3 days 19 hrs 56 mins.**

This record held good until just after the second world war.

REMINISCENCES OF AN END TO ENDER - BY LES MEYERS

I should like to relate here a few of my experiences during my Lands End to John o Groats record ride on the trike in 1929. There are some humorous and some otherwise.

My RRA observers on the first stage of the journey were Harold Johnson of the Finsbury Park CC and Harold Crocker of the Southgate CC and we travelled by car with the trike on the back down to Lands End, stopping at Exeter going down and at Mrs Nicholas's at Sennen the second night.

I pushed off from Lands End at 8 am on August 6th with the two Harolds in the car following. There was a strong S.W. wind blowing and I covered the first stretch to Penzance at evens, so I got there a bit early, the checker was not there. Luckily Harold Johnson had his address and knocked him up. After he turned up I signed his card and carried on. Then on to Bristol which was a busy town and no bypass then. Consequently my followers lost sight of me and I went into the centre of the town and, as it was getting dark, had to wait for the car which was carrying my lamp. The car had gone the other way through the town, so I had to purchase a 'bobby dodger' from a local cyclist and carried on. It was fortunate that I was well ahead of schedule when I got to Bristol, so after the delay of 20 minutes, I was still on schedule. I picked up the following car on the road the other side of the town. Picking up my own lamp, I surrendered the oil lamp to the followers. We got to the hotel at Berkeley Road in Gloucestershire about on schedule. This was the first real feed and rest, and I was ready for it.

From here I was followed by Mr and Mrs Mitchell the father and mother of Eddie Mitchell, who was a member of our Club at that time, and who made Stephens bikes and my trike. The fact that I was being followed by a car which had a lady in it caused a certain amount of embarrassment when I had to answer the call of nature. On through Worcester, Bridgnorth, Wellington to Warrington, where I was met by Tommy Hughes, who had lowered the standard time and set up a new time of 3 days 21 hours and some odd minutes previously in the year. He guided me through various by-roads which missed the main roads of Warrington and Wigan, but I don't think I missed any of the cobble setts of which all roads seem to be constructed round there.

I was beginning to get a bit sore by then and the vibration did not improve things. Somewhere north of Wigan I was followed by W.P. Cook of the Anfield B.C. I believe that he followed me through to Kendal where I had my first rest and sleep for five hours, after 422 miles. I was rather sore underneath by this time, but after a bath and a good sleep I felt quite fit again. I set off on the next stretch in the early hours of the morning followed by Maurice Draisey of the Century RC on his trike, carrying my spare tyres. We tackled the drag up Shap Fell which is quite a teaser. Being on a 64 fixed gear meant some twiddling on the downhill runs. By that time I wished I had a freewheel. This was before the days of Cyclo derailleur gears on trikes. Somewhere on the other side of Gretna Green we stopped to have a meal at the wayside out of Maurice's bag. He had been carrying all the weight and was getting a bit tired by this time. Then who should come along in a van but Doc Miller, a well known character in Scottish cycling circles. He promptly proceeded to take photos of us with a huge reflex camera. Then he threw the camera into the back of the van, and with Draisey's trike in the back and Maurice riding in front with Doc Miller they followed me. During this time Maurice was very thirsty and the worthy doctor asked him whether he would like a drink. Of course Maurice with visions of a large bottle of beer in his mind's eye, said he certainly would, and was handed up a bottle of milk. Maurice nearly fainted but managed to survive on it. When we got to Stirling we were met by Ron Winton who took over the following, while Draisey went by train up to Wick to meet me at John o Groats as official checker. From Stirling to Perth and from here to Pitlochry was fairly steady going and night had fallen. Then the gradual 24 mile climb uphill to Dalwhinnie at the top of the Drumochter Pass. While climbing this I heard the strains of the bagpipes being played at the side of the road. I don't know if they were being played for my benefit but they certainly cheered me up.

I was feeling very tired and looking forward to a nice feed at the top of the climb. However on arriving at the top there was nobody there and I nearly burst out crying. I was some time behind schedule and the feeders had gone back to Kingussie. I had a snack from Ron's car and then carried on to Kingussie where I had my next rest. Leaving in the early hours of Tuesday morning, I carried on to Inverness where I had breakfast. From here I was followed by 'Syd Collins and Jim Letts of the Ealing CC who lowered my record in 1949. On through Dingwall, Tain, Bonar Bridge, Helmsdale to Berriedale, where the road goes up 1 in 5 and then drops down a 1 in 5 gradient on the northern slope. My wrists by this time were so cramped that I could not grip my brake so I not only had to walk up, but also down the other side. From here to Wick I was very saddle sore and weary as the roads were in very bad condition for a trike.

At Wick I met George Knight, a great touring friend of mine, together with a crowd of Scottish boys, who set me up with a drink and feed. From here to John o Groats was purgatory as the road was all pot holes, it was pitch dark, and my lamp had decided to go on strike. When I eventually got to the END I was very thankful and about 5 hours behind on my schedule. Everybody in the Hotel had given me up. Nobody thought of ringing or knocking them up. After I had recovered myself I enquired if anyone had done so. Maurice Draisey who was the official timekeeper at 'Groats' turned out and clocked me in. So I must have lost some time there. After a hot bath and a feed I got to bed and slept until about ten in the morning Maurice sent my trike back from Wick Station and I returned in Sid Collins' car, a Morris Minor and my legs were so cramped that I had to sit in the back with my feet each side of Jim Letts, head resting on the back of his seat. They brought me down to Port Isaac in Cornwall to recuperate. It took us five days to come down in the car, longer than I took to go up on the trike.

I was very fortunate with the weather as it was fine the whole time.

I look back on the End to End ride as a glorified tour, as now things are completely different. The roads are faster and smoother and with the aid of variable gears and lorries following with spares and sleeping accommodation, times have considerably come down. I feel very grateful to Jock Ballantyne who did all the organising , and also to all those who turned out to help me during the ride.

Leslie J Meyers passed away in 1984 aged 89. He had been a member of the Southgate CC for 62 years. He did much for the Club, particularly in fostering the spirit of long distance cycling. He was a veteran of the First World War and also served in the Territorial Army at the beginning of the Second World War.

Sid Collins one of his helpers on the End to End also passed away in 1984 aged 79. He was a founder member of the Earling Paragon CC, a member of the Tricycle Association and the RRA. He was valued for his assistance on various record attempts and for his vast knowledge of the sport.

'Reminiscences of an End to Ender by Les Myers' courtesy of the Tricycle Association Gazette from August 1980, with additional text from Syd Parker and myself.

No 3 JACK ROSSITER AUGUST 1929 SOLO BICYCLE

The decision to ban the use of ferries in Scotland was taken by the RRA in 1925. This made the journey an extra 43 miles approximately. The new time standard they imposed was 2 days 22 hrs. Jack Rossiter, a member of the Century Road Club was the first solo cyclist to ride to this new standard. His apprenticeship into hard riding and all day racing was in 1920, winning the North Road 24 hr with 378.75 miles. He won many more 24 hr races in the next eight years sometimes riding two a year. He was also a prolific 100 mile and 12 hour rider. He won the Catford 24 hr in 1928 with 400.3 miles so came to the End to End attempt in 1929 with a very good pedigree. He was now a professional riding a Raleigh with Sturmey Archer 3 speed hub gears. The timekeeper was F.T. Bidlake and the month was August.

Jack Rossiter postponed his start by one day due to very heavy rain.. The next day was much the same but with a favourable wind. Apparently it was the worst conditions on record where a rider had made a start. Penzance was reached inside the half hour, where he crashed but remounted and carried on none the worse. By Bodmin he was 45 mins up on schedule, but took a short feed stop to be one hour up at Exeter, 120 miles, having sustained a puncture around Okehampton. Doubts as to whether he could sustain this turn of speed were soon dispelled as he stayed ahead of schedule in a crosswind to Bristol and beyond. By Tewkesbury, the rain was back to torrential force again. Rossiter had to have extra clothing going into the night just to keep warm. Whitchurch was reached at 2.20 am thanks to good navigation by his helping crew. After refreshments and dry clothing he was back out on the road into another torrential downpour, and on towards the slippery cobbles and tramlines of Warrington and Wigan, in the black of the night. The weather improved slightly as he pressed on through Preston and Lancaster, stopping at Kendal for a short sleep and hot bath. A proper meal, the first one since Lands End, was eaten. He had now completed 422 miles in 27 hours.

He climbed Shap and all it had to throw at him into a headwind and sharp stinging rain. He reached the summit of this barren landscape and pedalled on towards the border town of Carlisle, where he took on more food for the slog into a very cold wind which increased in strength so much he had to change to lower gearing just to maintain speed to Crawford for a quick feed stop. Here the road veered more favourably with the wind direction and took him to Lanark where he was nearly 2 hrs up. More clothing was donned on this stretch through Lanarkshire to Stirling to try and keep the cold from getting to his knees which were paining him after 580 miles and over 40 hours of riding. It is thought around the Perth area that a rabbit fetched him off further bruising his painful knees. At Perth he only took a few minutes rest instead of the full hour scheduled. He was eager to attack the Grampians and reach Blair Atholl before he took a well earned sleep there. Dangerous bends and thousands of rabbits made this area a nightmare of a ride on this second night. It's not so bad nowadays as the bends and villages are by-passed by straight main roads, but those narrow roads were used by riders up until the '70's. Pete Swinden said he recalls 'haring' along through the villages on the tandem record with John Withers in 1966, surrounded by rabbits and possibly hares.

Jack Rossiter was now over 3 hours up on schedule as dawn broke just after Dalwhinnie. However, dawn brought with it a considerable head wind that slowed his progress to Inverness, the capital of the Highlands. He had a short sleep and a bath here before racing on at just past 11 am on the third day, still 3hrs 45mins up on schedule now. The sun came out on a lovely warm day, although the wind was still troubling him as he climbed Aultnamain. This is a vicious climb and a hair raising drop down through road-works at the time.

Rossiter fought on now through Golspie and on towards Berriedale where he climbed the hill without dismounting, a rare feat in those days. By now the weather had turned heavily against him on the easterly tip of land known as the 'Ord of Caithness'. The name itself sounds daunting enough ! At Wick he took on extra clothing against the cold rain of dusk. The wind and rain on this last 17 miles were as bad as anybody had ever had, but F.J.Bidlake timed him home at John o Groats at 9.22 pm. The standard to beat now that ferries couldn't be used was 2 days 22 hrs. Rossiter had started at 8 am three days previously, so had broken the new standard by 8 hrs 38 mins in a time of 2 days, 13 hrs, 22 mins.

When questioned afterwards he said he now couldn't stop eating and felt surprisingly good, better than he expected to be. He said that at one stage the rain and wind nearly caused him to pack.

So ended another very successful record attempt. The next rider to tackle this would have to have either a good wind with him, warm weather, little rain or do without hardly any sleep. This record was now deemed to be getting 'tight'.

The 'Cycling' periodical of the day approached Harry Green, Rossiter's predecessor and the last man to use the ferries, as to his view on the future of the End to End. Green thought that sleep should be dispensed with entirely on further attempts as sleep disrupted a racing cyclists rhythm. He felt that dry weather should be waited for, thus reducing the risk of falling off on bad roads or slippery cobbles. Also getting soaked reduces ones physical output in such conditions. Even in those days, Harry Green felt that thundery conditions could enhance the quality of the air and he believed that the next record breaker, if given nearly those conditions, could possibly achieve close to 2 days 6 hrs. The next End to End wasn't quite that fast but only because severe stomach trouble hadn't been accounted for.

Rossiter went on to break three more records after the End to End. The bicycle 1000 miles based on a course north of London, in 3 days, 11 hrs 58 mins in 1930; the Lands End to London tricycle record in 19hrs 1 min in 1932; the 24 hrs tricycle record in 1933 with 385.5 miles. His long distance racing career had spanned at least 15 years, breaking no less than seven RRA records in that time.

Information courtesy of the Cycling Magazine, Alan J Ray, and myself.

No 4 HUBERT OPPERMAN MONDAY 16th JULY 1934 SOLO BICYCLE 24 HOUR END TO END 1000 MILES

Hubert Opperman from Australia, later to become Sir Hubert, as after his racing career he became a Government Minister and Ambassador in Australia, set out from Lands End on solo bike on Monday 16th July 1934. He rode as a professional for BSA whose bikes were made in my home suburb in Birmingham. The model he rode was a 'Malvern Star' which I later saw on display at either a cycle show or an RRA function. It was still in its original state as if it had done the End to End and been left in a garage until the day I saw it. I was tempted to touch it gingerly then I was later told he had suffered terrible stomach pains and had diarrhoea for hours on end in Scotland and saved time by staying on the bike if you know what I mean. I was glad I had resisted.

The first part of his journey was very fast, reaching Exeter 120 miles at virtually 'evens' (20 mph) His intention was to raise the 24 hr figure from 416 miles set in 1931 by E Brown, but he didn't want to push so hard as to jeopardise his overall attack on the End to End and 1000 miles. He surprised his helpers and manager Bruce Small by flying through without taking a scheduled break, a thing unheard of in those days. He reached Filton, just north of Bristol, with 200 miles 'in the bag' in 10 hrs 30 mins. Here he took a 20 minute break to freshen up before amassing 225 for the 12 hrs. By Worcester he had covered 256 miles in 13 hrs and 42 mins. Here he changed his gearing on his bike to a slightly lower ratio giving him a 64 inch bottom, a medium of 72 and a top of 77. At Shatterford Hill between Kidderminster and Bridgnorth a group of club cyclists tried to jump on his wheel. He responded to this in true continental fashion and jumped away, dancing on his pedals and out of the saddle. He was a past master at this, although he later had to stop for his lights and a feed in Bridgnorth. By Wellington at 11.08 pm 'Oppy' had topped 300 miles in just over 16 hrs, so still only approx 1 hr down on evens.

Peter Barlow recalls **"In 1934, I was taken out during the night to watch and follow Opperman on his End to End record. I suppose that we picked him up by Tarporley where we joined the entourage. This was exciting stuff for me for it was in the night and, for the first time, I had been allowed to stay up. I had a vague idea that Lands End was a long way away and that John o Groats was even farther. That, at the time, was of no consequence, but in later years I could recite the mileages with greater accuracy. What I do recall was the following car with its huge headlights, and Opperman riding in the middle of the road along the white line, out of his saddle, dancing on the pedals, and in the full glare of the powerful lights. He wore tights and I am fairly sure that he had a white cap. I say this because in those days, whilst tights were acceptable, white hats were certainly not. Nor had anyone seemingly seen hill climbing like this before, and apparently the purists were not impressed. I was, and it has stuck in my mind ever since. Mind you I did hear later that when Opperman was questioned about this new technique, he is reputed to have said that it was not a new technique, merely a way of easing a sore bottom !"**

A puncture and spoke breakage through Whitchurch to Wigan lost him another couple of minutes but more significant was the stomach problems that had come on over the last few hours as he sped on through industrial Lancashire and on to Kendal. Would he survive the 24 hrs ? The record stood at 416.5 miles. Sickness and diarrhoea was now setting in as he pressed on towards Shap. He had covered a great part of the climb when the car horn signalled the **24 hr point at 431.5 miles.** What a record, over 15 miles added, on not an easy course. He stopped in Shap Village on the way down. Sickness was preventing him from eating now and after a short rest and massage to his stomach, he pressed on through Carlisle and stopped at Carluke, south of Stirling for more treatment. He had now covered 549 miles in 1 day, 7 hrs and 52 mins but wanted to press on to Dunblane, north of Stirling, to pick up the A9 to Perth, and went through Perth still suffering almost intolerable pain from his stomach. He lost the best part of an hour off the bike at Blair Atholl to change his clothing and get on a bike with even lower gearing for the Grampian mountains. He had here taken 1 day 14 hrs and 12 mins for 642 miles. He now had to tackle the second dark night and it's very cold now in this northern outpost. He had virtually nothing left inside him; how could he possibly go on ! He was also still being sick.

Inverness was reached in 1 day 20 hours, where more broken spokes still failed to stop the rider, so determined was he. At Beauly just a few miles beyond Inverness, a doctor was found to try and help his sickness and stomach trouble. He had treatment and a rest but lost approximately 1.5 hours here. This didn't seem to worry him even though he was weakened by having no food inside, he pluckily pedalled on through Bonar Bridge and Golspie, 800 miles with 2 days 4hrs 11 mins elapsed. It was raining heavily in patches which further weakened the rider. On to the Ord of Caithness, he climbed at 6 mph using his lower gear of 53". Berriedale was tackled by the BSA rider in an attacking style without dismounting. Here he was over 4 hrs up on the old record which is amazing considering his physical discomforts 'en route'. By the time he reached Bill Best, the Timekeeper, at John o Groats, he had taken an incredible **2 days 9 hrs 1 min** giving him a speed of over 15 mph. This course was duly measured to give 866.06 miles. After a long rest in todays's terms of 6 hrs, he set out to tackle the remaining 134 miles of dark foggy wet and dreadful roads. The total time for the 1000 miles being **3 days 1 hr 52 mins.** I would think that the BSA Cycle Company were very proud of him, and also the Australian public would have been amazed on learning of his exploits, making this now truly a 'world record'.

Oppy's build up to the End to End had been pretty spectacular. He was already a seasoned professional both in Australia and on the European continent. He had gained glory in the Tour De France, and in 1931 he won the Paris-Brest-Paris, the longest single stage race ever. It doesn't exist nowadays because it proved unpopular with the riders as being too severe !

It is interesting to note that Gethin Butler was the first Briton home in the 2003 Audax/Randonee version of the Paris-Brest-Paris in 49 hrs.

'Oppy' started his working life as a telegraph messenger. In an exchange of information in later years with John Arnold, Sir Hubert Opperman mentions that his experiences over the cobbled roads on the 'Paris-Roubaix' stood him in good stead in Lancashire, on roads that a lot of other riders suffered on.

Mavys, his wife, helped him on his record attempts in England. She remembers being out on the road between 3 and 4 am after cutting his favourite sandwiches to carry on his back.

'Oppy' remembers the London to York record being delayed 30 mins because he was wearing a dark brown sweater and white socks whereas he should have been in all black. It wasn't until Bruce Small, his manager, pointed out that the RRA rule said 'a dark costume from neck to ankle' must be worn. They conceded by allowing him to wear his continental white cap, and his white 'Oppy' food bag on his back.

This famous Australian racing cyclist came to England in June 1934. In the short space of 15 days he broke 5 RRA records. At that time he was recognised as the greatest 'all round' bike rider of the English speaking nations. His continuation for another 140 miles after the End to End was over some of the toughest roads in the very north of Scotland. Hubert Opperman's organiser had relied on local knowledge for his route, overlooking the fact that in those times probably no villager knew what lay more than a few miles beyond his home. Opperman used his gears very successfully; they were 'Cyclo' made in England and had been available in Australia since 1932. He told John Arnold that if you've broken the End to End, you must be ahead of the 1000 mile schedule, so why not suffer a little more. You will feel just the same next day.

Hubert said that the reason why he slung a white Oppy bag over his shoulders was so that at night the passing traffic could see him. He'd found by experience on his long record attempts in Australia and France that after 16 hours of riding, solid food tasted like ashes and it was difficult to chew. He used thick soups, barley broth, peppermint water (for digestion) bananas and strong black coffee for the night. In France he'd learnt how to go to the toilet on the bike while riding in the bunch, such as in the Paris-Brest-Paris.

John Arnold had asked Hubert why he'd come to England to break records when there was much more money to make on the Continental race scene. Hubert replied that the BSA company was impressed with his Paris-Brest-Paris win in 1931. Bruce Small had fitted 'BSA' parts to his locally built 'Malvern Star' frames so his breaking of the End to End and other RRA records suited markets both here and in Australia. Just think of that, RRA and End to End records vying in importance with the 'Tour de France' and the 'Classics' in Europe. On a question of 'official betting' on sporting events in Australia, Hubert thought that even in the 1930's there was probably heavy wagering on the outcome of his rides.

In Australia Hubert Opperman was also famous for numerous cycle records such as Adelaide to Sydney, 1000 miles, in 63 hrs 37.5 mins; 885 miles in 24 hours motor paced; 107.5 miles in 2 hours and 585 miles paced by tandems in 24 hrs.

Once his racing career was over, Hubert Opperman channelled his energy into politics. He became the Australian Minister of Transport and Shipping, the Chief Government Whip and the first Australian High Commissioner to Malta. 'Oppy' was the only End to Ender to receive a Knighthood. In Australia when he died he had a state funeral.

Information courtesy of the Cycling Magazine, the 24 hr Journal, Alan J Ray, John Arnold and myself.

No 5 SID FERRIS SATURDAY 17th JULY 1937 SOLO BICYCLE END TO END AND 1000 MILES

After making an abortive start on the previous Wednesday which lasted only 31 miles against an adverse wind, Sid Ferris finally got underway 3 days later on Saturday 17th July 1937 at 10 am. Riding as a professional for Raleigh on a bicycle equipped with a close ratio Sturmey Archer gear with a medium of 78".

His build up years prior to 1937 had showed that he was a gifted 24 hr rider, having won 3 consecutive North Road 24 hr events with 429.75 in 1932, 431.25 in 1933, a new competition record, and 421 in 1934. He won the Catford 24 hr in 1936 with 418.30 on 2nd June, 6 weeks prior to his End to End attack. He broke E.B.Brown's Edinburgh to London 397 mile record by 1.5 hrs in a time of 20 hrs 19 mins, despite unfavourable winds. He had motored the End to End route with Charlie Davey , his Manager, and he had also covered the whole route on a bike with a rev. counter to gain accurate intermediate mileages between towns and cities.

The ride from Lands End started well and Ferris kept within a minute of Opperman's time at Bodmin but by Okehampton, 98 miles, Ferris had slipped to 17 mins down on schedule. He wasn't having such good wind conditions as 'Oppy', and remained down at Exeter, 120 miles. At Cullompton he stopped and asked his manager Charlie Davey, if it was worth continuing. By the time he reached Bristol 196 miles and after a sit-down feed at Redhill at 187 miles, he was over 50 mins down on the Australians time. At the 12 hour point between Bristol and

Gloucester, he'd covered just 210 miles, 15 less than 'Oppy'. From Gloucester onwards Ferris maintained his scheduled speed up to north Lancashire losing no more than the 50 mins he'd lost by Bristol. On through Worcester, Whitchurch to Warrington, 354 miles in 20 hrs 9 mins, just 49 mins down now but with a long way to go. He must have been worried as to his progress. The one factor that could make all the difference to Ferris was that he knew 'Oppy' had had a much slower second half of his ride due to sickness and stomach problems that had delayed him for over 2 hrs.

Preston was reached 383 miles at 7 am after 21 hrs, now only 44 mins behind Opperman's time to this point. At Lancaster he'd reduced his deficit to 34 mins. At the 24 hr point he had covered 422 miles, just 9.5 miles less than 'Oppy' in 1934. Ferris's second 12 hours being 2 miles further than his first. By Carlisle, 469 miles, a stifling wind had sprung up from the west, where the road goes close to the coastline, that hindered the rider, but after that the road climbs to Beattock and the wind turned to provide a helpful breeze. Ferris had taken a 16 mins stop near Carlisle which had now at Beattock increased his deficit back to 44 mins on 'Oppy'. His lack of progress in bridging the gap in time had started to worry him again. He'd taken another small stop of 12.5 mins between Ecclefechan and Lockerbie and had a lie down on the grass. He had been seen, probably by a checker, and this sparked off a rumour which spread a long way into Scotland, that he had retired. He got back on and continued to maintain a steady progress to reach Stirling 581 miles only 16 mins down on the record. Heavy rain over the Lammermuir Hills seemed to perk the rider up and refresh him. A puncture at Dunblane was the only mechanical problem on the ride.

By Perth he had gained enough to be a few minutes ahead of Oppermans time, but the long cold second night over the Grampians saw him lose time. He wasn't such a fast pedaller as 'Oppy'. Even though Opperman had spent 45 mins off the bike at Blair Atholl with sickness, Ferris was still 17 mins slower at Inverness. At Beauly where Opperman had consulted a doctor for his stomach pains and lost another 1.5 hrs, Ferris strove ahead by a decent margin for the first time. At Alness, 759 miles, he had gained 1 hr 40 mins on Oppy's time. Over Aultnamain, Bonar Bridge, Golspie and here Sid Ferris had gained 2 hrs 28 mins and it was by this amount he broke the record reaching John o Groats in **2 days 6 hrs 33 mins.**

At John o Groats he rested for 3 hours but refused to fall asleep fearing he would not wake in time to continue. In hindsight he should have stuck to his original plan of stopping for just one hour. Opperman had stayed 6 hrs at John o Groats before continuing for the 1000 miles.

Ferris re-started on his final 130 miles at 7.30 pm but within 2 hours of riding, weariness and exhaustion overtook him and forced him to take the first of a series of sleep stops. Three of his hours of riding had only put 15 miles onto his total. He was now suffering severe saddle soreness and had to have plasters stuck onto his damaged skin. His helpers fixed a layer of sponge on top of his saddle to alleviate some of the pain. He also reversed his handlebars to give him a more upright position to ease his backside.

The course Sid Ferris had chosen for the extra 130 miles was of quite a good surface and fairly level, but he was having a real battle against sleep deprivation. One saving grace is that it was a light night, a phenomenon in the far north of Scotland in mid-summer. He finished at 8.45am on the Tuesday morning in a time of 2 days 22 hrs 40 mins, taking over 3 hours off Oppermans previous record of **3 days 1 hr 52 mins.**

Recapping all that had happened a few months later, Sid Ferris recalls that breaking the End to End and 1000 miles record was the fulfilment of the greatest ambition of his life and it was to be the most momentous happening of his career. This remarkable rider had the use of only one eye, having lost the sight in his left eye due to a childhood illness. He had to wear a patch and protective shades for most of the journey. He paid tribute to the amazing unselfishness and sportsmanship of scores of helpers, south and north of the border, who had given up their time to give him help. His timekeeper was Bill Best, his manager was Charley Davey, himself an outstanding record breaker. Sid was helped by his wife and brother Harry. He started the record weighing 10 stone 7 lb and had only lost 1 lb by the end.

As a vegetarian he was pleased to report no eating problems except for indigestion caused by a banana at Carlisle. Sid felt that his preparation had gone well, paying as much importance to rest and sleep as he did to riding his bike. He breakfasted on 'emprote' which I assume was a supplementary protein solution, cornflakes and two poached eggs on toast. He had a rice and fruit sit down feed at Redhill just before Bristol. After that it was one or two tomato and cheese sandwiches. His drinks were of 'emprote' or egg and milk, orange, lemon or grape juice to which honey was added.

He mentions traffic between Bodmin and Exeter being heavy even in the late thirties. He got past a slow moving boiler being transported at about 80 miles into the ride, which held his helpers vehicles up quite considerably, and having to have his brother Harry chase him at a fair distance on one of the spare bikes in case of a mechanical breakdown or puncture. He said he felt glad that he'd been advised to carry on when making poor progress on various parts of the ride and recalls being so cold on his ride through the Grampian mountains that he wore a boiler suit over his normal night riding clothes.

Sid felt he could beat his own record if he was called to go again, by not taking scheduled stops, but by having everything available in the following lorry as and when needed, and that a fast first 24 hrs aided by a decent wind would now be essential for anybody trying to beat the 16 mph average speed of the record. He wished the next man good luck and thanked his sponsors, Messrs Sturmey Archer Gears Ltd, and Raleigh.

One year later in 1938 Sid went on and took the RRA 24 hr record from Cyril Hepplestone with 465.75 miles. This was his last record.

Sid's record breaking career had spanned 11 years starting in 1927 on a tandem with his brother Harry. He broke the London to Portsmouth record with 6 hrs 48 mins 12 secs, making a total of 5 RRA records.

Sid Ferris later received the Bidlake Trophy for his breaking of the End to End and 1000 miles.

Information courtesy of the Cycling Magazine and Alan J Ray.

No 6 LILIAN DREDGE WEDNESDAY 19th JULY 1938 LADIES SOLO BICYCLE END TO END AND 1000 MILES

By the mid 1930's Lilian Dredge had already proved she was made of the stuff End to Enders are made of.

Riding for Claud Butler on an Osgear 3 speed equipped bike, she put up new figures for the Lands End to London record with 22 hrs 13 mins 50 secs. She was a good all round rider who tackled anything from grass track to riding the world champs road race in Brussels in 1934.

At that time the Women's Road Records Association (WRRA) which existed until 1979 did not have the End to End listed as one of its records. Lilian, a keen cyclist since her school days, had realised she was more suited to long distance time trials such as the 12 hrs and long WRRA place to place records. She dreamed about tackling the 'longest record' and when in 1937 it was put on the list, she couldn't have been happier.

The difficulty now lay in finding a sponsor, and also there was widespread hostility from the Press who were the mouthpiece of big businessmen in the bike trade, who prophesied that a female tackling such a ride would 'die by the wayside' ! However, Claud Butler wanted to help and he agreed to back her 1938 attempt. Alan J Ray says that Lilian from then on practically lived on the bike so as not to give credence to the men who thought she wouldn't make it.

Lilian's husband, Freddie, himself a famous racing cyclist and record breaker, organised the attempt and Lilian was keen to acknowledge the help from all of the clubs involved on route.

It was difficult to know how to schedule a ride of this length and duration as a female rider had never tackled it before. A schedule of 5 days, 17 hrs was soon abandoned after only a day or so, as they realised she would be easily inside this. Helpers and official checkers en route had to be phoned or telegrammed that she would arrive much earlier than stated.

The 32 year old London professional had a 4 am start on Wednesday 19th July 1938 and on her first day in the saddle she got as far as Gloucester where she slept the night after covering 231 miles. The second day, Thursday, she got to Kendal, 424 miles before sleeping. Friday, another 219 miles was added totalling 643 miles, reaching Guay, not far from Blair Atholl. This days ride included the notorious climb of Shap Fell and the long haul into the Grampian Mountains.

Riding all of Saturday and finishing a few seconds to 1 am on Sunday morning, Lilian completed the final 234 miles to reach John o Groats. This mileage included an extra 8 miles travelled 'off-course' at Dingwall. She lost 1 hr 7 mins for this error, this being the only detrimental incident of the ride.

Lilian became the first female record holder over this route with a time of **3 days 20 hrs 54 mins.** Her average speed for the 870 miles being approximately 9.5 mph, including her three nights sleep. Her time was only 58 mins slower than the tricycle record put up by Les Meyers in 1929.

After a 10.75hr rest, Lilian continued for the 1000 mile record, recording 4 days, 19 hrs, 33 mins. Although at the time there wasn't an official recognition of the 1000 miles on the books of the WRRA, it was accepted later that year and when the course was measured a new time of **4 days 19 hrs 14 mins** was given.

What a remarkable achievement, a fifth of the ride was ridden in the rain. Lilian rode for 820 miles before she got off to walk a hill, and that was Berriedale. She climbed Shap on a 46" gear produced by Cyclo of Birmingham. She had a 6 speed system ranging from 46" to 74" on her Claud Butler. The timekeeper was Mr J.T. Wells. Her wheels were made with Conloy rims and Constrictor tyres, the best that money could buy at that time.

Lilian drank amongst other things 'Vita' grape juice and used 'Emprote' which seemed to be the in thing at the time as far as feeding was concerned.

Her WRRA record breaking career spanned just over 3 years, taking a total of 6 records in all. After the war Lilian played an active part in the WRRA and was an immense help on Edith Atkins and Eileen Sheridan's End to End and 1000 mile records.

I recently spoke to Ethel Brambleby who time trialled at all distances from 10 miles to 24 hrs with her racing career covering 50 years from the 1930's to the 1980's. She reminded me how much opposition there was from the male cycling fraternity to women racing. This bears out what Edie Atkin's husband, Ron, said about the Women's Road Records Association stipulating that the female record aspirants must not let the side down and appear unladylike during, or at the end of, their efforts, as this would fuel the ego's of the male hierarchy who ran the sport.

Ethel mentioned Lilian Dredge having to take asleep every night instead of carrying on until she was really tired. I think that with Lilian beating four days for the End to End and then taking less than another day to complete the 1000 miles was proof that women could stand the pace as well as the men. In fact when Marguerite Wilson went a year later she took nearly a day off Lilian's End to End figures purely by taking much shorter sleeps, as and when she wanted them, rather than at a set time.

Women's racing against the clock in time trials has until recently taken second place to the men. Ethel mentions having to start in time trials at 5.00 am in the dark and the cold, before the men. In fact in the mid 1960's Beryl Burton said that if she could start in the middle or end of the men's field I.e. some 1.5 hours later than normal, she could have improved Competition Record at most distances much sooner, due to being warmer and having had more sleep. It wasn't until 1988 that women were integrated into the mens field of riders which gives a much fairer balance of times and conditions.

Along with Lyn Stancer, better known as 'Petronella', Lilian Dredge became a pioneer for womens cycling issues in the 1930's. She rode the End to End against everyone's advice proving that a woman could do anything she made up her mind to do.

Lilian passed away in January 1987 aged 83 years.

No 7 INNES AND THOMPSON 5th JULY 1938 TANDEM END TO END

'Lol' Innes and Bill Thompson, two Yorkshire vegetarians, tried to establish new tandem figures for the End to End in July 1937. As true amateurs they attempted the record during their annual works holidays. They were lucky to have a following wind and felt that with even more luck they could beat the RRA standard by 3.5 hours.

However, luck was against them just after Auchterarder with 600 miles covered. They crashed heavily and the 'stoker' Bill Thompson was stunned and badly cut and bruised. The tandem was beyond repair out there in the middle of the Highlands of Scotland. It had broken handlebars, buckled wheels and bent cranks. They sadly had to abandon the attempt, only to try again one year later.

Our valiant pair tried again on July 5th - 7th 1938, during their holiday week. They didn't have much luck with the wind on this second attempt, but they still made fine progress to cover 420 miles in the first 24 hours and at Auchterarder where they had crashed the previous year, they took a three hour rest.

When they arrived at John o Groats they had set a new record of **2 days,14 hours, 48 mins** which stood f or 14 years. They then rested for seven hours, travelled back to Yorkshire, went out on the Club run on the Sunday and back to work on the Monday !

The RRA had set a standard of 3 days for the tandem. This record hadn't been attempted since 1895, when G.P. Mills and T.A.Edge put up a paced ride using ferries in Scotland, to record 3 days, 4 hrs, 46 mins.

As I mentioned earlier Innes and Thompson were unlucky with the wind. They had to start on the prescribed date as it was part of their annual holiday, and was the only way of getting helpers, unlike nowadays where people seem to get time off quite easily, which is good for End to Enders.

The Air Ministry supplied a forecast which gave Northerly winds in Scotland and turned out to be very accurate.

They started very strongly with a westerly wind at 9 am, which got them to Exeter, 120 miles, in 6 hrs 5 mins, even after stops for chain trouble, road repairs and very heavy traffic. They ran into heavy rain at Bristol, 196 miles at 7.00 pm having taken just 10 hrs to here, they stopped for a 10 mins feed. They ran out their 12 hr mileage near Gloucester with 228 miles. The night started calmly and they reached Kidderminster 270 miles at 11.28pm. Just beyond Whitchurch at 327 miles, Bill Thompson suffered stomach trouble and took an 8 min stop. The riders took the hilly main road through Tarporley instead of the flatter route through Eaton village, which Opperman and Ferris had used.

The cold dawn brought an unwelcome freshening North-west wind accompanied by torrential rain. They arrived at Warrington at 4.32 am with 351 miles covered. Just beyond Warrington at Newton le Willows, the riders took a 20 mins feed stop at Phil Johnson's house.

The wind was now well against them as they continued their ride to run out the 24 hours with 420 miles covered. A brilliant mileage in such conditions. They reached Kendal 424 miles, 11 mins later. They took a 30 mins break here but had to continue against a headwind.

They reached Carlisle 50 mins inside schedule, 469 miles, in 27 hours 40 mins up to there, in spite of the tough conditions they were gradually gaining on their schedule hour by hour. At

Beattock 508 miles, they had started to drop and were only 36 mins inside the schedule. Stirling and then Auchterarder where they had to abandon on their first attempt the previous year, was reached. They took a 3 hour break here for a bath, sleep and a meal at 9.40 pm on the second evening.

At 2 am Thursday they resumed their ride in freezing thick mist. It was now bitterly cold, they suffered these conditions for another 3 hours. Along this section including the climb out of Perth to the summit of Drumochter, they dropped behind their schedule for the first time since the start. For the next 100 miles through the Grampians, the riders were fed and helped solely by their following car. I would imagine that the lack of telephone HQ and indeed telephones in this remote area was to blame.

The wind was now coming in from the North east and they reached Aviemore 696 miles just 17 mins down on schedule now. Inverness 728 miles saw them 10 mins behind schedule at noon. They were due to take a four hours stop here, it being the last major outpost on route for hospitality, however they decided instead to press on and forego a rest, putting them at an advantage of 4 hours which they knew they would need to overcome the hostile conditions waiting for them on the coast road and the 'Ord of Caithness'.

Another scheduled stop at Bonar Bridge, 777 miles, was omitted which put them a total of 5 hours in hand. The road conditions at Golspie and Brora were atrocious making it hard for the tired riders, despite this, they gamely rode up the 'Ord of Caithness' and Berriedale, to reach Wick 852 miles at 10.30 pm.

They covered the last 17 miles in thick mist and heavy rain to reach John o Groats at 11.48 pm. A new record for the 869 miles now stood at **2 days 14 hours 48 mins.**

They rode gears of 62, 78 and 89" to Auchterarder and 59, 69, 78" for the remainder of the journey.

Information for this article was supplied courtesy of 'Cycling' with text from myself.

No 8 MARGUERITE WILSON 1st SEPTEMBER 1939
LADIES SOLO BICYCLE END TO END AND 1000 MILES

On Tuesday September 1st 1939 at 10 am Marguerite Wilson set out on her attempt on the End to End and 1000 miles. The first leg of the journey runs easterly and she battled into a stiff headwind. In fact a cameraman at the start at Lands End had been blown from his vantage point a few feet up on stepladders. So hard was the ride over Bodmin Moor that Marguerite wondered whether the wrong decision had been taken to start at all, but of course one must remember that the start of the war was looming and daily becoming ever closer. Apparently when she was waiting at Lands end, she waited three days with a gale blowing the wrong way off the land. On the third day a Hercules official said to her 'you are starting tomorrow whatever the wind is doing' ! Marguerites reply turned everybody pale, but on the fourth day the wind turned enough to make a start. In fact it turned out to be the very last day she could have started on, as when she arrived at John O Groats, blackout restrictions were being put into place, making night time movement almost impossible and even more so in that region with

'Scapa Flow' and the British Navy's operation so close to land. As she battled on from Bodmin the spirit and determination that had made this beautiful blonde athlete the fastest woman of her day prevailed, and she continued on to Okehampton to be 52 mins down on schedule, taking just 6 hrs 4 mins for 98 miles, all done against the wind. At Bristol the road bears north, putting the wind on the riders right shoulder, although still not favourable. A 40 mins stop was made here. She was now 1.5 hrs behind her schedule having ridden 193 miles in 12 hours.

At Kidderminster 272 miles, Marguerite stopped for a sleep in a specially equipped caravan that was following the event. Just after this stop the following cars lost sight of the rider, and not believing she could have travelled so far ahead of them they discontinued the chase and started to go back and look down other roads thinking she had taken a wrong turning with the signposts not being easy to see in the moonlight. In fact she had recuperated so well from the sleep and feed that she rode off as if riding a 10 mile time trial. She was now far ahead of the helpers cars even with the wind still not favourable.

All through the Midlands and on towards the Industrial North, Marguerite started to pick up lost time to be at Wigan 364 miles in 24 hours. She was now only 30 mins behind schedule. After a short rest she picked up speed to average 18 mph for the next part of the journey to the foot of Shap. Records show that at the bottom of Shap she was a few minutes down on schedule, but she climbed so strongly that by the summit she was a quarter of an hour ahead. After the ride, Marguerite said the climb of Shap was the part of the ride she most enjoyed. She climbed on gears of 66" 72" and 84" on her Hercules bike. Shap is 1,304 ft high and she had a strong crosswind to battle against. By 6 pm on the Wednesday she reached Carlisle 470 miles and over the border to Gretna. One local resident who had seen her flash by pursued by a line of cars asked if it was a runaway wedding, and if so where was the groom ? She was now faced with a series of climbs as she entered into her second cold dark night. Her hands were now getting very sore, so helpers put double the layers of tape on the handlebars to cushion the road shocks. On this lonely stretch she sang to herself as she rode steadily on to reach Lanark in the early hours of Thursday morning where she took a three hour stop for sleep and food. This put the rider behind schedule once again. She pressed on refreshed to reach Perth 612 miles, 1.5 hrs down on schedule. After 48 hours of riding, she'd covered 632 miles at an average speed of 13.25 miles per hour.

On Thursday morning Marguerite climbed into the Grampian Mountains. The purple coloured hills dwarfing the little black clad figure as she strove northwards towards John o Groats. At Glengarry the rain fell heavily on the mountain tops and after a while the sun broke through the clouds to glint on the riders blonde hair. As she descended Glengarry, the wind turned quite strongly in her favour, and this combined with the warm sun revived the rider and she picked up speed again to be just an hour behind schedule at Aviemore.

By Inverness where her schedule was made to run at 10 mph, she gained enough speed to be three quarters of an hour ahead of schedule and was gaining, with the wind still in her favour. At Dingwall, 749 miles, she was over 2 hrs up.

By Bonar Bridge with 100 miles to go she had gained another hour and was now well into her third night with a silvery moon glinting on the sea out on the right. A short break at Lybster was taken before the last stage from Wick was undertaken at a steady 20 mph. She finished with a sprint over the last 200 yards, taking the record by 22 hours in **2 days 22 hrs 52 mins.**

After the congratulations were over Marguerite wanted to be on her way again to complete the 1000 miles and she took quite a lot of persuading to stop for a breakfast and rest break first. She left John o Groats at 11 am and turned into the wind that had blown her to the finish of her greatest record. As she left the hotel yard, she looked out to sea where a destroyer could be seen in the distance. There was a tension in the air as the helpers had heard radio bulletins at the Hotel saying war was imminent. She completed the final miles in the dark looking for the lights of the town at Wick. She looked in vain until the outskirts of the town were reached. There the police and soldiers gave the information that 'blackout' had come into force. The 1000 miles was finally completed in **3 days 11 hrs 44 mins.** On route she ate cream buns, bananas, chops, sandwiches, eggs and chocolate. She drank milk, tea, cream soda and coffee.

Marguerite Wilson started cycling at 17 years of age, winning her first 10 mile time trial in 29 mins 14 secs. She had been very good at lots of different sports at her school in Bournemouth, playing hockey, tennis and netball. She was a good runner and had won a gold medal for her County at hurdling. She was 21 years old when she tackled the End to End and 5ft 10" tall, definitely the youngest female End to Ender, in fact the youngest person ever, since G.P. Mills in the 19th Century. She excelled at riding in hard conditions, tackling a lot of her records against adverse winds. In 1938, when preparing for her End to End by attacking the London to York and 12 hr records, she had ridden like this as if in defiance of the unfavourable wind. She was an amateur rider at the time, and G.H.Stancer suggested the conditions were totally wrong and she was pushing too high a gear to succeed, but succeed she did taking the London to York in 10 hrs 54 mins and improving the 12 hrs to 215 miles. She repeated this feat as a professional in 1939 before her End to End and improved the London-York by 51 mins to 10 hrs 3 mins and raised the 12 hr mileage to 230 miles.

She won the Bidlake Memorial Trophy for her outstanding performances in 1939 and it was presented to her by G.H. Stancer. She was the first woman recipient.

Marguerite went on to take the 25 and 50 mile records in 1940 plus London to Liverpool, London to Birmingham, London to Brighton and back, and finally the Edinburgh to Glasgow and back. In 1941 she reclaimed the 50 mile record after it was taken from her by A. Briercliffe in 1940. This brought her final tally of records to 22.

It would be six years before women's record breaking resumed in 1947

Most of the information for this article was courtesy of The Cycling Magazine and Alan J Ray's book 'Cycling Lands End to John O Groats'.

No 9 J.K.LETTS AND S.W.PARKER AUGUST 2nd 1947
TANDEM TRICYCLE END TO END AND 1000 MILES

Letts and Parker beat the tandem-trike RRA standard by 1 day 1 hr 19 mins with 2 days 22 hrs 41 mins, going on for the 1000 miles in 3 days 12 hrs 25 mins, between August 2nd and August 5th 1947.

They left Lands End at 8 am on the Saturday morning. The timekeeper was F.W.' Robby' Robinson. All went well until Camborne where Syd, the stoker, recalls that a local cyclist came out of a left hand turning, collided with them and bent their handlebars slightly, cutting Jim Lett's finger in the process. Syd reckons the chap was drunk as he was staggering all over the road. They lost approximately 1 minute. Bodmin was passed in 3 hrs 17 mins and at Okehampton they had a sit down feed and rest. Between Taunton and Bridgwater, Syd recalls them stopping for a call of nature when Jim tripped and fell into a ditch filled with stagnant smelly water which left Syd on the back getting the full odour until Almondsbury was reached beyond Bristol where the local club had arranged a sit down feed and change of clothing.

In the first 12 hours 181.5 miles were covered. At 1.58 am on August 3rd they got to Worcester and another sit down feed was taken under a railway arch. A loose cotter pin was dealt with by a large hammer wielded by a local clubman, so much so, that when the hammer struck, the noise was magnified by the arch and Jim Letts nearly jumped out of his skin, thinking that the tandem trike had been ruined. Needless to say everything was OK and no more mechanical problems arose. On through Wellington at 4.57 am and they reached 24 hours just before Tarporley producing 333 miles. Another stop for a rest and feed at Newton-le-Willows, Warrington, at 9.19 am. The house of a local clubman, Phil Johnson, was used and a large table had been laid with two of three big bowls of cornflakes and different types of cereals, brown and white bread, sandwiches, coffee, tea, soft drinks and considering there was food rationing due to the war years it was a wonderful spread. Syd's wife Ivy had arranged most of these sit down feed stops by letter in the previous months leading up to August. Syd recalls her sending out about 80 letters to club folks on route as there were very few telephones in those days.

Wigan 10.21 am, Preston 11.30 am and on to Kendal for another stop at Mrs Braithwaites, where Syd was suffering with his feet. Taking his shoes off did the trick, probably cooling his feet down. They left Kendal at 3.04 pm, and even with the stops they were still considerably hours up on schedule. Shap was climbed at 4.22 to bring them to Carlisle where another trike record breaker, Ed Tweddle had laid on a steak dinner as befitting the fact he was a butcher Lockerbie was reached at 8.21 pm just over 36 hours for about 490 miles and these chaps were regarded as just fast tourists, although Syd had broken the London-York and 12 hour trike record in 1938. Now on through Crawford 10.38 pm to Lanark at half past midnight into August 4th. The only time Syd and Jim fell out and had cross words on this trip was when they approached Beattock Summit. Jim who had ridden over it on a previous training trip kept saying it was a tough climb, which unnerved them both. When they reached the summit Syd felt it wasn't a very hard climb and told Jim so. They stopped and walked away from each other. The timekeeper 'Robby' Robinson spoke to them both separately and got them to patch things up. Honour was soon restored and they got back on the tandem trike and resumed their ride still way up on schedule. In fact, being so many hours up on schedule was causing problems with helpers and feed stations on route. Syd's wife had to ring the police in Glasgow from Carlisle to forewarn a local Glasgow clubman that his services would be required much sooner than planned at Stirling. Syd recalls a trike rider approaching them just as they left the town. He was sweating profusely as he handed over a large bag of sandwiches to the pair. Syd thanked him as they pedalled away but when he sampled the sandwiches later, he realised they were soaked in paraffin which had leaked out of the primus stove kept in his saddlebag.

Perth was reached at 6.08 am and their gain in time was extended even further still. They had actually missed a feed at Auchterarder due to not being able to contact the helper. At Dunkeld they had another sit down feed on the grass verge very early in the morning, 7.40 am, bathed in sunshine and feeling very pleased in the knowledge that they could tackle the Grampians in warm daylight. The 48 hours ran out here at 622 miles and they were now approximately 10 hrs up on schedule.

Pitlochry and Dalwhinnie were reached before midday. Through Aviemore and on to Inverness where another steak dinner was served up thanks to another clubman who was a butcher. Syd remembers Jim insisting on having a shave with his 'cut-throat' razor, not a wise move after so many hours steering a tandem trike. Syd preferred to spend his time eating and resting, but was safe in the knowledge that his wife Ivy, being an accomplished red cross volunteer, could save Jim from bleeding to death if the razor had slipped. Approximately 1 hour was taken for this rest. At Tain, Syd recalls hallucinating, seeing an old-time ferryman on the side of the road beckoning to him. Its not surprising when you think they hadn't had a sleep at any of their stops.

The left turn and climb out of Helmsdale was the toughest climb on the route, and they walked Berriedale with the timekeeper alongside them. At the top, one of the helpers patted Syd on the back and said 'you're OK now, its straight on'. That statement nearly lost them the record as before Dunbeath is entered you descend rapidly and strike a very sharp left hand hairpin bend. Its pitch black now, middle of the night, lights not much use. Syd reckons they were 'bobby dodgers' - battery lights which were prone to flickering on and off. Jim shouted as they hit the bend, Syd instinctively swung his full weight over the inner wheel just in time. Years later when Syd went over the course on a touring holiday, he was amazed to see in daylight how close they had been to the edge of a fatal sheer drop into the sea and the rocks below.

Just beyond Wick the road turns right at the village of Reiss and in the pitch dark and enveloping mist they missed the turn and went straight on to just outside of Castletown where there was a water pumping station. They stopped and went inside to find the attendant to ask him the way. Syd says they gave him quite a fright seeing two figures dressed in black tights and alpaca jackets turning up in the middle of the night. He directed them across country to John o Groats and it turned out to be a rutted track and not the proper road. The tandem trike was bucking in all directions and they felt more and more lost. The first cottage they came to they knocked the door for someone to help them. A very frightened lady appeared and pointed in the general direction through a window. They eventually came to a main road and after enquiring more directions from an hotel, they finally reached John o Groats from the opposite direction. The timekeeper was waiting on the bench outside the hotel, fast asleep, but awoke when they rang their bell. The helpers had been scouring the ditches looking for the lost riders. In retrospect they should have retraced their steps to Reiss as soon as they realised they were off course, but as Syd says, when one has been without sleep for 3 nights, one doesn't think straight or logically. They had made it at 6.40 am to take 1 day 1 hr 19 mins off the RRA standard with **2 days 22 hrs 41 mins** - a truly remarkable achievement.

After food and a short rest, they continued for the 1000 with just 121 miles to do. The weather was fine and warm as they set off to Castletown, 892 miles at 10.45 am. At Dunnet Head, Jim said he felt very sleepy so they swapped positions and Syd took over on the front. They had practised for this eventuality so didn't have to change or alter anything on the machine. At 'Reay Water Bridge' 908 miles at 1.30 pm they stopped at the turning point and lay on the grass for a ten minute sleep, the first since Lands End - 3 days days ago. 'Robby' the timekeeper went over to a farm and collected some eggs for a quick meal to see them through Thurso to Wick. Jim now resumed his steering duties and they had one more stop for afternoon tea at

Thurso Hotel much to the amazement of the guests. Syd settled for a kipper. Then on to Castletown again, back to Reiss, return to Castletown for the last time at 992 miles at 8.05 pm. On past the Post Office at Mey running out some extra miles over the 1000 just to be safe, finishing eventually at the cross roads between Wick and Canisbay at just after 9 pm to record **3 days, 12 hrs, 25 mins,** beating the RRA 1000 miles standard by virtually a whole day - not bad for fast tourists !

Both riders had used their annual holiday for the attempt. They had to go whatever the weather, which turned out OK with just a variable wind. Syd says everything was rationed. Food and petrol coupons were issued and dated. Everyone mucked in and saved what coupons they could for them. The system used for getting rid of out-of-date petrol coupons was to hand over coupons and money last thing when the engine was running, for a quick get-away. They had wonderful help from lots of club folk throughout the ride. Syd has no recollection of the cost of the attempt as most folk gave them what they had. A trait that seems to have carried on in the cycling circles to this present day. You realise how kind and generous people are in this sport of ours.

Syd was 31 years of age and a coach builder by trade. Jim was 41 and a manager of a timber yard. They trained every weekend for nine months prior to the attempt, but Syd says he had never ridden a tandem trike before, or since !

Apart from the End to End and 1000 miles the other highlight of Syd's record breaking days was in 1938 on a Trike - London to York in 10 hrs 24 mins, going on for the 12 hr record with 230 miles This record was broken by Dave Duffield seventeen years later by only three quarters of a mile.

Jim Letts took a total of 4 RRA records and Syd Parker took 5.

Some of the details for this account were courtesy of The Cycling Magazine; extra information was supplied by Syd Parker, with comments and text from myself.

No 10 HERBERT PARKES 18th JUNE 1949 TRICYCLE END TO END

Bert Parkes, the 38 year old Mersey RC rider, set off from Lands end at the very unorthodox time of 10 pm on Friday 18th June 1949. He'd started by using the 10 pm signal from the BBC radio, possibly the one at the Hotel, and with credible witnesses in place, this method was quite common practice until the 80's. It could still be used today providing there is an Official Observer and another witness to confirm the start. The last pip of the hourly signal is used to despatch the rider, also the BT speaking clock could be used if required.

The record Bert was attacking was the trike record put up by Les Meyers in 1929, some twenty years earlier, one of the first records put up without the use of ferries in Scotland. He was riding without any motorised help at all, relying on a saddle bag to carry waterproofs and sandwiches etc. He had a double bottle cage on his handlebars and used a 4 speed derailleur with fairly low gears, from 52" to 72". His lights were already mounted on the trike so he probably had spare batteries in his saddlebag as well.

At the time of this first attempt by Bert, the 1939-45 war had only been over for 3 years so a major lack of food could have indeed been a problem but we were reckoning without the generosity of club folk the length of the country who gave the rider his much needed feeds by dipping into their own rations. Petrol, food and clothing were still on ration due to the war, so a following car would be difficult to find fuel for.

He had no previous experience of record breaking, was a pure amateur time triallist of no more than 'average ability' which I find an amazing description considering what he was about to undertake. Les Meyers, the previous record holder was regarded as a 'fast tourist' again a statement I find hard to swallow - Lands End to John o Groats inside 4 days on a trike in 1929 ! I find these riders performances worthy of a better description.

Bert was a regular Mersey RC member. He lived at Queensferry and worked in the steel works at Shotton. I also have reliable information from Peter Barlow that on Bert's record, he had another hard riding clubman follow him from Bristol to Perth at a fair distance behind. His name was Harry Okell, he was carrying a few tools and spares and food etc, but it was so cold by Perth he had to retire and let Bert carry on alone. That's got to be close on 400 miles - what a heroic undertaking. Harry, I noticed, was listed as winning the Mersey RC 24 hr race in 1948 with 412 miles, and came 7th in the same event in 1949 with exactly the same mileage - so you could say he was consistent.

The marshalling through towns and the feeding was provided by clubmen and women the whole length of the 872 miles. A telephone relay system called 'Operation Spanish Armada' with the HQ at Tommy Barlow's house near Manchester was used to gather information as to the riders progress for marshalling and feeding purposes. It was probably the first ever time a telephone HQ had been used in this way for the End to End record. Tom and Peter Barlow manned it and organised the ride for 4 days.

Bert Parkes a popular member of the Mersey RC was using his annual works holiday which was a fixed date, so he had to be lucky with the weather, unlike nowadays, with up to five weeks holiday a year and numerous bank holidays along with flexi time, most people can now afford to wait for good conditions to be forecasted before booking time off. Its amazing when you read through the accounts of the End to End rides, just how many were reliant upon the annual fortnights holiday, either for themselves or for a team of helpers comprising of clubmates and workmates, using the same holiday period to give their valuable assistance.

He rode on through the night, reaching Exeter 121 miles on Saturday morning at 7.41am. It had been a chilly night over Bodmin Moor and then skirting along the edge of Dartmoor, but at least it hadn't rained and there wasn't much wind. By the 12 hour point, he'd got nearly to Taunton 155 miles. He was riding to a schedule that would give him a 4 hour beating of Les Meyers record. Parkes schedule was split into 4 stages. Lands End to Newton le Willows - 357 miles, at 12.5 mph. Newton le Willows to Stirling, Stirling to Inverness - 373 miles at 11 mph, and a final 141 miles at 8 mph.

After Taunton, Bert had several rather long stops for food and by Bridgnorth at 285 miles he was an hour behind schedule to reach his first major stop at Newton le Willows, he was still riding comfortably up to that point. He stopped at Phil Johnson's house for three hours and had a massage, a sleep and a breakfast of cereal and fish. He set back out on the road to Carnforth, 409 miles, with renewed vigour maintaining a steady 14 mph. He reached Kendal,

424 miles, bang on schedule, climbed the whole of Shap without walking and crossed the border into Scotland at 4 pm on Sunday.

The next big climb took him to the Beattock Summit and after a run through the industrial area, he reached Stirling, 580 miles, some time after midnight Sunday. He took another long break for a wash, a good sleep at George Elrick's bike shop run by a clubman, leaving after another 'hearty' breakfast at 4.20 am Monday morning at 'first light'.

Bert Parkes took the road through Perth to Bankfoot where the Mersey Roads Club President, Guy Pullan, had a feed ready for him. Then came the ascent of the Grampians to Dalwhinnie, just over the summit, where another feed awaited him. At that point Bert was down on schedule but was still riding smoothly and with confidence. Apart from the day being hot, in fact, that hot it had melted the tar on the road, causing his tyres to sink in, rather like riding in sand. The wind was favourable and helped him over a fast stretch off the mountains to Inverness, 730 miles, at 6.20 pm Monday.

By now, after nearly three days on the road, he'd grown himself a light beard and was starting to look 'swarthy' with his limbs and face tanned by the hot sun. At Inverness he was supposed to take a three hour break but decided to cut it down to two hours to bring him back onto schedule. After a good meal of steak and chips and hospitality from the Clachnacuddin CC, he set back out on the road to tackle the last daunting hills at 8.20 pm on that Monday. He had two trike riders following him at a fair distance, in case he had a mechanical failure, and turned due north over the shorter hillier route over Aultnamain instead of going the longer low road route through Tain.

At Helmsdale, 817 miles, he was 2.5 hours up on his schedule, using his low range of gears to good effect over the Ord of Caithness. He passed through Wick, 854 miles, at 9.15 am Tuesday morning and using two Observers, was timed in at John o Groats at 3 minutes past eleven, breaking the previous record by nearly seven hours.

Quite why he started late at night in Cornwall, I do not know, whether it was to miss traffic in towns or to finish in daylight, or to climb certain hills in daylight. For whatever reason, it worked well for him, giving him a new time of **3 days 13 hours 3 mins.**

Little did he know the success would be short lived !

Some information was courtesy of The Cycling Magazine with additional material from Peter Barlow and comments from myself.

No 11 J.K. LETTS 16th JULY 1949 TRICYCLE END TO END

Almost exactly one month after Bert Parkes improved the trike record to 3 days 13 hours 3 mins, Jim Letts set out from Lands end at 8 am on Friday 16th July. He was timed away by F W 'Robby' Robinson, the same timekeeper who had officiated on the successful tandem trike record that Jim had put up with Syd Parker in 1947.

The 45 years old Ealing Paragon CC rider had a favourable wind from the start although it was accompanied by heavy rain. By Launceston at 78 miles he was 53 minutes ahead of his schedule and at Okehampton 97 miles he was 1.5 hours ahead. After a sit down feed at Exeter he sped on still gaining time to be 100 mins ahead at Taunton, 151 miles. After another feed at Bristol, he reached Berkeley Road, 216 miles, done by 1 am on Saturday. On through the night he passed through Gloucester and Tewkesbury, still holding his speed. By Worcester he had gained two hours, but had to stop for another feed.

By the time he reached Kidderminster at 5.35 am, the wind had turned against him and although he pushed on strongly his lead in time was beginning to slip. After 24 hours of riding he had amassed 298 miles. A stop for refreshments at the usual house belonging to Phil Johnson at Newton le Willows on the A49 at 355 miles, he was now 1 hr 44 mins ahead of schedule. By Preston he'd lost a little more time and so decided to take only a 45 mins stop at Kendal instead of the scheduled 1 hour.

Jim then set off to climb Shap. He had now reached the half way point - he rode into heavy rain on this tortuous climb and lost another 10 mins on schedule. At the Parkhouse Café, just beyond Carlisle at 469 miles he took a 20 minute break at midnight. He was steadily losing time as he entered Scotland. On through Gretna, Crawford, Lanark and all through that second night reaching just beyond Carluke in 48 hours, with 550 miles done.

Jim stopped at Stirling, 575 miles, for a much needed rest and feed and left there at 11 am Sunday with just 37 mins gain on schedule. The wind was troubling him on this next section of road but at least the weather was brighter. Past the Bridge of Allan, Dunblane and Perth, he battled on to Dunkeld, where another feed was provided. With 622 miles done he was now entering the Grampians, through Blair Atholl, Dalwhinnie and Aviemore to Inverness, now down on his schedule by 23 minutes that allowed a one hour stop here. He bravely made the decision to cut short his stop and started off again only 3 mins down, just before 2 am Monday.

By then sleep deprivation was affecting him and some twelve miles later at Beauly he was persuaded to take a sleep in the following car for 15 minutes. Refreshed by this, he pressed on towards Dingwall, 746 miles, where another delay lost him time. His freewheel had broken and he had to ride a spare trike belonging to his tandem trike partner Syd. The helpers repaired his machine and had him reunited with it after only 10 miles. He was now 20 mins down at 4.30am and took a feed at Bonar Bridge, 786 miles, with just over 3 days riding 'under his belt'. It was around this point that he turned round in the road and started to ride back the opposite way towards the helpers and had to be forced to turn back in the right direction. When questioned at the end of the ride, Jim said he had hallucinated and seen an old lady on the side of the road who told him to go back home ! When you analyse the ride, he had been on the road for well over three days with no more than about 15 mins sleep in total.

He was due at Helmsdale, 825 miles, at 11.20 am, and arrived at 12.15 am, but with the schedule being made 'generous' at this far point of the ride, he knew that barring accidents, the record was assured. He rode strongly through Wick and took the correct turning, unlike his previous tandem trike record where they missed the right turning at Reiss, and headed towards Castletown.

Even with a puncture sustained in the last closing miles Jim reached John o Groats at 5.27 pm Monday 19th July, timed at the finish by R W Robinson, with **3 days 9 hours 27 mins,** taking 3 hrs 36 mins off Bert Parkes's record that had stood for just one month.

So, for Jim Letts, that was two End to End records - one on Tandem Trike and one on Trike, plus the 1000 miles on tandem trike and much earlier in 1932 he had broken the London to Bath and back tandem trike record with S.W. O'Shea, in 11 hrs 36 mins 31 secs. A total of four RRA records in all.

Jim Letts passed away in April 1989 at 84 years of age. He was a founder member and the first Chairman of the Ealing Paragon C.C. He was also a member of the Royal Zoological Society and an accomplished photographer.

Some of this information was courtesy of The Cycling Magazine with additional comments from Syd Parker and myself.

No 12 BERT PARKES 16th JUNE 1950
TRICYCLE END TO END

Now 39 years of age, one year older and wiser than for his previous record, Bert Parkes set out again at the unorthodox time of 9 pm on a Friday from Lands End Hotel south door. The Cycling Magazine of that week reports it was a fresh westerly wind but John Williams says there was a 'raging wind' on the first day , strong enough to get him to Lancashire in 25 hours.

Parkes was trying to regain his record back off Jim Letts who had taken it in 1949 after Bert had held it for just one month. He was riding a narrow 27" width axle trike with 4 gears ranging from 52" to 72". Again he was carrying his own food and requirements for the journey up to Bridgnorth, where he would pick up a following car with Peter Barlow, and Tommy Barlow who would do the timekeeping at the end.

He encountered rain over Bodmin Moor during the night but managed to reach Exeter at 5.36 am Saturday. He had already gained just over one hour on schedule; by Taunton at 152 miles at 7.42 am he had gained another 24 mins to be 1 hr 28 mins up. At Taunton one of the Observers sent telegrams to helpers further up the country informing them he had started and that he would probably be well up on schedule. He reached Bristol, 199 miles at 10.54 am, and was now two hours up. He continued to make excellent progress reaching Worcester, 269 miles, at 3.06 pm. Now over 2.5 hours up, the wind direction at this stage was a freshening north westerly which technically for the direction he was travelling in, was over 50% against him.

He was timed through Bridgnorth 287 miles at 5.21pm. He stopped for his third feed. As he proceeded north he now had a following car containing full back up for the rest of the journey, including a spare trike. Bert reached Tarporley at 9 pm having covered 337 miles in the first 24 hours. He was now on home territory as the Mersey Road Club 24 hour race passes through here in its early stages. By the time he had reached his major rest stop at Newton Le Willows, with 360 miles done at 10.45 pm, he had actually gained three hours on his schedule. He stopped for three hours sleep here and his machine was checked over for the remaining part of the journey. He left at 1.58 am Sunday with rain now falling, on into the darkness through industrial Lancashire and over Shap.

The rain continued as he crossed the border, he rode steadily on reaching Beattock Summit, 510 miles, where the rain had stopped. He stopped for a complete change of clothing. From this point the weather began to improve, the wind was now just from the west, but dying down as the day wore on.

Abington was reached at 3.20 pm, Sunday. He had managed to get three hours ahead of schedule despite the rain, the terrain, the stops for food etc. He passed through Stirling at 7.45 pm, riding strongly to complete his second full day in the saddle. By Perth as he headed for the Grampians the weather was near perfect with a warm westerly breeze. Into the small hours of Monday morning he started to feel sleepy and so took a 'nap' in the following car. This revived him considerably and as dawn broke he felt refreshed and strong again; strong enough to cut his two hour scheduled break at Inverness, down by half, leaving at 9.43 am. He was still nearly three hours ahead of schedule here.

Bert reached Bonar Bridge at 2.15 pm and was now 4 hrs 8 mins ahead of schedule. By Helmsdale at 818 miles he'd gained nearly another hour at 5.34 pm. He rode all of the 'Ord of Caithness' except for the last 100 yards which he ran up. He did the last seven miles to Wick, 855 miles, at 'evens' passing through at 8.25 pm, now six and a half hours gained. He got an enthusiastic reception at Wick and eventually reached that northern most tip of land at 9.38 pm, regaining his record from Jim Letts with a ride of **3 days 38 mins** a beating of 8 hrs 49 mins, one of the largest 'chunks' of time since 1905. Only one record has taken more time off than that; Crimes and Arnold's in 1954 with an 18 hours beating of Letts and Parkers tandem trike record.

The interest in the record was 'terrific', 159 telephone calls were received at the Barlow household, this I think set a precedent for attempts in future years. John Williams Senior (Father of Bob and John) was on this momentous record as an Observer, John junior also rode out to meet the following car, going as far as Scotland. He recalls getting the train back from Scotland. He must have been a teenager at the time and in later years went on to organise three or four very successful End to Ends in the late 90's and at the turn of the 21st century.

Apparently it was Bert Parkes who 'discovered' John Arnold. It was on Bert's ride home from work where he would be overtaken by this young chap on a rickety old bike. He told Bert he had ridden one or two club time trials. The times that John had produced as a novice were pretty impressive to Bert. A few weeks later, John bought a trike, rode the Tricycle Association 100 that Whitsun winning the event beating some 'star' riders and as Peter Barlow who related the story to me says, 'the rest is history'.

Another note of interest here, neither Albert Crimes nor John Arnold would contemplate attacking Bert Parkes Trike End to End record because he was a fellow clubman and a friend of theirs. Albert wanted Dave Duffield to attack it first, so that he could himself feel justified in attempting the record at a later date. Such was the comradeship of amateur club riders at the time.

This article was formed using passages from The Cycling Magazine, with additional material from Peter Barlow and John Williams.

No 13 S.F. (FRANK) COWSILL and A.E. (ALEC) DENTON 28th JULY 1952
TANDEM END TO END AND 1000 MILES

Monday 28th July saw Cowsill and Denton of the Lancashire Road Club start their assault on the tandem End to End record held by Innes and Thompson since 1938. The time to beat was 2 days 14 hrs 48 mins and a standard of 3 days 18 hrs set by the RRA, to beat for the 1000 miles.

They scheduled to cover the 870 miles in 2 days 10 hrs and during daylight hours they maintained a small lead on that schedule, but after a meal stop north of Kidderminster, they were delayed by a burst tyre, and then repeated bulb failure in their lamps. So at the 19 hr point after 345 miles they were 40 min behind schedule but with a proposed two hour forty mins break just before Warrington cut to two hours, they left on time and on schedule.

Members of their own club saw them through Buxton (Lancs) and from here to Bankfoot 623 miles they lost no more time. They heeded the advice given to them by the previous record holder Thompson, to wrap up warm against the freezing cold in the Grampians They were so cold on this second night through the Highlands they had to stop regularly to 'thaw out' and keep awake. By Inverness they had dropped an hour on schedule. One can't imagine such cold at the end of July.

After a stop for a meal with the Clachnacuddin CC in their clubroom at Inverness they continued to Bonar Bridge 778 miles to arrive 15 mins down on schedule. The final 93 miles to John o Groats were ridden with a good wind all the way, gaining all the while on their schedule to arrive at the John o Groats hotel mid afternoon 3.47 pm, Wednesday, clocking **2 days 8 hrs 47 mins.** A truly magnificent ride.

After a meal and a bath the riders decided to continue for the 1000 miles with over 1day 9 hrs to do 130 miles to beat the standard. They rode back along the route they had used to Dunbeath where they slept for 9 hrs, continuing for just over 100 miles to Dingwall, just north of Inverness, with a time of **3 days 7 hrs 41 mins.** The last 28 miles were done at 18 mph. They are, to the best of my knowledge the only modern day riders to just turn and virtually retrace the route for their remaining mileage for the 1000.

I spoke very recently in 2004 to Leslie Brown who at 91 years is the sole survivor of this epic voyage and he recalled the names of the other helpers and officials at that time.

The timekeeper was Mark Haslam, and Tommy Barlow was the Observer. Tom joined the team in Lancashire. The other members of the team were Frank Hart, Cliff Baxter, Austin Bridge, Les Brown and finally John Dearden who was a solicitor. Les said that apart from Tommy Barlow, the rest of the team were novices at helping on long distance rides, so really were unprepared for any problems that would have arisen.

He recalled a few, off the record incidents that occurred during the three days on the road. The first was on the road to Stirling at Cumbernauld, where the road goes down a hill to a 'T' junction with a halt sign. A policeman was stood by the junction with his bike; in those days they slung their large cape over the handlebars. When the helpers asked him if the tandem could just go left at the junction without stopping he replied "No, the rules must be obeyed" The lads were disappointed at this and stood by as the tandem came down the hill. At the last minute the policeman threw his cape over the halt sign and stood in the road to let the riders through. What a man !

The next memory he had was of the ride through the Grampians being absolutely freezing, so cold in fact that he had to lend his 'zipper' jacket to Frank Cowsill on the front of the tandem. Les said that the jacket fitted him like a glove as Frank was somewhat taller and larger than him.

By the time the riders had got to Inverness, they were both tired and cold. They stopped for a meal at the Clachnacuddin CC HQ cooked over an open hearth. Alec was very hungry and devoured everything put before him, but Frank was so tired and cold he couldn't eat. Les said he just sat and stared in front of him as if in a trance, which in hindsight was probably mild hypothermia.

They resumed their journey and after a couple of hours had passed they stopped again at a transport café. While waiting to get served Les noticed Frank taking a piece of cold half eaten toast somebody had left on a plate. He hid the toast behind his hand thinking nobody would notice and started eating. That was the turning point , they fed him up with as much as he could eat and from then on he was fine all the way to the end of the ride, although he had a few words with a post box in one of the villages on route, thinking it was Les's wife who always wore a red jumper - how tiredness can play tricks ! Actually Les's wife 'Jess' was helping at the telephone HQ in Manchester.

They broke the record and retraced their journey for the 1000. They stopped at Dunbeath for a sleep as there was still over a day to complete the remaining 100 miles. Les recalls the team trying to find a B&B and lodgings for the night. The riders slept at the pub. Tommy Barlow and the timekeeper stopped a mile or two down the road, which left two without a bed. The pub landlord said "If you've got camp beds, I've got the keys to the bank next door and you can sleep in there, but I'll have to lock you in mind !"

After a long sleep which really was too long for the riders as they had stiffened up very badly, Les recollected it was two to three hours of riding before they loosened up. The tandem took the coast road instead of going back over the Aultnamain climb. The 1000 miles ran out at Dingwall. It was a fortunate way of breaking the record as it meant they were three hours closer to home making for a much shorter journey back to Lancashire in the car, as the whole entourage and riders had to be back at work the following morning.

The tandem they used was borrowed off a clubmate and was a Claud Butler 'ultra short wheelbase' with 3 speed gears. There was a big difference in the size of the two riders. Alec Denton was only short and very thin and 'wiry' weighing about 9 stone, and approximately 5ft 6". Frank Cowsill was a big 'six footer' of a man and much larger than his 'stoker', and most of the helpers.

On looking though past 24 hr results, I noticed Alec Denton in 1954 went on to get third place with 441.76 miles behind John Arnold and Stan Bray. A very creditable ride on the Mersey course.

Les kept in touch with the riders over the years and said that Alec Denton had passed away in 1978 from kidney failure aged about 65, before dialysis was readily available. Frank Cowsill died two years ago in a nursing home. He had suffered a stroke and could hear and understand Les but could only communicate by nodding his head.

Les Brown at 91 is still very fit and active still 'getting the miles in' on his bike on local lanes, being a very keen DIY man he has just finished building a conservatory onto his home at Lochmaben near Lockerbie. He's in an ideal position as an observer for the Liverpool to Edinburgh record and of course the End to End. He said he'd had the pleasure of seeing virtually everybody go through over the years . His last one being Lynne in 2002. He remembers her dropping the bottle he'd handed up.

Over the years he's been in the helping teams on many great rides, including Albert Crimes Trike End to End, Bailey and Forrest tandem End to End, and of course Cowsill and Denton in 1952, plus many more over the years. I wish him well and hope he sees many more go through his 'patch' in the next few years.

Cowsill and Denton's record ride details were courtesy of The Cycling Magazine with additional material from Les Brown and comments from myself.

No 14 EDITH ATKINS JULY 27th 1953 END TO END LADY SOLO BICYCLE

At 4 am on Monday July 27th 1953, Edith Atkins set out from Lands End to become the first lady amateur to tackle the End to End.

She had already proved herself as a 'stayer', a term affectionately given normally to hard riding 'mile eating' male members of a cycling club. Edith had already taken the Women's RRA amateur record for the Lands End to London 287 miles in 17 hrs 13 mins in 1952. This was only 4.5 mins outside Marguerite Wilsons professional record some 14 years earlier.

In the months preceding her End to End Edith collected six national road records. She rode from Holyhead to London, 264 miles in 13 hrs 31 mins 57 secs. Then in one notable ride she broke the London to York record, 195 miles in 9 hrs 56 mins 20 secs; continued north to pass 234.75 miles in 12 hours; reached Edinburgh 385 miles in 21 hrs 37 mins, and at 24 hrs had amassed 422 miles, becoming the first woman to exceed 400 miles in 24 hours. Six days later she covered the Edinburgh to Glasgow and back 88.5 miles in 4hrs 38 mins 56 secs. What a year so far, followed two weeks later by the End to End.

There was a strong south westerly wind and bright moonlight as she was sent on her way by timekeeper Alan Gordon. Rain heralded a wet dawn before 25 miles was completed. She donned wet weather clothing and sped onwards to be at Exeter after a tough 120 miles in 6 hrs 28 mins. This was very heartening for her as it put her an hour up on schedule and two hours ahead of Marguerite Wilson's figures.

She reached Bristol in under 11 hours. Between Bristol and Gloucester the first 12 hours yielded 217 miles. A stop was made for a massage and warm food, she was now 24 miles ahead of Miss Wilsons mileage at this point in time.

On through Worcestershire and Shropshire where Whitchurch was reached by 11pm, having covered 320 miles. She stopped here for approximately 3.5 hours for food and sleep. At 2.30 am Tuesday 28th July Edie set off from Whitchurch and along the Cheshire lanes in bright moonlight towards Warrington and by the 24 hour point had amassed 347 miles. She was now slower by 17 miles at this point compared with Marguerite Wilson.

The wind wasn't much help now as she pushed on through Lancashire. She climbed Shap Fell in bright sunshine which really spurred her on to make a great 'out of the saddle' effort on this long tortuous climb which brought Edie back inside her schedule once again.

By Carlisle, reached in 32 hrs 23mins she was starting to feel sleepy and as she crossed the border at Gretna Green the weather was against her.

The climb over Beattock Summit had her battling into driving rain and wind. By Lanark, early Tuesday evening, Edie was only 23 mins inside her schedule. A 42 min stop was called for at Stirling for sustenance and massage. Food was provided by local club folk for her and the helpers.

Edie was scheduled to take another stop at Perth but not wanting to lose any more time she went straight through to Pitlochry to take a stop of nearly two hours. At the 48 hr point Mrs Atkins had covered 649 miles to Miss Wilson's 632. Quite an appreciable margin after so many hours in the saddle.

Edie was entering the Grampians, the hardest section of the ride as sleep deprivation was not only affecting her, but also her small band of dedicated helpers that included Lilian Dredge, who's husband Freddie was manning the phone HQ in London, her husband Ron, Lyn Stancer and timekeeper Alan Gordon. The times at various checkpoints on route testified as to Edie's courage and determination.

At Dalwhinnie 670 miles, she was 1 hr 19 mins ahead of her schedule. At Tomatin, 710 miles she was nearly two hours up. Inverness was reached but there is no report of her stopping here, only that she stopped before the 'Muir of Ord' to change her rear wheel to give a much lower set of gears for the climbs ahead.

At Aultnamain 770 miles came the heavy cold rain which soaked her through. At this point her following car was a long way behind, probably trying to negotiate the 'hair raising' drops and hairpin bends with poor camber on that section of road. Edie had to ride this section without any waterproof clothing at all. At Bonar Bridge with just 100 miles to go she stopped for a complete change of clothes and tried to get warm, not easy with just one car and not much room to manoeuvre. She lost 15 mins here.

She was still feeling the effects of her soaking as she started the climbs on the 'Ord of Caithness'. She rode all of the hills but by Berriedale Edie was really exhausted and suffering badly. The last 30 miles took her 2 hrs 34 mins and it was an exhausted rider who reached the John o Groats Hotel at four minutes past ten that Wednesday night, with a time of **2 days 18 hrs 4 mins.** Edith Atkins had beaten the professional ladies record by 4 hrs 48 mins. A remarkable record time that only three men had ever achieved before her; Rossiter, Opperman and Ferris.

After a near 5.5 hrs stop to sleep and get warm, Edith chose to go on for the 1000 miles which left her with 129 miles to complete in 12 hrs 13 mins to beat Miss Wilson's professional record, or 21 hrs 49 mins to beat Wynn Wrightson's amateur record produced only a few weeks earlier in 1953. Even after a rest and refreshment Edie was still badly affected by the cold rain her muscles had endured that last few hours riding up the north east coast. However, at 3.31 am on Thursday, almost 3 days after she had originally started in Cornwall, so far away now, Edith set off on the last daunting part of the journey.

The going was very tough and every time Edie turned into that cold rain with the wind coming off the sea she slowed down dramatically. She needed to do the last 80 miles at nearly 10 mph, the conditions were awful, and after seeing Edith continue to lose speed, Ron abandoned the ride to save her anymore suffering. When she stopped she was shivering from the cold and exhaustion. Her shoes were soaked causing her feet to be very chaffed and raw. She still had plasters on her toes from the recent 24 hr record ride.

So ended one of the most heroic post war records ever. Edith had taken so much out of herself from the 'borders' onwards and had so many soakings its amazing that she increased her advantage over Marguerite Wilson's record to an hour, let alone nearly five !

Compared to today's gearing she rode with very low gears between 54" and 82". This plucky housewife and mother of two children had as an amateur beaten the professionals time over this most arduous of routes. She rode for the Coventry Road Club who, like her family, must have been mighty proud of her.

Her diet was not a fussy one, just fairly standard food as far as reports go. Edith doesn't appear to have suffered any problems with what she ate on the ride. She consumed milky foods, barley water, eggs, tea, coffee, meat and vegetables. Ron, Edith's husband successfully organised her record attempts. He was an active racing member of the Coventry Road Club and when Edie joined the club it was 1949 before she took her riding and racing seriously. She maintained that she was not a 'natural' at cycling, but after seeing her successes at all distances, one would disagree with that statement. She was a member of the ladies racing team and had to work hard to maintain good results. They won many team titles and in 1950 they broke competition record at 50 miles.

Ron noticed at the end of long club rides Edie had a better recovery rate and seemed fresher than he did. In the winter prior to her End to End of 1953, she intensified her training when weather permitted. From January onwards she trained every other day putting in 20 to 30 miles at a time. In the months just prior to the End to End she had upped her mileage to over 300 miles a week. Her children John and Joy were at school so she was able to concentrate on her other interest which was 'physical culture', a mixture of posture, gymnastics, dance and balance, all adding to her physical stamina. With the team from the Physical Culture Club, she entered and won many competitions.

At 33 years of age, standing just 4 ft 11.5" and weighting just 7 stone 6 lbs, Edie was, along with Eileen Sheridan, among the shortest and lightest record breakers ever, yet she seemed absolutely tireless, which goes to prove that there is no set ideal average size for people to be able to break records, or excel at cycle racing. Also, one must remember in those days there were no women's specifically designed bikes. They rode just the smallest gents bike available with the saddle pushed as far forwards as possible, and virtually touching the top tube.

Nowadays the manufacturers have excelled at producing bikes that are designed for shorter upper body and arms, also the advent of 'compact' frames with sloping back top tubes has meant that virtually 'tailor made' bikes can be bought, 'off the peg'.

The bicycle she rode was an 'R.O.Harrison' frame, made in London and assembled in Coventry by Tom Bromwich, to Edie's specific requirements. It is currently on display along with Eileen Sheridan's 'Hercules' in the Coventry Transport Museum. I find it amazing that Coventry provided two of the toughest yet petite female cycle record breakers ever. Both taking the 'Blue Riband' in consecutive years, Edith in 1953 and Eileen in 1954. Both 7 stone and 4 ft 11".

Edie became a sought after 'guest of honour' and after dinner speaker at many cycling club dinners in the 50's, 60's and 70's. she was a very active and enthusiastic WRRA (Women's Road Record Association) member and voted against a separate amateur and professional set of records. From 1980 onwards the WRRA recognised just the one time and record to beat, and that was the fastest, whether performed by a professional or amateur status rider.

When I contacted Ron Atkins in 2004 he was 88 years of age and he still enthuses about Edie's achievements as if they had happened last year, let alone 50 years ago.

At John o Groats at the end of the record, he and Edie were sitting on the rocks after dinner looking out to sea, and she said 'how on earth did they ride Penny Farthings up to here at the turn of the century ? Ron recalls asking her if she would contemplate doing it all again, knowing that out of the six hours 'off the bike' time, she really only needed about 3 hours. She had been advised that a lengthy night time stop was the 'done-thing'. Edie said she was quite happy with what she had done, after all it was and still is the 'Blue Riband' of cycling records!

He praised her representing Birmingham and Coventry in gymnastics competitions gaining over 70 medals and winning 5 championships. She had been competing from 8 years of age. The confidence gained from performing and competing in gymnastics helped her tackle challenges that cropped up later when cycling took priority, and record breaking was her main aim.

Ron recalled Edie being summoned to an interview with the heads of Raleigh and Dunlop with a view to sponsorship for her record breaking, particularly the End to End and 1000, and afterwards driving her home from the meeting and she was quite upset at the outcome of the interview and said to him that she didn't want to be put under pressure by a stranger and that she wanted Ron to manage and organise her End to End.

Ron became interested in record breaking when he got involved in helping Jack Middleton and the tandem pairing of Raby and Mizzen. He said that financially, record breaking put a great strain on their resources. The End to End obviously being the largest financial outlay. One of the main reasons for taking a longer stop than necessary was to put her back on schedule so that helpers and checkers coming out wouldn't miss her. Don't forget that with only one small van, all the extra help they could get was important. Although Edie had told reporters at John o Groats she would love to have another try, as she was sure that with shorter stops and better weather she could take at least two hours off the time. Deep down however, she knew that without financial backing she would not be able to go again.

Ron remembers soft-soaping Edie and on the way home he bought her something she'd always wanted - a kilt. When asked what tartan she wanted, she said "I haven't a clue but I like the colour of that one there !" The shopkeeper said "That's the Gordon Clan Tartan" and she said "That one's fine, that's the name of our timekeeper, Alan Gordon".

Ron reckoned that she rated her Lands End - London and London - Holyhead and a 12 hr of 234.75, as rides that gave her great satisfaction. The important thing to him was that she had come through this tough period of record breaking looking and feeling non the worse for it. The WRRA had insisted that nothing should affect their image of women breaking records and ending up looking less feminine for it. Remember in 1953 it was still, as in the 20's and 30's, very much a man's world and there would have been quite a lot of male opposition to women proving they were a fair match to the men in athletic pursuits. He said that Edie played down the effort she had put in to break the End to End, likening it to a weekends hard ride with the club lads to the coast and back.

One or two amusing incidents he recalls, when Edie being well ahead of the following vehicle as she entered Perth in the 'wee small hours' took a wrong turn and got lost. She rode on looking for road signs until she spotted a policeman. Remember it is the middle of the night and she asked him the way to Inverness. He advised her to turn and retrace back into town and pick up the correct road. He was also inquisitive and asked her what she was doing out on her own at that time of night, to which she replied "I'm going to John o Groats!" I bet he thought 'Hmm a likely story'. Another time months later on holiday on the side of Ullswater in the Lake District, they were sleeping in the camper van. Edie awoke with a start, looked up, saw the roof rack through the sunroof of the van, and thought she was still on the record attempt, and panicked saying she'd got to get back on the bike !

During the record Ron recalls having to hand over the driving to Lilian Dredge on Berriedale as he had lost his powers of focus, he'd been driving so long, he'd almost lost his sight. Edie was right in front of him one minute, and the next she was way up the road. Luckily after a short sleep his vision returned to normal.

In her younger days, Edith's mother had won a bicycle in a whist drive at a social club, and from that she had gone on to be a founder member of 'The Coventry Meteor CC', to which Edie joined as her first club. Ron came along and whisked her away to the Coventry Road Club and that was really the start of the story.

At 75 years of age in her last racing season she rode 45 events and had completed the 'Wild Wales Challenge' ride five years running. The onset of Alzheimer's disease curtailed her riding to just local trips with Ron.

Edith died tragically in an accident while crossing the main A45 road near to home in 1999. She was 79 years of age.

John Atkins, her son, went on to become the British Cyclo-Cross Champion on numerous occasions. Parents Edie and Ron's determination and fitness had rubbed off on him to keep the Atkins name held high in competitive cycling circles.

Some of the details of Edith's record were courtesy of The Cycling Magazine, with additional material by Ron Atkins and Alan J Ray

No 15 EILEEN SHERIDAN FRIDAY JULY 9TH 1954
LADIES SOLO BICYCLE END TO END AND 1000 MILES

Eileen Sheridan's rise to fame started much the same as Edith Atkins. Both girls came from Coventry although rode for different clubs, Eileen for the Coventry Cycling Club and Edith for the Coventry Road Club. Eileen came into cycle racing through club life, going out on Sundays and weekend tours with the local C,T,C, she soon started to prove herself against other girls winning many time trials from 10 miles up to 12 hours and regularly would have been placed in the first five riders in the men's event, as in those days the ladies and men's events were run off separately.

Eileen's amateur time trialling career lasted about eight years, winning her first club 10 in 1944 in the days of 'alpaca jackets and tights'. She won or came well placed in virtually everything she rode., Her domination of the sport was very similar to Beryl Burton's a few years later. Eileen, like Beryl, was successful on the track, and road racing saw even more wins. The longer the distance the better she went.

In April 1946 Eileen's son Clive was born which curtailed her racing for virtually the whole year. In 1949 she won her first 12 hr race with 236.6 miles beating the existing ladies record by almost 17 miles. The winner of the men's race only covered just 6 miles more. Mary Rawlinson, the secretary of the W.R.R.A. persuaded her to tackle some longer distance records and in 1950 Eileen won the first Ladies National Championship '100', with 4 hrs 37 mins 53 secs, breaking competition record by over 5.5 mins. In 1951 she was presented with the Bidlake Memorial Trophy for her outstanding achievements.

Her professional career started in 1952 with 'Hercules Cycles' who expected her to attack and break all the womens's professional road records, most of them held by Marguerite Wilson, who also rode for Hercules prior to 1941. Frank Southall, himself a prolific record breaker for Hercules, was to be her manager. During the next two years Eileen went on to break no less than 28 place to place and distance records including the End to End and 1000 miles. She rode many of the records in unfavourable conditions so as to fit in with Hercules Cycles busy promotion schedules, however all of these 'middle of the night' starts in frosty conditions and riding against a wind instead of with it, stood Eileen in good stead for the big records to come.

In 1953 Eileen tested herself on the Lands End to London record which she took in 14 hours 36 mins 18 secs , also taking the 12 hour record on the way with 250.5 miles. This was followed by going on for the 24 hrs giving her a new record at 442.75 miles. What a ride in 1953 ! Eileen says she had already proved her ability to ride through one night, but what of a second night, and to continue for the 1000 miles would mean a third night also, however, the thought of it did not deter her in the slightest, as it was her ambition to break and hold the records. She looked forward to the test with great excitement. This formidable cyclist weighing just 7 stone 12 lb and standing 4 ft 11" had earned herself the nickname of 'The Pocket Hercules' She had built up her upper body and torso by rigorous exercise with weights and barbells.

On Friday July 9th 1954 at 10 am on a dull gloomy morning, Alan Gordon timed Eileen away from the south door of the Lands End Hotel, on what was to be the ride of her life. The wind was more southerly and proved a hinderance over Bodmin, past the 'Jamaica Inn' packed with tourists, all keen to get a photo of her taking a drink from one of the club lads on route. It was possibly Stan Butler, Gethin's grandfather, not realizing that nearly 50 years later his grandson would be doing the same journey. The weather continued to deteriorate and just past Okehampton the cold rain came. Exeter was reached in 6 hrs 26 mins however, the first 120 miles had put her 30 mins behind schedule. Here the road veers slightly more north, so the wind was more helpful, and Eileen reached Bristol in 10 hrs 29 mins.

Lilian Dredge, the very first End to End lady record breaker, had now joined the ride with extra transport for the helpers. Her car was very useful for by-passing the rider where roads permitted. Eileen had now started taking solid foods, comprising of pieces of chicken and sliced banana. The banana taking the dryness away from the chicken.

Bristol as ever was very busy it being 8.30 pm by then, but was marshalled as usual from 'the downs' to Filton by helpful club folk, seeing her safely through. A brief stop before Gloucester to fit lights and put on night clothes took but a few minutes and at 12 hrs she had done 227 miles.

Worcester was reached at 260 miles and took just under 14 hours. Eileen was 45 mins faster than Edith Atkins and 36 mins up on Sid Ferris. It was a moonless pitch black night with a warm following breeze. Eileen recalls that as the roads became deserted and the trail of cat's eyes were illuminated by the following cars a queer feeling of unreality came over her. The silence was broken only by the faint hum of the car and the swish of her tyres. The towns and villages had a deserted haunted look and when the road passed between avenues of overhanging trees she seemed to be riding through a vast tunnel.

Just before dawn at Whitchurch 323 miles at 3.37 am, it started to rain steadily. Despite the prospect of riding through the industrial areas of Warrington and Wigan in the early hours of a damp and misty morning Eileen still felt in high spirits as she had completed virtually a third of her journey. Although she had been running between 30 and 45 mins behind her schedule for a long time, Frank Southall wasn't too bothered, knowing that his rider was a strong finisher. The rain eased off after Preston 385 miles, done at just 8 mins past 7 am.

On now through Garstang, Lancaster and Kendal. Just before the 24 hours was up a broken gear cable called for a change of bike and the fresh saddle seemed much more comfy than the original one. Eileen climbed Shap on a 72" gear and her speed never dropped below 10 mph. When the 24 hrs were completed just before the summit of Shap she had topped 432 miles. This was the furthest anyone had travelled on the End to End route in 24 hrs, covering a mile more than Hubert Opperman's distance in 1934. At Penrith the 'Hercules' caravan, which was mounted on a low loader lorry, joined the entourage. This was to prove very useful as the ride progressed, having a resident nurse, who was Frank Southalls's sister Ruby. There was a huge crowd of helpers and pressmen waiting for Eileen to stop at the caravan, but she still felt strong and sailed straight past.

At Carlisle she was starting to slow with the cold and fatigue, having covered 470 miles in 27 hrs, 24 mins. Eileen recalls as she climbed into the caravan and was helped by Ruby 'Nurse Crew' "there was an understanding before we started that on no account was she to let me sleep when I should really be on the bike. It was essential that she should be strict on this and promised whole-hearted co-operation. While I sat by a gas fire warming my frozen limbs, Ruby served up some delicious hot broth, then after a blanket bath and a change of clothing I had a short nap of fifteen minutes. I was ready to go and Monty Southall (Frank's brother) insisted on carrying me to my cycle to reserve energy". Eileen's total stop time was 56 minutes and she was now 102 mins down on schedule.

It is just as well she had had a break at Carlisle because as soon as she got on the A74, the wind turned against her and cold stinging rain buffeted her from all angles. Eileen recalls that the climb of Beattock was the worst part of the ride and she had to keep giving herself pep talks. It was late afternoon when Lanark was reached, 546 miles, and after being pushed in every direction by the wind she was surprisingly now 11 minutes up on schedule. Another 40 miles and Stirling was reached, bathed in a beautiful rose pink sunset. At Perth with 615 miles covered at 11.18 pm, Eileen took on lights and extra clothing for the second night. She was now 82 mins up on schedule but was starting to experience a nagging pain in her right knee, possibly from the cold rain and excessive climbing in the last 12 hours.

At midnight she passed through Bankfoot at 625 miles, on to Dunkeld and Pitlochry, when an overturned lorry blocked the road and the policeman who was diverting the traffic told her that the accident had had fatal consequences. The pass of Killiecrankie led to the forests around Blair Atholl and the climb into the Grampian mountains. Through this second night the midnight sun lit up a strip of sky on the northern horizon, but all around, the mountains appeared like monstrous forbidding shadows, streaked here and there with patches of white - snowdrifts in the gullies.

As the opalescent dawn came the temperatures dropped still further until the intense cold was almost unbearable. At one point Frank Southall gave Eileen his own socks to put on over her shoes. Don't forget in those days there were no such things as overshoes or neoprene and roubaix tights. These materials hadn't been discovered and it would be 1985 before they became generally available for cycling use.

Eileen recalls feeling very sorry for the helpers who appeared at intervals hugging flasks to their chests to keep the drink warm for her. At Dalwhinnie she took a much needed break. She had ridden 673 miles and had gone through two nights on only 15 mins actual sleep. Both hands were now badly blistered and she had been holding the bars with her thumbs only. She was 109 mins up on schedule and still riding well despite the cold. She donned a plastic coat and two pairs of gloves to keep out the cold. Sponges were taped to her handlebars to reduce the vibration.

After dropping down through Kingussie and Aviemore, Eileen had almost reached Carrbridge 701 miles, when Frank seeing that fatigue and cold were slowing her, called a halt for 70 mins. Hot towels were held over her legs and a sleep was taken for 25 mins. Eileen asked for an extra few minutes and Nurse Crew, true to her promise, was firm and said "No". She told Eileen afterwards that she had never seen a long distance cycling event before, and although she had been duty bound to refuse extra minutes sleep, she wept after Eileen left the caravan.

7.30 am, Sunday, still 53 minutes up on schedule, Eileen pedals on to reach Inverness at 9 am in brilliant sunshine, where several club folk turned out to speed her on. A coach that had passed her on Saturday caught up with her again on Sunday morning after stopping at a hotel for the night. The passengers waved her on, amazed to see her still going, and so far up the country from the previous day. Past the Beauly Firth and on to Dingwall, 752 miles, now 96 mins up. Round the Cromarty Firth to Aultnamain and climbing the 1000 ft summit with ease on her lower range of gears, even though the morning was getting warm, she kept her extra clothing on to get some warmth into her weary limbs and tired muscles.

Bonar Bridge and the Dornoch Firth were passed amidst lovely scenery. Golspie, 801 miles was reached at 2.47 pm, and she was now over 2 hrs up on schedule and feeling very confident. Helmsdale was the first hill on the 'Ord of Caithness' and she walked the hairpin section, then swooped down to the valley at Berriedale. It had been pre-arranged for her to walk the hill on the other side as Frank Southall reckoned the energy saved by walking was well worth the extra few minutes taken. The whole team walked with her up Berriedale. Even the Editor of 'Cycling' H.H. England walked with her, obviously anxious to relay any of her feelings and thoughts into text for the following week's magazine.

Later as Eileen climbed a hill at Dunbeath and looked back and down to see the following cars, she waves and the drivers waved back. Eileen said later that one of the drivers, Jack Howe, told her that her cheerfulness when they knew she was desperately tired, bought a lump to their throats.

On this last section, the road appears to go on forever and at this point 835 miles, at 5.49 pm, the wind had turned against her to blow in off the sea. The telegraph poles went on for miles into the distance. Eileen was losing a lot of body heat now from sheer fatigue. She had put virtually all of her tracksuit tops on and even had Frank's polo neck sweater over top. The helpers said she looked a forlorn pathetic figure struggling along. She wanted another sleep but was afraid she would never wake up in time to get the record. Even the journey from Wick, 17 miles, took one hour and forty minutes.

Eileen arrived at John o Groats at 9.07 pm, having taken **2 days, 11 hours, 07 mins,** breaking Edith Atkin's amateur record by 6 hrs 57 mins. Her average speed to John o Groats had been 14.75 mph. Everyone was jubilant., her husband Ken being the first to congratulate her. The official observer, Mrs Mary Rawlinson was very upset, saying it had been awful watching her over those last miles. Many photos were taken. Eileen climbed into the caravan in desperate need of a sleep. Frank told her she had just over 130 miles to do for the 1000 and that he was very proud of her, and sure she could do it.

So, after 1 hr 48 mins rest, Eileen set off to ride though the third cold night on the next hardest ride of her life. Eileen recalls starting off on what was to be the greatest trial of all - the fight against mental and physical weariness ! She was only able to roll gently away from the John o Groats Hotel, her muscles had stiffened up and become painful. It was a fairly dark night, but out to sea the midnight sun lit a streak of sky on the horizon with a fiery glow, making objects on the shoreline stand out starkly, silhouetted against the brilliance. Everything about that third night was unreal; Eileen recalls having no sense of direction on unfamiliar roads, doing short 'legs' to Castletown, then Reiss, back to Thurso, Wick and then back to Thurso, Castletown and back to John o Groats.

She remembers stopping to turn at a marshall in the middle of the road, and then finding no-one there. Those final miles were a dream, hedges became rows of animals, beautiful coloured images would appear. Even people in the following car were 'seeing' things. Eileen didn't worry about speed, she just concentrated on pedalling and keeping her eyes open. She imagined things lying in the road and swerved to miss them. She realised she was very close to crashing which would end her record attempt, so decided to have another sleep. About 70 miles remained to do but when she re-started she rode very close to the grass verge for mile after mile. Officials in the following car told her to ride in the middle of the road, but she said she felt drawn towards the edge as if by a magnet.

Just around dawn was her lowest point and she recalls crying from sheer exhaustion. As she rode past Frank he looked worried but she said "I'm ok". The helpers and drivers ran for miles with her, chatting and joking just to keep her spirits up. She had another hours sleep in the caravan. Nurse Ruby woke her and Eileen recalls sitting up in the bunk bed whispering so as not to wake the helper in the opposite bunk. Ruby insisted there was nobody in the bed, it was just Eileen's imagination. Eileen had a cooked breakfast to eat but her hands were so swollen she had to be spoon fed by Frank. She was dropping in and out of sleep as she was eating.

As Eileen climbed out of the caravan dawn had broken at last, a sunny morning with just 40 miles left to do, she started to come alive again, and over the last 20 miles she averaged 18-20 mph. Lilian Dredge was the last marshall to turn her on those final miles. Towards the end a car load of spectators unaware of procedure, got in front of the official car. This got Frank annoyed and he leaned out of the window and bellowed "Get a move on". Eileen took it that the remark was meant for her and tired as she was she bristled with indignation shouting back "What the devil do you think I'm doing" anger making her go a little bit faster. At long last the John o Groats Hotel was reached in **3 days 1 hour,** smashing the existing women's record by 10 hrs 44 mins - what a beating ! Eileen was only 2 hrs 20 mins slower than Sid Ferris at 1000 miles.

Eileen recalls putting on a summer frock afterwards for the photographs with the group of helpers, but her whole body had become swollen and she had a job doing the zip up. When she weighed herself she had gained 8 lbs. She said she felt bruised all over and her legs were swollen.

Two hours after she had finished, the tandem trike pair, Crimes and Arnold completed their End to End in 2 days, 4 hours. With food still short and on ration, the Hercules helpers gave their left over cooked chickens to the tandem trike crew for use on their 1000 miles. John Arnold told me years later that he only ever had poultry at Christmas as a treat.

This concludes the story of one of the worlds finest female athletes. Eileen Sheridan had won the imagination and hearts of not just cyclists, but everyone who had heard about her exploits. She had just two records to get, the 25 mile and 50 mile, which she duly broke in October the same year, taking all of the women's 21 professional road records. In the Autumn of 1955, Eileen gave birth to a daughter, Louise, and this was to be the start of normal family life for her.

Eileen's professional skill as a glass engraver and artist has kept her busy since her record breaking days. She has produced many commemorative vases and bowls, all beautifully engraved. One of the most famous of these is the crystal vase for the ladies End to End . Commissioned by Mrs Christine Watts and presented to the RRA in 1991. The first recipient was Pauline Strong in 1990 and Lynne Taylor in 2001 and 2002. The vase takes pride of place in our lounge and is admired by everyone.

Now, at 80 years of age, Eileen is feted at all of the top cycling functions she still attends, 50 year after her records, and is President of her cycling club. I met up with Eileen at the CTT prize presentation at Derby in January 2005 where she always attends with her lifelong friend Ivy Thorpe. Eileen remembered one or two amusing incidents from her End to End, such as being pushed up the steps to the lorry and into the caravan by Monty Southall, as her legs didn't work properly after nearly 500 miles. Another funny moment was recalled when Stan Butler (Gethin's grandad) who helped from start to finish, drove his van full of helpers over the border into Scotland. They sat on the wheel arches and hung onto cords and straps hanging from the roof of the van. They approached a hump backed bridge at speed, the van took off, coughed and spluttered, landed back on the road and stalled. Luckily the van and its occupants were non the worse for the episode.

Eileen stressed to me the importance of upper body fitness, being so short it was even more so. She worked with weights and could easily lift her own body weight over her head. She did gym movements in the swimming pool, helped by her husband Ken. Onlookers thought they were training for a visiting circus act. Press ups were her speciality, putting the men to shame.

Eileen has an old map of Great Britain and to this day is still amazed as to how anyone can ride a bicycle non stop from End to End.

Alan J Ray's book 'Cycling Lands End to John o Groats' and Eileen Sheridan's autobiography 'Wonder Wheels' by Nicholas Kay, provided some of the information for this article, with additional material from The Cycling Magazine, plus comments from Eileen and myself.

No 16 ALBERT CRIMES AND JOHN ARNOLD 10th JULY 1954 TANDEM TRICYCLE

Lands End to John o Groats in 2 days 4 hrs 26 mins
1000 miles in 2 days 13 hrs 59 mins 12 hrs 257.745 miles 24 hrs 466.25 miles

This article uses information printed in 'The Cycling Magazine' and 'The Sporting Cyclist' with passages from Jock Wadley, Alf Arnold and myself.

Before I start to chronicle their record tandem trike or 'long barrow' ride, I would like to put in perspective the magnitude of the ride. In 1954, Albert Crimes and John Arnold, became the fastest riders ever, on any type of machine, over the End to End and 1000 miles.

The strength and talent of the two riders shows through when you consider a tricycle is rated at least 10% less efficient speed wise to a solo bicycle. It would be four years before Dave Keeler on solo bike took just over an hour off their time and 3 hrs 24 mins off Ferris's 1937 record. It isn't until Paul Carbutt's ride in 1979, of 1 day 23 hrs 23 mins, which equates to a near 10% beating, that the situation is redressed, some 25 years later. That's how ahead of their time Crimes and Arnold were.

They started at 9 am Saturday 10th July 1954, some 23 hours after Eileen Sheridan. They had a fresh westerly wind, very helpful at the start. When braking fiercely at Launceston, they burst a front tyre, and they damaged a front wheel at Taunton. Despite stopping and changing the wheel they were still gaining on an ambitious schedule set to beat the tandem trike 12 hour record of 242.5 miles set by Tweddell and Stott in 1951, and also their 24 hour record of 412.5 miles set in 1952.

The pair reached Exeter, 119 miles, in 5 hrs 26 mins despite a delay of 7 minutes at Taunton. They reached Bristol 32 mins up on schedule. The road alters direction here and the wind strength had gone. They sped on through Gloucester and Tewkesbury to run out their 12 hours, 1.5 miles south of Worcester with 257.75 miles. This was the first of their magnificent records which, along with their 24 hrs, End to End and 1000 miles, still stands today - some 50 years later. They were now well up on a schedule to beat 2 days, 6 hrs, but later on as they approached Whitchurch, Albert started to suffer with his stomach, probably due to the extreme exertion of the first 12 hours.

A stop was called for just after midnight at the café at Whitchurch. A lot of their club mates from the Crewe Wheelers and Middleton CC were there to lend a hand. They stopped for 30 mins but Albert's stomach was still troubling him when they continued, towards Warrington and Wigan. John's mother greeted them as they passed through Warrington, it was the first time she had seen either of them in competition. They pushed on through home territory to reach Carnforth, where the existing 24 hr record point was passed with 3.5 hrs still to go.

Albert and John climbed Shap but had to rest two thirds of the way up and again another 25 minutes break at Penrith, 452 miles, was taken for Albert's stomach to recover. They lay on the grass verge covered with coats just after their own 24 hr time was up on the Sunday morning. They had covered 466.25 miles, only 1.25 miles short of the 24 hr solo bike record held by Cyril Heppleston, and all this after having over one and a half hours off the bike for illness. This is worth 30 miles at least, so would have put them near to 500 miles in real terms.

Just after Carlisle, Crimes had the worst stomach pains of the ride. They agreed to stop for another 30 minutes but it extended to 55 mins, poor Albert couldn't move, the pain was so bad. By sheer willpower he forced himself back into the saddle looking really rough, but after about half an hour the pain eased and the pair pushed on to Beattock 508 miles, where a 3 hr sleep and hot bath awaited them. As they left to resume their ride they were just 7 mins down on schedule, the time now being 4.18 pm, Sunday afternoon.

They stopped for a feed at Auchterarder, 601 miles, and again at Pitlochry for night clothes and lamps ready for crossing the cold wet Grampians. Capes were donned to keep out the chilling heavy rain. Another stop at Kingussie when the front wheel was badly damaged hitting a deep rut in the road. Three front wheels wrecked in one ride, that's got to be a record in its own right !

Inverness, 730 miles, was reached at 4.57 am. The Clachnacuddin CC played host to the pair and their clubroom became a bathroom and a breakfast room, such was their dedication to helping riders on the greatest ride of all, the End to End. The modern day equivalent to this is the welcome and help one gets from the Caithness CC and Wick Wheelers at John o Groats and 1000 miles.

Crimes and Arnold got to Bonar Bridge 778 miles in 46 hrs 24 mins, gaining speed and feeling better as the time went on. They flew up the coast and the 'Ord of Caithness' and arrived at

John o Groats in 2 days 4 hrs 26 mins. The fastest ride ever over this journey in spite of having over 6 hours off for one reason or another.

One very sad detail of the ride is recorded here, that J.G. McDonald of the Speedwell R.C. had died on route, helping the lads in the north of Scotland.

When they arrived at John o Groats at lunchtime Monday, the pair sat astride their machine chatting to Eileen Sheridan who had just finished her 1000 mile record 2 hours earlier. They all looked remarkably fresh. Albert and John had a meal and an hours sleep and resumed their ride for the 1000 miles after just a 2.5 hr break. John recalls him and Albert being given two whole chickens by Frank Southall, Eileen's manager, to eat on their next 130 miles. John says what a delicacy it was as they only ever had poultry at Christmas. He broke it up and filled Albert's back pockets with legs and portions.

The remaining 129 miles were completed in approximately 7 hours to give them 2 days, 13 hrs, 59min. The fastest ride ever on record for 1000 miles on any machine. John recalls their exploits over those last few hours, finishing at 1 minute after 11 pm, not quite dark due to almost permanent daylight in Scotland at that time of the year. They had cornered tight bends in true trike riding style leaning out over the back wheel to keep the machine from tipping over. Their agility after two and a half days of riding was amazing, on some of the stretches they reached speeds of over 30 mph. Their tandem trike was a 'Higgins' only the second one ever made.

Peter Barlow, the record organiser, had directed operations from his home in Manchester by telephone as he had done for Bert Parkes' ride in 1950. With Peter was his mother and Pat Sirett of the Mercury RC. All three maintained a day and night watch until the record was over, checking helpers were in place, getting weather forecasts to the team. They in turn were kept in touch by phone by Peter's father, the famous Tommy Barlow, who for years had organised and run the country's Best All Rounder competition.

An amusing detail, Alf Arnold recalled was that the Middleton Cycling Club girls, who were helping on the road between Ashton-in-Makerfield to Preston, were given instructions as to what to say, in case a policeman wanted to know what they were doing out on their bikes all night ! "We're waiting for two men on three wheels" - "Oh yes, a likely story" !

The record ride had taken 6 months to organise with over 500 helpers spread throughout the journey, but it was well worth the effort, those four records still stand today, over 50 years later.

Two weeks later, John Arnold went on to win the Mersey RC 24 hr championship time trial with 466.73 miles on his bike, again putting up the greatest distance ever in the Mersey 24 to that point in time, what a remarkable man .

Jock Wadley, a famous 'Sporting Cyclist' correspondent for nearly forty years, followed both Eileen Sheridan's attempt to Carlisle, then got a train back to Manchester to join the Crimes and Arnold record. Here are a few 'snippets' from his extensive coverage of that epic weekend.

"Waiting at Brent Knoll for Eileen who was half an hour late. At last Eileen appeared looking bright and perky. From the following car, timekeeper, Alan Gordon handed us a note showing her progress from Lands End, and then Frank Southall, her manager, gave the picture of the

ride so far in his usual 'clipped' manner. ***'Rough ride to Exeter; no wind to start with, then a south east got up across Bodmin Moor; I told her not to fight the hills; she had cold rain into Exeter, since Taunton she's been going great'.***

As Eileen headed north out of Bristol with the Severn lying like a silver ribbon at the foot of the welsh hills, beautiful, yes; but more comforting to Eileen and the helpers was the sight of flags and chimneys giving evidence of a gentle breeze coming from the south.

Following Eileen was a fascinating experience as the car headlamps picked out a trail of cats eyes winding its way to the north. The white sweater not only was a great advantage in spotting the rider, it served to emphasise the way in which Eileen sways a good deal even on the flat stretches.

As we approached the hills we could see the clouds swirling round the higher peaks and we knew that soon Eileen must be tackling the first major obstacle of the ride, Shap Fell. Halfway up the climb the 24 hrs had passed by with 432 miles on the clock. Another hour or so in the saddle, and then nearly into Carlisle to stop for her first rest in the giant Hercules caravan. While Eileen rested I went on into Carlisle and phoned Manchester HQ to find out what my future movements would be. The voice from Manchester said 'they've started'; the only news I've got through so far is that they're four minutes up on schedule at Penzance" ! 'They' of course, being Crimes and Arnold on the tandem trike.

Jock Wadley then had to catch the train back to Manchester and describes how the train hurtled down Shap 'roaring' at nearly 100 mph. He had a snatched sleep at Peter Barlow's house, interspersed by telephone calls the team were receiving. Peter came to wake Jock and said 'two hundred and fifty six and a half miles in 12 hrs and father says they're 'going like the clappers'.

After a pillion passenger ride out to the End to End route Jock describes clambering into a car with Bill Davies, Stan Smith, Jack (John) Williams, Mersey Roads, and Tommy Barlow himself *"and so there I was for the second time within 24 hrs following the red light of a record breaking machine through the industrial north. They celebrated reaching their local 'Brock' time trial course by clocking 16 mins for a six mile stretch. Hereabouts John Arnold reached back to turn the rear light off and I could really see for the first time this tremendous trike and its skilled 'propellers'. But were those side wheels really wobbling like that or was it just my lack of sleep? Arnold was out of the saddle just as he had been in the national championship 24 hr.*

It was predicted the riders could get to the Scottish border inside 24 hrs and possibly top 480 miles. Jock Wadley recalls 'alas, this was not to be'. We heard the riders calling out for peppermint and soon learned the reason, the pair stopped for 20 mins at the foot of Shap with Crimes undergoing a spot of stomach trouble. They topped Shap and dropped down to Penrith. 'They won't do 480 now' we said 'but they'll get into Scotland' We were wrong again, for a mile beyond Penrith poor Albert just had to stop again and another 28 mins was lost before he was fit enough to restart. They completed the 24 hrs with 466 miles and then shortly after Carlisle, Albert flopped down on the grass verge, again in severe pain.

Between them they decided on another half hour stop, the pair of them were rolled up in blankets by their helpers at the side of the road. When 'reveille' came Crimes managed to get

1

3

2

4

5

6
B.S.A
Hubert Opper
23-7-34

7

8

9

10

12

11

13

14

15

16

17

19

18

20

21

22

23

24

25

27
Viking
Viking

LOCTITE
28

26

29

30

32

31

33

34

to his feet, stagger a couple of paces, only to collapse in the grass. Now quite frankly, great as the reputation of Crimes is, I thought this was the end of the End to End road, and I began to wonder how I could get up to Inverness to catch up with the Sheridan record.

Surely, I thought, Crimes cannot possibly restart in a state like that, and if he does, then the pair will only be able to creep towards the Grampian mountains and probably 'die' in them. Wrong for the third time !

With 55 mins gone by the pair were on their way again, having lost the equivalent of 30 miles in the last three hours. Just over the Scottish border, Albert started to pick up fine, he even took aboard some specially ordered jam sandwiches. They were due to take a three hour stop at Abington and the helpers were confident that if only Crimes could get there his troubles would be over. They 'pounded' away at 'evens' and climbed to Beattock Summit at 1000 ft in grand style. By Abington they were only 11 minutes behind their schedule. There they had a bath (it looked like a tank of oil after they got out, said one of their bathroom attendants) They also ate and slept here. We hoped their troubles were over, and they were.

When they resumed their ride up through Lanarkshire, they punched the pedals and leaned and lunged and before long old Albert was actually laughing and John told him off for singing. The evening drew close, the Grampians did not loom up in the distance, but rose gracefully. The road moved gradually up from the greenery of wheat and potato crops into forests of stately pines. Soon we saw little but the rear light of the trike moving rapidly ahead. It was a cold night in those hills and the boys wrapped up well, Arnold putting on a pair of long trousers. They caped up against the rain.

With the Grampians behind them they dropped early morning into Inverness. There was a half hour stop in a wonderful atmosphere of homeliness from the Clachnacuddin CC. Oil lanterns hung from the roof, there were cups of tea all round and for Crimes and Arnold bacon and eggs fried on a roaring coal fire. Crimes was a new man: 'just look at him' he taunted, pointing to Arnold stretched out on a camp bed while he himself tucked into his meal with relish; 'take a picture of me with my foot on top of him, will you?'

The rest of the ride was an absolute triumph for the revived pair. They laughed at the Aultnamain crossing where everyone else grovels. They stopped for a meal at Helmsdale to fuel them for the last section of the ride. They climbed the 'Ord of Caithness' at 12mph, cornered beautifully on the descent into Berriedale and climbed it like a couple of 'Koblets' (Koblet was a famous climber in the Tour de france who won mountain stages) They sprinted down to the John o Groats Hotel where Eileen Sheridan (who had only finished her 'thousand' two hours previously) downed her dinner tools to greet the boys.

After a two and a half hour rest they continued for the 1000 miles and what a ride it was, as I have said Crimes and Arnold just don't know how to go slowly. To the end it was a 130 mile time trial. They actually did the first 100 miles in 5 hrs 15 mins !

Never shall I forget their final 15 miles from Thurso. It was past 10 o'clock at night but up there in Caithness still light enough for me to read and write in the car. A great moon was rising; the cliffs of 'Hoy' on the Orkneys rose sheer from the sea. Ahead a pair of madmen were tearing that tricycle to bits riding on the flat at 25's and uphill at 'evens', swooping down at 35's and cornering on two wheels with the third wheel a full foot in the air" "I screamed out loud during those last miles, said Stan Smith (who had put off a trip to New Zealand so he could follow the ride) because it seemed that even with all their skill at handling the 'barrow' they must fall off".

But Albert and John did not fall, and neither, I think will the four records they achieved.

1954 saw not only the most remarkable quadruple record ever in the RRA's history but two weeks later John won the Mersey RC 24 hr on his bike with 466.73 miles despite a recurring foot problem made worse by his strenuous years efforts. John saw a Specialist and in the winter of that year had a short spell in hospital for treatment. Despite his doctor telling him his racing days were over, he continued to ride, his enthusiasm was not letting him give up that easily.

Despite retiring in the North Road 24 hr the following year with swollen feet again he went on to ride the Mersey 24 hr with specially made wooden clogs bolted to his pedals and he finished with 431 miles. In 1959 his feet had improved enough for him to get 4th place in the Catford CC 24 hr Championships with 460 miles on his bike

Johns feet did get better and three years later he put up two more great performances. The first was in the 1962 North R.C. 24 hr beating Cliff Smith with 463 miles despite injuring his leg at one of the turns after falling off. His second performance, probably his last, was the York to Edinburgh trike record in 1963 taking over 1.75 hours off the previous record with 8 hrs 48 mins 28 secs. His brother Alf recalled that he had a favourable wind and that the following car had a job to keep up with him around the Darlington area, doing nearly 60 mph.

Years later John told me he had arthritic problems in and around the years of his long distance racing career. He said even on the day of his End to End he remembers finding it impossible to walk more than 10 yards without sitting down to rest, because of the pain in his feet.

At the Guest House where Albert and he stayed, John recalls trying to stand and have a wash and then having to sit and rest on the side of the bath, with Albert laughing and saying how could they be attempting the End to End when John couldn't even stand up !

John has in recent years suffered similar problems and in 1984 had gout in his big toe. He changed his diet and cut out anything that contained sugars, even fruit. He started eating fish instead of meat, swapped to wholemeal bread, oats and bran cakes, cheese and potatoes, halibut oil capsules, yeast tablets and vitamin 'c'. Within two weeks he was back on the bike and feeling much better.

I'm told gout, which is a form of arthritis, occurs when your kidneys stop excreting the solids from your blood and deposits them in crystal form in the joints.

One of the accolades Albert gave to John at a later date was "What John Arnold can do, I can almost do" !

John was a classy rider, not particularly tall but with broad straight shoulders obviously a very tough rider but a very smooth pedaller. He could regularly be seen out of the saddle forcing the pace back above 'evens'. Albert remarks that if it weren't for Johns underlying foot problems he's sure he would have taken the trike End to End record inside 2 days. I'm inclined to agree wholeheartedly !

In 1976 J.B. (Jock) Wadley wrote an article for 'Cycling' headed **"1954, one machine, two men, three wheels - and four records shattered - Tricycling Tandemons".** Jock Wadley said "As a journalist who had followed umpteen Tours de France, all the Classics, knows the British and Continental scene inside out - can you honestly say that any worthwhile performance has ever been put up on an obsolete contraption like a tandem tricycle? There can't be a dozen of the things left in the world."

Jock recalls Tom Simpson telling him about his early days with the Harworth Wheelers. "I was about 16 at the time and out with some of the lads on the Sunday clubrun. We came across a dozen or so club chaps standing round an island near Ollerton. Thinking it might be a road race we stopped and asked what event it was. They said they were marshalling a record attempt by Crimes and Arnold on a tandem tricycle and that they were due any minute now. We waited expecting to see a pair of old codgers ambling along about 15 mph. Instead we saw two real athletes approaching at 25 mph, taking the wide island on two wheels and leaning out like sidecar passengers, flattening out and tearing off down the road. That is one of my most thrilling memories of British cycling sport."

Jock recorded: **I first met Crimes and Arnold during the 1953 Mersey Roads Club 24 hr trial which that year incorporated the RTTC national championship. They were both riding tricycles, separated by 22 minutes on the start card. A dozen entries in the competition records section of the RTTC handbook gave the reason why. Three lines under '24 hours tricycle' is a fair sample.**

1949	**A. Crimes**	**Crewe Wheelers**	**411.79 miles**
1951	**J.R. Arnold**	**Middleton CC**	**419.26 miles**
1952	**A. Crimes**	**Crewe Wheelers**	**422.40 miles**

Albert Crimes was No 15 on the card. John Arnold 37. That represented about 7.5 miles, a gap which Arnold set out to bridge with an opening "100" of 4.47. Within another 100 miles he had caught and dropped Crimes and was leading on the road. I waited at dawn at the 241 mile feeding station, but instead of the crack tricycles coming through first it was P.E.A. (Nick) Carter, No 61 who had then been riding for exactly 12 hours. He said he had passed John changing a tyre a few miles down the road. Nick stopped for a 10 minute feed, Arnold went through non stop to resume the path finding role which he was to keep for the whole of the second half of a sensational bike v trike match.

Carter and Arnold were easily leading on elapsed time and when they reached the start of the finishing circuit at 402 miles, 'Nick' had a 13 minute lead. That looked safe enough because the 'lap' included many sharp bends and corners which favoured the two wheeler rather than the three.

Arnold (who as a youth nearly had a trial for Manchester United!) fought hard for the equalizer, pushing and lunging and leaning round the circuit with such determination that he gained back six minutes in three hours riding. Carter's winning total was 459.48 miles, Arnold had the second greatest distance with 457.33, and defending champion, Eddy Mundy (Addiscombe) next with 448. And Crimes? He rode splendidly but could do nothing - indeed he had the wisdom not even to try - to match the extra 1.5mph that his rival had found. I remember him arriving at that 241 miles check for a quick sit

down feed and tersely giving a victims view of the Middleton menace. "Bugger him" said Albert spooning into a bowl of cereal.

In fact, Crimes finished with 425 miles, a 2.5 miles improvement on his own 1952 competition record. (In the less permissive days of 1953 my report in 'The Bicycle' had Crimes as saying "Blow him". An unlikely story indeed !

Although second in that Mersey Roads 24, Arnold was unplaced in the incorporated championship which was open, said the rules, only to riders of bicycles ! The club worlds indignation on learning this was soothed by the decision of the RTTC to make a special presentation to Arnold at the Champions Concert in the Royal Albert Hall, London, and at the next National Council meeting, delegates voted that tricycles would be eligible for future national championships, and the BBAR competition.

At the Champions Concert John Arnold told me of his 1954 plans to attack several tandem tricycle records, "with Albert of course". Red hot rivals on solo trikes, great friends off them, and a fine team on the long three wheeler, Crimes-Arnold (yes, in that order, it was John's machine but he liked Albert up front where he could see him working)

Jock takes up the story of Crimes and Arnold's End to End in the Lancashire area: **Thirty miles farther on lay formidable Shap Fell, halfway hill of the End to End trail and even a tandem trike driven by Crimes and Arnold would take some pushing over that. Lights had been turned off soon after the Brock display, and in the growing daylight we followed through Kendal (426 miles) where the mint cake comes from, with the first slopes of Shap only a few miles away.**

"Ten minutes inside evens" I wrote. We reckoned that this could all be lost and a bit more, but regained comfortably on the fast descent to Penrith (452) and consolidated on the next 28 miles to give 480 in the 24 hours. While we worked out such matters in our heads. Things were going round in Albert Crimes stomach. A worried looking breathless helper waved a refused bidon for us to stop our car. 'Albert is not so good' he said. 'He wants peppermint'. Already the long barrow had pulled up at the foot of Shap. What a place to feel poorly. On flat roads he could have taken things easily but still progressed slowly northwards but here ... the proposed five minute stop doubled, and doubled again. Twenty minutes lost before the 1.5 man power machine began a painful climb of Shap.

'They can't do 480 now' said Tommy Barlow, 'but they could just get into Scotland'. After an unspectacular drop into Penrith even that seemed unlikely, and soon afterwards impossible The tandem trike had stopped again for what was to be a further 28 minutes wiped off the profit. Then, after an 11 mile slow trike ride the first 24 hours was at last over, at a spot only a few hundred yards from where Eileen Sheridan had made her first big stop. Crimes and Arnold's 466.25 miles was a 54 mile beating of the previous tandem trike best, but a disappointment to them nevertheless.

Like Beryl a decade later, they were so superior that they were not content just to beat a record in the minor world of three wheeling, but to do so in a way that would command the respect of all. Their 466.25 miles, incidentally, was only just short of a closely packed list of other records standing at the time. Competition bicycle: E. Mundy 467.52 miles;

RRA bicycle: C. Heppleston 467.5 miles: RRA tandem: R.C. Smith and A.E. Collins 467 miles.

Had the youthful Tom Simpson happened to meet Crimes and Arnold passing through Carlisle that day he would not have been impressed. Far from taking the corners on two wheels, their mount seemed to have half a dozen and all of them glued to the road. Albert Crimes face matched his once white hat and neckerchief, now grey with the dust and grime of a 10 high pile of English counties. More than 400 miles of Scotland lay ahead. Normally helpers on a long road record spread out every ten miles with food, drink and encouragement, but since the Crimes 'parcel' they fell in behind the official observer's car. Beyond Carlisle and seven miles short of Gretna Green came stop number three. As steersman, the stricken Crimes was able to choose his own place to suffer, a bed of grass and scrub on the verge of the A74. There he flopped down, muttering that he would be all right in half an hour. Helpers rolled a blanket round him and he was soon asleep. Arnold was also wrapped in a bundle and posted off to Nod.

Half an hour up .. Reveille .. Arnold up like a Lancashire lark (he was born in Yorkshire though) ... Crimes not so perky. He managed to get to his feet, staggered a few yards, collapsed again on the grass. After a while Albert was up again and this time stayed up. It was John who grunted in the grass and lay abed for an extra minute. A quick wash and brush up, a drink of tea, and they were off.

A few miles into Scotland there was a nice touch when a clubman handed up a drink with a shouted 'Congratulations - and good luck for the other two'. 'Thanks Wilson' the tandem mates called back to J.W. Stott, who with E. Tweddell had held the 12 and 24 hour records. On the fast A74 through Ecclefechan and Lockerbie, the car speedos showed a steady 20 mph even when Crimes was steering one handed to deal with a specially ordered packet of bread and jam sandwiches. As a roving reporter-photographer, I was able now and then to transfer to a feeding van for a few miles and drop off with the first hander upper. There was now usually a grin on the steersman's face which had been so sad and grey south of the Border. I remarked on this when they made another scheduled stop at Auchterarder (601 miles). John said he preferred Albert with the stomach ache. 'The silly so and so was actually singing climbing a hill' he said.

So far I have said little about Arnold in this End to End story. He was quietly tucked away on the back getting on with his own job and a good bit of Alberts during those difficult hours. Few riders have impressed me as much as the Middleton man, and I have been club cycling for nearly 50 years. He reminded me of the tough old roadmen of the 'Heroic Age' of the Tour de France with its 250 mile stages and fix-your -own-bike rules.

There was another half hour stop at Helmsdale (817 miles - 54 to go) for a snack kept deliberately light since the next seven miles included the severe hill climbs of the Ord of Caithness and Berriedale. C & A went steadily up and daringly down the tortuous road, playing hide-and-seek with the sea hundreds of feet below. The A9 became less restless, settling down to a sober route through 'one minute to the sea' townships of Dunbeath, Latherton and Lybster up to Wick and the last 17 miles of the ordeal.

They arrived at the famous John o Groats Hotel in 2 days 4 hours 26 minutes - 18.25 hours better than Letts-Parker. The bicycle record (by S.H. FERRIS) was 2 days 6 hours!

Albert worked as a Locomotive Inspector on the Railways and John was a Cabinet Maker and Joiner. They wore white handkerchiefs around their necks, a trend that was copied by a lot of aspiring long distance road riders of that era. Albert died aged 64, a victim to cancer, in 1985.

John Arnold is, I am glad to say, still with us and has been out to help on record attempts as recently at 2002 turning up to watch the Anfield 100 at Prees and the Mersey 24 hr with Harry Wilkinson. Both were present when Lynne and Gethin broke their respective End to Ends in 2001. Harry and John organised four or five comfort stops with Harry's van on Lynne's first solo End to End, and then retraced to see Gethin into Scotland for his successful End to End and 1000 miles in 2001. Harry was very well placed in long distance events from the 1930's up until the 70's riding and winning numerous 12 hr races. He was a regular help to Gethin over the years.

On a more amusing note, the photo of Crimes and Arnold taken at Cholmondley in Cheshire, hurtling through their first dark night, had them in a blind panic for about 30 seconds or more, and should have a caption underneath, saying 'Crikey, where are we, I can't see a bloody thing !', or very similar words to that effect. John Arnold said the photo had been taken by flashlight straight into their eyes just before a winding downhill section at about 30 mph, both riders being temporarily blinded. (This information comes to me via Johnny Pardoe).

The two reports of Jock Wadley's were written 22 years apart and both contain different and interesting information. This is why I've included them both.

No 17 DAVID DUFFIELD FRIDAY 7th JUNE 1957 TRICYCLE
North to South - John o Groats to Lands End

This event had taken Mick de Mouilpied six months to organise with petrol rationing in force as a result of the Suez crisis, it was not an easy job. The reasons for going from North to South were because you were more likely to have petrol available in the South. Another reason David felt was important, was that it gets warmer as you ride south and the hills are less severe on a trike the further south you get. The reason for going relatively early in the year was because he'd heard along the grapevine, that a big adversary of his, Albert Crimes, was planning to attack the record that same year. The downside of going from North to South is that it's a long way to get to the start unless you're a Scotsman. This journey was achieved on a sleeper train from Birmingham to Wick with his trike in the guards van. David was also worried that he'd never been north of Penrith, or south of Exeter, so didn't really know what to expect.

His preparation for the ride was hampered by daily driving as a cycle company sales representative, so having to cram 4000 miles in just 5 months of weekend and holiday riding. When he beat the 1000 mile trike record the previous year, he simply regarded it as just good training for what he knew lay ahead.

In 1957 on Friday 7th June at 8.00 pm in the evening Dave Duffield at 26 years of age, started the attempt from John o Groats with a north west wind to **Wick**. He had all of his warm clothing on as it was bitterly cold with an icy wind drifting down from the snowy peaks, making the 142 miles to Inverness really hard. Luckily at the last minute before the attempt, petrol had been taken off ration, so he knew he would get a helping van from Perth with timekeeper, Tommy Barlow on board as an Observer.

As he rode towards Inverness, he disturbed a herd of deer on Berriedale but luckily with it being nearly the season for the midnight sun, it was not too dark. Later he had to contend with weaving in and out of sheep wandering across the road from where they were sheltering in the hollows at the bottom of the hedgerows.

A puncture at **Golspie 71** miles was fixed with freezing numb fingers, but stopping helped him regain the circulation in his frozen feet. Don't forget 1957 was long before overshoes were available. At **Aultnamain**, a very steep climb at **103 miles**, he strained both knee caps in the cold, the pain of which remained throughout the rest of the ride. At **Inverness 142 miles,** David was on schedule at 14.5 mph. He had a stop here and was ably looked after as usual by the 'Clachnacuddin CC' who soaked his feet in hot water and fed him hot soup, as this was all he could take due to an unsettled stomach.

As he rode on into the Grampians, the wind turned against him and his stomach pains got worse, causing him to stop several times and sit on his side wheel doubled up in pain. He was sick a few times and resorted to lying down to ease the pain. In the last 60 miles he had lost 1 hour due to stops. He was in a very bad state and felt 'all in'. At 200 miles he met John Arnold, the great long distance specialist. John promptly dosed David up with hot tea and peppermint and after some more hot soup, sent him on his way 1.5 hours down on schedule but with the knowledge that it was 'all downhill to Perth'! David battled on to regain a half hour back off his losses.

At **Perth 257 miles**, he met up with his following van . The Barlow's, Tom and Peter, dosed him with regular 'Andrews Salts' followed by hot soups and drinks from the helpers. After this he made good progress to make **Stirling 291 miles** with a following wind.

By **Beattock 364 miles** he was only 30 mins down. It had been so cold through the Highlands that his knee caps had become detached, so at the transport café stop at Abington, he had to have bandages put on to keep his kneecaps in place. I'm reliably informed that he kept the bandages on to the end of the ride. Another bad bout of sickness at Carlisle caused him to stop and take a 2.5 hr sleep.

He got back on at 4.15 am and set off into a cold damp and dismal dawn over **Shap**. At **430 miles** he was now approximately half way with the hard parts mostly done. He started to have trouble with loose chain ring bolts and broken spokes in the front wheel due to extreme pressure from climbing out of the saddle. His stomach troubles were improving due to regular drinks of Lucozade which he continued to take for the rest of the journey.

At **Kendal 446 miles** David had gained an hour on schedule and took more hot soup to keep a cold drizzle at bay. After a windless ride through industrial Lancashire, he picked up a following breeze which took him to **Whitchurch 551 miles**, still an hour up. He stopped for a decent meal, his first for a long time. Here the wind suddenly dropped and brought with it torrential rain which continued on and off for the next 26 hours. Flooded roads caused his drive wheel to spin on the hills between Bridgnorth and Worcester.

He was now on home territory and was being cheered on by many local club folk from the Beacon RC and Oldbury and District CC. By **Worcester 614 miles** he was still making good progress into the third night to go through **Bristol 675 miles** still one hour up. He was due a scheduled sleep and felt so strong he contemplated riding through non-stop but knowing there was still 200 miles to go, he felt he would benefit from stopping and getting into dry clothes.

As he re-started at **Highbridge 703 miles**, the forecasted north west wind arrived, but so did a cold rain to accompany it. He could only ride slowly as the cold and wet was penetrating his legs. By Exeter the rain had stopped and after a feed stop he had a hard ride to Okehampton. Those 22 hilly miles took over two hours to do with wind buffeting him from all angles as the road twisted and turned. At Okehampton conditions were perfect and with the full force of the wind Dave flew over the last 96 hilly miles to Lands End, despite the pains in his knees caused by the freezing conditions in Scotland. He gained another one hour to finish at 4.09 pm on Monday 10th June to record **2 days 20 hours 9 mins**, taking 4 hrs 29 minutes off Bert Parkes 1950 ride. Bert was one of the first to congratulate Dave Duffield at Lands End, having followed him over the last few miles.

After the local photographers had recorded the scene, the helpers loaded the car back up to take two trikes and a bike on top. The drivers were tired, so Duffield drove most of the way home, pleased with the successful ride and the help he'd received on the way.

Duffield had no following car until Auchterarder, where Peter and Tommy Barlow picked him up and followed him through to Whitchurch. From there to Worcester, Alan Tomkins and Beacon RC President, Jack Clements assisted and for the final 260 miles, Jack Wrightson and Idris David were the Observers. Mick de Mouilpied was the overall organizer and was to go on and organise many successful records over the coming years.

Attempting the record from North to South was a very brave decision to make and David is the only rider to succeed. The wind direction needed for success is North, North east, and as one can imagine, its usually a very cold wind. If rain occurs the rider has to work so hard just to remain warm let alone travel at racing speed The doubts he must have had in his mind, over that first 200 mile stretch, riding without following helpers made this a brave performance.

Lots of theories have been put forward in favour of the North to South route. It must be very tempting for a rider or attempt organiser to put in a reverse schedule after waiting for a south west wind and getting nothing but northerlies day after day.

Pat Kenny attempted the north-south route in 1980 when attacking Duffields second successful trike End to End put up in 1960. He abandoned between Penicuik and Moffat due to lack of help from the wind. I was on that attempt as a helper and I know Pat had waited for ages for the right conditions.

This article uses passages from 'The Sporting Cyclist' with additional information provided by John Arnold and myself.

No 18 ALBERT CRIMES 16th AUGUST 1957 TRICYCLE END TO END

Following Duffields successful North to South record earlier in 1957, Albert Crimes, the steersman of the famous Tandem Trike duo, Crimes and Arnold, who had taken the End to End in 1954, decided he was about ready for an attempt on the solo trike record. Why hadn't John Arnold attempted the trike End to End you may ask, and the reason is two fold. Firstly he had suffered badly with his feet and ankles since the tandem trike record in 1954, and secondly he would not attempt to break Bert Parkes trike record because he was a great mate of Johns and he had a lot of respect for him. Albert Crimes likewise had waited until Duffield broke the record for the same reason.

Albert recalls in his own story of the record, how his club mates had pestered him for over a year to attempt it, and such was their enthusiasm, he agreed in the end. Peter Barlow heard about it and set about organizing it with Alf Arnold, John's brother who was also an organising wizard. Both men had played a crucial role in the tandem trike record. Jokingly Albert says they enjoy organizing and are always waiting for some mug to say he wants to go for it !

Albert was told all he had to do was train and get fit which he already was, and turn up at Lands End ready to go. His training consisted of 180 to 200 miles each Sunday, and two rides in the week of 40 miles. During a holiday in July he put in about 1,700 miles and felt very fit. His weight tumbled from 11stone 12lbs to 10 stone 4 lb. He was now race fit, one more run to Bristol and back approximately 300 miles and he was ready.

The forecast he was given was a south west wind turning north west later which meant starting as fast as possible to make use of the wind, before it turned.

He started at 4 pm at Lands End on Friday 16th August 1957, a very unusual unorthodox starting time, I must admit. I don't know whether it was to tie in with passing through various towns avoiding rush hours , or whether he thought if he was successful and broke the End to End by the scheduled amount, with a normal early morning start at Lands End it would almost certainly mean he would ride well into the third night, and by starting 12 hours later, he could avoid this and finish his 1000 miles completely in daylight.

By Exeter he was two hours up on schedule and still gaining with a favourable wind. At Highbridge he had a sit down feed just as rain set in. He continued on his journey still at a good speed and remembers looking forward to poached eggs on toast at Gloucester. From here onward he suffered a slow patch of riding until Bridgnorth suffering some stomach discomfort which diminished as he got on to well known roads, looking forward to another feed at Whitchurch.

He had been helped and cheered on by many Midlands club folk and recalls there being no finer tonic than seeing familiar faces at the roadside, although quite a lot of his club mates missed him as he was still over two hours up on schedule. Excellent police cooperation helped him through Wigan and while waiting at traffic lights a voice quietly said 'best wishes and good luck, I once held this record'. I can only assume it was probably Bert Parkes who broke it in 1949 and 1950.

At Brock which is the home of the Lancashire time trial courses he stopped for a two and half hour sleep. He was physically lifted of the trike by Alf and John Arnold. They and other members of the Middleton CC gave him a good wash and put him to bed. After a meal, he was sent on his way again through Lancaster and Kendal where he was handed some of the nicest soup he had ever tasted.

On to the climb of Shap which he took in his stride. Albert was greeted at the top by Ed Green and his wife, who offered up a musette full of food, which Albert declined, much to Ed's disdain. An extra sit down feed was taken between Penrith and Carlisle of liver, bacon, egg, tomatoes and chips, which was to set him up for the next tough section where he turned into the wind.

For the next few hours he really suffered in this border region. At the top of Beattock he took a 10 minutes sleep in the car and then struggled on towards Abington where another 15 minutes sleep was had. He was now suffering the worst time of the whole ride. He felt he could sleep for 12 hours he was so tired. He had lost interest in everything.

Peter Barlow gave Albert the 'father and mother' of all dressing downs saying there was nothing physically wrong with him and that '10 mph was better than nothing at all, and although the wind was against him from the north west, it would soon change and come from the south west'. Albert took a lot of convincing but gradually pulled through, crediting the team of helpers for getting him through a very bad patch. It was now a matter of plodding on and trying to hold on to what was left of his early gains on schedule which was approximately two hours as he left Abington.

Onwards through Stirling and Perth onto the A9. To Dunkeld, Pitlochry to the assault of 'The Grampians' at Blair Atholl. Albert recalls passing over what he thought was the first summit and then struggling on the descent against the wind and getting nowhere, going slower and slower. He decided to take a 5 minute rest, by then the following car had caught him and told him he still hadn't reached the summit. He said he felt much better knowing he was still climbing.

He began to get more help from the wind now and his speed went up accordingly. He was now starting to enjoy the ride, if that is possible. After an exciting drop into Inverness he took a 30 mins sleep in a tent. After 45 mins total stop he was on his way again with a following wind and only 140 miles to do. The tent and food was again provided by Maisie McLeod and The Clachnacuddin CC.

The next major hurdle to Albert was the 'Ord of Caithness', Berriedale in particular he wasn't looking forward to. He was worried that his brakes wouldn't cope on the wet descent. What a lot of people don't realise is that a racing trike generally only has 2 brakes acting on the front wheel which makes it tend to skid and lose steering in severe conditions. Often the rider has to lean out over the left or right wheel on a bend just to keep the wheel down. Uneven and severe road camber can be very exhausting to a rider.

Albert remembers slowing down in a series of skids to the bottom and then began the tortuous climb with its infamous left hand hairpin bend of roughly 1 in 4. He knew he'd got to take the bend wide to get round, but in the dark and wet conditions he cut the corner. The inside drive wheel skidded and stopped, he paused for a second or two and stood on the pedals, and before he knew what was happening he was on his back having tipped the trike up on top of him. It took him a long time to get to grips with the situation, in fact, it was Wick before he'd settled down, taking some hot tea there. The trike was a 'Higgins' who was one of the main trike builders of that time.

At last the lights of John o Groats Hotel hove into view. He was so relieved to have got there. Albert remarks in his article "It was a tremendous thrill to be met by RRA officials and be told I had got the record subject to confirmation. The record was ours, and I do mean ours. No long distance record can ever be broken by an individual, it is the result of a terrific amount of team work and I am quite sure no one could have a better team than I." Albert had taken 7.5 hrs off Duffields time to record **2 days 12 hrs 37 mins.**

A selection of details now recalled in an article by Alf Arnold who organized Alberts attempt

"We were in the North of Scotland in Mr and Mrs Brown's car, Maurice Woodcock, John Arnold, Harold Nelson and myself, with Chris Riley on motor bike, helping Albert on his way to Inverness. During this section of the ride, Albert had been crying out for something for his sore backside, so John and myself set off looking for 'Fullers Earth'. We travelled round the villages asking but to no avail. In the end Les Brown managed to get some Nivea Crème which did the trick. Les Brown now took over as observer and they got to Inverness around 6 pm. It was calm with a slight southerly wind. We left Inverness in front of Albert to give him drinks and food.

Around 7.30 pm the wind got up stronger and with rain falling it reached gale force, but Albert was lucky as it was behind him all the way up the coast road. I realised that we could be at John o Groats very early in the morning, well in front of schedule time, so I phoned the hotel from Golspie to put them in the picture. The landlord said everything would be all right for us whatever time we arrived.

Albert went up the road like 'the clappers'. I later transferred to Bill Davies car to get in front to John O Groats. I was very worried about the RRA witnesses who were supposed to be at John o Groats. They had made no contact with us at all and I could not risk taking any chances. I can recall going through Wick and seeing the Wick police on the steps of a large building with tea for the helpers, and seeing a Sergeant with a bottle to hand up to Albert when he came through at 3 am. The phone HQ for the North of Scotland was manned by the borough police at Inverness. This was the second time they had volunteered to do it for us. They supplied all the information to everyone who required it. Many did use this service, which was vital in that area.

We arrived at John o Groats around 4.15 am and managed to wake the landlord. It was pouring with rain and there was no sign of the RRA witnesses, so I immediately phoned the speaking clock and checked the watches of members of the team who were with me at John o Groats. Albert arrived at the front door of the hotel at 4.37 am. What a great performance.

My brother John's party had broken down on the coast road. They were stranded but managed to get a message to John o Groats to say a half shaft had broken on the car. I told them there was a spare one in the boot. They replaced it and carried on to the end with some amusing stories.

One character who was with us on this and many other record attempts was Harold Nelson of Wythenshaw. After the attempt he made a tablecloth and embroidered on it the map of England with the signatures of all who took part, with all the clubs round the edge. It was presented to Albert at a later club dinner."

Harold Nelson became a notable official of the NRRA and the RRA. He ran the hospitality HQ on the Mersey 24 hr for many years providing a team of masseurs and feeding facilities for tired riders. He was also instrumental in Eric Mathews rise to prominence in long distance racing. In later years he was awarded the 'B.E.M' for his services to the sport.

In March 1958 Albert was presented with the Bidlake Memorial Plaque at the North West TA Luncheon, and he received a minutes ovation in praise of his deeds. Peter Barlow gave a moving tribute to Albert stating how he had broken 4 competition records in 1949, his most notable being the trike 24 hr record of 411.75 miles, in the Mersey Championship event. Then how Albert had teamed up with John Arnold and took the 12 hr, 24 hr, End to End and 1000 on Tandem Trike, followed by taking the solo trike End to End in 1957.

Albert gave his thanks to his great team, including, Alf Arnold and Peter Barlow, his organisers. He thanked Gerald Clowes who had given up his own racing season to train with him. He concluded by saying that if John Arnold hadn't suffered so badly with his feet and ankles after 1954 and had attacked the trike End to End, John would surely have reduced the record to inside two days.

So, this great performer and Bidlake recipient of 1957 modestly placed the credits to others, rather than himself. Albert went on in 1958 to take the solo trike 1000 miles record, about which I have devoted space elsewhere in this book, on separate 1000 mile record successes.

Certain passages in this article were taken from the Cycling Magazine with additional material from Alf Arnold and myself.

No 19 DAVE KEELER FRIDAY 30TH MAY 1958 SOLO BICYCLE END TO END

At 9.00 am Dave Keeler set out from Lands End to try and break Sid Ferris's 21 year old record of 2 days, 6 hours, 33 mins and also to attempt Arthur Renders 1000 mile record of 2 days 16 hrs 50 mins. He had postponed his start from the Wednesday because of unfavourable winds. His attempt was unusual in as much as it was very early in the year. His job as a scientist working in Paris and living partly in France and partly in England, meant fitting in the attempt whenever possible.

The weather was favourable and warm but only a moderate wind. He gradually dropped behind schedule to be 10 mins down at Bristol. His first 12 hrs produced 242 miles getting him just south of Tewkesbury. He lost more time to be 57 mins down at Lancaster - 403 miles.

It was around the Shap area he complained of a bad back, he got held up in Carlisle on the Saturday at 9.30am due to the 'Tour of Britain' starting there. The police had diverted traffic and the record breaker got completely lost and covered only 9 miles on the correct route in that hour. Worse was to come for Dave. He completely lost contact with his helping team who were also delayed by the diversions. He rolled along steadily waiting for them to catch up and make contact. He did a great deal of freewheeling from Gretna Green onwards.

Dave was going through a very bad patch, although he was well up on Sid Ferrris's time at this point, probably by about four hours. He must have realised his ambition to beat two days was falling apart; he'd still got 400 miles to cover and couldn't afford to be complacent.

I suppose freewheeling is better than stopping, at least you are reducing your distance to be covered and having a rest at the same time. At Beattock he was nearly two hours down on his 2 day schedule, and after a second night climbing The Grampians, he arrived at Inverness 728 miles in a thick 'pea-soup' mist after dropping to sea level. He stopped for warm clothing and with struggling to find his way through the mist he lost more time here. In the third 12 hour section he had covered only 118 miles.

On the very steep stretches of 'Aultnamain' he got off and 'trotted'. His helpers thought they could run with him but with his long legs they had a job to keep up. On the steep badly surfaced hairpin bends of Helmsdale and Berriedale he found it easier to walk up due to the gradients being 1 in 6. He said he felt very fresh at this point and knowing that he was still well inside Ferris's time must have been some consolation to him.

He flew through Wick holding his schedule speed and reached John o Groats in 2 days 3 hrs 9 minutes taking 3 hrs 24 mins off Sid Ferris's 21 year old record. Its interesting to note that Ferris was also a vegetarian.

A two hour rest was scheduled here, but Keeler only took 40 minutes before continuing for the 1000 miles. He had 13 hours left to cover the remaining 130 miles, but nature had taken its toll and Dave was almost asleep in the saddle on this hot afternoon. After another 50 miles making 920 miles covered, Charlie Davey called the attempt off.

This classy 29 year old Yorkshire Vegetarian C and AC rider had now brought the two days barrier closer to reality, given a stronger wind and no delays at Carlisle who knows what could have been achieved?

Dave was the first amateur solo bike rider to attack the record in more than 50 years. His preparation for the record had been a Southern RRA 'London-Southampton-Dover-London' record around 300 miles in total which he broke. He fitted his training and racing into a busy work schedule also compounded by living in two countries.

He was one of the first men to ride the End to End in shorts and a racing jersey as opposed to Alpaca jacket and tights. At the time of the record in 1958, he was a well known fast 25 mile and 50 mile time triallist having broken the hour and two hours and winning events on many occasions.

More importantly, his long distance pedigree was equally impressive having won the 1957 North Road 24 hr with 480 miles. This proved he had a very good basic background to make an 'End to Ender'. He stood 6' 2" and weighed 13 stone, taller and heavier than any of his predecessors who were mainly of medium height and build.

Charlie Davey, also a vegetarian record breaker in earlier years was his Organiser and Manager, having looked after Sid Ferris some 21 years previously. Frank Armond, another record breaker in the 1920's, was his timekeeper on this epic journey.

When questioned about attempting the record as early as May, Dave explained that although most riders would want to cram in thousands of miles early in the year, he felt it was possible to find a balance between peak fitness and rest, so that the body is ready to respond to a great effort.

He used a new unconventional Campagnolo 'Paris Roubaix' rear gear mechanism which gave five gears from 61" to 94". Gear changes were made by twisting a long lever on the seat stay to unlock the wheel, while a quick back pedal action switched the chain onto another sprocket. Helpers blamed Keeler's backache in later stages of his attempt on his frequent rear-ward leaning to change gear, but Dave thought this unlikely. .So ended another chapter in the history of the End to End.

Three months later, he won the North Road 24 hr with 490 miles, even after being sent 'off course' several miles by drunks pretending to be marshalls in the night !

In an interview with Dennis Donovan 'Cycling Weekly' in 1991, Dave Keeler, who was 76 on Christmas Day 2004, talked about his record and his cycling before and after it. He was the first man to beat the hour for 25 miles in Wales, and took the Welsh 50 miles record about the same time. Also in the early 1950's he broke the Scottish 25 miles record, beating Stan Higginson on Clydeside, and although he also won the Scottish 25 mile championship, Dave never won an English time trial championship.

On the Coventry track 'The Butts Stadium' he won the 4000m pursuit championship in 1951 and then in 1958 after getting the End to End record, he broke the 24 hr 'Competition record' in the North Road event with 490 miles.

Dave worked in Baldock and lived in Letchworth in the 1950's and then got a job in France and married a French girl. Three of his four children were born in Versailles, the fourth in Watford, and they all have dual nationality. He came back to England on a fortnights holiday to ride the Lands End to John o Groats record, and when the party got there on the Sunday dinnertime, they stayed overnight at a hotel in Wick. Dave said the journey home seemed endless, finally arriving home on Wednesday lunchtime.

He remembers Jock Wadley questioning him repeatedly about this new fangled rod change, Campagnolo 'Paris Roubaix' rear gear, as used by Fausto Coppi to win the Paris Roubaix Classic in 1950, and whether its lever being positioned on the rear seat stay had contributed to Dave's bad back ache. Dave said that being so tall he often got back ache anyway.

Ten weeks later, Dave Keeler had lost his record to Reg Randall. He only found out about it by accident when he rang Jim Hannings at his local bike shop and he said "I suppose you know you have lost your record !" Dave was so shocked, he left the phone hanging on its cord and has no recollection of riding back to Letchworth. He said he was so disappointed he felt like packing in and taking up golf. However, later he did 4 hrs 24 mins in the Bath Road 100 and it helped him get over it.

After riding a few road races in France, he returned in 1959 to have another crack to get his record back off Reg. It was a hot sticky August day with no real help from the wind and the tar was melting on the road. Between Okehampton and Tiverton he abandoned after dropping 30 mins behind schedule.

Dave made a three year 'come back' in the mid '70's at 48 years of age and got within seconds of his 25 and 50 mile times done in 1951. He also took 4 mins off his best 100 time with 4 hrs 11 mins in 1975.

He has made a few forays back to ride in Vet's events but the last time I saw him was at the John Woodburn film show in 2002, looking very tanned and very fit for his age.

Information courtesy of Dennis Donovan 'Cycling Weekly' with additional text from myself.

No 20 REG RANDALL 29th JULY 1958 SOLO BICYCLE END TO END

Reg Randall was a stocky cheerful rider who had to plan his End to End record around his work's annual holiday, so he couldn't really choose when to go or wait for a good wind or dry conditions. His large band of helpers were under the same obstacles of an annual fortnights holiday.

Out of all the record breakers, Reg was one of the shortest compared to the man who's record he was hoping to beat. He came very well prepared being an avid continental tourist and long distance man. He had won the Catford 24 hr time trial in 1953 and 1954 with mileages of 457 and 453 miles, and in 1955 had put up 458 in the same event. He rode a 5 speed bike with gears ranging from 61" to 92", very similar to Dave Keeler's who's record of 2 days 3 hrs 9 mins, Reg was trying to beat.

Reg's one ambition was to break the End to End but he always had doubts about his speed, although he was confident of his reserves and stamina. He was surrounded by lots of friends and clubmates who managed to convince him that 'the farther he went, the faster he got'.

When talking to Eileen Sheridan at the 'Greenford CC' dinner where she had been guest speaker, Eileen managed to instill in him a need to do it. Her enthusiasm was such that she arranged for Reg to see Frank Southall and he was also very positive he should go for it. Reg says he always knew he could 'go the distance' but whether it would be fast enough he wasn't sure, but only time would tell. From January 1958 it was 'all systems go'. George Dixon from the Greenford CC was to manage and organise a team to take Reg to the Scottish borders and Jack Spencer from the Harlequins , Reg's own club, was to take him from the Borders to John o Groats. He was told 'all you've got to do is ride, and leave the worrying to us'.

Roy Haynes, one of Claud Butler's mechanics helped Reg with his bike and took over the mechanical side of things. Syd Parker, another tandem trike End to Ender also gave him lots of helpful advice. Reg says, apart from all his own helpers who were magnificent throughout, there was Les Brown and his wife who gave him such help at the top of Shap with all sorts of food and drink an End to Ender would require.

His record attempt started at 10am on July 29th 1958, and he experienced torrential rain. He had a bad fall at Preston and took a wrong turning which cost him a lot of time. He got absolutely chilled to the bone after Beattock by the cold wet conditions, but just stopped long enough to change clothes. At Dunblane he was 27 minutes up on Keeler's record at that point and seemed to be moving very well.

Reg took another drenching as he conquered the Grampians to be three quarters of an hour up at Inverness. Between there and the end he came close to disaster when a brake cable broke at a crucial moment. He also suffered another fall and spent some time 'off course'! but he was still in control and as he rode up Helmsdale he waved cheerfully to his followers.

He reached John o Groats and continued for the 1000 but after falling twice more and suffering sleep deprivation he abandoned after 35 miles.

Apart from the height difference between Dave Keeler and Reg, there was a difference in riding style. Keeler was a smooth pedaller, Reg was a puncher of the pedals and seemed to fight the bike when in full flight, and although his time trial results prior to the End to End at 100 miles and 24 hours were slower than Keeler's, Reg was always up on Keeler even if only 1 minute at Shap 440 miles. His biggest advantages came later on in Scotland where he'd gained 16 minutes by Blair Atholl, 50 mins by Muir of Ord, and at the end he'd gained 1 hr 11 mins to take the record with **2 days 1 hour 58 mins.**

A report of Reg Randall's End to End printed in Cycling - August 6th 1958 - author was John Mathews:

"In appalling weather conditions, with no sit down feeds, no rest, no scheduled stops and with mechanical and other delays which totalled over 30 minutes, Reg Randall smashed his way into the record books.

With his right wrist swollen and painful so that changing gear was difficult and pulling on the handlebars almost impossible for nearly 100 miles, Reg had battled through to take 71 mins off Dave Keelers 10 weeks old record".

The author describes Reg Randall as virtually an **'unknown from the Harlequins CC'**. 'I would dispute unknown' - one only has to look at his Catford 24 hour wins in 1953 and 1954 with 457 and 453 miles. Both very respectable mileages and good performances to base an End to End on. He goes on to say that **with Reg failing to get the 24 hr and 1000 mile records, this proves that 'in future the three records must be attempted separately'** How fortunate to have the 'wisdom of hindsight' with Coupe and Woodburn both getting the 24 hr record in the same ride and Gethin Butler getting all three in one ride !

Reg, an engineer from Hayes in Middlesex, was racing on multiple gears for the first time. He was short, stocky dark haired, 32 years of age, 5ft 2" and weighted 10 stone 7 lb, and was known as 'Tubby' to his friends. He was an extremely modest man, who's first thought was always for the team of helpers who assisted him on his way. He always made a point of thanking all the marshalls and helpers as he flashed past. He was a tourist and clubman first of all, and a racing man secondly.

After a 10 am start with the wind swinging round to blow strongly from the South and after riding himself in steadily on lower gears, he continued to Bristol to be up on Keeler's time at this point. He just missed the rush hour in Bristol at 7.32 pm by going straight through the town centre, cutting out the usual 3 mile detour. Bristol as ever was well marshalled.

He had scheduled to get to Gloucester in the 12 hours but even after a 5 min stop for lights

and night clothing he was still nearly 30 mins up on this schedule, completing 246 miles for the first 12 hours, 4 miles up on Keeler.

Worcester 10.36 pm, Kidderminster 11.22pm, Bridgnorth 12.07am, Wellington 12.52am and with Whitchurch behind him, he reached Stockton Heath, just south of Warrington, when a near calamity threatened the record. Its here that the route crosses the Manchester Ship Canal, and the swing bridge was closed to allow ships through. Fortunately, just as Reg reached the bridge, it started swinging back to link the roads, and the delay was reduced to 5 mins.

Its just after Warrington at 353 miles that the heavy rains started. It was now 3.46 am and he was nearly an hour up on schedule. At Wigan he stopped to get out of wet night clothes, take off lights, and replace a broken rear brake cable.

At Preston after 382 miles in 19 hours 38 mins, he went off course and when retracing at a roundabout, he slipped on the greasy road and fell heavily. This fall shook his confidence on bends for the remainder of the ride. His handlebars and brake levers had to be straightened. In all he lost another 5 mins but by Kendal, 42 miles later, he was still 38 mins up on schedule. Then came the rugged road out of Kendal up into the Lake District. It was pouring with rain as he tackled the drag up onto the bleak moors of Shap. At the foot he was handed a glucose drink. He shouted "once I get rid of this lot (the hills) I'll start moving". He reached the top having covered 15 hard miles in the hour. At the top two club folk offered him a choice of various cooked foods, but Reg didn't want to stop so gratefully accepted a drink of sliced peaches and pounded on.

The rain had stopped by the time the first 24 hours had expired at Low Hesket, between Penrith and Carlisle - 459.5 miles. By Carlisle at 10.31 am Wednesday, Randall was 49 minutes up on his schedule, which commanded a fast second day. He crossed into Scotland at Gretna Green 478 miles in 25 hrs 3 mins, and from then on he stopped taking heavy solid foods. Even though the first 24 hours had been tough, the second 24 hrs had to be just as tough to get the record.

After 500 miles came the long bleak drag up into the Beattocks to the summit at 1,029 ft, where down came the heaviest rain so far on the attempt. The roads were flooded with muddy water from road works. He took a severe battering from the weather and got, in his words 'chilled to the bone'. He stopped before Lanark for a change of clothing at 3.15 pm still 20 mins up on schedule. He took an extra sweater to keep warm in this hilly terrain. At Stirling the cold rain came back with a vengeance. Through Perth at 7.14 pm still 10 mins up on schedule, but time is getting tight as he battles on towards Pitlochry and 'The Grampians'. Along the fast relatively flat roads on the 'Pass of Killiecrankie' enshrouded with heavy mist, rain and black clouds swirling round the mountain tops to Drumochter Pass at 1,484 ft in the Cairngorms. He'd lost all of his gains on schedule over this last 100 miles. He stopped to replace a bulb and put on a race cape to keep out the cold. He passed through a well marshalled Inverness at 2.35 am on Thursday, now 20 mins down. He said later "If I hadn't been so pigheaded about not wearing a race cape early on, I would have felt a lot better". He praised the club folk of the Clachnacuddin CC for their wonderful help at an unearthly hour.

Just outside Beauly at 3.20 am, a car had crashed on a hairpin bend. Reg stopped, turned and tried to see if he could help. He was sent on his way, assured that a following car would attend to the crash, but he lost several valuable minutes here. Then, with 107 miles to go, as dawn was breaking on the last day, on the turning off the A9, came a 1 in 10 descent before 'Aultnamain' At the foot of the drop was a sharp right hand bend, on went his brakes, the front cable snapped, he snaked down the hill in one long uncontrollable skid, half jumped, half fell off at the bottom, and lost some 5 mins while a cable was fitted.

As he approached Aultnamain, he'd gained enough time through not taking lengthy stops, to be an hour ahead of Keeler's ride at this point. Then at Bonar Bridge, 777 miles in 43 hours, came the first sign of wrist trouble. He had to pull his gear lever back with his left hand, due to his right hand being too painful to use, except for the easier job of pushing the lever forward. With John o Groats over a 100 hilly miles away, this was going to be an agonising last stretch along the coast. The wind which had dropped during the night was getting stronger now, and for the first time the weather was getting better, with sunshine and blue skies for the first time in over 50 hours.

As he rode the 3 mile long climb out of Helmsdale at 816 miles up to the Ord of Caithness, he took off his woollen hat, waved it cheerily to the caravan of following cars, as he rounded a hairpin 's' bend, and climbed steadily to the top in 15 mins 'the worst climb of the ride' he said. At the top he turned and waved again as he crossed the last County border into Caithness. Down the steep one mile drop into Berriedale, over two bridges in the valley and then came the short, sharp, notorious End to End 'wrecker' - Berriedale hill. Out of the cars jumped his helpers, running alongside, they pleaded with him to get off and walk, but he outrode them and stormed to the top, covering the climb in 7 minutes. Beyond Lybster the 48 hours was up and he was well up on Keeler's ride - 17 miles in fact. At Wick he knew the record was his, barring accidents.

He had a last drink 8.5 miles from John o Groats, two long drags remained. Each time he expected to see the coast ahead 'I thought it would never come' he said. Then over the bare moors to the last ridge and straight ahead lay the finish, the sea and the Orkney's in the background. Now desperately tired, the long, shallow downhill drop made little difference to his speed. Exhausted he pulled into the first hotel on the road, but it was the wrong one! Frantically he was beeped by the following cars and he continued another three quarters of a mile to the sea. Reg is not the first or the last to make this mistake at the end of this exhausting journey.

Timekeeper G.M. Collins looked at his watch to record : 2 days 1 hour 58 mins.

As a large enthusiastic crowd of helpers, campers, and coach trippers, crowded around he had his wrist bandaged, changed his racing vest, and finally set off on his 1000 mile bid after a 23 minute break. He had 14 hours 29 mins to cover 130 miles to equal the record. He planned to have a roadside sleep after covering some of the extra miles. Instead he went 'off course' soon after he started, producing only 28 miles in 2 hrs 9 mins. He fell off at the dead turn. At Reiss 898 miles, alas and sadly, the end was in sight. He hadn't got the strength to turn a decent gear with the wind, let alone against. Reg now had very little fight left in him and midway between Reiss and Castleton with 905 miles covered in 2 days 5 hrs, he took the advice of his helpers and abandoned his 1000 mile attempt.

When questioned by the author, Reg gave his own version of the ride *"The End to End has been my ambition for a long time. I started serious training with the Brentwood Utility 100 mile at the end of February, and since then I've averaged over 500 miles a week. I'm really a tourist at heart and that's why I like long distance events. I've 'suffered' more in 24 hour events than I did on the End to End. In fact, I didn't feel rough at any point although the cold rain in the Beattocks 'chilled me to the marrow'. The half light was the worst time for riding, I kept imagining things that just weren't there. Passing through one village at dawn, I swear I saw three women standing at the roadside, but when I got there they were petrol pumps !*

It's funny the things one thinks about, I was handed up a drink at Redruth and dropped the bottle on an island on the right of the road. For two days, I wondered whether the clubman had found his bottle. At one time I though I stood a chance for the 24 hr but decided the End to End was more important, and given good conditions, I am convinced the record can go inside 2 days"

And of the notorious climb up Berrriedale which End to Enders usually walk, he said ***"I couldn't get off. My legs are so short it would have taken too long to walk it".***

Reg trained harder for his separate 1000 mile record in 1960 which he broke with 2 days 10 hrs 40 mins, one of the reasons was to confound those who said he couldn't do it. During his 1000 miles he was so tired he promised himself when he finished he would sleep for 1000 hours.

Reg says looking back at his End to End record he should have taken more time off the existing figures but knowing he was inside the schedule he became complacent and he says he lost the urgency to try himself to the limit although he still rode hard at the end. He thoroughly enjoyed his 1000 miles achieved in 1960, being an avid tourist and 'mile eater' he relished in the ride, one of the out and home legs being over 200 miles long.

After the 1000 miles, his enthusiasm for riding the bike was such that a few days afterwards he rode with the lads from the club, to a beer festival in Munich and remembers riding back on his own through Holland and Belgium to be in work for the following Monday. He rode his record rides without sponsorship and most of the expenses for his two records were paid for by his team of friends and helpers who all chipped in. They also gave up their holidays for him. He says he owes his two records to all his friends help. He just enjoyed riding his bike.

Since 1958 Reg has regularly been part of the End to End and record breaking scene, being a helper and observer on many attempts. His love for the sport is immense and he has put a lot back into it with his support and enthusiasm. When reading through other riders accounts, his name crops up regularly.

Although he loved riding his bike, he hated proper training and would often pray for rain when at work so that he wouldn't have to go ! Reg recalls years later after having ridden his first 24 hr event, he insisted on riding to the club tea rendezvous on the Sunday afternoon, then riding back to the usual pub to finish off the ride, adding another 32 miles onto his grand total, and some more liquid into his body.

In 1963, Reg moved from Enfield to Bidford on Avon to work for the 'Revolutionary' new 'Moulton' Cycles. He had two more attempts at the End to End, both on a Moulton. On the first attempt he retired at Preston, being well behind schedule against a headwind On the second, he abandoned at the Scottish border for the same reason.

.Johnny Pardoe, one of the Stalwarts of marshalling the End to End route in the Warrington and Preston area over the last 40 years, says one of his first connections with the End to End came on a holiday in Scotland. Riding his trike along the top of Scotland from Cape Wrath to John o Groats, he arrived in time to see a short stocky dishevelled rider slumped in a chair outside the hotel. When he enquired as to what had happened to him, the helper replied "that's Reg Randall, he's just broken the Lands End to John o Groats record with **2 days, 1 hr, 58 mins**!" From that moment onwards, Johnny said he was hooked on long distance records.

Information courtesy of 'Cycling', Reg Randall, and Johnny Pardoe, with text from myself.

No 21 DAVID DUFFIELD MONDAY 11th JULY 1960
HIS 2nd TRIKE END TO END

An article written by Peter Thorne, one of the band of helpers on David's epic ride
(with additions from myself)

On Monday 11th July 1960, David set off from Lands End at 8.00 am, timed away by Ted Bricknell. In a strong south west wind, an early rainstorm didn't deter him. His progress was so rapid the following vehicles had a job to by-pass or keep up with him. David Duffield, the famous 29 year old, 6ft 3" Beacon Road Club Trike rider was now trying to re-claim his record taken from him in 1957 by Albert Crimes with a performance of 2 days 12 hrs 37 mins.

Around the Taunton area, the Perry brothers put in a very useful appearance with drinks and sponges for the rider all across and beyond the Bridgwater flats and up to Bristol; their knowledge of the local roads enabling them to by-pass the rider. Keith Edwards, a Midland Reporter for the Cycling press was phoned with Duffields progress. Heavy evening traffic in **Bristol 198 miles** didn't slow David down as local club folk gave him a swift passage through the city. At Gloucester, Lewis Morris and his crew saw him through safely.

Dave lost a shoe-plate in this area; ***in those days of toe clips and straps, shoe-plates were generally a short thin block of slotted aluminium nailed onto the leather sole of the shoe. The slot clipped onto the back-plate of the pedal and provided as secure a fitting as today's clip-less pedals.*** The helpers phoned through to various people in the Midlands who would bring out a selection of shoe plates for Gerry, one of the helpers, to choose from, and nail on, using the car jack as a 'shoe last'. ***Percy Stallard brought out a selection of shoeplates and a hammer at Wolverhampton, but it didn't get mended until Abington in Scotland.***

Jack Clements, President of the Beacon Roads, and Dicky Bowes, Solihull CC took over helping at Gloucester to give the following car a chance to get ahead, and have a break at Stourbridge, before going on ahead to Newcastle under Lyme to resume helping again. They barely had time to wash, eat and re-stock the van with hot flasks etc, than it was time to catch a very fast moving Duffield, so happy to be on home territory, and being one of the first to use the flatter well lit roads through Wolverhampton, Stafford and Stone. ***He suffered severe stomach pains around this area, which had him writhing in agony. Dr Hamley was contacted at Loughborough University and suggested the helpers gave him porridge, which eventually cured him.***

At Newcastle under Lyme, George Ward, Jack Duckers, and Wilf (all VTTA riders) provided a van to be used for feeding all the way to John o Groats. North West Tricycle Association members were out in force between Newcastle and Warrington, dashing around the dark Cheshire lanes with drinks and encouragement. Dave took a bad patch on this stretch and lost all the 'gains' he had made on his schedule. Preston was reached at 6.29 am on Tuesday. Peter Barlow who was directing the ride gave instructions to the helpers to 'keep Duffield moving, even at 5 mph, its better than stationary'. At Wigan David took a 'rub-down' and a change of clothing in the back of the van at 5.30 am. A local policeman passing by asked if the rider was undergoing an 'endurance test?'.

At Lancaster Gordon Tait and his club mates had set up a table at the side of the road and a most efficient 'wash and brush up' was achieved. David had a wash, a massage and a feed and was back on the road within a few minutes of his arrival. The helping crew also got a chance to 'freshen up' at this point. From here on the wind blew from the north for most of the remainder of the ride; only the last 40 miles saw the wind generally on his left shoulder as the road swings eastwards. He climbed Shap and had to stay out of the saddle on the descent due to the wind strength. Conditions were so bad here, he threatened to pack.

Through Penrith and Carlisle to cross the border at Gretna, greeted by the sounds of the bagpipes. Duffield was feeling very sleepy on this stretch and the sound of bagpipes made him think he'd reached the 'golden gates'.

At **Abington 526 miles** there is a famous pull in transport stop where a scheduled break was taken, although David didn't really want to stop, it proved to be worth it with Mrs McInnes administering motherly attention on the rider.

This was the lady who had bandaged both his kneecaps on his north to south ride in 1957. The severe cold on his first night had caused the kneecaps to lift and become painful. I only found out about this from John Arnold who chatted to Mrs McInnes when helping on Albert Crimes trike End to End, two months later. She mentioned having some poor devil turn up in the middle of the night and having bandages put on to relieve the pain.

This break at Abington in 1960 was a much less painful one. David even had time to listen to Acker Bilk on the Juke Box for a minute or two. I wonder what Peter Barlow would have said if he'd have known ! Back on the road again, Acker Bilk must have had magical powers as Duffield reduced his outstanding time deficit of 20 mins to be back on schedule as he passed through Lanark and Stirling to Perth, where he took on lights for his second night on the road. He had 'Neads Foot Oil' rubbed into his legs, to keep out the cold and wet one is likely to experience in the Grampians. ***Neads Foot Oil is extracted from sheep's hooves after being crushed and is a natural waterproofing.*** Gerry, one of the helpers, reckons it adds quite a distinctive flavour to fish and chips when eaten from the same fingers !

Over the Grampians from Perth to Inverness they came across David lying on the ground with his feet up on the axle of his trike. He was tackling the unbroken climb to the summit at

Dalwhinnie and had experienced numbness in his legs. After a quick rub-down the feeling soon returned and he was back on the road, pedalling on once more. ***He had suffered with a bad back some months prior to his attempt. The cause was fibrositis.***

At Tomatin on the A9 before Inverness, David stopped for the support car to go ahead to make sure the sit down feed was all in hand. He was about 50 minutes down on schedule at this point. As on all other attempts over the last 30 odd years, this hospitality stop organised at Maisie and Ian Mcleod's home was superb; from a motor bike marshal who by-passed the rider to warn of his approach, to the wash, change and feed, not just for Duffield, but also the helping team as well. To Maisie's husband guiding the entourage back out to Dingwall on his bike in the pouring rain, nothing was too much trouble and David was back on the road in 30 mins. He wasn't too tired to tell them all about a small Scots lad who had asked him 'do ye no think ye're a bit tae big to ride one o' them ?'

Back on course now with approximately 130 miles to do, Dave was showing signs of sleep deprivation, which isn't surprising considering he hadn't had any for over 50 hours. He persevered on through repeated rain showers and although still an hour down on a schedule aimed to beat Albert Crimes record by 2 hours, he maintained a steady pace to lose no more time.

He had heard at Inverness that Albert had walked Berriedale which made David determined to ride up, and this he did ! ***Peter Thorne, one of the helpers and also the author of this story, believes David is the first Tricyclist to ride all of the hills, and also the first to go without sleep.***

Due to roadworks and repairs, the surface on both Helmsdale and Berriedale was atrocious, and progress was so slow in places that he was almost at a standstill. Every turn of the pedals must have been agony, the helpers walking alongside were struggling with aching muscles, but at the top, Dave still had the time and strength to chat to two girls whom he had just met. Freewheeling down the other side for a breather, David would never have thought that the next day on the way home, he would be helping to push a fuel-less van to the top from the opposite direction !

At last the wind turned more favourable onto his shoulder and he settled down to the last 40 miles, in fact, he went 'mad' at it, and mile after mile was reeled off at over 'evens' and all this after 850 miles and 58 hours, the last 17 miles from Wick was covered in 50 minutes.

During this story, I have said little or nothing about the splendid work undertaken by George Ward and his crew of helpers, who fed David using a calor gas stove in the back of the van. They prepared fresh porridge and hot drinks along the whole of the journey. Although I reckon as much porridge was spilt in the van as went in the bottles !

For the first and last time, the van went past Duffield with about 9 miles to go to 'Groats', so that Ted Bricknell could time the finish. I would have given a lot for a picture of David's face as we passed him , though I shall carry a mental picture of his contorted, determined features for many years ! Despite the isolation of John o Groats, there was quite a crowd to welcome David as he crossed the line at 1.5 minutes to seven to record a time of **2 days 10 hours 58 mins** taking 1 hr 39 mins off Albert Crimes 1957 record.

To the uninitiated this would appear to be 'the end' but no, after a short 25 minute sleep in the van, David was back up again. Photographs, Telegrams, another penn'orth on the scales, now showing 12 stone 5 lb, he'd lost a complete stone since the start. After talking to reporters and making phone calls, the team made their way to the hotel for a bath and well deserved meal, and sleep.

Sandy, a coach driver who was staggered to hear of David's 2.5 day ride, told us it had taken him three days to get to Glasgow with his coach party, and generously treated us to drinks.

Finally at 10.30 pm, we made our way slowly up the stairs and to bed. The journey home to Birmingham took 2 days.

My thanks once again to Peter Thorne for this 'spirited' description of Dave Duffield's second successful End to End ride, and to the Tricycle association Gazette, where it first appeared in print.

As most readers are probably aware, David went on to become a famous 'Tour de France' Commentator on Television. His in depth knowledge of the riders, the history of the race, and his comments as the race unfolds, warms him to his audience. As well as 'the tour' David has covered most major continental races.

At 74 years of age, I wonder if he can still remember his two successful End to Ends in as much detail ?

No 22 JIM BAILEY AND JACK FORREST 26th JULY 1960 TANDEM END TO END

Jim and Jack set off on Tuesday July 26th 1960 at 10 am from Lands End with Stan Churnage doing the time keeping honours. He was to stay with them throughout the tandem ride. They were attacking Cowsill and Denton's record of 2 days 8 hours 47 mins set in 1952.

A light north westerly helped them to Exeter where they were 20 mins up on schedule despite very heavy traffic which prevented the following cars from keeping up with the riders, making feeding very difficult.

At Tewkesbury they had covered 243 miles to be 2 miles up on schedule at the 12 hr point. They stopped for night clothes although it was a warm evening, Jim recalls when they got to Nantwich they were suddenly stopped and led down a dark alley into Jack Duckers house for supper just after 2.00 pm. Jack was a well known local clubman.

Nearing dawn a cold ground mist appeared as they travelled along the edge of the Lake District. They had a sit down feed at Kendal 424 miles, before they climbed Shap Fell. They were originally going to stop for a feed on the summit but Jim says in hindsight he's glad they changed their minds as it was very cold at the top and they would have rapidly cooled off if they had stopped.

The stop at Kendal took 12 minutes which left them just over an hour down on schedule. Near Penrith the 24 hr point was reached giving 448 miles. Heavy traffic caused them to lose time in Carlisle at approximately 10.30 am.

After crossing the border they took a break for food at Gretna. The road from Ecclefechan over the Beattock Summit proved very painful for Jack Forrest on the back as road widening had made the surface like a cart track. This always magnifies the shock waves for the person on the back of the tandem, sitting directly over the back wheel.

At Abington where there is a large transport café and is a popular stopping place for End to Enders, they took only 1 hour of a scheduled 2 hr stop. This was to cut their losses on schedule back to three quarters of an hour. They had covered 526 miles in just over 27 hours. The road to Stirling is a trying one in the heat of a summers afternoon. Jack started to nod off to sleep on Jim's back and Jim recalls singing loudly at him to keep him awake, a rare sight and sound for bystanders !

At Stirling 578 miles they were given hospitality by the Central Scotland Wheelers with a sit down feed laid on in their clubroom. This helped Jack through his weary patch.

Nearing Perth, Jim was starting to get a severe pain in his right knee. Warm clothing and massage partially resolved the problem as dusk began to fall on this second night heading towards the 'Grampians'. It was a fine night but they still had no help from the wind as they attacked the long drag up to the 'Pass of Drumochter'.

Recalling the climb out of Blair Atholl at about 650 miles, Jim had one of the most frightening moments of the ride. A deep loud rumbling came from the hill ahead of them. Two glaring headlights seemed to fill the straight road coming nearer and nearer. It was two enormous 'DUKW' amphibious landing craft vehicles, probably on manoeuvres in the area. Then further on they had another scare as a diesel train appeared to be hurtling towards them like a ghost train in the night. The road ran alongside the track making it even more frightening.

The run into Inverness reached speeds of 45 mph with rabbits dashing across the road dazzled by the headlights of the following cars. Jim's wife, Marjorie, said she feared for the lads safety on this stretch.

North of Inverness they had their only puncture of the ride and this happened just when the mechanic was being sick. Later on they suffered broken spokes in the front wheel, which also delayed them. At Dingwall on the north east coast, dawn was rising, they had covered 750 miles with 120 still to do.

Jack was again feeling very drowsy. They took another 20 mins halt for sleep which proved valuable as it gave them the energy to tackle 'Aultnamain' even though they had to walk the initial slopes. From here on the wind and weather took a turn for the worse against them, and when the road veered to the east they were often battling into the teeth of a gale blowing off the North sea with cold drenching rain. They were forced to walk many of the hills due to the severity of the conditions.

Jim recalls at one stage they were going so slow the helpers ordered them off the tandem, wrapped them in warm blankets and made them sleep for a while. With 90 miles still to go they had only to do 15 mph to stick to schedule. From Wick the going was easier for them and the last 17 miles were covered at 20 mph.

They arrived at 2.48 pm, only 48 mins outside schedule but beating the record by nearly four hours. With **2 days 4 hours 48 mins.**

Although there remained 25 hours left to get the 1000 mile record, another 130 miles approximately, the last few hours had taken its toll and with the weather that had plagued them from Inverness getting worse, they called it a day, or even 2 days !

The riders praised the magnificent help they had received from the teams and the club folk on route, saying this was the main reason for keeping going, so as not to let anybody down. Ian Appleby, Alistair White, Jim's wife, Marjorie, Les Brown and his wife, providing food on the move for the riders and helpers, including Albert Crimes, Tommy Barlow (RRA Observer) Dave Duffield, and timekeeper Stan Churnage.

Jim was 31 years old when they broke the record. Jack was a touch older. Both men were of average height, Jim was more of a racing man being seeded at most distances from 25 miles to 24 hrs. Jack enjoyed club touring with the CTC and prior to 1959 he raced only a few times a year. His 25 mile time was 1hr 7mins, 234 miles for 12 hours and 408 miles on a trike for a 24 hr, whereas Jim's was 1-2-43 for 25 miles and 439 for a 24 hr.

Nine days after finishing the End to End Jim put up a personal best 100 miles of 4-23-26.

The only other National RRA record they broke was ridden in 1959, the 24 hr with 492 miles, a superb record that still stands at present day. This fine performance prompted Tommy Barlow to suggest they tackle the End to End.

The tandem they used was originally owned by the famous short distance Higginson twins on which they broke competition record for 30 miles with 1 hr 1 min 35 secs in 1954. It was made by 'Mercian' of Derby.

Their RRA certificates were signed by 'George Herbert Stancer' possibly the last ones signed by this famous man.

Jack Forrest died in 1986 aged 62. Jim Bailey still competes in time trials at 74 years of age.

This article used original text by Roy Green printed in the 'Cycling magazine' with comments from Jim Bailey and myself.

No 23 DICK POOLE MONDAY JUNE 14TH 1965 SOLO BICYLE END TO END

The first man inside 2 days

This was indeed a landmark to me and indeed lots of other cyclists. More important to me than the breaking of the 4 minute mile or the 4 hour 100, purely due to the sheer distance and time involved. I had seen Dick riding 24hr events earlier with his team mates, Arch Harding and Freddie Burrell, such steady smooth riders all. The most memorable one for me was the 1961 Mersey RC Championship event. When dusk was falling I saw six or seven top line riders all within 5 mins of each other. Cliff Smith, Ken Usher, Dick Poole, Fred Burrell and Arch Harding. If I remember rightly, Arch loved a pint and a smoke, preferably while riding.

This year, at our house, we have the large team plaque presented by the Charlotteville in 1948 for the 24 hrs RTTC championship event and what a piece of history that is. The reason we have it at home is because the Walsall Roads Ladies Team of Marina Bloom, Lynne Taylor and Tracy Maund were the fastest team from all the men in 2003 and also now in 2004. The first time ever in the history of the event being run. On the plaque the Middlesex Road Club team with Dick Poole's name on appears no less than five times !

I always remember Dick as being a 'classy' rider especially in appearance, always donned in white track mitts, cap and long white ankle socks and quite often white handlebar ribbon with his club name Middlesex RC printed on shorts. We all wondered how he managed to keep so clean. He was a dedicated club man who gave up lots of his precious 'racing' time to support other aspects of cycling club life. Apart from being the first man inside 2 days, I think he was also the first to use a double chainset on his 'Mercian' bike, giving him gears of 59-102".

Just two minutes before his 10 am start , Dick gets on his bike. A young man walks out of the Hotel and casually remarks "I suppose he is going to John o Groats? Please give my regards to Mrs Mackenzie at the hotel !"

Using extracts from timekeeper Frank Fischer's article on Dick's End to End, he states that after a misty foggy start, Cornwall and Devon posed no problems except for a bit of a 'packet' on the hills around Okehampton, leaving Dick a few minutes behind schedule. This was compounded by detouring through back streets in Exeter, plus a nagging wind to Cullompton, where, while trying to negotiate rough surfaces due to roadworks, Dick was thrown from his machine and fell heavily injuring his hip. He quickly remounted.

The heavy traffic going towards Bristol was hindering the rider and helpers alike and by Bristol where Reg Randall marshalled him through, he was 23 minutes down on Randall's time here, and after a feed at Cambridge village he was 35 minutes down at Gloucester. The breeze was now only slight and not much use for any speed but by Worcester Dick had pulled back 12 mins. Up through the West Midlands his losses weren't helped by a now windless dark night, Dave Duffield the trike man saw him through all of this area. When he crossed the A5 at Wellington he was riding into heavy rain. I saw him go through Bridgnorth and he seemed to be riding very smoothly, his eyes fixed on the road ahead. He experienced problems with his lights and by Whitchurch he was wet through and 49 mins down.

Dick's **first** 100 miles was in 4 hrs 48 mins; his **second** 100 miles - 5 hrs 22 mins; **third** 100 - 5 hrs 24 mins. On through Cheshire where lots of clubmen had turned out; cartoonist Johnny Helms, John Arnold, Tom and Peter Barlow to name but a few. .By Lancaster the wind had picked up favourably and the rain was easing, thus enabling him to regain time and only be 28 mins down now.

Dick went off course at Kirkby Lonsdale and was re-directed by a helpful observer after losing a handful of minutes. A foggy misty climb on Shap was hampered by slow moving circus lorries on their way to Penrith. It posed dire problems for the following helpers cars and by this time they were 30 mins behind Dick. They had all caught up by Shap Wells but Dick took another long-winded route here which put another mile or more onto the distance. At Penrith he was just 5 miles or approx 15 mins down on Reg Randall's time.

The 24 hr yielded 454 miles to Reg's 459.5. On through Carlisle to Ecclefechan, rain falling steadily now but Dick is pedalling smoothly and strongly. By Crawford he was 4 mins up on Randall and by Lanark he had 21 minutes in hand. He had one or two stops in the next 100 miles to eat 'off the bike' and put dry clothing on. He was also having to have his wounds dressed from his earlier fall.

Dick's **fourth** 100 miles was done in 5 hrs 16 mins and his **fifth** 100 in 5 hrs 40 mins; **sixth** 100 miles in 5 hrs 31mins and his **seventh** 100 was in 5 hrs 58 mins.

Now for a second night which was quite a pleasant one for a change, and a full moon. By Dalwhinnie - 673 miles he had 41 mins in hand. The trip through the Grampians was an outstanding one and Dick recalls 'one of the most enjoyable rides of his life'! Inverness was reached nearly an hour up on Reg's time. The profusion of early morning wildlife on the road over Aultnamain kept Dick awake. He saw rabbits, squirrels and deer. He asked for an accurate time check and was obviously calculating whether he could beat two days at this point. His efforts on the hills and his skilled descending were thrilling for the helpers to watch.

His **eighth** 100 miles was in 5 hrs 58 mins.

Cromarty Firth and a lovely clear summer morning; 3.30 am with the glorious Scottish scenery unfolding. Dick races on to be 1 hr and 22 mins up on Reg at Bonar Bridge. His climb of Berriedale was described as 'fantastic' by Mike Rees, one of the helpers, who likened him to 'Charley Gaul' a prolific climber in 'Le Tour'. He averaged over 16 mph from Helmsdale to Berriedale, and this after 818 miles. After Wick he had a couple of near misses with traffic pulling out on him which alarmed those watching from the following car, but Dick was completely unruffled., and the rest is history.

He was timed in by Frank Fischer at John o Groats, in **1 day 23 hrs 46 mins 35 secs**. What a tremendous achievement - **" the first man ever inside 2 days ".**

There was some doubt as to whether Dick would continue for the 1000 miles but after 30 mins off the bike for rest and food, he was away again. The shortest rest anyone has ever taken. He was going much better than any previous rider has ever done He had only to do 13 mph to get the record.

His **ninth** 100 miles was done in 6 hrs 22 mins including a half hour stop. His **tenth** 100 in 5 hr 47 mins.

For about three hours the weather held good then a strong 'westerly' set in bringing cold rain, but apart from asking for frequent hot drinks, it seemed to have little affect on the rider. He was doing approximately 15 mph into the wind and 20 mph with it. On the last 5 miles of 'safety' mileage he rode into very heavy rain and wind and Bernard Thompson called a halt as the timekeeper timed him at **2 days 8 hrs 6 mins.**

Unfortunately and tragically, this mileage when meticulously measured at a later date was found to be 1.5 miles short. Words cannot describe the disappointment. Dick doesn't dwell on it though and the RRA, although they couldn't pass it, they did commend Dicks brave ride to their books 'history' section with a special mention. In hindsight, once again, if you allowed another 10 minutes or so for the missing 1.5 miles, making 2 days 8 hrs 16 minutes and then look at Gethin's 1000 mile record of 2 days 7 hrs 59 mins, some 36 years later, you realise what a tough battle Gethin would have had with only 17 minutes to play with, instead of 2 hrs 41 mins, the amount he beat Reg Randall's record by.

Dick's ten consecutive 100 mile times show such a smooth evenly paced ride, considering the severity of the route and the delays involved.

En route, Dick consumed one gallon of rice and fruit salad, 20 or more 'Complan' meals, 6 rice and raisin mix feed, and 12 oranges. So even in 1965, Polymer feeding was being introduced into sports feeding, although Mike Rees, a contributor to the 24 hr Fellowship Magazine, reckons Dick consumed mainly liquids, and it was his helpers who had most of the food ! Dick goes on to say that 17 days after his End to End he did a 'PB' at 25 miles with 58.10 and three weeks later a 'PB' in the Mersey 24 hrs with 480 miles, for which he won a gold medal.

Dick said the End to End changed his life. It had an impact on his involvement with the sport, and he qualified as a coach after a year, and was asked to set up a scheme for the RTTC. He went on to be National Coach for about 10 years nurturing our 4 up World TTT team of Ant Taylor, Jeff Marshall, Martin Roach and John Tooby, to ride at Leicester. Then he turned to the new sport of Triathlon.

He later ran three marathons, became a founder member and treasurer for the European Triathlon Union and represented Great Britain in the European Masters duathlon championship in Madrid. Later he returned to time trialling and at 71 years of age he managed to set a local vets record at 10 miles of 24-36, so he's not past it yet !

One of his memories afterwards, was in the form of a telegram from Dave Duffield, saying 'The End to End to end all End to Ends - Well Done'; so it really did change his life !

Dick Poole's 1000 miles discrepancy came from taking the shorter route over Aultnamain (which he had scheduled to do) but using the measurements of the route that uses the lower road through Tain which is some 2 miles further.

This article uses extracts from The Cycling Magazine, plus comments from Dick Poole, and text from Frank Fischer and myself.

No 24 SWINDEN AND WITHERS TANDEM END TO END 6th JUNE 1966

After several years of road record breaking, the national trend for long distance riders is towards the 'blue riband' record of the road - Lands End to John O Groats.

Towards the end of 1965 this trend materialised into a set plan for my club mates from Birmingham St Christophers c.c, Pete Swinden and John Withers, who had during their five years of record attempting, broken five Midlands Road Records as well as the longest RRA record, the 1000 miles.

The previous year, Pete, the steersman, had married and spent his honeymoon in Cornwall, reconnoitring the route by car, whilst John had a fortnights cycling holiday in Scotland to examine the northern end of the course. The attempt organising was put in the hands of the Beacon roads Clubman, Mick de Mouilpied, who set to work in February to contact the huge band of helpers who always assist on an End to End record attempt. He also organised a phone HQ in Birmingham which was to prove so invaluable during the ride. His HQ was at the home of Mick's club mate, the Clements family, who had to handle over 400 calls in less than 3 days!

Pete recalls that Mick enlisted the help of clubs 'on course' to marshall, and Pat Kenny remembers only one occasion when he had to stop the car and refer to the map. Even desolate parts of Scotland in the middle of the night were well marshalled. Inverness seemed alive with club folk and in the Midlands, Cheshire and Lancashire, they were very well looked after. Two teams of helpers who were particularly prominent were the then holders of the Tandem End to End, Jim Bailey and Jack Forest, and teams from Liverpool and Glasgow St Christopher's also followed for great distances, feeding the riders.

At 10 am on Monday 6th June 1966, timekeeper Eric Wilkinson sent the riders off from Lands End with a promising forecast from Plymouth Met Office of moderate to fresh south to southwest winds. Right away the riders started to gain on their schedule, aimed at 2 days, 3hrs, compared with the 2 days, 4 hrs, 48 mins 3 secs of current holders, Bailey and Forrest. All along the 'give and take' roads of Cornwall, Pete and John averaged over 21 mph and reached Exeter 119 miles, taking 5 hrs 36 mins.

Just before Launceston they were stopped because two lorries travelling in opposite directions had scraped each other as they passed and were stuck, completely blocking the road. The riders couldn't walk up the verge because there was a deep ditch, so they lifted the tandem over a gate and ran up the field until they found a gap in the hedge to rejoin the road. It was some miles before the following car caught up. Approaching the centre of Exeter, a butcher complete with striped apron dashed into the road and marshalled them into a sharp left hand turn. Other club folk then took up the marshalling so that they completely avoided the city centre.

Only one point was unmarshalled and so when the tandem stopped at a 'T' junction, Pat jumped out of the following car to direct them. Unfortunately Eric's chronometer was on Pat's lap at the time and bounced on the road. The case was a bit battered but the mechanism was OK. Another amusing thing happened crossing the Bridgwater Flats, where the Perry brothers who had been regular helpers throughout the Somerset region over the years, fed the riders with battered aluminium bottles, one of which bounced into the road from the grass verge and was flattened by a lorry. This caused John Withers to impersonate their broad Somerset accents with "Oi aard thard bottle since we fed Rossitrr". When the Perry brothers passed away years later they bequeathed a substantial donation to the RRA in 1999, for the continuance of the Associations good work.

A veer left in the road in this area had put the crosswind to a tail wind and the riders galloped to a 29 mins gain on schedule at Bridgwater - 165 miles in 7hrs 43 mins. The Bridgwater Flats were a welcome relief from the hills of Devon and Cornwall producing a further gain of 8 mins in the 32 miles to Bristol which was reached at 7.15 pm.

Amongst the many club folk who were out to marshall the riders through here, was Reg Randall, former bicycle End to Ender, who had 'detoured' on his way home from work to turn a 4 mile journey into a 40 mile one.

In virtually all of the larger towns of Cornwall, Devon and Somerset, there were traffic jams, as there were very few bypasses in those days. The riders were generally able to trickle along inside or outside of the traffic, so not too much time was lost. The following cars were unable to keep up with them in the traffic and by Bridgwater the riders had had to stop twice to fill the tandems bottles from shops at the side of the road.

They had a very good wind to Bristol where they encountered very heavy traffic. They had been advised by the locals that the city centre route would be quicker than via the familiar Avon gorge. This was probably right, although at the time they were quite concerned about getting lost. At one point they overtook a marshall, also hampered by the traffic, who shouted directions as they passed him by. The wind had now virtually dropped but they were still going well.

With the course heading through Gloucestershire, the riders, who were also inveterate tourists, were on really local roads, and after passing through the centre of Gloucester, 53 mins up on schedule, they made their first stop of 4 mins at Tewkesbury to take on lights and night clothing. Here their steersman Pete, first complained of an ache in his right knee and algipan was massaged into it to ease the pain.

The riders were quite cheerful as they headed into the first night and the first 12 hrs were completed with 257 miles at Worcester. This virtually equalled the Crimes and Arnold mileage of 257.75 set in 1954 on their End to End, and at that time they were the fastest on any machine at 12 hrs on the End to End course, and by 1966 nobody had beaten that A large contingent of Midland club folk were now out on the route and the miles quickly slipped past with dawn breaking near Wigan and gains still mounting to 40 mins. Roadside helpers through Lancashire included John Arnold and Bailey and Forest.

The climb of Shap was a tough one and a heavy mist shrouded the summit making the descent very tricky. The 24 hr point ran out at Carlisle - 470 miles, definitely the largest mileage by any rider on any machine at that time on the End to End route . In fact it would be another 16 years before Mick Coupe bettered this by producing 482 miles on his End to End in 1982.

Pete and John were still minutes up on schedule and carried on over the border to Ecclefechan and Beattock to Lanark. Three miles south of Lanark, Pete's wife Barbara had to work on his knee again. It had been troubling him now for over 15 hours and was getting worse. A doctor at Perth Royal Infirmary was contacted and Perth was reached by 6.32pm on the 2nd day, 50 mins up on schedule. They were marshalled into the hospital and straight into Casualty, but by the time Pete had been treated with an injection everyone was feeling queasy because of the heat in the small treatment room. The doctor was a bit concerned about the cartilage in Pete's knee but only time would tell. By the time they were back on the road, they had all but lost their 50 mins gain on schedule. They soon settled down to face a cool but dry evening, as they rode towards the Grampians.

It is interesting to note that at Perth, 614 miles, they were still exactly 30 mins faster than Dick Poole's time in 1965. It wasn't until Inverness that Dick started to draw level and then pull over two hours out over the tandem by John o Groats. After a 14 mins sleep at Aviemore, the organiser Mick de Mouilpied, advised the helpers by phone that Pete was to receive another injection at Inverness. When they reached there they were 71 mins ahead of schedule and in spite of it being 2.10am, the place was alive with club folk from the Clachnacuddin Cycling Club, who marshalled the tandem through the dark and into the hospital. Pete recalls years later, being once again ushered into a very hot room with all the helpers, and the lady doctor trying to put a circle of injections around his knee cap. The syringe fell apart, leaving the needle dangling from his grime and algipan encrusted knee, at which point he passed out !

Pete says that as he came round he remembered thinking he'd dreamt about racing and then awoke to find it was true. The doctor was arguing with Barbara, saying he shouldn't go on, at which Barbara replied, "I'm his wife, he always gets like this, and what would you expect to be like after 700 miles ?"

They had lost 25 mins at Inverness but by not taking a scheduled sleep here, they were soon on their way and now 1.5 hours up, feeling very fragile, with 140 miles of the toughest road still to come, Aultnamain, Ord of Caithness and Berriedale. They achieved this in approximately 8.5 hours, and Pete recalls it being over an hour from Inverness before they were both 'firing on all cylinders'.

They tackled the climb to Aultnamain Inn okay, but had a problem descending in the thick mist with dawn breaking, when a large ram appeared only a few yards ahead. Pete estimates their speed was probably 40 mph and as the road was very wet he didn't dare brake, but did the next best thing and closed his eyes. It worked well and to his surprise the ram moved out of the way.

From here the road hugs the coastline, and with an unhelpful crosswind off the sea, they realised they weren't going to join Dick Poole in the 'sub two day club'. At Golspie a sudden crack heralded three broken spokes in the front wheel and the wheel swap cost them just 2 mins.

Climbing Helmsdale a lady suddenly appeared, dashing across the road from a milk float, narrowly missing a car and offered them a 'pinta' milk which was their regular tipple in those days, but with the severity of the climb, neither Pete nor John could take the bottle. Pete said it was a shame considering she had risked her life doing it. After climbing the next rise with ease and having heard many stories about the steepness of Berriedale, Pete said to John he would walk the hill rather than aggravate his knee. He asked how far to the hill and John replied 'that was it, we've just climbed it' !

John was becoming very sleepy now but didn't want to stop, so asked Pete to talk to him to keep him awake. Pete even resorted to singing to him, but John still succumbed. Curiously enough, it didn't slow them down as John still kept pedalling even when asleep. After about half an hour he came round but not fully, describing his condition as like being in a tunnel - all echo'ey. He was also mildly hallucinating, talking all sorts of nonsense, but able to respond sensibly when Pete spoke to him, and all the time pedalling quite normally. After a near-miss on the road from Wick with a head-on overtaking car, they arrived at John o Groats. As they rode over the car park to the finish, the rear tyre gave out with a terrific bang. How lucky can you get !

Eric Wilkinson recorded a time of **2 days, 2 hours, 14 mins**, bettering the previous record by 2 hrs, 34 mins. Pat Kenny had been in charge on the road, Mick de Mouilpied and the Clements family had kept the phone HQ up and running and Pete's work colleagues from English Electric, Stafford, none of whom were cyclists, had again given up part of their annual holiday to help on the feeding team. The Observers, were Ed Zoller and Jack Wrightson.

Pete and John decided not to continue for the 1000 miles, a decision they regretted later, as they realised a week or so after, that they could have possibly bettered the Crimes and Arnold figures and even Reg Randalls, but the 1000 miles was already a record Pete and John held, breaking it in 1964 with 2 days, 18 hours, 9 mins.

John Withers passed away in 1990 aged 52 and is still sadly missed. He died of a heart attack whilst touring on his bike in France. I knew him personally, and I'm sure if he was still with us he would have loved assisting with contributions to this book. His memory and knowledge of time trialling and record breaking was immense. He taught me a lot about life as well as teaching me how not to fall off a trike. Along with Pete and Pat Kenny as a team, he was always the one who said "which 24 hrs are we riding next year chaps?"

Physically John was Spartan to look at, standing about 5ft 10 and less than 10 stone racing fit, but like many record breakers, he had remarkable stamina and determination which I think are the two leading features a record breaker needs.

Pete on the other hand, was shortish, stockily built standing 5ft 4" and 10 stone racing fit. He would only swim underwater, not on top, which suggests heavy bone density, and terrific lung capacity. One more feature that makes Pete unique is that since a boyhood accident, he has the use of only one eye. Like Sid Ferris, Pete's main worry was keeping anything from damaging his good eye, by wearing glasses or shades.

Again, like John his tandem partner, he had built up tremendous stamina over the preceding years of club riding, time trialling up to 24 hours, 438 miles being Pete's best, and riding the 1000 miles in 1964. All things that make for a good End to Ender.

The tandem they used was a 1948 Hobbs ultra short wheelbase which basically meant it was built for speed and not comfort as were most of the tandems at that time. It cost Pete £ 10 in 1963 and after considerable restoration it was proven to be well worth it. At the time of the record Pete was a Production Engineer at English Electric, Stafford, and John was a Clerk in an Accountants office. Pete was 30 years of age and John 27 years.

Their feeding regime was fairly normal food, milk, fruit cocktail, sandwiches, bread pudding and rice pudding. The favourite drink in the '60's was ice cold milk from milk machines situated on main roads in most towns and villages. Its bright white light stood out like a beacon and was a very welcoming sight for thirsty riders.

Dr Hamley from Loughborough University had tested Pete and John on fitness apparatus in the laboratory and gymnasium at Loughborough. Things such as heart monitoring and lung capacity could only be checked on indoor equipment in those days. He was obviously one of the early pioneers of 'sports science'. He knew the lads well and knew that it wasn't just a physical strength they needed. It was almost more important to have a very strong willpower.

Dr Hamley was the person who co-ordinated the hospital help in Scotland, and its safe to say he played a big part in their physical well-being.

In hindsight, if Pete had carried on riding instead of getting hospital treatment they could have gone inside two days, however, one can always say 'what if ?' He may have done permanent damage to his knees by not stopping - who knows ? A bent pedal, worn shoe plate, saddle out of alignment or a physical problem, may not appear if riding up to 12 hours, but after 30 or more hours it shows up. One very rarely gets a second shot at the End to End, once in a lifetime is usually enough !

(This episode was from an article by Pat Kenny, with additions from Pete Swinden and myself)

No 25 JANET TEBBUTT JULY 1976 AMATEUR LADIES BICYCLE END TO END

After two postponements in weeks prior to her success, Janet at the age of 40, finally got away from Lands End at 5 am on Sunday 18th July 1976. One of her previous postponements was due to lack of a timekeeper but on this occasion Vernon Wright travelled from Cardiff to time her away from this famous landmark. The Sunday was chosen to give even better starting conditions than Saturday.

The reason for a 5 am start was to get over the exposed Bodmin Moor before the sun got too hot as this had been one of the factors in the previous years failure, when she had been forced to retire in the Lancaster area. Heatstroke or the effects of it can drain you physically to the point where the fittest of athletes give a jaded performance, and there is no antidote, medicine, treatment or quick cure that can resurrect you for an effort of this magnitude.

Pearl Wellington of the WRRA, herself a prolific record breaker at all distances to 24 hrs, was the Official Observer in the following car to Taunton. Janet's husband Alan and his brother Mike were 'on duty' in the feeding car. Janet was 12 minutes up on schedule at the Launceston bypass at 9.40 am. At Okehampton Fred Baker and his wife Marjorie appeared. Midday at Exeter and just on schedule here, Exeter as always, checked and marshalled by the Luxton family.

Although it was sunny there was always a following breeze and Janet knew she must keep cool. The traffic was so quiet in Exeter, Ivy Thorpe managed to take a photo standing in the middle of the main road ! At Taunton Reg Randall came on board as following Observer, Janet took the alternative route through Congresbury to Bristol. It's a quieter route and less hilly compared with the main road. It was around this point that she started to feel hot and then cold, and her stomach was in turmoil. It was something she had never experienced before but she was determined to ride through it although she lost about 10 mins against her schedule along here.

Alan Windsor replaced Reg Randall as Observer at Rudgeway with Philip Wilson and his young son, fellow members of the Clevedon and District Road Club joining Alan in the feeding car and stayed on board until the end. Although Janet had a helpful wind along here through Gloucestershire, she arrived at Worcester some 8 minutes down. She was marshalled through with members of the Redditch Road and Path Club on every corner, in the most efficient way.

Three miles further on a stop was made for lights and night clothing and as darkness fell she reached Kidderminster some 30 mins behind schedule. Don Barker and other local CTC members made sure she didn't get lost through the town. Janet took a half hour sleep just beyond Whitchurch but was eager to get going again so as to be clear of the big towns in the Industrial north, before Monday morning's rush hour. Although she kept a steady pace through Warrington, she arrived at Preston some 80 minutes behind schedule. The wind had now veered to come from the West and was troubling her. One consolation though, she had now got beyond the spot where she was forced to retire in 1975.

The traffic in Kendal at 9 am was hectic but Janet had managed to pull back over 20 minutes here. Now came the hard climb of Shap, shrouded in mist and rain. At 430 miles it was a testing time. Once over the top she took a 20 minute break. The main A6 road was now quiet and the rain had cleared. She was now feeling remarkably fit, which was just as well because the wind had now veered from the North west. At Carlisle with 472 miles covered Janet joined the heavy traffic on the A74. She said it was dreadful, so bad, she had to have a break at Ecclefechan. Her helpers had a hard job, all they could do was to give her vocal support and hope that Janet could keep going.

Moffat was reached and the climb of the 'Devils Beeftub' saw her reach the biggest drop on schedule, some 2 hrs 28 mins. She was now virtually level with Edith Atkins ride in 1953, but Janet felt that having got that far and still feeling in reasonable shape, she stood a fair chance of getting to John o Groats even with 344 miles still to cover.

Janet had now crossed over from the West coast and was heading towards Edinburgh and the East side of Scotland. At Penicuik, 554 miles, she'd gained 15 minutes and with Ed Zoller and his team of marshalls seeing her through the streets of Edinburgh another few minutes were gained by the time the Forth Road Bridge was crossed.

This was a major landmark for Janet and she thought about her husband Alan and the helping team. They'd got her this far and she couldn't let them down now. At Perth she rode into a very dark second night, on roads she didn't know. The car's headlights helped her pick out the edge of the road and her memories of this section of road were wandering hedgehogs, a large owl and a herd of frightened deer.

As she headed into the Grampians, a southerly wind picked up and this enabled Janet to pull back from being 2 hrs down on schedule to being only 1 hr down at Dalwhinnie. Along this section of road the helpers lost contact with the telephone HQ manned by clubmate John Ford. Meanwhile Janet had negotiated Inverness, after a very cold second night, she said it was busy with rush hour traffic and people going to work.

After riding through the scheduled stop at Evanton and making the most of the tailwind, Janet had got to the top of Aultnamain just 5 mins behind schedule. Telephone contact was regained at Golspie and John Ford said it was the best news he could have had, and now the record looked like a possibility.

The first cold rain storms hit her as she climbed the Ord of Caithness making descents very tricky, she walked the steepest part of Berriedale, but was soon back on the bike after Ron McQueen told her that the cemetery at the top contained record aspirants who hadn't made it! At Dunbeath she was 21 minutes up on schedule.

Lack of sleep made those last 44 miles something of a nightmare as Janet had only taken one hours sleep since the start, some two and a half days ago. She felt she was riding round in circles and twice thought she was back at the same spot. The weather was now deteriorating, the rain and wind was against her, blowing in off the sea. The helpers had to persuade her she was on the right road and was going in the right direction for John o Groats.

At last she dropped down that last long slope to the hotel, suddenly it was all over, she had beaten her schedule by 34 minutes to take the record with **2 days 15 hours 24 mins 20 secs.** Janet couldn't thank her team enough for the help they'd given her throughout the ride. Her husband Alan had spent many hours masterminding the whole project and had produced a well estimated schedule.

Janet had ridden the last 360 miles without a stop, a hard task at anytime let alone after 500 miles. In an interview with Radio Bristol she said she was very relieved to get the record after all the preparation and the previous disappointments, although she felt in despair at times when she was way behind schedule and it felt like an almost impossible task to perform.

But what a performance, taking 2 hrs 40 mins off Edith Atkins amateur record. It was also a first time success for Ron McQueen who went on in 1979 to time Paul Carbutt, and in 1980 Pat Kenny, over this famous route.

Eleven years later in June 1987, Janet Tebbutt tried once again on this arduous road. She was now attacking Eileen Sheridan's 1954 professional record. Starting at 6 am Sunday June 21st, Janet was soon up on schedule. By Exeter she was 15 minutes to the good but by the Bridgwater Flats had lost all of her gain and by Bristol was 20 minutes down. At the end of her first night she was 3 hrs 30 mins adrift of her schedule and by 4.40 pm on Tuesday, after reaching Golspie, 778 miles, the attempt was abandoned. So near, yet, so far.

This ride description uses extracts from the Cycling Magazine with comments from Janet and additions from myself.

No 26 PAUL CARBUTT - SOLO BICYCLE END TO END WEDNESDAY 11th JULY 1979

Paul Carbutt started racing at 17 years of age with a 1-13-49 for 25 miles. Since then he's ridden track, hill climbs, road race, time trials, a true all rounder.

A National Champion at 50 miles, 100 miles and 12 hours. He won the 1977 'BBAR', and rode the World Championships in 1974 and 1975. The Montreal Olympics saw him riding the team time trial, three Milk Races gave him a best place overall of 3rd in 1977. Paul won the Girvan 3 day road race earlier in 1977, and his last mission that year was to finish 16th in the

World Road Championship in Venezuela. He rated his ride in the Tour of Belgium to be one of his best.

Paul viewed the End to End as a great adventure and during the ride he says he learned a lot about himself in two days. Although he turned professional for 'Viking' he still worked during the week as a Pattern Maker Designer for the Rover Car Company. He still belonged to his native local club, the Saracen Road Club, and later the famous Solihull C.C. He is the first End to End rider to ride for a charity and raised thousands of pounds for the physically handicapped charity 'PHAB'.

I asked Paul how he trained for the End to End and he said his longest ride was 140 miles, but he would regularly cover 100 miles at close to evens on a fairly low gear. He was always happier at the longer distances and always finished in high positions in all six of his 12 hour races, his best being 276.9 miles. In training he tried one 'all night' ride but wasn't impressed, he'd been over most of the End to End route so knew what lay in waiting for him.

So July 1979 saw Paul set off at 10 am on a tight schedule which he only kept to for about 70 miles. This was the first professional End to End since pre-war days. The attempt was nearly stopped at Penzance after Paul went past a lorry trying to reverse the length of the High Street. The police took a dislike and stopped him and the following car for a 'talking to'. He was eventually allowed on his way.

The wind after Bodmin played tricks and hampered his progress. It was a humid sticky day and he just managed to stay above 'evens' without a helping wind. At Gloucester he was 42 mins down on his schedule and 5 mins slower than Dick Poole's time.

Paul stopped for lights and extra clothing and picked up a police escort through the town. At this point he realised he probably wouldn't break Ken Joys 24 hr record of 475.75 miles, but he was quite happy and riding within himself. A lot of people were out through the Midlands to see him through and by Whitchurch he had got back ahead of Poole's time.

By Warrington 353 miles, the dawn was showing signs of coming up. Paul was now taking more milky foods, rice pudding etc. as like many riders before him, the ability to consume solids and proteins diminishes after a day on the bike. Shap was reached just ahead of Dick Poole's time. After the first real stop of the ride he seemed composed and was away again in 10 mins. From this point onwards Paul started to haul back the minutes to record 460 miles in 24 hrs.

On his passage over the 'Beeftub' his aggressive climbing style snapped a spoke which locked his 28 spoke rear wheel up. A quick wheel change was made. The temperature at this point in the ride was very high, in the 80's farenheit. His pedalling became very erratic, something was seriously wrong, he weaved to a halt and Keith Audas just caught him before he fell off. Heatstroke and sheer exhaustion had caused the collapse. His pulse was very high as you would expect from the climb. After a while his pulse returned to normal and once he'd cooled off and had a sleep he was deemed fit to continue. Paul said it was like waking from a nightmare, he struggled to stay focussed but knew he had got to get back on. He put on a lightweight silk track vest and packed ice on his neck to cool him down. Once back on the bike he started to pick back up on speed, taking advantage of the downhill drop towards Edinburgh. He got lost going round Edinburgh and lost valuable minutes asking the way.

Going over the Forth Road Bridge cooled him down with the sea breezes being very welcome. It was turning into a perfect second evening as he pedalled swiftly towards Perth getting there at 6.15 pm over 45 mins faster than Dick Poole's time.

As the sun went down Paul started to struggle, again riding erratically, out of the saddle trying to pick up speed and then freewheeling again. A halt was called for on Drumochter Pass, where a change of clothing and a short break did the trick. After a few minutes he was away, heading for Inverness with a tailwind.

At Inverness the team lost their way again but luckily Paul was well directed by local clubmen. He was still 40 mins up on the previous record at this point. He had rain after Inverness which made descending on the mountainous roads a bit tricky. Paul didn't know what lay in store for him on the 'Ord of Caithness' as he hadn't reconnoitred this far north. The hills of Helmsdale and Berriedale cut into his lead and by Wick he was just 28 mins up on Poole's time.

He was struggling very hard on this last section, against a northerly headwind and with a pulled leg muscle, he still pedalled fluently to reach Ron McQueen the timekeeper in **1 day 23 hours 23 mins l sec.** He had beaten the record by 23 minutes.

Paul looked all in, his eyes were dark and sunken, his cheeks hollow and he's aged considerably, again another common factor seen in End to End riders. They look ten years older when they arrive. The first words he uttered were 'I'm not going for the 1000 miles'. What a plucky ride from a man who had virtually collapsed from the effects of heatstroke twice. Paul summed it all up by saying he'd done a full seasons work in two days !

His back up team comprised of Keith Audas, Dave Binns, Frank Westell, Brenda and Keith Robins. P.R. man Alan Rushton who went on to organize lots of well promoted bike races for TV, and last but not least the RRA officials, Joe Pilling, Peter Barlow, and timekeeper Ron Mcqueen.

Paul had been a 'hero' of mine since his BBAR win in 1977 and his 12 hour performances ranked him alongside Phil Griffiths, John Woodburn, Ian Cammish etc. The fact that he was riding professionally in road races just prior to his End to End makes his ride unique, going from riding in a team with a large bunch of riders, to the exact opposite, a totally lonely solo performance covering not 80 miles, but over 10 times that distance, approximately 860 miles.

My own club mates didn't really know much about Paul Carbutt except for one or two high profile time trial wins and BBAR placings. The fact that they hadn't seen him riding in 24 hr events made them sceptical as to his abilities. Even when standing at the island at Bridgnorth, they were questioning me and were saying we wonder how far he will reach ? I had no doubt about his ability to succeed. When riding road races he often rode 'from the front', he was an aggressive rider very similar in style to Phil Bayton. Paul was usually at the front of a bunch, dictating the speed, and this is how I knew he'd got the grit and determination to do it.

I met up again with Paul at an afternoon film show of John Woodburn's End to End in Hammersmith in January 2003. Paul had been invited there along with other solo End to End record breakers to appear in front of quite a large audience of avid cycling fans.

Paul had been diagnosed a year or so previously with motor neurone disease. A debilitating illness for which there is no known cure. He entered the room to a standing ovation which was heartfelt by everyone there. Along with all the other record breakers he signed autographs and answered questions, but was perplexed by the esteem that is given to those who break the record. He obviously hadn't realised the enormity of his ride and at that particular time he was the only one who was capable of the feat. After all, there had been a 14 year gap waiting for someone to tackle it. If it was easy there would be two or three attempts a year. Although he was now wheelchair bound, he was still getting out on a hand controlled recumbent machine.

Paul phoned me in early March 2004 and asked how the book was progressing. I said "OK, but how are you going ?" He was very matter of fact, and told me he had stopped driving and couldn't work any more as his arms and shoulders, the only limbs he had some limited control left in, were failing him. He still sounded positive and said how good it was to chat to someone who had raced and ridden in the same era.

Less than two months later Paul had passed away, aged 53, leaving our world a sadder place. He was a good family man and even when he was a busy professional rider he still had time to coach the youngsters at his local cycling club, of which he had been a life long member. He always encouraged riders of all abilities .

Paul's last big ride was in 2000 with ex tour rider Harry Reynolds. They both rode the 'Etape de Tour' and received gold medals.

Paul was an outstanding person who had shown great courage in everything he did. He leaves a wife Janet whom he married in 1976, and two sons, Anthony aged 20 and David aged 18.

Paul's end to end story was courtesy of 'Cycling' reworked for this book with additional thoughts from Paul Carbutt and myself.

No 27 PAT KENNY 4th AUGUST 1980 TRICYCLE END TO END

"Would you like a three day all expenses paid trip to Scotland?" was the question I posed to Steve Howes, a young lad just about to be pushed off by me in the VC Toutourien '50'. "Well, I'd have to think about it" he replied. The question obviously didn't upset his concentration, because he went on to record a 2.12 personal best time, and turned out at Gailey Island to assist in this epic voyage to Scotland.

This 'epic' was of course, Pat Kenny's tricycle ride from Lands End to John o Groats, taking 2 days 10 hours. This successful ride came after many setbacks, three unsuccessful rides on tandem trike in 1979 with yours truly, and one failure 4 weeks earlier attempting to ride downhill from Groats direction.

After a good weather forecast seen on a portable TV outside Wolverhampton Station, we picked up Ron McQueen of Mersey RC 24 hr fame, having timed 34 Mersey's on the trot. The arrows on the weather chart pointed up, with lots of low pressures out in the Atlantic waiting to blow in a south westerly direction. We motored down to Sennen, to Mrs Woods's bed and breakfast house. The weather was grey, windy and very daunting.

4th August 1980, up at 6.30 am for an 8 o'clock start. After a good breakfast at Mrs Woods she said she thought it was about time one of us broke the record. I said to her that this one was the one ! Down to Lands End Hotel, just Pat, Ron and myself, no crowds, no one else but the occasional seagull with its beak pointing into the wind. The wind was tugging at our clothes, 8o'clock pips and Ron sent him on his way. We were glad to be away from Lands End, a desolate sort of place without sunshine, as desolate as John o Groats in similar conditions.

Penzance was reached 5 mins up, Pat was averaging a steady 22's, Bodmin 57 miles was reached 25 mins up. The holiday traffic a bit of a nuisance until the wide dual carriageways and by passes were reached. Pat was moving at a really forceful pace at over evens. It was such a joy to ring headquarters and inform Hazel, his wife, of his progress. Okehampton 98 miles was reached in 4 hrs 57 mins, 35 mins up on schedule. The one or two touring cyclists we saw riding the other way were really struggling into the wind. Exeter was reached 29 mins up on schedule. Our usual checker make it just in time; there was Jean Luxton emerging from a side street just in time to see Pat flash past. At Cullompton two riders approached riding the opposite way; one was Martin Donelly who'd had many a time trial battle with Pat, and both wished him well.

Pat's average had now dropped just below evens, but still very creditable. Wellington then Taunton, and onto the Bridgwater Flats, back up to evens now, one or two climbs left just after Churchill to take the back route through Bristol. Here we met Eric and Jan Wilkinson, Eric almost uncontrollable with the prospect of him being so far up on schedule. Jan hanging on to him to have a calming effect so that I could get a word in edgeways. Eric said the wind had only appeared an hour before the rider. Eric had timed the Swinden-Withers tandem record in 1966.

We'd just missed most of the rush hour traffic at 6 0'clock in Bristol. For me it was most important to ring up to HQ so that helpers and well wishers in the Midlands wouldn't miss him. He was also fed and watered on his way out of Bristol by S.W. Tricycle Association members who we regularly see on End to End attempts - many thanks to them. Thornbury was reached in very wet conditions. Pat had already spent one hour in heavy rain and it was getting through his clothing. I arranged a bus shelter to sit down in so he could change and perhaps put on dry kit and waterproof clothing, ready for the night ahead. Everything was ready for a quick stop, but no ! Pat jokingly said, 'its bright up ahead' and he would carry on. My only worry was that he would get cold and wet on his first night; anyway, on to Gloucester, 56 mins up. Here we picked up Bill Griffiths (father of Phil) who'd expressed a desire to go on a successful End to End attempt. 12 hours produced 229 miles, a fine ride on its own. Lets hope the next 12 hours would show as many miles. At Gloucester, Pat was 15 mins down on Duffield's figures at this point.

A quick 9 mins at Tewkesbury to put lights on and dry clothes and toilet stop. Pat showed his desire for chips in Worcester, so a chip shop, telephone and garage were found in that order. Alan Richards and Sandy had now joined us along with Dave Duffield, the present trike End to End record holder. The two cars by-passing and helping, saved me leaving the rider at this point. Dave Duffield helping until the Wolverhampton area. Pete Swinden and family were out from about Kingswinford onward. Gailey Island was reached 1.25 hours up and he was still gaining. All the families were out 1 mile north of Gailey, all Pat's children, Hazel, Liz and our kids plus lots of local club folk and friends - a great encouragement. The wind at the Four Ashes Tar Distillery was blowing straight along the route.

Stafford was reached 1 hr 25 mins up, this was to be the highest gain on schedule. Reg and 'Nan' Pearce and the lads from the Stafford RCC were out. Pat's front light was looking a bit dicky at this point so I suggested we put in new batteries and a 'clip on' front light. This was accomplished in a 4 min stop at Stone. Timekeeper Ron McQueen ordered him 'on his way'. Here, the well known health and fitness food fan, Graham Dayman, a staunch helper in many past attempts, joined us. Steve Howes, the young time triallist, decided to take the free holiday in Scotland as mentioned earlier, and became a driver in the following car with Bill Griffiths. I joined Graham and Wayne Verdon, both of the Royal Sutton in the 'SURF CITY' car. I was to become chief cook and bottle washer from now on, providing coffee for everyone with water boiled by a heater run off the car battery as we drove along.

We were stopped by Police in Newcastle under Lyme on a routine vehicle check. When they saw the muddle of equipment in the back of Graham's car and his difficulties in finding his documents, they accepted our explanation, that we were following a madman on three wheels up to John o Groats. What a relief ! We were well past the 10 hr point and could pass every 20 mins, which proved to be a perfect set up. Holmes Chapel, where a plastic kiddies blow up dolphin was taken on board, rather like an albatross brings good luck to a ship in troubled waters. It was quite a startling sight, a 3 ft long fluorescent pink dolphin bobbing along the road in the wind. If it had been the second night, Pat would have put it down to hallucinations, which one gets from lack of sleep, exhaustion and loneliness.

Anyway, on towards Knutsford. We were wished well from three lads who'd seen many a Mersey 24 and many an End to End go through Warrington, where we were also marshalled through by a well known Mersey man, Dave Denman, with another type of motorised three wheeler (Reliant Robin) In this way he was able to short cut through the back roads and appear at many important junctions. John Arnold, himself a holder of the Tandem Trike End to End and many other records, marshalled us through a right turn at Winwick Church,.. He was offering his usual peppermint tonic. He offered me some which I accepted gladly having already sampled some in the middle of the night in the Mersey 24. This latest brew had a different taste and he said he had run out of sugar and had used black treacle. We bade him farewell at about 3.30 am. Pat was slowing now, his gain on schedule was down to less that one hour. 40 miles of 'Coronation Street' type suburbs took us through Wigan and on to Preston and Lancaster.

By Preston he'd pulled back time to be 29 mins up on Dufffield. The main aim was to keep his spirits high, shout at him and make him laugh. On towards Kendal and the Lake District. **The 24 hours ran out with 413 miles;** as you can see a large drop in the second 12 hours (184 miles) As Pat climbed Shap I ran alongside and he said he would have preferred conditions like our first tandem trike attempt when Shap was wet and shrouded in mist, and the rider couldn't see the tortuous climb ahead. Also on our first attempt, the late Ed Green had produced a bellowing shout and a large bag of Mars Bars along with other ribald quips. Alas the great man has gone from us, but perhaps his jovial ghost will loom on Shap when an End to End rider goes through.

We'd gone ahead to set up a sit down feed at Penrith in the corner of the garage we'd used the year before. Pat's right knee was troubling him here and our soothing hands were loosening the muscles behind the knee. Seven minutes here and more dry clothes. The wind over the last 150 miles had been from the west and had been troubling Pat more mentally than just physically, in as much as what was going to happen later in the day, knowing that at Carlisle he had to turn left on the A74 to Beattock and into the wind.

In an interview with Dennis Donovan, Pat related some of his feelings about the ride.

"The climb of Shap Fell was a struggle on a bottom gear of 54 inches and the entry into Scotland was hard. I accepted the fact that the climb up to the Devil's Beeftub would be hard" Kenny said, "but I would get some time back down the other side. The speed Harold Harvey and I did on the tandem trike three years ago, when setting up the Scottish tandem trike 25 just didn't materialise. I became very despondent and depressed. I wondered how I could break the news to the lads that I wanted to pack, then a side wheel punctured. Good, I thought, Now I can have a rest, but John Taylor thought otherwise. They changed the wheel, forced me on the trike, and I didn't get a rest after all".

Taylor said afterwards "We had to do something drastic, so at Penicuik, we spotted a concrete bus shelter which Pat said looked like a dungeon., and the first thing we saw among the graffiti was the name 'Kenny'. Kilroy had been there too ! Pat was stripped , washed and his clothes changed, then came the 'lies' that conditions would be better when he got to Aviemore. At Edinburgh he was down to a crawl".

The weather chart in Tuesday's Daily Telegraph gave westerly wind arrows but didn't give any clear details about low pressures or winds to follow. Carlisle was reached and his lead was slowly dropping . The following car had to take a protective course to avoid the continuous flow of 70 mph juggernauts coming straight off the M6. Approx 40 miles of this had to be suffered along the Ecclefechan and Lockerbie by passes. Pat was hoping for a relief from the wind when he turned right off the A74 at Moffat, but no, if anything the wind appeared to be against him up the 8 mile climb to the top of the Devil's Beeftub, then a 40 mile descent to the outskirts of Edinburgh. Pat at this point was at an all time low and was losing his gain. The time was about 3 pm on the second afternoon. He punctured his front wheel tub on the descent of the 'Beeftub' At Penicuik we found a bus shelter with the name 'Kenny' painted on, a good omen, and decided here he ought to have more clothing and lights on so that he needn't stop again. A bit more rub on that knee and away again. A clubman of the Edinburgh RC who knew his way around the short cuts and back streets here, popped up two or three times at very important junctions, and saw Pat safely through. We saw John Randall who had helped Pat and myself on the Edinburgh-York tandem tricycle record a few years earlier. He lives virtually on the course here. We also saw Ken Price and the motorbike marshall (natives here). They bypassed and helped Pat through many junctions prior to the bridge. The Forth Road Bridge loomed up ominously. Pat crossed with ease. I showed Wayne the old railway bridge used in the film 'The 39 steps' (repeated on the BBC TV about 10 times a year !)

I'd already shown Pat the 'Telegraph' weather chart at Moffat and he'd accepted his fate quite jovially. I'd told him to pack in this mental battle of miles per hour and what he'd got to do it in. I said he was torturing his mind and that he ought to sit on and try to enjoy himself for an hour or two because however much he was dropping his mph I was not going to let him pack until it was irretrievable I.e. two hours down. I was ringing into HQ every two hours and around about 8 pm on this the second night, at Cowdenbeath, Hazel said she'd seen a weather chart with arrows pointing up in Scotland. Graham had also rung his wife Sheila and she gave the same news. On this (it turned out to be false information - one day too late) we kept him going. I told him he only had to do 12 mph to the finish, and anyone can do 12 mph cant they? This part of the route seemed to be a twisting, turning, badly surfaced 50 miles.

Kinross now and on to Perth where a scheduled 15 minutes stop was forsaken to put him only 27 mins down on schedule. Now started the 13 mile climb ending on the top of the Pass of Drumochter. Pat rode very well up here, but requested warm clothes when he got to the top. We detoured in to Dalwhinnie off the by pass and rang Hazel, only 1 hr 5 mins down now and holding it quite well. We must have woken the entire rabbit population of the area, as they were everywhere. Back onto the main A9 now ahead of the rider. At this point he was 1 hr down on schedule and the only thing in his favour was possibly 30 of the next 60 miles were downhill between Dalwhinnie and Inverness. Gradually he began to haul the time deficit back. I shouted at him to grab a minute at a time and try to get a quarter of an hour back by Inverness, which would put him 48 mins down on his schedule. The self-same amount he hoped to break the record by.

On the last two descents into Inverness we realized that he was going to do it, he didn't want food, just encouragement. He flew into Inverness but the cold and rain over the last two hours had turned his toes white. He got off the trike into a warm car. He wanted dry socks, over trousers, kagoul, thick gloves and overshoes. Ron McQueen said "This is the last time you get off between here and Groats" and wagged his finger. We were parked just outside a butcher's shop in Inverness and the proprietor must have seen what was going on, and generously offered us his shop for warmth, but we thanked him kindly, said how tight time was, and he sent us on our way with a bag of pork pies. Pat actually left Inverness with 140 miles to go and just over 10.5 hours to do it in. at this point we realised how lucky we were with the weather, with just a cool drizzle and hardly any wind at all, so that the sections around the Beauly Firth and Dornoch Firth would be easier than previously visualized. The morning got warmer but he still didn't take off his over clothes. He told me later that he was scared to in case Ron McQueen told him off again. Pat still recalls to this day how Ron Mcqueen's words rang in his ears for those last 100 miles or more "I've not come all this way for you to lose the record by a few minutes - no more stops !"

Through Dingwall and on to Aultnamain like a man possessed - a steady 12-14 mph over the top and down he rode beautifully. Young Wayne could not believe it was possible that a man could ride for two whole days and still have the strength to ride up a mountain at these speeds. Off Aultnamain, 100 miles to do and in just under 8 hours, but still the climbs of Helmsdale and Berriedale to come. Bonar Bridge was reached; we knew he was in with a chance.

Around the Inverness area we noticed that his drive wheel tub was showing signs of the tread lifting. Now it was noticed there was a large bulge. We had Alan Richard's machine to use as a spare, so that no time would be lost. We decided it would be quicker if he rode the spare machine and we would put a new tub on his own. It was also very wet and damp and I felt it would stick better if done in the dry. Anyway, all went well, machines swapped, tub replaced and we motored on past Pat using our 20 minute passing point. We got Pat's 'Higgins' trike down off the roof rack and then calamity. The following car came racing up with the news that Pat was off and walking because the drive spline was slipping round inside the hub of the drive wheel. I leapt on Pat's trike and wobbled for 3 miles, luckily, downhill. I was wearing sandals and with the saddle 6 inches too high for me I got into a dangerous wobble and realized what trouble I was in if I damaged the machine. As it happened all went well. Pat lost about 3 or 4 mins but said he enjoyed the walk in the company of Wayne. Off he went once more. He then passed the spot on the Dornoch Firth where we 'packed' on our first attempt. His deficit was now being whittled down even with the delays.

Helmsdale was reached only 30 mins down on schedule but don't forget in terms of mileage he still had a long way to go. It was about this point that Graham noticed his movie camera missing, having left it on a wall in a lay by. He said he had visions of Sheila tearing him apart when he got home and told her, as his previous camera was dropped in the sea ! Pat's imminent success, dare we say it, overcame his anxiety at this point and I promised to see Sheila and get him a free pardon. About this point Wayne spotted a fawn in a large driveway of a house, and as it was good daylight, I dismissed the possibility of him hallucinating.

On the climb of Helmsdale and the Ord of Caithness, we thought we could run alongside him round the hair pin area, but no, he flashed past at 14-15 mph urged on by now hysterical voices. For the past 24 hours I hadn't managed to get a smile out of Pat, normally one who can see the funny side of life. Graham and I conferred as to what would make him laugh. We told him Alan Richards would let him have anything out of his bike shop if he got the record, even the promise of a harem of voluptuous young ladies at John o Groats, but no, not a smile. Then I noticed the schedule for the 1000 miles and the first directions were for a left turn at Castletown. The next time I ran alongside Pat I said quite seriously 'I'm not too sure of this left turn at Castletown Pat" and he put a questioning look on his face. "I'm not going for the 1000" he said, and then a silence and he twigged it and smiled, and rode off into the distance, shaking his head and laughing to himself.

He had shown concern on our previous journeys through Berriedale braes as to the severity of the drop into Berriedale with a sharp left hander at the bottom. Pat felt that on his trike he would have to take the bend wide at the bottom and may run into something coming across the bridge the other way, so I promised to slow the traffic down from the opposite direction. Wayne and Graham had positioned themselves on the hill to warn me of his approach. I wore a very bright yellow marshal's jacket and felt very conspicuous. The shout went up 'he's coming' and by now it was drizzling and the road was wet and slippery. Would he make it round the bend ? I managed to stop a car and caravan going across the bridge. Great sighs of relief as he managed to control the trike on his own side of the bend. We all ran with him up the hairpins out of Berriedale, his drive wheel spinning on the grease and oil, with us trying to find dry patches for him to ride on. His face was very grim at this point, and he started to look very old. His face was puffed up from exposure, one eye half closed. He rode on without faltering on one of the toughest hills in the UK and would have put a fresh bike rider to shame.

On to Lybster now and only 31 miles to go, and exactly 2.5 hours to do it in.

He hammered through Wick knowing that he had 1 hr 35 mins to do the last 17 miles. Duffield had done these last 17 miles in 52 mins so we quickly calculated him to be 43 mins up on Duffield here. The local inhabitants were unaware of history in the making. Graham had suggested earlier that we ring John o Groats hotel and hire a room and bath for 2-3 hours. This I did and said to expect the rider at 6.30 to 7.00 pm. Just one more right turn after Wick, apparently a junction where many tired End to Enders have gone off course. Just 10 miles to do now, I felt that we could now say it was safely in the bag. The timekeeper told us he would go ahead 3 three miles from the end., No one realised just how vulnerable the rider was at this point, no spare machine or tools and Ron's three miles turned out to be seven. We shouted encouragement to Pat until we were almost hoarse.

There are two rises to climb before John o Groats and Pat's heart must have sunk when he struggled up what he thought was the last one into a strong head wind, only to find another 2 miles of road going up into the distance, but as he climbed the final rise, there he saw it, the odd shaped towers of John o Groats hotel, now only minutes away. We followed him down the last half mile with horns blaring and lights flashing, at just after 6.30 pm. The sort of success one feels like telling the whole world about.

Ron McQueen timed him in **2 days 10 hours 36 mins and 52 secs.** A whole 22 mins beating of the record. A record which at one time around the Edinburgh area looked never to be on. I shook Pat's hand and went into the hotel to see about the room. The lady at the desk informed me there was no hot water at all as the boiler had broken down. Oh dear, never mind; we cleaned the rider up a bit, put the machine back on top of the car, and whisked him off to Wick where we found ample digs, which we had frequented only a month earlier before the previous unsuccessful attempt. Pat was all smiles now and I realised that a great burden had been lifted off him mentally. He rang Hazel at HQ himself and I can imagine a few tears of relief rolling down cheeks back at home. Ron McQueen was very pleased as he drew on his 100th cigarette of the attempt. He had become the first living timekeeper to time three successful End to Ends, second only to the great Bidlake. Janet Tebbutt and Paul Carbutt being his previous successes. All this in his year of retirement with just a Mersey 24 to do to complete an unbroken run of 35, and a gold badge to honour him at 76 years of age.

A great evening was had by all over a meal. A few tired vacant looks, and heads dropping towards soup bowls after a 3 day round the clock non-stop no-sleep performance, and that was just the helpers. Pat showed few signs of the ride he'd just completed, other than the skin peeling off his chin, this being from all the sponges. Apart from riding in waterproofs the last 12 hours, he'd also ridden with a thick woolly hat tied to his saddle from the Pitlochry area. His backside will probably take a few weeks to get right.

From an original article written by myself and printed in the 24 hr Fellowship Journal in December 1980

The two years prior to Pat's successful End to End had seen four failed attempts. Three of them were on tandem trike with myself. Our first attempt got to Bonar Bridge where we were left with 80 miles to do at evens against a north easterly wind. The second attempt the wind dropped completely in the Midlands in an 80 degree temperature. We climbed off at Trentham, near Stone. A month later we took the west coast route through Glasgow, but climbed off at the end of Loch Lomond after 20 hours of cold rain.

Pat was determined one way or another he was going to break the End to End. He attacked it from the North on his trike in 1980, but climbed off after only a few hours ridden behind schedule. Such was his determination to take Dave Duffield's record, happily he was successful at last. People reading down the list of record breakers cant start to imagine the trials and tribulations that lead up to those records being broken. It shows the 'true grit' of a person when they can mentally and physically hold themselves in good enough condition for nearly two years running, having sustained 4 failures and then still going on to attempt and break the record in 1980. Most record breakers I know are not of a 'laid back' nature and Pat fell into this category, always planning and thinking about future efforts.

Pat's record was the second closest-run contest time-wise after Wilko's 58 second beating of Woodie's record. Pat took nearly 22 mins off Duffields 1960 record.

So finally Pat Kenny had got his End to End record, the fifth attempt he had made on a variety of machines. **"It had been my burning ambition to get the End to End since 1966, when Swinden and Withers broke the tandem record. I had a feeling I would get there one day, but an element of luck was needed. I persevered knowing that in my own mind I could do it, and that I had to be at my best, both mentally and physically".**

Pat's foray into RRA record breaking started in 1965 when he took over 3 hours off Ed Tweddell's Edinburgh to London trike record and in the same ride broke John Arnold's 24 hour trike record, by adding 3 miles on with 431.5 miles. Like me he joined Birmingham St Christophers Catholic CC when he was a teenager. Immersing himself in club life, touring, Sunday club runs, time trialling, and organising events on a regular basis. Apart from National RRA records of which he broke a total of 9, he broke numerous Midland Road records with various partners including myself. He rode mainly trike and tandem trike.

Pat became a National RRA committee man; he is a Course measurer, Observer and still finds time to be a regular RTTC and RRA Timekeeper over a period exceeding 30 years. He has timed National Championship time trials and road records from 25 miles to End to Ends. All this and in his 66th year has amassed nearly 780,000 miles being the second greatest mile-eater after Chris Davies.

He has been a driving force behind many successful road records since the late 70's organising, advising, weather watching, his knowledge of record breaking is immense. Needless to say he has been a great help to me when writing this book.

No 28 MICK COUPE SOLO BICYCLE END TO END 29th JUNE 1982

The team travelled down on the Sunday for a Monday start, however there was too much west in the wind, so it was decided that Tuesday was to be the day, come what may. A start would be made at 12 noon. The reason for this start time was simply so as not to arrive very early in the morning, at some 'ungodly' hour, as Mick put it. Tuesdays weather looked no better with a fairly strong westerly wind and a thick coastal fog. The decision to start was made anyway.

Pat Kenny timed him away from the Lands End Hotel south door at midday on Tuesday 29th June 1982. The time to beat was 1 day 23 hrs 23 mins, a record held by Paul Carbutt since 1979. This midday start nearly proved disastrous as you will see when the record breaker travels through Scotland.

The first 50 miles was done in 1 hr 53 mins, the 100 miles took 3 hrs 50 mins, this being the fastest start to any End to End attempt. Mick recalls his brother Roger trying to slow him down, but as he said, he had a very strong westerly wind behind him and was making good use of it. He knew that as he turned more northerly after Bristol it would be on his left side. He was always confident he would break the record, and viewed the End to End as an extension of the few 24 hr races he'd ridden. Mick was a fast finisher and knew in his mind that this would be how he would tackle it.

As he came out of Cornwall, he was nearly an hour up on Carbutt's figures, but Mick paid for his fast start with a bout of cramp in both legs on the Bridgwater Flats. By Worcester his lead had reached its highest peak being 1 hr and 21 mins up on Carbutt's time here. When I joined the team as an observer in the feeding car at Gailey, his lead had been pegged to 1 hr up. At 12 hours he'd covered 261 miles, the fastest anybody had ridden up to this point on the End to End route.

The wind at this point was just about favourable, as he progressed in the dark, along familiar roads and on up through the Potteries with lots of club folk out to see him through. Dawn started to break at around 340 miles in the Knutsford area, and on now through Warrington towards Preston, still maintaining a very impressive 'evens' pace. I remember his helpers feeding him syrupy pancakes purchased at a 'Little Chef' very early in the morning. At Garstang he'd had his fill of these and I was invited to try one of his favourite snacks. I'm always one to try out new foods to add to a long distance diet, but they were horrible and so sweet !

The weather as I recall was by midmorning quite favourable, a hazy sun, not too hot, a following breeze, and Mick was riding very well with his effortless style. Up through Lancashire, Kendal, and over Shap in good conditions, he took it all in his stride, he was a good climber being very slight although well muscled in the legs. On now, beyond Carlisle we realised the 24 hrs record of 475 miles held by Ken Joy since 1954 was about to be broken. We shouldn't have been surprised at Mick breaking the 24 hr record as he'd won the National Championship with a distance of 492 miles.

We were waiting in a lay by on the A74 when we had to take shelter as a terrific thunderstorm followed Mick up the road. Pat timed him out here at 482.5 miles, the first man to get from Lands End into Scotland ever in 24 hours. What an achievement ! There were tears of joy all round, followed by a rainbow across the A74. Almost fairy tale conditions.

He had added 7 miles onto the record distance and had averaged over 20 mph up to here. After a brief stop for a freshen up, Mick pressed on through the Dumfries and Galloway region, leading up to the big climb to Edinburgh, the 'Devils Beeftub'. He climbed well here and arrived on the outskirts of Edinburgh where one catches an occasional glimpse of the Forth Road bridge. He said the jubilation of getting the 24 hr record and being the first man into Scotland in 24 hours made him feel very good. He remembers going well until he turned left onto the wide dual carriageway leading to the bridge and taking a 'right hammering' riding into a gale-force wind. He recalls seeing a lad coming down the opposite carriageway doing about 40 mph and free wheeling.

It was at this point one of the official observer's, suggested to Mick's brother Bill, that he might as well get him off the bike as he would never get the record being so far down on time and riding into such a head wind, to which Bill replied "You don't know my brother Mick !" The observer had forgotten that Mick had started at 12 noon and not 10 am.

By the time he reached the bridge he needed a rest, and I recall him slumped on the grass verge with his back against a wall. He'd had a real battle with the wind and was worried about going over the bridge. I had gone over it a couple of years previously on the tandem trike and apart from a little bit of buffeting from a side wind I wasn't perturbed, but then a tandem trike is a lot heavier and much more stable than a bike. The wind coming across the Firth of Forth was pretty strong when Mick got there. He stopped at the side for a rest, a feed and some warmer clothes before going over. One of his helpers said "We can't get him back on his bike, he's absolutely petrified of going over". Mick had thought he could ride over the bridge on the road, but was told he could be disqualified for taking pace from the traffic if he did, and would have to ride on the footpath along the edge. He had a terrible fear of heights, and he had also seen some workmen on the bridge a little way down, welding a new piece of barrier and handrail back into place and that worried him. After what seemed like ages, actually only 7 mins, his helpers managed to cajole him to go over. He hadn't realised he would be detached from the motor traffic, as previously, on training trips over the bridge with the lads from the Edinburgh RC, they had ridden over on the main carriageway with the cars. The cycle and walkway is suspended at the side and below the level of the traffic, when you are going across it feels like you are on a gangplank about a quarter of a mile high, suspended above the sea, protected only by a mesh fence. If you dare look down, the large ships below look like toy boats about two inches long. Mick gingerly rode over, looking only at the path in front of him and trying to stay upright in the very strong crosswinds. He lost so much time after doing so well, we thought it might have affected him badly enough to lose the record.

Once safely over he still had a very strong wind to contend with all the way to Perth, another 33 miles. Mick battled on and in his head he knew the only way he could get the time back that he'd lost on the bridge, was to forego a planned stop at Blair Atholl. This posed a problem as he went through., as the helping and feeding cars were parked up on a big lay by at Blair Atholl. They were caught by surprise and they realised they couldn't go past him again for another half hour, as there was no bypass or detour the cars could take to get by. He was hungry and tired but maintained his speed to gradually be an hour up on Paul Carbutt's figures.

From Perth to Inverness, riding into the second night over the Grampians the wind that had been nagging away and troubling Mick suddenly disappeared and he recalled how easy it became. The last climb before Inverness was done and he felt really good. He was the first rider to officially use the newly opened Kessock Bridge, where he had his only mechanical problem of the ride, a broken spoke in the back wheel, it being quite a steep gradient over the Beauly Firth requiring an out of the saddle effort. The feed car soon had him on his way again.

Mick's brother, Roger, had worried him about a cattle grid at Bonar Bridge that goes across the road. The helpers had gone on ahead and opened a little side gate for him to go through. They'd even gone to the trouble of sweeping debris off the pathway for him. Mick recalls hurtling through at about 45 mph and going straight over the cattle grid. Roger said later to Mick that at the time he wasn't amused ! He made good progress over Helmsdale and Berriedale, as I mentioned, he's a good climber and sat in the saddle up both of them. When his helpers said he'd got 25 miles to go, he though of all the 25 mile time trials he'd ridden and felt he could beat the hour.

He thought of all the thousand's of training miles he'd done in preparation to get here and felt pleased. He got to Wick and then had forgotten where the right turn was. There was no signpost. He looked back, where were the cars ? He stopped and asked an old lady the way and carried on. By now he is flying down the road. The following car came past with the timekeeper and it was a good job, as sheep had strayed onto the road and completely blocked it.

The car cleared a path through and Mick continued at speed towards John o Groats. He took what he thought was the drive to the hotel, a large white building, but after 200 yards he realised it wasn't the right one. He'd still got three miles to go !

He recalls virtually sprinting the remaining distance and then the last mile downhill to the coast and the hotel. Pat Kenny said it was the fastest he'd seen anybody finish - 30 mph. Mick hadn't realised there was a 10 ft wall at the end. Pats only regret was that he couldn't persuade him to continue for the 1000 miles. he recalls a couple of memorable incidents. The first obviously was the joy at Mick getting the 24 hr record in a thunderstorm, and the second was a stag leaping out of a wood on the 'Ord of Caithness' A common sight at certain times of the year to see three or four large deer standing proudly on the hillside watching the rider go past. Probably their ancestors had watched as G.P Mills, Tom Peck and Rossiter had made their way north.

Mick gave me a brief family history of cycling dating back over 80 years. His father Bill Coupe (Senior) was a good rider before the second world war and in 1929 he rode his first 25 mile race. His mother's family were also racing cyclists with Jim Carr winning the Anfield 100 in 1935, the year Mick was born. Aubrey Cahill, his uncle raced in Ireland and won the 25 mile championship twice. His uncle's on his dads side of the family, Frank, Oswald, Roger and Freddy Brown, were all racing men. At six years of age, Mick contracted rheumatic fever, and it was feared he wouldn't be following his famous family into cycling as a sport. Mick remembers the illness took seven months to recover from, leaving him unable to walk properly, as it not only affects your heart but also your joints. He had to have special shoes made for him.

At nine years of age his family moved from the very strong cycling region of the Potteries, to Daventry, where cycling clubs were virtually non-existent. As a teenager he remembered becoming interested in golf and motor cycles and in 1949 he became the Northampton junior golf champion. So, he did have a competitive streak, and this is a sport Mick still plays today.

At sixteen, his father bought him a new 'Velocette 350cc' motor bike and Mick says this is what changed his life. A long trip back from Skegness in the rain triggered off his rheumatic fever again. The doctors told his parents that he now had a heart problem and must pack up the motor bike riding. He was advised to take up cycling, but to take it easy !

The family moved back up north to Lancashire where they all joined the South Lanc's road club. Mick was now seventeen and was starting to get the competitive urge. He rode on the track and in short distance time trials. He worked at H.J.Heinz Foods on a rotating 3 shift system, which played havoc with his training and sleep pattern. At 24 years of age he packed up racing. He was surrounded by his relatives all racing competitively. His dad and his brother were riding all distances up to 12 hours.

When Mick was 34 years old his cousin, John Cahill, contacted him with a view to getting a 24 hr championship team together and would he be interested ? He joined the North Staffs

St Christopher's cc and that was basically the start of his voyage into long distance racing and eventually the End to End in 1982.

John Cahill's idea of training was going out for at least 100 miles a day, a recipe which Mick says at first nearly crippled him, but eventually paid off. They were joined by Tom Finney and Mick Parker. In the space of three weekends they rode a 100 mile , a 12 hr, and another 100 mile. John won the first 100 with 4 hrs 9 mins. Mick did 4 hrs 35 mins after borrowing Bernadette Swinnerton's bike at 70 miles due to his cranks falling off ! The 12 hr John won and Mick came 3rd. The following week he won the South Staffs 100 with 4 hrs 19 mins. Rheumatic Fever had changed his life completely the second time, and his heart condition had now corrected itself.

Mick says that although he hadn't raced long distance until he was 34 years old, he was used to riding with his dad and brother Bill, who would regularly stretch him on journeys over 100 miles. He remembers working at Warrington and riding there and back home to Leigh every day. On one occasion they were too late to post a 25 mile entry form off, so they rode after work to Blackpool and back ! His dad and brother were on gears, he was on a 69" fixed and they still couldn't drop him.

Mick was now working regular daytime hours which gave him a chance to train properly, and in 1979 at 44 years of age he won the National Championship 24 hr, beating cousin John, and 'Ticker' Mullins, and along with Mick Parker they broke the team 24 hr comp record.

The talk quickly got round to 'End to Ends', but he realised they would need a lot of money as it would be an 'all or nothing' effort. They set about looking for a sponsor with the same enthusiasm and belief in them that they had in themselves.

Derek Partington who owned 'Partington Cycles' in Bolton was the main sponsor behind the 'Horwich Cycling Club' and agreed to put up the financial support needed. His brother Roger would do the organising, Mick's wife Brenda was a charge nurse at a young persons disabled unit at Preston and they were trying to get funds for an ambulance, and this was all to tie in with his ride, raising money for this cause. The workforce of 2000 people at Heinz all donating one pound made this a good start to the fund.

Derek Partington supplied him with his race equipment and running costs, plus transport. Heinz donated enough food for all the helpers in the various cars. The helpers and officials had all donated their holiday time, free of charge. The Horwich cc were magnificent, but most of all his wife Brenda, had made it easy for him to train for the six months prior to the attempt. With a family of five teenagers to look after it wasn't easy, but she coped, making sure at the same time that Mick ate properly. Roger had set him a realistic schedule to keep to and had sorted out all the arrangements with the RRA. They knew they were limited to start times, and couldn't afford to stay at Lands End with 14 helpers to be paid for, for more than 2 nights.

I knew he had ridden a few 24 hr races including the 'Mersey' as I used to chat to him and his team mates. His original club when I first knew him was North Staffs St Christopher's cc, my original club was Birmingham St Christopher's cc, so we got on well. John Cahill, Tom Finney and Mick Parker formed many winning teams with him in championship years and this stood Mick in good stead for his End to End. The support in Scotland from the clubs was as ever superb. Tears of joy from his helpers at the end and a congratulations telegram from Paul

Carbutt minutes after he finished topped off a wonderful 2 days. Later at a club do they thanked Pat and myself and presented us with 'pot owls', a traditional custom done in the Potteries.

In hindsight, I always thought Mick looked a bit pale and washed out. I hadn't realised he'd had two brushes with rheumatic fever and I also found out 20 years after his attempt he was diagnosed with a thyroid problem. It's a condition that can bring on fear of heights and open spaces, so was this perhaps the underlying problem at the Forth Road bridge. It's a thought isn't it ? It put his ride into an ever greater perspective in my mind. A ride that raised over £ 3,000 for his local disabled charity in 1982.

I spoke to Mick recently and he said that the End to End was a dream fulfilled and couldn't thank his helpers and family enough for making it come true. He doesn't ride much anymore but still plays golf and ski's as much as he can when he goes abroad in the winter.

Mick is the oldest man in modern day times to break the record at 46 years of age, taking 44 mins off Paul Carbutt's 1979 record with **1 day 22 hrs 39 mins 49 secs.**

Information courtesy of 'Cycling' with additional text by Mick Coupe and myself.

No 29 ERIC TREMAINE TRICYCLE END TO END 5th JULY 1982

Between the 5th and 7th July 1982, Eric Tremaine of the Leicestershire Road Club, broke the tricycle End to End record by 4 hrs 18 mins with a time of 2 days, 6 hours, 18 mins, 35 secs, beating Pat Kenny's 1980 record. This new record by this 'classy' trike rider at the peak of his career sounds plain sailing but was quite the opposite. Although he was up on schedule from start to finish, his ride was anything but easy.

On Friday July 2nd, only the Glasgow weather station predicted winds from the south; by Saturday the forecast was more favourable, the southerly winds now looking more promising; on Sunday at Lands End the wind was south westerly and very strong. After phoning the weather stations again on Sunday, Eric and his team decided to start as scheduled, Monday 8 am.

Waking at 6 am after a poor nights sleep, Eric tackled his last 'normal' meal for two and a half days, cereal, scrambled egg on toast and tea, then after taking a leisurely ride down to Lands End he awaited the 8 am start from timekeeper Joe Summerlin.

Eric started at a steady pace, the sun already warming the air. Clifford, Eric's brother recalls cyclists en route cheering Eric on, also an elderly lady with a walking stick waving encouragement and checking the time and number plates of the following vehicles. Penzance saw a slight gain on schedule, Eric trying not to stretch himself too early. By Bodmin with 50 miles done, the sun was now hotter, not Eric's favourite weather but one consolation, the wind was near perfect in direction. Exeter was reached and although well marshalled Eric was glad he'd checked the route through the town on his way to Lands End, as being up on schedule he had beaten some of the marshals to the roundabouts.

On his way now through Taunton and Bridgwater, where the cycling magazine reported that Eric fought a nagging headwind on the Bridgwater Flats that gave him severe back pain. On reflection, Eric remembers the head wind and remembers a new 'see through' drinking bottle disintegrating as it hit the road, but does not remember a bad back. He recalls a sore back later on in the ride (after 24 hrs) and had to have regular massage relief from John Osborne, an Australian cycling enthusiast and masseur whom Eric had invited on the trip the week prior to the attempt.

On towards Bristol now, Eric said he had programmed his mind to think in short steps of 15 to 20 miles and this worked well for him. With the hills of Cornwall, Devon and Somerset nearly all behind him, Eric tackled one last climb after passing under the Clifton Suspension Bridge, the steep rise up to Bristol Zoo, ably assisted by the marshalling of Arthur Comer, Jack Spencer, Geoff Lonsdale and members of the South West Tricycle Association. Clifford also a trike man and on the team as a driver/mechanic, recalls Eric going through feeding stations with people handing up much needed sponges, spread out along the back route through Bristol, all giving Eric much appreciated encouragement.

12 hours passed with 225 miles covered just before Gloucester, slightly down on Pat Kenny's record at this point but up on schedule.

The first reinforcements to the team, Dianne and Brian Thorp joined just after Gloucester, just in time to get to know 'the ropes' before an unscheduled stop just before Worcester. Twenty minutes were taken for a feed, massage, put on night clothing and fit lights to the trike. At Worcester Eric started seeing people he knew, that other famous tall record breaking tricyclist, Dave Duffield, started to appear at various places, giving his loud unique encouragement, along with Les Lowe and the gallery of Midlands enthusiasts.

The battery lights in those days were pretty useless and by Wolverhampton fresh lamps were called for, the original ones having flickered themselves out. Eric was now nearly an hour up on schedule, but still behind Pat Kenny's time. Indications from flags flying on garage forecourts showed a helping wind. The night was warm.

More members of the Leicestershire R.C. joined the entourage at Gailey Island where the A5 crosses the A449 End to End route. On through Stafford, Newcastle, Knutsford, Warrington. During this phase Eric was going through a relatively 'slow' period. It was now the middle of the night, not a time conducive to speed, plus the constant problems with lights made the 100 miles between Stafford and Lancaster a slow one, taking nearly 7 hours, still on schedule despite the slow patch, he was now just ahead of Pat Kenny.

Tuesday's dawn began to break as he approached Wigan, light rain showers started. Along this stretch, out of Cheshire and into Lancashire, there were lots of North West Tricycle Association supporters including John Arnold, who joined the cortege on his well laden bike, riding behind the support van for quite a way, exchanging greetings and asking how Eric was. Clifford describes it as a fantastic experience, no longer like an extended 24 hr but different in some subtle indefinable way, racing through built up areas, getting involved with numerous traffic lights, seeing cyclists appearing mysteriously out of the half light, running with bottles and reappearing later on up the road by way of local bypasses, springing into action to support a single tricyclist hell bent on riding from Lands End to John o Groats.

On towards Preston, the wind had shifted to the west, accompanied by more showery rain, the next town was Lancaster, still on schedule he passed through the deserted town centre, by the bus station with 'checkers' seeing him out of the town on towards Kendal. A message was relayed to Eric on this stretch of road, he had 55 mins to do 17 miles for the 24 hr record. With the wind and rain Eric felt this was an impossible task, and try as he might, the 24 hrs elapsed as he passed through the busy streets of Kendal, with Clifford and timekeeper Joe Summerlin correlating relevant land marks in the town just in case the record went. Alas this was not to be with 429.6 miles covered.

I had helped on Pat Kenny's 24 hr record of 431.5 miles in 1965, starting at Edinburgh, taking the Edinburgh to London record and then continuing out to the south coast for the 24 hrs. Pat had a good wind for about two thirds of the ride, but of course he could 'give it his all' knowing he could stop at the end of it. Eric couldn't afford to jeopardize his End to End just to break the 24 hr record.

The 'slow' patch over the last few hours, possibly from losing time with dodgy lights, had taken its toll on Eric. Don't forget in those days, decent battery lights were virtually non-existent. I remember before all of my 24 hr races, experimenting with batteries and bulbs trying to find something that would last at least 3 hrs, packing batteries and light casings with bits of rubber to avoid 'flickering' bulbs usually to no avail. Any rechargeable systems were real 'Heath Robinson' looking with lots of wires and sticky tape, looking more like a home made bomb, and weighing as much. It would be at least the late 90's before rear L.E.D.'s and decent front lamps became bright enough for acceptance; rechargeable lights at an affordable price appeared in about 1998.

After getting out of Kendal, Eric chose a good lay by and had a break. He got out of his wet clothes and took a feed; the masseur worked hard on his back and legs for 20 mins to prepare him for the climb up Shap and beyond. Dianne Thorp, Brian and Eric's wife, Carol, had taken a break from feeding and had tried to sleep in Paul Bowler's back up car. Paul drove up the M6 in preference to the record route and from Kendal onwards they became quite agitated as to what was happening to Eric, resolving not the leave him again if they could avoid it. The suspense was 'killing' not knowing where he was and what state he would be in. Don't forget this is long before mobile phones. After a frantic search they found Eric off his trike at the bottom of Shap.

Eric, on his way again, tackled the lower slopes of Shap climbing in thick mist. It was here that the double freewheel differential axle proved its worth. The road was damp and a single wheel drive would have lost traction. Remember Albert Crimes' mishap on the 'Ord of Caithness'. Eric's gamble of extra weight for the two wheel drive had paid off. The trike was a 'George Longstaff' himself a T.A. member. It was an early model made especially for Eric in George's back shed workshop before he expanded his business.

From the top of Shap the mist cleared and by the time Eric had descended through Shap village, the sun was shining bright and warm, with the wind now helping from behind. Penrith was reached without taking the scheduled stop. Clifford describes following Eric in the van and being almost mesmerised by his younger brother's long legs pumping the gear rhythmically, like a very efficient engine, for mile after mile. He felt at that stage, convinced that in some peculiar way, the whole effort was pre-destined and that this was an example of how we have so little control of our own actions, or fate !

Eric was now fast approaching the border country but the road to Carlisle proved to be one of the hardest parts of the ride. During his reconnaissance of the area, he had noticed a number of steep hills from the car but in reality on the second day they seemed much worse than he had imagined and was glad to see the signs for Carlisle.

At Carlisle he took an 'Oppy' bag of food ready for the long haul up the A74 through Gretna to Beattock. He really wasn't looking forward to this stretch of dual carriageway with few features and heavy traffic, it being the main road into Scotland via Edinburgh, Glasgow and Perth. There was now a slight headwind but Eric maintained a steady 18 mph.

Road works on a five mile section meant a reduction to a single carriageway and Eric ended up with a huge backlog of traffic waiting to pass, and what was the cause of the road works, yes, you've guessed it, council men drain cleaning right at the very end of the closed section ! Pat and I had suffered the same problem in exactly the same place, some three years earlier on our attempt. I remember as the 'stoker' being able to turn my head to the left and ignore the abuse from the car occupants as they passed us after the road works. Eric said he felt that the waves he got from the cars were ones of courteous admiration, or were they ?

Just before turning onto the A701, he was handed a musette from an unknown lady, containing a piece of cake which Eric recalls was absolutely superb. The sun was now hotter and a short stop was called for a massage and cooler clothing. Eric was now complaining of backache and saddle sores. Clifford recalls looking at Eric lying on the grass, shattered and very tired, and he thought 'is this the time where we need to use the tough approach' ? He felt that a medical person like a Loughborough 'boffin' could be of great use at a time like this, reassuring the rider and the team that the body's resources are capable of meeting the demands made upon it.

Eric resumed his ride and was now on the slopes of the Devils Beef Tub and felt encouraged by the way he was climbing. Over the top and with the steady 50 mile downhill run to Edinburgh further gain on schedule looked inevitable. At Broughton he had another unscheduled stop after getting neat 'Eau de Cologne' in his eyes from a sponge.

The schedule had him arriving at Edinburgh at 8 pm, but in reality he was now 2.5 hours up and had heavy rush hour traffic to contend with, plus promised marshals seemed to be missing so Eric relied on his memory of the route to find the Forth Bridge. The marshalling confusion was caused by a mix up with the schedules of Eric and John Woodburn and how the marshals would be contacted on the day.

All went well on the Forth Road Bridge; Joe Summerlin rode the spare trike over behind Eric in case of mechanical trouble, but the crossing caused no problems and he was soon turning off the A90 to Inverkeithing to follow the old road to Perth. The surface of the road, as Clifford recalls, was appalling, some of the worst he'd come across; 'Clement 10' tubular tyres are not the best for these conditions. A puncture occurred but with Clifford's swift mechanical skills a quick wheel change was performed. Eric had a chance to 'water the grass' and was soon on his way again. Eric described the road surface as the worst of the attempt. He 'honked' out of the saddle for nearly 5 miles downhill, and then up the 2.5 mile climb towards Perth, the resulting severe swelling and numbness in both hands made gear changing and feeding very difficult. People don't realise that a trike, having three points of contact with the road, gives at least 30% more bruising than a bike.

At this point Eric was still well ahead of schedule but wanted to get as much road covered in daylight as possible before stopping for night clothing. This left the following van and support vehicles in a bit of a quandary. They needed to fuel up knowing there would be no garages between Perth and Inverness. Having missed a feed before Perth they were required to wait another 30 mins, due to RRA rules about passing, Clifford recalls catching up with Eric as he waited at traffic lights in Perth and shoving a bag of goodies in his back pocket before the lights changed.

After covering another 14 miles Eric was beginning to feel cold and felt unsettled inside, he knew he wasn't moving as fast as he should be so decided to stop. It lasted one and a half hours and Eric recalls sitting under a pile of blankets for most of that time. The team was concerned and anxious thinking that Eric had had enough. Hot food was prepared, but he could not eat it, his hands were swollen and his backside sore.

Perth had been a critical barrier for him to get past (anyone can get to Perth syndrome) and by getting as far past there as possible, he felt he was now on the last stage of the ride. Clifford recalls it being the most crucial point of the ride, the cold swollen hands and the general disposition of the rider made one feel almost ashamed to be urging him to carry on and take yet more punishment. Time was passing by all too quickly and the margin over Pat Kenny at this point was rapidly disappearing. Eventually Eric found the strength to continue, wearing a pair of well padded ski gloves, a warm top and tracksuit bottoms, he made his way up the A9 with the still inconsistent battery lighting. The roads ahead were of recent construction, levelling out some of the gradients that must have confronted John Arnold, Albert Crimes and David Duffield, but no doubt available to Pat Kenny.

Eric soon started to feel better; his helpers were now feeding him with soup, sandwiches, whole cold boiled potatoes and Complan to build up his strength. He felt good as he tackled the long drags maintaining a good average speed he reached Aviemore at 2.50 am with 690 miles covered. The moonlit sky soon dawned to another sunny day, in spite of his physical discomforts his morale was high.

Inverness was reached and Eric could now cut a few miles off the original journey which went through the city by using the Kessock Bridge over the Beauly Firth. It was still under construction and permission had been obtained in advance to use the bridge but a disclaimer form needed to be signed by all those crossing just in cast of an accident. Once off the bridge Eric made the Aultnamain climb his next objective before taking a stop a Bonar Bridge. Eric recalls going over this section of the road when on a holiday in Scotland with Carol and viewing it with great respect for the riders who had ridden it previously, little realising that within 12 months he would be traversing the 'hallowed ground' himself. Eric felt that even with his bad hands he performed the descent off Aultnamain with the skills and agility all good trike riders have.

With less than 100 miles to go, Eric suddenly had a craving for cornflakes which posed a problem as none of the support vehicles had any; his wrists were also giving him real pain. Bernard Thompson, the famous 'cyclists' photographer with his wife Ethel, who had followed the attempt from Carlisle, went off in search of supplies, obtaining some elastic bandages from a local hospital and cornflakes from a bemused shopkeeper. At Golspie Eric stopped again for his cornflakes, a change of clothing , had his wrists strapped up, a large blister on his hand burst with a needle, finishing off by borrowing Ivy Mitton's Savlon to rub into his sore backside. Eric is almost 4 hours up on Pat Kenny and determined not to stop again before John o Groats.

The wind was beginning to get up directly behind the rider just as the Met Office had promised on Sunday. Eric had now already made up his mind not to continue for the 1000 miles due to his severe discomforts. He had no fears about the climbs of Helmsdale and Berriedale and realised, barring disasters, he would now get the record. Climbing the Ord of Caithness the helpers took it in turns to run alongside Eric. The lorries driving behind them were very patient, the drivers putting the vehicles into crawler gear and sitting behind the entourage then wishing the rider well when they eventually went past. Dianne who had prepared an orange for Eric just after climbing Berriedale remembers Eric had climbed so quickly that John Osborne had to sprint to put the orange into Eric's mouth as he went past. John, who had never seen a trike raced before this trip was amazed as he watched Eric climb and descend.

Eric was now pulling out all the stops; feeding was now tinned fruit and lemonade. He gave instructions for everyone to get ready for the photographs at the finish. He was now riding at a pace similar to that at Penzance.

Through Wick and turn right - 14 miles to go. The hills seemed to go on and on. At last the final drop down and that final corner to the Hotel. He had arrived and his ambition had been realised. Joe Summerlin timed him in with a new record of 2 days 6 hours 18 mins 35 secs taking 4 hrs 18 mins off Pat Kenny's time of 1980.

Before dismounting the trike he sipped champagne, then posed for group photographs in the warm sunshine, ate an ice cream and was checked out by the local doctor before having a welcomed bath. In the space of two weeks, the John o Groats hotel had witnessed the setting of another superb record.

Eric thanked his team of helpers and officials; Joe Summerlin the timekeeper, Ivy Mitton and John Williams, the RRA observers; his wife Carol, Dianne and Brian Thorp, brother Clifford, John Osborne, Frank Wildman, Paul Bowler, Steve Hill, Jeff White, Bernard and Ethel Thompson. At the telephone HQ Mavis Wildman, Janet Preston, David Roome, Dave and Barbara Binks. Pat Kenny for his advice, help and assistance during the planning of the ride, and finally the club folk the length of the country who came out to cheer him along on his 'experience of a lifetime'.

The turn of events that led up to Eric tackling the record in 1982 was pretty amazing, almost down to fate itself He had always wanted to ride the End to End but always felt he wasn't quite ready for it. He worked at the time for Rolls Royce in the Design Office at Ansty; he had made plans around 1980 to emigrate to Canada having been offered a job there. Whilst finalising plans to move, the job fell through, the result of a Canadian recession. One of his regrets had been that he had never attacked the End to End, and given this second chance, he set about the task with vengeance looking forward to an experience and the fulfilment of a lifetimes ambition.

In 1982 he was 40 years of age and as ready as ever for an End to End. Since 1963 he had ridden seven 24 hr races on a bike, his best being the Wessex in 1966 with 475 miles, and three on a trike taking comp record in 1972 with 457.895, beating John Arnold's previous record by over half a mile. He'd also broken comp record three times for 100 miles; 4-31-20 in 1969, 4-30-48 in 1971 and finally 4-27-51 in 1972.

Eric had thought the cost of an End to End would be prohibitive but with the sponsorship committee of the Leicestershire RC/Kirby and West taking over most of the financial burden and getting the advice of Pat Kenny, he decided it could be done and arranged the attempt within three months. An introductory letter requesting help was sent out to known End to End helpers, the response was overwhelming. Clarke's of Leicester generously loaned a Sherpa Van and a Minibus, Paul Bowler provided an estate car as back up.

After a weekend trip by car with Carol to John o Groats to check out the route, Eric arrived back on the Monday with a greater respect for the record and for those who had broken it. He wondered if he had bitten off more than he could chew, and had to convince himself that Pat Kenny was only human, had admitted to having bad weather on the second and third days of his attempt, whose time trial performances were no better, and with the hour bonus for using the Kessock Bridge, the record could be his.

Clifford, Eric's older brother who was on the record as a driver and mechanic is a pretty hard-riding trike man himself. I watched him ride the Anfield 100 this year (2004) and at 69 years of age he recorded 5 hrs 10 mins on a trike, and that's a course that's quite hilly, using the new Mersey 24 hr 33 mile circuit and this the day after riding a Tricycle Association 50 mile event in the same area, awarding him the combined tricycle prize.

Eric himself finally emigrated to Canada in 1984 and nowadays rides a bike during the summer months doing regular rides of over 60 miles with his cycle computer as company. He says, for him, anything less than 60 miles isn't worth the effort. He still had that competitive time trial mentality every time he goes out for a ride on the road or on the stationary bike in the gym.

In 2003 at 61 years of age he came back to visit his family and rode the Anfield 100 and the Bruce Kingsford 50, recording times of 5-37-48 and 2-40-40 respectively.

I spoke to Eric in June 2004 and he says he still remembers the record as if it were yesterday. The anticipation of waiting for the right wind, the build up for weeks beforehand and then the 'euphoria' of breaking the record made it a unique occasion.

It was the pinnacle of his career and he was so glad he didn't miss doing it. He was 40 years old and at 6ft 2"inches tall weighed in at 12 stone 12 lbs. During the ride he gained over 10 lbs in weight through water retention. He says the End to End was the main objective of the attempt and the 1000 would have been a pure bonus. Upon reflection, going on for the 1000 would have spoiled the End to End experience and he has never had any regrets about the abandonment.

I asked him about hallucinations and he recalled having an almost 'out of body' experience just before Wick. The wind was pushing him along and he remembers as if looking down on himself from above ! At the finish Eric said it was a funny sensation when everybody starts talking about the ride. The rider although the central 'star' of the activity is oblivious of the turmoil going on around him, when the helpers started talking about the panics they've had and the worries he's caused them. Eric said it was like attending your own funeral, central attraction but not aware of what is going on.

Another amusing incident occurred when the following vehicle thought he was waving to somebody 'on high'. It happened near Aviemore; Eric wanted to know the time and so lifted his watch hand up in the air to catch the light from the van's headlights. Obviously the 'waving' was misinterpreted.

The only equipment change Eric said he would make is that he would have the latest in multiple gearing with a triple chainset, silk tubular tyres and obviously the latest in lighting technology. No hesitation, the double freewheel drive would definitely be used.

Sadly, George Longstaff, the man who designed and made Eric's trike passed away in 2003 after suffering a severe stroke while out riding. Since his early beginnings he had produced bikes, tricycles, tandems and tandem tricycles for all aspects of cycling. A lot of famous cyclists ride his machines, and he was a brilliant engineer and a gifted perfectionist. He also made machines for the disabled and people with 'special needs'. Everything was custom built.

George had been present when his first wife Cynthia, had been tragically killed at the end of a time trial in June 1982, aged 35, but he had bounced back and concentrated himself into his demanding work. He still managed to devote time to record breaking activities, helping and observing whenever he could. I recall George being out through the Potteries and into Cheshire on most End to Ends I've been on and he was out on Lynne's three End to Ends. Like Tommy Greep and John Arnold, I doubt he's missed many in over 40 years. He leaves his family and second wife, Beverly, who he was riding with at the time. The cycling fraternity is much poorer for his passing. Luckily his business is being carried on, hopefully for many years to come, to keep this famous man's name going.

Eric still has his trike in Canada. He doesn't ride it at present but gives it a regular polish, keeping it as a memento of his unforgettable End to End.

This record ride description had input from Eric Tremaine, Clifford Tremaine, Cycling Magazine, and myself.

No 30 JOHN WOODBURN SOLO BICYCLE END TO END FRIDAY 13th JULY 1982

John won his first RTTC Championship '25' in 1961 with a 56-01. 20 years later in 1981 he won the Mersey RC 24 hr with 488.43 miles. In between those years, apart from winning lots of time trials, he broke no less than eight RRA records, the 24 hr and End to End, making a tally of ten, by 1982.

He failed on his first End to End attempt in 1981 which terminated at Blair Athol, when attacking Paul Carbutt's record of 1 day 23 hrs 23 mins. I saw him when he came through Wellington (Telford). He was freewheeling a lot and was already down on schedule. John recalls with a fortnight to go before the End to End he decided to attack the London to Bath and back. He broke Les West's 1973 record by nearly 4 minutes, a record which still stands today at 9hrs 3 mins 7 secs. John rates this as probably one of his best performances ever, but reflects that the effort involved probably took too much out of him. Either that or he had contracted a virus which started on the Monday prior to his End to End attempt. By the Wednesday he was too weak to stick tubs on wheels !

After travelling down on the Thursday he did some gentle rides around St Just but couldn't climb hills at anything more than walking pace. He had a check up with a local G.P. who advised he needed at least a months rest. He went to bed to rest but there was so much pressure on him to ride he gave in two days later and started on the Monday.

John remembers starting with a high temperature and just 'rolling' the bike along to Preston ! A rider of John's capabilities could probably do that, ride at just over evens and get away with it, but it probably would severely damage any 'lesser mortal'. He remembered reading a letter in 'Cycling Weekly' from a doctor saying the effort could have killed him. After Preston he continued but was gradually losing time and finally abandoned the ride on the Pass of Killiecrankie, a mile or so short of Blair Atholl. Not bad for someone with a high temperature and a virus.

As well as his London to Bath and back, John also rates his 1961 National 25 mile championship win; his 14th place overall in the Warsaw-Berlin-Prague (Peace Race) in 1963; BBAR winner in 1978, the first and only rider over 40 to do so, and finally his Lands End to John o Groats at 45 years of age, the 2nd oldest man to achieve it in modern times.

1982 saw John training in January doing 30 to 40 miles a night and between 80 and 100 miles on Saturday and Sunday, weather permitting. The end of May saw him race-fit and ready. He waited down at Lands End for a week or two for a good wind. Friday 13th July was going to be the strongest south westerly wind and John, not being superstitious planned for that day. By this time, Mick Coupe had updated the record to be 1 day 22 hrs 39 mins 49 secs, and had improved Ken Joy's 1954 24 hrs record from 475.75 miles to 482.5 miles, so John had to work to a tighter schedule than his original one. The attempt was funded by his Manchester Wheelers Club sponsor, Jack Fletcher.

It was a sunny start at 10 am with a very strong south westerly wind. When he reached 'Indian Queens' on Bodmin Moor, he ran into torrential rain which lasted to Okehampton, probably explaining why he didn't start to overhaul Mick Coupe's figures until Bristol where he had gained 6 mins. The summertime traffic through Cornwall, Devon and Somerset was very heavy and whereas the rider managed to squeeze through the jams, the cars got stuck and John missed a couple of feeds.

Dusk, just south of Tewkesbury saw him take on lights and a 13 mins stop for a sit down feed, provided by his helping team, comprising of the current RRA President, Keith Robins and his wife Brenda, with Johns partner Anne. Observers were Edwin Hargraves, Pat Kenny and timekeeper George Hunton. Lots of supporters had seen John on the A38. Bill Griffiths and Dave Duffield were out to support him.

At the 12 hr point he had covered 263 miles to Coupe's 261. At Kidderminster he was helped on his way by Phil Bayton, the 'Staffordshire Engine' who was the current National Criterium Champion. John was one of the first to use the Wolverhampton route and found the hordes of club folk on route a great encouragement. An old adversary of John's, Phil Griffiths, saw him through Stafford. He had a piece of fried fish along here, so no fancy diets for his man, just normal food; rice pudding, fruit cocktail, biscuits, soup, tea, fruit juice and sandwiches.

The first night was uneventful, out through Warrington and Preston. By Lancaster 400 miles, he was 26 minutes up on Mick Coupe with 19 hrs, 04 mins. Dawn brought a cold start to the day as John climbed Shap, 415 miles at 7.19 am. He said it was a very cold descent. He had his only puncture at Penrith.

On now through Carlisle, still a good breeze and the sun was bringing the warmth back to him. Along the A74 his 24 hrs ran out in the Ecclefechan area, just south of Lockerbie Bridge, with 494.25 miles, which took John to a new RRA record by nearly 12 miles.

He took a 20 mins breakfast stop where he had cereal and a change of clothes, another warm day and still in luck with the wind. John turned off through Moffat and was soon attacking the Devils Beeftub. Soon Edinburgh was reached and John felt happier now to have reached another landmark. Out on the by pass with the Forth Road Bridge looming up in the distance, 573 miles at 2.30 pm. Keith Robins rode John's spare bike over the bridge just in case John punctured but everything was okay.

At Perth 607 miles he was nearly 1.5 hrs up on Coupe but still with a second night to get through it wasn't all over yet. John recalls climbing Drumochter feeling very cold especially on the downhill runs. Inverness was reached and he had surpassed his 1981 distance and was still feeling good.

Dawn broke as he climbed Berriedale with ease, on his Campagnolo equipped 'Stan Pike' bike with a 52/42chainset and 12-20 rear cogs. John remembers the roads being very quiet on the 'Ord of Caithness' allowing him to take wide sweeps on the hairpins both up and down. The last two miles drop to the hotel was the best part with the Orkneys as a backdrop. At John o Groats he'd taken 1 hr 36 mins off the record to record **1 day 21 hrs 3 mins 16 secs.**

The month of July 1982 was in RRA terms a very historical one, seeing no less than **three** successful End to Ends. When George Hunton, John's timekeeper, asked John if he would be going on for the 1000 miles there was a definite **no**, as John had been suffering with stiff and swollen ankles over the last period of the ride. So ends the last chapter of his record breaking career, at 45 years of age.

In John's words "After two years of chasing the record, it was such a relief to get it over and done with". There was no pressure to continue for the 1000 miles from his sponsor, Jack Fletcher of 'Trueman Steels'. John made a separate attempt on the 1000 record some 2 years later, but packed at 21 hours with unfavourable winds.

On a lighter note, he did a 10 day sponsored 'Brewery crawl' on his 'End to End' bike, calling at all of the major breweries, probably 20 in all, from as far afield as Faversham in Kent to Warrington and Sheffield. John had to drink a pint at all of them and raised £ 45,000 for charities. He said at least he could get off the bike and have a rest at each stop.

In about centenary year, some rare film footage of John's End to End was discovered on a shelf in a garage. The film was produced by Pete Dansie and Ray Pascoe, and was titled '2 days + 2 nights'. It was in colour with a musical background and a running commentary. It shows John amidst heavy traffic in Devon and Cornwall; taking on lights at dusk near Tewkesbury; taking sit down feeds at night; crossing the Forth Road Bridge; riding through Scotland, and finally the drop down to John o Groats. Interviews with John before and after give an insight to the nature of this remarkable man, who is still competing at top level at 67 years of age.

The film was turned into Video format and shown at the 'Riverside Theatre' in Hammersmith in January 2003. Being a Charlie Woods promotion, it was a 'sell-out' with the theatre packed to capacity. Invited End to End guests included Eileen Sheridan, Pauline Strong, Lynne Taylor, Paul Carbutt, Dick Poole, Dave Keeler, Andy Wilkinson, and of course John Woodburn. John said he was overwhelmed by the amount of famous cyclists and friends who had turned up to watch what John describes as a very slow ride, 18.9 mph ! The film highlights the loneliness of the long distance rider and the team work involved to ensure success. A good film for any aspiring record breakers to watch. John makes it look so easy, but we all know it isn't.

As you can see from his bike description, John pushes quite big gears and when you see him on the road in time trials he seems to roll the gear effortlessly. At the time of his record he stood 5ft 9" and weighed approximately 11.5 stone, with wide shoulders and a large rib cage encasing a very effective pair of lungs !

When you see him saunter up to collect his numerous awards at CTT functions, you wouldn't think you were looking at one of the fastest men of all times, yes, even at nearly 67 years of age he is still winning time trials.

An article in Cycling Weekly headed: Woodburn has 54 feeds in 45 hrs End to End

"I couldn't have done it without you" he told his band of tired helpers after his 847 mile trek. He had had 54 actual, feeds, and refreshment every half hour. "The biggest headache for helpers is the RRA passing rule" said Keith Robbins who was the feed organiser. The rule is designed to stop the rider from receiving any advantage from a moving vehicle and states that the rider cannot be passed more than twice in any one hour, each 'helping' car that passes must have an RRA observer on board. In 1982 the only way to provide more frequent help was to by-pass the rider on another road or motorway to emerge hopefully in front of him. Former trike End to Ender Pat Kenny was a master of these detours on Woodburn's ride, and upset courting couples as he and the helpers blasted down quiet country lanes late at night to get in front of their man. One detour took in an extra 18 miles. They needed to get ahead from Inverness onwards, where some of the steep descents had cattle grids going across the road and with John plunging down the winding descents at 40 mph. He needed to be guided through the paths at the side of the grids to save him puncturing his light tubulars with the impact.

John suffered problems with his batteries, the front light only lasting 2 hrs, one of the cars that was ahead of John, came across a walker in the pitch dark. Fearing that John wouldn't see him until it was too late to swerve. They gave the walker a green fluorescent 'glow' stick, so that John could avoid him. (Back in the 70's and 80's Dr Barbara Moore started a trend of walking from Lands End to John o Groats) The feeding team found that John preferred being fed on the flat, rather than on an uphill section. He found he could control his bike better and wasn't out of breath. One of his favourite hot meals was mince with vegetables, followed by tinned custard with cherries or melon. He had a craving for ginger beer, fish and chips on the first night at Stafford, and ice cream in Scotland. Keith Robbins said they used a primus stove and saucepans to cook with, but hot water was provided mainly by a water heater, run off a cigarette lighter socket, when the engine was running. He said "we used it so much that in the end it burnt out".

Over the last few years, the rules on passing have been scrapped, so there is now no restriction whatsoever to passing a rider, as long as there is an observer on board who records all the details such as time and place of passing. Funnily enough 'old habits die hard' and it usually is about 30 minutes or twice in an hour, which generally is enough. The only exception to this is if an emergency crops up where the rider needs passing sooner, perhaps to be marshalled through a tricky junction etc. So the kamikaze by-passing of the rider down narrow lanes, is no longer required.

The main story was John Woodburn's own account with extracts from Cycling Weekly plus additions from myself.

No 31 PAULINE STRONG LADIES SOLO BICYCLE END TO END 28th to 30th JULY 1990

"Pauline cuts End to End record by four hours"
Article by Ken Mathews courtesy of Cycling Weekly

Pauline Strong (Wyvern CC) a Liverpudlian who lives in Gwent, South Wales, is the new holder of the women's RRA bicycle record for 847 miles from Lands End to John o Groats, taking four hours and 17 minutes off the record which had stood to Hercules professional Eileen Sheridan since 1954. Sheridan set the record at two days 11 hours and 7 minutes, but when Strong reached the John o Groats hotel at 2.50 pm on Monday afternoon the record had been updated to two days six hours 49 minutes and 45 seconds. This was a remarkable effort after she had overcome a broken collarbone six weeks earlier to the day.

Strong had postponed her ride by a day to try for a better wind and when she set off on Saturday at 8 am from Lands End, conditions were more favourable. As evening drew in, people in the north west heard she was something like an hour down on schedule. When she eventually arrived at Knutsford after 342 miles the deficit was almost two hours. It was said that the schedule card had been drawn up too ambitiously for her early stages. She said she was suffering from bad knees, a bad back and extreme tiredness. The broken collar bone had precluded her from taking part in a planned 24 hour event, and although much preparation had been done on the turbo trainer, she was going into the unknown.

At Wigan (365 miles) she was asked what she wanted by her husband Alan. "Just sleep" she said and she was allowed 15 minutes. A short while earlier there was talk of retiring either at Knutsford, Warrington or Preston but she was determined to go on. At that time, 6 am, on day two, it was calculated she needed to do 12.9 miles in every hour, provided she kept going for another 32 hours. Twelve people were on the road as back up, plus others manning the 24 hour phones for news

A trip off course did not help. By 7.30 on Sunday morning, at Forton near Lancaster, she rode through the early morning 25 start and was going smoothly as the promised freshening wind was getting up in her favour. A quick hot meal in the caravan at Galgate, and she came out looking good. Touring expert and record holder Gordon Brennan saw her through his home patch at Lancaster. Through Kendal and on to the climb to Shap, which she took extremely well, she arrived at 10.15 am, a couple of hours down on schedule.

Pauline grabbed a jacket for the descent of Shap, while her husband shouted "You are doing a stormer". She reached Kendal by 11 am but there was heavy traffic through Carlisle and by 12.30 it was the "Welcome to Scotland" sign which merited a one-arm punch in the air. A short stop in a lay-by on the A74 at 12.40 was a chance to tell her she had picked up 40 minutes on her schedule and timekeeper Roy Moss said 'from here on the schedule becomes very generous'. Another stop at 1.40 and she left with heavy knee bandages over what she called her Nora Batty's (wrinkled tights).

The 500 miles came up around 2 pm and heavy rain came down. By 2.50 she was through Moffat for the start of the Beef Tubs climb. Partway up through the mist and the rain, she turned and said "It looks just like the Isle of Man on a rainy day". A quick stop for soup at the top and it was on again. The descent left her freezing cold all over and lost her the time she had just made on the climb.

The Edinburgh RCC and the local CTC turned out in force to marshal her through and over the Forth Road bridge. By now it was established that she had three and a half hours in hand to beat the record. Through Sunday night and a record number of changes of clothing due to heavy rain. By 4 am she was on the road to Inverness with only 153 miles to do. Timekeeper Moss and experienced record follower Eddie Mundy said the A9 road to the Slochd summit was much improved. The other timekeeper, Nobby Clarke, calculated her average overall speed to this point was 15.8 mph. To break the record she needed to do 10.7 mph to finish.

Soon after this there was almost a one hour delay as she was hallucinating and not feeling at all like going on. However, the former women's Tour de France regular got going again and from there on, despite a painful left buttock, she showed tremendous fortitude. She amazed everyone by starting to pull back time, despite having to negotiate some nasty climbs in the closing stages.

Soon Pauline was riding into the record books and then the champagne corks started to pop. The team of unshaven men and emotional women clamoured round their heroine who was generous in her praises for the tremendous support she had received, from sponsors beforehand, and the back up team during the attempt.

"NOW FOR SOME SHORTER RECORDS" - SAYS PAULINE

IN AN INTERVIEW WITH DENNIS DONOVAN - ASSISTANT EDITOR - CYCLING WEEKLY

Ten hours after finishing her record breaking ride Pauline Strong was back to her old self, cracking jokes as she relived her epic ride. **"At the moment I am aching all over. Most people had already written me off before I started but it was tattooed on my brain that I had to finish - that is if you have a brain at all to do this kind of thing"**, said the 34 year old ex-international.

"I did the last 150 miles by memory. My knees were so swollen that I was unable to bend them, and I was out of the saddle trying to bend them. There were problems from the beginning as well as at the end. We had traffic jams in Cornwall. There was a 13 mile tailback and I wasn't too sure as I weaved my way through, whether someone would

suddenly open a car door on me after they had been waiting for so long. At one point I was two hours down and I was ready to retire. The first night was the worse as I was down on my schedule and I knew there was harder to come.

Helen Edwards was in Warrington and she gave me a kick in the pants and told me to go on Its all her fault that I got the record. One problem was that I was falling asleep on my bike. I did have 20 minutes off the bike and had 10 minutes sleep I am told. When we got to Inverness I asked for a change of clothing. 'I'm not going into town looking like this' I said. I had bandages over my tights and a hood over my head. I looked like Batwoman.

Once I knew I had the record, I began to slow down. It was a horrible feeling and I could do nothing about it. I thought, oh my god, its slipping away from me, its slipping away from me. When I got to John o Groats it was just a sense of relief. I don't think the attempt had sunk in. I was just suffering from exhaustion and lack of sleep. I sat down, we drank some champagne, and then I got into the bath. Having got into the bath, the problem was getting out again. I had a massage, then we all had dinner, but everyone was falling asleep. If I had gone straight to bed I would never have got up again. As it was I had a good night's sleep and now I'm ready to do it all over again !

I shall take three weeks off and going for any more records is not on my mind at the moment. Perhaps, maybe I will try some shorter ones like Cardiff-London, but not anything longer.

It was unbelievable the amount of people who were out. At 3 am you would see someone sitting on a fence and urging me on. All I had to do was ride the bike, my back-up team were fantastic. Some people will say that I didn't ride as far as Eileen did in 1954, and I was aware of that before I started. I set out to do a faster average speed than she did, and if I hadn't beaten that then I would have gone again. I know it's a place to place record and I wouldn't have refused it, but if I had beaten her record by ten hours, it would not have meant the same if I hadn't have gone any faster.

The first thing that I got when I finished was congratulations from Eileen. She gave me lots of tips and advice beforehand and it was almost as if she was glad that I had got it".

There was a slight tinge of regret in Eileen Sheridan's voice when asked for her comments now that her End to End record had been broken. *"No one likes to lose a record" she said "but I loved holding it. I can't grumble I held it for a long while, but I have always said that I knew it could be well and truly smashed, and she's beaten the record well. It was a marvellous ride and she rode through a bad patch early on and fought back. Now that takes guts".*

With new roads, bridges and the like the distance has been reduced by some 25 miles from the 870 miles that Sheridan rode in 1954, and in some people's minds the Sheridan record was a better one. *"Oh dear, you cannot put her record exactly against mine and I'm just proud that she has got it. It had been left on the shelf for far too long. It isn't an easy thing to ride at all, and no-one knows how they will react until they have done it. There were never any doubts in my mind that she would get it. She was the right age, what I would call a strong, strapping girl.*

Its something you never forget. The other end of the ride was worse for me, it was the most difficult part. It was very tiring, I was asleep on my bike and there is a limit to what the body can take. I had no problems through Cornwall and Devon as you are stomping along at the beginning. Everyone involved suffers on the End to End, and do you know I was thinking of Pauline all last weekend, just how long she had been riding. There was I doing the chores, going to bed, then waking up and she was still riding."

Pauline at the time of her End to End record, ran a cycle shop in Caldicot, just over the Severn Bridge in Wales where she lives. Five weeks prior to the attempt she was hit from behind by a car, and broke her collar bone. This meant she could only train on a turbo home trainer. Despite this set back she started as planned. Pauline rode it like she would a 12 hr event, counting down the miles she had done, not the hundreds still to do. She suffered pain from her collar bone and also her back and knees. Her knees were so swollen at one stage, she was advised to consider giving up. She met an old racing partner at Warrington who said 'you must keep going, think how you'd feel if you did pack'. Pauline said she knew she was right.

Aside from the physical discomfort, the mental exhaustion caused its own problems, not least of which was a period of hallucinations - I was seeing dogs at one point ! I remember somewhere around the halfway mark, thinking I wouldn't wish all this on my worst enemy. Now when I recall it, I think "fancy sitting on a bike for two and a half days, I cant believe I did it" ! Pauline went on to thank her willing helpers and officials.

Pauline did go on to break some shorter records. In 1991 she broke the **Cardiff to London with 6 hrs 52 mins 14 secs.** That same year she broke the **100 mile record with 3 hrs 49 mins 42 secs,** and also took 7 mins off Eileen Sheridan's **London to York with 8 hrs 57 mins 42 secs.** Like her End to End it was a record Eileen had kept for over 38 years. In 1992 Pauline went on to take the **12 hour record with 259.5 miles.** With Pauline's first record, the **25 miles in 56m 5secs in 1980** and her very last RRA record, the **50 mile with Ray Hughes on tandem in 1993**, the record being **1hr 34 mins 54 secs,** this concluded a 13 year record breaking career, bringing in all, seven records.

Pauline had been a professional rider for Raleigh for a number of years, having been a regular 'Tour de Feminine' (ladies tour de France) rider. After a successful number of years at road racing, interspersed with time trialling, Pauline produced what I think was her toughest, pluckiest, best-ever ride, the End to End. Considering her training had been thwarted by a broken collar bone which prevented her from using a 24hr race as a useful build up for her record, I think Pauline's ride was also a very brave one.

I saw Pauline at Gailey Island on the Saturday night. I was kept informed as to her progress on the Sunday, and when I rang Roy Moss, the timekeeper in the following car, things didn't look good at all. It was about 10 pm and she was going into the Grampians. Roy said she was struggling with her knees, due to very heavy rain, also she wanted a sleep, but with over 200 miles still to do, Pauline was pushing on so as not to lose any more time.

I went to bed that night re-living our tandem trike ride through the Grampians, but then it was dry for us, even though I had a problem knee like Pauline's. I could just imagine that desolate dark wet road going steadily up over the three summits, and I hoped she would make it, and not succumb to pain and tiredness. In fact you are almost afraid to ring again in case its bad news.

When I found out on Monday morning that she was still going, I knew she stood a good chance, having got that far; then the good news - 'Record broken' by over 4 hours, what a relief, lump in throat, tear in eye; once again the sheer enormity of her ride, against all odds.

One small detail, the mobile phone in Pauline's following car in 1990, was the first to be used on an End to End record. I bet you couldn't slip that one into your pocket !

One amusing incident - the following car got a call on the phone from a woman who said her husband had only gone out to see Pauline pass by, and she hadn't seen him for a day and a half, and did they know of his whereabouts. Alan Strong managed to convey to her that he was alive and well and was following in the convoy.

A year later in August 1991, Pauline tried again to put the record 'on the shelf' - but it wasn't to be. With 500 miles covered, Team Raleigh's Pauline Strong abandoned her attempt although three hours up on the record. We had reached the Warrington area and the wind was due west and getting up to gale-force. **"Our contacts in Edinburgh were surprised that I had got that far as the wind was definitely swinging the wrong way round up there. I was well into the record, covering the 100 miles in 4-35-0 and doing 247 miles for 12 hours, but it was veering from a cross-wind to a headwind on the A74. I wanted to put the record on the shelf for a long time, and it isn't something that I want to do every year. We are hoping to go again either in September or October and we will be talking to Raleigh about the possibilities".** She had set off from Lands End at 8 am on Saturday and by the evening was 30 mins up on schedule, but during the night the weather turned against her. After 24 hours she had covered 430 miles but by Sunday afternoon she was riding into a gale force wind and from a scheduled 17.5 mph she was down to only 10 mph, and the attempt was cancelled.

At the **end of May 1992**, Pauline tried again to reduce her own End to End record to two days. She had an unfavourable wind through Cornwall and was struggling to get back onto her ambitious schedule. In the Taunton area at around 150 miles she fell heavily while taking a sponge and a banana, suffering a cut to the back of her head and bruising of the ribs. Although Pauline only lost three minutes off the bike, the incident clearly upset her rhythm and soon she was 28 minutes down.

She soldiered on into the warm evening, but around midnight it became evident that the record was falling away. She said "I carried on for as long as I could, but my ribs were hurting and it just got so bad in the end that I couldn't breathe properly, and I couldn't put any weight on one side to get out of the saddle to climb. That was when I finally knew it was time to climb off".

At the **end of August** that same year, Pauline made another attempt, and in an article by Ken Mathews entitled ***"Never Again"***, he tells of Pauline's third and final abandonment.

Pauline Strong (Team Raleigh) made a brave attempt to lower her own RRA Lands End to John o Groats record at the weekend, but was forced to abandon after 420 miles at Carnforth. At the time she was about three hours down on her tight schedule which was set at becoming the first woman in history to beat two days for the 840 miles. She still had nearly four hours in hand inside her own record, set in 1990 with 2 days 6 hrs 49 mins and 45 secs, but the strained tendon in her right leg sealed her fate, proving too painful to allow massage. Add to that the constant overnight rain which she said 'chilled her to the bones' and it was a merciful relief when she eventually stopped after a couple of resumptions following pep talks from her husband Alan.

It started so well when she left from the lands End Hotel, and looked good in the early stages as she was about level with the tight schedule. By Exeter (120 miles) she was seven minutes up on schedule and looking well with fine conditions and a helpful breeze. One hundred miles was reached in 4-47-30. She was two minutes outside 10 hours for the 200 miles and as the light was fading she donned night clothing and switched to her other machine, without tri-bars and fitted with powerful halogen lights.

By 8.35pm on Saturday night it was raining heavily and at Gloucester (231 miles) she had pulled back some time and was only two minutes outside her schedule. Twelve hours came up after 236 miles had been covered. A quick halt for a chicken leg at 11.25pm marked a third of the way and the target now was to go for the 24 hour record of 446.5 miles set by Eileen Sheridan in 1954. The 300 mile point was passed in 15 hours and 40 minutes. At Stafford (302) miles in heavy rain she missed her turn into a pedestrianised shopping centre but re-traced after escaping a gang of youths who threatened to pinch her bike when she asked directions. By Newcastle under Lyme town centre she was 33 minutes down on schedule and at 2.30 am she passed the sign into Cheshire. Another rear wheel puncture at 3 am plus report of a pain in the back of her right knee did not help. At Knutsford (341 miles) the deficit was one hour and a decision was made to call in at the home of Prescot Eagle's Ian Murray. Pauline left his home at 5 am after a complete change of clothing and a brief lie down.

The pace was noticeably slow and despite two stops and two pep talks from her husband, she struggled to complete 403 miles in 24 hours. Lancaster bus station at 404 miles, and the arrears were approaching three hours. She still had another four hours left on the schedule to beat her own record but even Alan Strong had to admit it was all over, and at 9.30 am just north of Carnforth at 423 miles he called an end to the attempt.

"Never, never, again" said Strong soon after and this time she appeared to mean it. "If anyone decides to go for my record, I will give them the trophy to save them all that pain I have been through" she added.

Extracts used from Cycling, Ken Mathews and interpretations from myself.

No 32 ANDY WILKINSON 26th SEPTEMBER 1990 BICYCLE END TO END

Andy Wilkinson, 'Wilko' to his friends, at 27 years old, 5' 9", 10.5 stone, started out on September 26th 1990 against all the advice of the 'experts' to tackle the longest place to place record on the RRA's books. The 'Blue Riband' record, Lands End to John o Groats. A member of Port Sunlight Wheelers, an avid tourist and Rough Stuff Fellowship member, a good all round road race man and time trialist. Anfield 100 winner that year, he had already postponed 4 times due to adverse winds and weather and the End to End season was fast coming to a close.

Keith Boardman, father of Chris, was the organiser and was about to call the attempt off for the fifth weekend running, but Wilko had other plans and reckoned he could pull it off. They mustered a helping team who knew Wilko's determination and self belief. He finally got away after a mechanical delay at 10.20 am. One feature of the ride was the heavy rain which started early on and continued well past the Highlands.

Andy was the first to use tri-bars, pulse meter and most importantly 'polymer' or liquid feeding. The traffic down in Cornwall and Devon was so heavy some of the helping cars lost contact with Andy till well past Exeter, heavy mist and rain making road conditions very poor. Pauline Strong, a month earlier had experienced the same heavy traffic conditions.

Wilko didn't stop until he was just south of Bristol, by this time he was soaked through and had a complete change of clothes and due to misty conditions he put his lights on here. When he restarted, John Williams who was the Ride Director reckoned Andy was about 2.5 hours up on a schedule to beat 'Woody's' ride by 16 minutes. The expected adverse winds hadn't arrived, in fact apart from the rain, the winds were quite helpful.

Ken Mathews article tells us **"Andy recalls the heavy traffic in Cornwall forced him to take more risks than normal as he weaved his way past cars stuck in jams. He was just happy that no one opened a car door on him. He was on his own for miles due to the conditions in the West Country. Despite these conditions his first 12 hours produced 266 miles. He didn't rest again until his scheduled stop at Grappenhall after 350 miles at clubmate Ian Murray's house, he was greeted by an army of helpers who gave him a complete change into dry clothes in the kitchen".** At that point he was over 4 hrs ahead of schedule. The planned stop was for 1 hour but Wilko was persuaded to cut it short. Perhaps in hindsight a good decision as further up the road a closed level crossing and a road closed for major repairs required the rider to climb the gate with his bike over his shoulders, cyclo-cross style, over the railway line. Jonathan Williams used his knowledge of the local roads to get the cars back onto the correct route.

"By Wigan 366 miles, he was soaked through again as the heavens opened once more. At Preston 382 miles he was having trouble with a convoy of cars passing him looking for an 'acid house party'. Apparently Pauline Strong had suffered the same nuisance on her ride having to contend with a police helicopter overhead monitoring the situation". I'd forgotten all about 'acid house parties' - I must be showing my age?

Wilko was now starting to take regular toilet stops, he was wearing bib shorts and this made the process take much longer than necessary, also he was having to change clothing on a regular basis due to the heavy rain soaking him through. John Williams recalls stopping at Garstang, Kendal, Penrith, Gretna, Mofatt and Broughton. Peter Keen who was a sports scientist and nutritionalist was consulted, and he suggested reducing Andy's liquid intake, as with the heavy cold rain, Andy had stopped sweating out the fluid intake from his polymer feeds.

"At Lancaster with 69 minutes inside schedule Andy stopped again for dry clothes - Race cape, thermal top and dry gloves. Edwin Hargraves reports 423 miles in 20 hours, will we have a new 24 hr record ? Shap was climbed into a headwind and pouring rain.

Andy was now starting to look a bit rough. They thought about making him have a sleep

but opted instead for him to stop and have beans on toast sheltering under a lorry trailer in a lay by at Penrith". John Williams recalls that Wilko had had a brief sleepy spell near the end of his first 24 hours, but a complete change of clothing by Gretna services and his first drink of coffee soon revived him. The stop at Gretna was enlivened by the arrival of a police patrol car and the Scottish policemen were far from amused by a gang of 'scousers' trying to hide a near naked 'Wilko' trying to struggle out of wet clothing at the side of the main road. **"Andy battled on to produce 489.9 miles for the 24 hrs, so failed to beat John Woodburns figures also produced on the End to End route, of 494.25 miles. On through Moffat and over the devils Beeftub, Andy now looked very grim and it was a worrying time for all the team".**

By this time Wilko was running out of fresh dry clothes, John Williams recalls the Scottish timekeeper Dave Harris, who was to time the finish, suggesting his wife could pick up all of the wet clothing, which by now was quite a considerable amount, take it back to their home in Edinburgh where she commandeered her neighbour's washing machines and tumble dryers to dry the lot. She also took Edwin Hargraves who had observed from south of Bristol to the railway station after another job well done. Edwin at that time was the current secretary of the RRA. The dry clothes were then driven up to Inverness by Dave Harris's wife Margaret, what a saviour.

The heavy rain was now affecting Andy's transmission to a point where on the regular toilet stops, the team had to spray all the moving parts with WD40. When Edinburgh was reached Wilko was just over 4 hours ahead of schedule, which meant he had 6 hours in hand on the record if he maintained his scheduled speed which after Inverness would be 17 mph.

"It was now 2 pm on day two. Andy had a brief stop on the Edinburgh ring road which was still usable by cyclists in those days. He changed into dry clothes so as not to get chilled off going over the Forth Bridge. Jonathan Williams rode a spare bike over behind Andy just in cast of a mechanical failure, but all was well here. Andy seemed to have ridden through a bad patch and had gained a new lease of life. A brief spell of afternoon sunshine was also a great help on this next section to Perth".

Unfortunately by the time he had reached Perth, he was showing definite signs of sleep deprivation. Beyond Perth and now well into the second 24 hours Andy's need for sleep was not put off by more coffee, and near Dunkeld he had to take a brief rest. He responded well and although not as perky as after his first sleep he got to Inverness and the Kessock Bridge for his next stop. Wilko took a 20 mins break and changed into fresh dry clothes delivered from Edinburgh. It was here that he was feeling a lot of soreness and pain in his left knee. At this point he was still 3 hrs 50 mins up on schedule.

John recalls following Andy from this point. The rain had resumed but Andy was making good progress and once over the Cromarty Firth Bridge he was really getting stuck in. After the left turn at Alness he was attacking all the climbs to 'Aultnamain Inn'. Wilko was now demonstrating his roadman skills on the hairy descents around steep wet hairpins in the dark. The following car trying to keep up was aquaplaning on the bends. The occupants of the following car were very relieved when Andy got to Bonar Bridge and on to flatter roads but he was to lose a lot of valuable time on this next section of undulating road. The adrenalin and fight was draining from him.

It was here on the A9 with 756 miles completed that Andy started to falter and fall asleep on the relatively monotonous flat roads. He was still 43 mins up on schedule so a total of 59 minutes in hand. He had another brief stop for approximately 10 mins to have his knees rubbed and a drink of hot coffee but the main problem was he was too tired and sleepy to eat. As his time advantage was quickly slipping away, a decision was made to bully him into keeping going, with the incentive of another sleep at the top of Helmsdale.

At Golspie 777 miles, he was still 40 mins up on schedule but at 3.15 am, he really was starting to struggle. He stopped to change lights, stuff newspapers down his thermal top to keep out the cold. He changed his rear wheel to one which would give him lower gears for the remaining severe climbs of Helmsdale and Berriedale. While he was stopped, the convoy of about 7 cars got ahead for the first time since Inverness so the helpers in turn could give Wilko a good shout on the hard climbs.

On Helmsdale, Andy stopped just short of the summit and refused to go on without sleep. Jim Turner and Ken Mathews decided to give him a wash and rub down and wrapped him in all the blankets they could find to let him sleep in the car. Jim was worried that Andy was becoming hypothermic. After about 30 minutes Andy had gone into a deep sleep and it took what seemed an age to rouse him enough to steer and pedal a bike.

Andy continued with very little enthusiasm and only crept along shivering a lot and struggling to keep a straight line. On Berriedale he began to perk up a bit but appeared to be very confused by literally dozens of mainly very young rabbits scuttling around on the road, several times he ran over rabbits that nearly brought him down.

The next climb at Dunbeath saw his speed fall and Andy was creeping again and complaining about his knee being sore and now obviously swollen.

At Latheron he stopped again to have his knee treated, he desperately wanted sleep. He was refusing all food and drink. After about 20 mins he resumed and after that it was a pattern of slow progress with brief stops at virtually every road junction ! By now the advantage in time had all been frittered away. All calculations now were being made as to how much time remained against the old record.

At Lybster, Dave Harris, said Andy had exactly 2 hours to get to John o Groats, about 27 miles. On the bike, Andy was maintaining 15 to 17 mph, but two more stops before Wick left just 60 mins to do the last 17 hard soul destroying miles.

At last with the finish nearly in sight, Wilko woke up enough to finish without stopping. It was a nail biting climax and nobody knew until the final seconds as to whether he would get the record. He flew over the line at the hotel and collapsed into the arms of the waiting helpers, he was absolutely exhausted.

Timekeeper Dave Harris recorded a 58 second beating of John Woodburn's 1982 record. This is the closest margin anyone has broken the record by, **ever**. A new record of **1 day 21 hrs 2 mins 18 secs.**

"After champagne and then breakfast, served by the kilted manager at the John o Groat's Hotel, Andy had a bath and a 4 hour sleep in a warm bed before being woken up

for an interview for BBC Radio Merseyside, to give a live account of how he achieved his great record. He'd even made the front page of the 'Liverpool Echo' - fame at last" !

On reflection years later, Andy recollects that tri-bars in the latter half of the ride were a mistake to use, as the fixed upper torso and head position lulled him into sleep. Instead of the rider pulling against the tri bars in an aero dynamic 'tuck' position, the tired rider tends to lean on the bars and 'nod off '.

The classic hypothermia symptoms seen in Andy towards the latter quarter of the ride, I've seen him suffer many times since, on practically all of his great rides. His winning 24 hr rides, his record 24 hr of 525 miles, his mixed tandem End to End with Lynne, his winning BBAR 12 hour race; at the end of all these events he's pushed his body so far he collapses in a shivering sleep and has to be covered in blankets to preserve what body warmth he has left. He told me only recently that he doesn't remember hardly any of the last 120 miles of the End to End and didn't realise until the last few minutes that he was so close to missing the record.

He praised his helpers and back up team, Keith and Carol Boardman, also their daughter Lisa who manned the phones. Ken Mathews, John and Jonathan Williams, Jim Turner, and finally his three sponsors 'Cycles Peugeot UK', 'K' Cycles of Eastham and 'Raby' Nurseries where Andy worked with his father, timekeepers Eric Wilkinson and Dave Harris, both of whom have now sadly passed away, and finally observers Bob Williams, Edwin Hargraves and Les Lowe.

At 27 years of age, Andy is one of the youngest riders in modern times to break the record. The very youngest was G.P.Mills in 1886 at 19 years of age in the days of 'paced' records.

Andy was using advice given by Keith Boardman (father of Chris) as to his training for the attempt. Keith had helped Roy Cromack with a training schedule for his epic 24 hr record in 1969. It wasn't based on lots of long hard miles, but used more intense interval type training where no two days or two weeks are the same. Like Cromack, Andy worked full time, so had to fit his training in after work as well as race at weekends. The months prior to his End to End he rode lots of 50's, a few 100's and some very useful 80 or 90 mile road races, either getting high placings or winning every event he rode.

He had to have something constructive to take him through his wait and build up for the End to End. In mid-July he had an appointment in Chichester with Peter Keen who ran a Sports Physio Testing Laboratory. Peter went on to test and coach our National Cycling Squad, taking many riders to Olympic medals and International and Commonwealth honours.

With the intense type of training Andy had been doing plus the riding every weekend, Peter felt that Andy had built up a massive engine that was very efficient at running very fast, but he didn't consider that it would cope with running at a slower speed for a very long duration. He now felt that Andy needed some long steady training miles, so to fit all of this in Wilko had to put the attempt back a month, to suit the training schedule. We must not forget that up until now most of the individuals Peter Keen had prepared were only competing over a fairly short time span with sometimes no more than just a few minutes effort required, so there was no data to look at and compare Andy's efforts with.

In recent years Andy has gone on to break more records including his 525 mile 24 hr in 1997. He won the Anfield 100 seven consecutive times from 1990-1996. He rode a Peugeot cycle fitted with Michelin Hi-lite tyres.

Wilko's latest adventure was appearing on BBC TV in 2003 in a twelve man Hercules Challenge in which he came a very creditable third. The twelve arduous tasks were all designed to be an endurance punishment to a different part of the body on 12 consecutive days, each day lasting up to 7 hours. Andy showed his overall body strength and terrific stamina.

My sincere thanks to Ken Mathews and John Williams for the text and background information on Andy's ride, also with descriptions of the record by 'Cycling Magazine' and comments from Andy and myself.

No 33 RALPH DADSWELL 10th AUGUST 1992 TRICYCLE END TO END

The idea for Ralph Dadswell to tackle the Trike End to End was put into his head by Pauline and Alan Strong. Pauline had broken the women's record in 1990 and was obviously eager to see someone else suffer over this, the longest of record routes. Ralph already had 1991 planned out so it was to be in 1992.

Ralphs already impressive tally of records included Trike 50 miles in 1-45-50 and Trike 100 miles in 3-41-11 in 1990. Trike London to Edinburgh in 19 hrs 27 mins 54 secs in 1991, taking approximately 1 hr 20 mins off Pat Kenny's 1995 figures and the 24 hr record of 447 miles adding 15.5 miles to Pat's 1965 figures. The trike 12 hr record of Stuart Jackson was also broken with 248.75 miles adding 3/8th mile on. Also Jackson's London to Bath and back became Ralph's in 1991, with a ride of 10 hrs 19 mins, a beating by over 14 mins, so he came to 1992 well prepared. In May he travelled north to 'sus' out the route with none other than John Woodburn, with John's partner Anne driving the back up car.

In four days they covered the stretch from Kidderminster to John o Groats on bikes and it gave Ralph a good insight of what lay beyond the border. In June he checked out Lands End to Bristol. Preparations were made and a team of helpers and observers etc was formed. They included Martin Purser, Hedley Stennett and Bob Fotheringham who formed the team to help through Scotland while John Dalton, Audrey and Roger Hughes, Pat Kenny and Tim Dadswell would do south of the border. The ride was generously supported by Radford Sons and Co of Southampton, the sponsors of the Antelope Racing Team.

Ralph has kindly given me permission to use extracts and passages from his own account of his ride updated in 1996.

At 8 o'clock on 10th August 1992 Audrey Hughes timed him away from Lands End. He had to start even closer to the cliff edge as the south door of the hotel was blocked with a coach picking up passengers and cases. After picking his way through the cobbles and obstructions he was finally on his way. As he left the car park he remembered to switch on his computer. The first 10 miles to Penzance Ralph reckons are the twistiest of the ride. Penzance was very busy; the wind he recalls was very helpful. Redruth, Bodmin and Launceston were passed and the 100 miles at beyond Okehampton produced 4 hrs 45 mins , giving 30 mins up on schedule.

Exeter was reached at lunchtime but he got through without delay. The road to Cullompton was poorly surfaced but as it swung round towards Taunton conditions seemed to improve. The miles past Bridgwater Ralph recalls were 'fabulous with wind directly behind me!' Unfortunately the terrain starts to get tough as Bristol is approached. Once over the Mendips at Churchill there are several more vicious ascents before the final freewheel towards Bedminster. A profusion of marshalls guided him off the A38. It is very tricky here to pick out the correct route through this very populated area. On to the Avon Gorge and under the Clifton Suspension Bridge to climb onto the Downs., an area where he had lived as a student. Then a slight descent to Filton and back out onto the A38 again. There was an anxious moment when a motorist decided Ralph was holding him up (on an empty road), he overtook, cut in, then jammed his brakes on for a pedestrian crossing, causing Ralph to swerve to avoid him.

Two hundred miles had been covered in less than 10 hrs. He was still 30 minutes ahead of schedule. There now followed another terrific section of tailwind riding. The road to Gloucester was also memorable for the number of supporters who had turned out to see him. Ralph recalls over that 25 mile stretch there were people every mile. Pauline Strong handed him up a bag of seedless grapes, which were very refreshing when he eventually managed to get them out of the bag. Ralph hadn't mastered the art of riding the trike 'no handed', an impossibility I would have thought.

Several miles later Ralph spotted seven of his work colleagues who had travelled across from High Wycombe to give him a shout and a cheer. It was great for him to see some familiar faces, they had produced some banners and they have even developed a cheer-leading routine. They by-passed him several times using the M5 and saw him all the way to Stafford.

By Tewkesbury at 8 pm, Ralph had covered 240 miles in 12 hours. Tim, his brother, joined the helping team here with hot food from the Tewkesbury 'chippy'. Clothes and lights were stopped for at Worcester, on towards Kidderminster where a short sharp but heavy rain shower quickly demoralised him. Fortunately it was brief and Ralph convinced himself that it wasn't going to rain again for the whole remainder of the ride. Its amazing what goes through your mind on a record attempt of this magnitude.

Pat Kenny joined the ride at Wolverhampton providing them with experience and an extra car, thus reducing the pressure on the others. 300 miles were completed by Stafford in 15 hrs 35 mins, still over 20 mins up on schedule. At Stafford, the local club lads tried to marshall him around the ring road instead of his chosen planned route through the pedestrianised area. This threw him a little but he soon recovered.

At Newcastle under Lyme he started to feel very sleepy and so immediately took a 10 minute cat nap in the car. He continued towards Holmes Chapel and Knutsford completely refreshed. By now the wind had dropped causing him to lose his earlier gains on schedule. By Warrington he was 10 mins down, but numerous marshalls on route at 3 am raised his spirits and kept him on course through Wigan and Preston. He was still losing time, arriving at Lancaster 35 mins down. This, Ralph says, was not a major concern as the schedule was (theoretically) to beat the record by 4 hours. He could afford to lose time as long as it didn't get out of hand. The 400 miles had taken 22 hours. As daylight returned Ralph started to feel a bit depressed. There was no wind and he seemed to be riding rather sluggishly.

He told the team he wasn't sure whether he wanted to continue, as there was still over 400 miles to go. Their reaction was obviously to shake him out of that idea. He realised he wouldn't be able to improve on his own 24 hr record of 447 miles, so he wanted to stop soon for a wash, fresh clothes and a massage. At Carnforth, Martin, Hedley, Bob and Roger joined the entourage, however Ralph didn't exactly welcome them as he was still in his 'slough of despond'!

He took his break at Kendal at approximately 7.15 am, and after being re-vitalised he set off again, this time on Tim's trike with a wider range of gears as his own only had a bottom gear of 58". He completed 428 miles in 24 hours. He used the low gears to good advantage to give him an easier more relaxed climb of Shap Fell. The weather at the top was unusually quite pleasant. Ralph took a feed at the top and just as he was finishing his sandwich he sheared the inner ring off the chainset. After a brief delay he was reunited with his own trike which he'd discarded less than an hour earlier. Ralph set off for Penrith wondering what the team would do with the disabled machine. As it turned out the decision was made to buy a new chainset at the bike shop in Carlisle. Pat and Tim returned home having done their stint.

The weather turned for the worst at Carlisle with heavy rain making the trip on the A74 a very unpleasant one. 500 miles was completed in 28 hrs 20 mins at Beattock and the A74 is left behind as Ralph turns towards Edinburgh. After swapping back to Tim's machine he bounded up the Devils Beeftub climb in 16th gear. His enthusiasm was soon dampened by another heavy downpour which flooded the road. Fortunately it was short lived and as he approached Edinburgh the sun shone at last. Feeling drowsy Ralph took another 10 mins sleep here. Along this stretch he was musing at the job ahead of him. He was fairly relaxed and he decided to deal with the 'Grampians' after a good nights sleep. It sounded like a good idea as he's already covered a lot of ground, then of course it struck him, he couldn't do that. The whole point is not to stop. This shook Ralph up a bit.

He hit the Edinburgh ring road at 4.30 pm and it was busy. After a feed taken at high speed he negotiated several well marshalled roundabouts to join the A90 to the Forth Road Bridge. After crossing the bridge he noticed he'd picked up a large stone in one of his rear tyres so stopped for a wheel change. This proved difficult as the wheel wouldn't come off the trike, however after about 5 mins the job was done and he was off towards Cowdenbeath, where the road had been freshly 'tarred and chipped' earlier in the day. Ralph got a bit confused when confronted with two roads ahead, both saying Cowdenbeath, but realised in time that one was for heavy lorries. It was now a steady drizzle as he carried straight on through enormous puddles and under overcast skies.

John and Audrey had stopped earlier for a break at Moffat having been driving and on duty for 500 miles. They rejoined the entourage on the road from Cowdenbeath to Kinross. After another brief check on the map they left a deserted Kinross behind and began descending Glenfarg towards Perth. This stretch of road was probably last resurfaced before it was replaced by the M90. It is now (1992) in a disgraceful state and even though largely downhill, it was highly unpleasant on a tricycle. Finding a smooth line for three wheels was impossible.

After the sharp climb from the 'Bridge of Earn' Ralph arrived at Perth having passed the 600 mile point in 34 hrs 50 mins, one hour and 40 mins behind schedule. Ralph recalls " some months before, John Woodburn had quoted to me that 'any fool can get to Perth', rather harsh

I thought but at least I've passed that test ". At least he had retained his sense of humour up to this point.

The next target was the summit of the Pass of Drumochter, 50 miles ahead; first though he had to negotiate a rough stretch of the A9 to Dunkeld. Once there he stopped for lights and extra clothing. After Pitlochry darkness fell and by Blair Atholl it was definitely night, with the hint of a headwind. Somehow, including the stop for lights etc, he had lost more time and was now just over two hours down. It's a steady 15 mile climb to the summit and Ralph in his mind had split it into 3 sections. The first is around the Blair By pass to Calvine; then you climb for five miles to Dalnacardoch Lodge where the dual carriageway starts and finally you strain your eyes for five miles watching for the sign to 'Dalnaspidal Lodge'. When this finally happens you know you are near the top with just two miles to go. By that time your enthusiasm is up and ready for the descent.

Ralph reached the summit at 11.25 pm, 2 hrs 10 mins down on schedule. Ralph recalls "There then followed perhaps ten miles of descent, but it wasn't steep enough to freewheel down. This was confusing because I'd freewheeled down it in May. I seemed to be slowing dramatically whenever I stopped pedalling. I might as well have been still climbing for the effort I was putting in !" Passing Dalwhinie, Newtonmore and Kingussie, he was feeling sleepy again and so took another 10 minutes break.

The road now starts to climb and he optimistically presumed he was on the run up to the Slochd Summit, however after several miles of easy climbing he recognised the hotels of Aviemore. What a drag - the real work hadn't even started. If Drumochter had seemed a long time coming then the Slochd Summit signs took forever. Ralph still felt good and was climbing quite positively; he hadn't been off the big 48 tooth chainring since Cowdenbeath, however, after three or four false ends he knew that the summit had got to come soon, or he would be at risk of fading.

At last it was there and he began the freewheel to Inverness or so he thought. Life isn't that easy and simple! There are two interruptions to the downhill slope to Inverness and the second one brought him down to walking pace. 700 miles passed in 42 hours, about 2 hrs 10 mins down, but of course still comfortably ahead of the record. Eventually the lights of Inverness appeared, at about 3.30 am - what a set of lights. He was convinced that there must have been an all night celebration going on, as everything seemed to be fully illuminated, however, when he finally reached the Kessock Bridge, it was clear that nothing was going on as the only sign of life was a solitary marshall pointing the way for him. He climbed the bridge as it goes up in a large arc; he was down to 8 mph. Once over he zoomed onto the Black Isle where there is the prospect of over 5 miles of climbing.

Ralph was now suffering from hallucinations, a common feature for many riders when you investigate their accounts of an End to End. He recalls 'any traffic which may have kept me company as far as Inverness had now disappeared, consequently, the hallucinations which had surfaced sporadically now became more intense. I had already become accustomed to seeing people ahead with drinks who turned into trees etc. The ultimate vision was the group of four people in the lay by. As I approached they turned into three plants and a sack of rubbish. Another quote from Mr Woodburn sprang into mind at this stage. He had said in his sage-like way "when you start, all you want to do is beat the record. When you get to Inverness you know you're going to make it, then you can start thinking about how much you'll knock off the record". Personally, I think that a home-straight of 120 miles is something more than a formality !

Meanwhile I was climbing towards the roundabout at Tore. I was given advance warning of the roundabout by a huge sign saying that there was one mile to go. Several minutes later, there was another huge sign, this time it was half a mile to go. Around the bend and there was the final approach with another giant sign. After all that preparation, there were no cars, just a solitary marshall'.

Ralph was now getting more and more affected by tiredness and sleep deprivation. He worries about the bridge going across the Cromarty Firth. He says 'I knew there was a bridge, however, I couldn't see the bridge as I tore (Ha Ha) down the slope. I got so worried and I wondered what to do if the bridge wasn't there any more. I guess I was tired'. Once over the bridge he took a short break and was told that to break the record by 2 hrs 30 mins he had got to average 15 mph for the final 105 miles.

The road to Tain was ridden at 15 mph and then Ralph made history by being the first End to Ender to cross the new bridge over the Dornoch Firth. Crossing this bridge effectively cuts 7 miles off the journey. It is obviously worth 30 mins off the record so Ralph wanted to make sure he broke it by at least that much to feel that he had done a better ride.

The ride from Golspie to Helmsdale had Ralph struggling over the light undulations. Suddenly a problem developed in his left ankle. For a while he panicked and then tried the exercises he knew had overcome his previous Achilles problem. By Helmsdale the pain had subsided but there was a definite swelling. He had planned a triumphant romp up the climbs of Helmsdale and Berriedale but had to settle for any easy gear so as not to aggravate his injuries.

It was here at the top of Helmsdale with the mist closing in that Ralph describes the start of his final 'forty miles of delusions!' "Visibility fell alarmingly, I guess my delusions started here. After several miles I believed that I had been through Berriedale but had somehow not noticed it. This idea was soon ditched, as the road suddenly dropped away and I started to accelerate. I had forgotten that my brakes would be wet. You can imagine my alarm as I approached the escape lane and couldn't stop. After a short time I was able to slow down. As with Helmsdale, Berriedale was carefully done, I was chatting with Roger Hughes (who was running) as I went up the hill. He says this was the last sensible conversation I made until after the finish. The weather was now pretty grim. It seems that a depression was not behaving as forecast (how inconsiderate); instead of keeping well out of my way, it was providing me with a wet easterly wind off the sea.

I cannot be sure of quite what went wrong but my brain seemed to be playing tricks on me. I was looking out for Latheron followed by Dunbeath. I knew to recognise Dunbeath by the bridge across the valley, so imagine my surprise when I saw the signs for Dunbeath but no bridge. In fact you don't see the bridge until you're almost on it and so I was left wondering what had happened to Latheron. I remembered a sign before Latheron saying 39 miles to John o Groats. My computer indicated that I had passed the 30 miles to go point, so I was very confused. I decided Latheron must still be up the road, I suppose eventually I must have got there. As I passed the B & B bungalow, I saw someone look out of the window and so I waved. I wonder if the connection was made between a bedraggled tricyclist and the person who stayed there in May promising that he would do Lands End - John o Groats on a three wheeler.

Shortly after that I became unhappy with the road I was on, surely I've been along here before. I decided to stop and look at the map. Hedley assured me that I was going in the right direction on the right road and I hadn't been there before. Unconvinced, I carried on. Lybster is a bit of a blur but I do remember the signs for the 'Portland Arms Hotel'. The conditions now were so miserable that I decided that I couldn't still be on the record attempt. Hence, logically I must have already finished and I must now be dreaming or something? However, I was trying to be logical, so if I had finished then I am sure I would know my finish time, and I didn't know that. Also the wind and rain were rather realistic; no, I decided that I wasn't dreaming; this was real life. Reluctantly I pressed on but not for long.

I soon stopped and demanded to know what was going on.. Why was I out on my trike when they were all sitting in the van ? I bet they're loving this, sitting in there laughing at me getting blown around and soaked. Why can't I get in the van or why aren't they out here with me ? Martin did his best to explain. Audrey tried as well "what have you been doing for the last two days Ralph" "getting the End to End" "well you haven't got it yet. You have to get to John o Groats first !" Silence.

I continued for a bit further, then stopped to complain about the weather. John assured me that in a couple of miles I'd stop climbing and I'd get a tailwind run in to Wick. Unconvinced again, I continued, less than a quarter heartedly. By this time the team were wondering what was wrong with me and had considered the possibility of hypothermia. Fortunately they didn't tell me.

At Wick my brain must have recovered slightly and I left the town still on the A9 with 17 miles left, then started to look for the right turn towards John o Groats. At a junction which was obviously not the right one, I turned around in the road and had another look at the map. I really can't believe what is happening, as I knew the course perfectly before starting. I was told to look for the junction in a placed called Reiss. I continued. That right turn meant the weather and wind was against me and I began stopping regularly without good reason. I was also sure that I was on the wrong road.

My prior recollections of the Wick to John o Groats stretch were of peat fields and telegraph poles. There were none of either. To add to the confusion, helpers from different cars would tell me different mileages whenever I stopped. This fuelled my paranoia about being on a wild goose chase. The words 'John o Groats' now meant nothing to me. Several times I was implored to ride along just over the next hill, then you can finish. This continual promise of the will o the wisp finish enhanced my suspicions about the motives of these people around me. I seemed to be on a conveyor belt being soaked by a perpetual shower.

The team were having more and more trouble getting me to restart. At one point I rode into a side road and then into a field entrance. Martin despairingly asked me to get back on the road and told me to carry on. I just wanted to do anything to make them let me get into the van. At around this time, Audrey, the timekeeper switched into scolding school teacher mode. She informed me that she had gone for two days without sleep to get me this far, and I was not to mess things up now ! Funny - no response from Ralph ! She told me that all I had to do was ride along this road. I asked how far I had to go. She said to continue until I saw a large hotel at the end on the left. I didn't really understand what the fuss was about. I actually worked out that she meant the John o Groat's hotel. I still didn't know why she wanted me to get there.

Martin and Audrey were running alongside me now, Roger also ran but had to take his shoes off as they were getting uncomfortable. I think that routine happened several times, with Audrey being accompanied by any one of Martin, Hedley or Bob. Martin tells me he ran for 2 miles not having slept for 30 hours and that coming straight after riding a 12 hour race. Audrey must have run for miles - What a Star ! At one point, I was handed.the mobile phone and told to speak to my dad. Even this failed to convince me of anything. I wasn't even positive that I was talking to who they said I was!

Eventually we saw the John o Groats novelty house where many riders have started to burn it up at this stage. No reaction from me. I see from photos that I passed the John o Groats sign - I don't remember it. John now drove ahead with Hedley to get to the finish. It seems that I then started to go faster although it is downhill. No sooner had Hedley stood on the finish line than I came around the final corner towards the hotel. I was pleased to get there, as Audrey had promised that I could get in the van at the hotel.

I had no conception that I had now finished the record attempt. I also had no idea of the time. It turned out that I had taken **2 days 5 hours 29 mins** and had beaten Eric Tremaine's 1982 time by 49 mins 35 secs.

Things flooded back to my brain as people shook my hand and congratulated me. Suddenly it all made sense. Oh dear - why oh why had I wasted all that time ?"

The latter stages of Ralph's ride were very similar to Andy Wilkinson's except that Andy did have hypothermia. Andy, years later remembers being very confused from Tain onwards, and also kept stopping, not knowing that he was on a record attempt where every second counts. Luckily in both cases the record was broken; Ralph's by at least the margin he wanted for the shorter mileage because of the new bridge, and Andy's was by 58 seconds !

Ralph suffered no lasting effects from his ride, although his ankle plagued him for a week or two and he had 'pins and needles' in his hands which is quite a common complaint with cyclists of all age groups. It is caused by minor damage of the nerves that run through the carpal tunnel in the wrist. Ralph says following treatment he will probably live !

He rode tubular tyres on his 'Longstaff' two wheel drive trike with gears ranging from 58.5" to 117" and on Tims trike the Scottish section was covered with a top of 93" and a bottom low enough to climb 'Ben Nevis'. (Now there's an idea !) His feeding regime was flavoured Maxim carbo polymer drinks plus sandwiches, rice pudding , bananas, sultana's. Coffee and brandy were consumed towards the end in small quantities.

His tally of records done including his End to End up to present day is 34 in all, including 10 ridden with Marina Bloom on Tandem Trike. I would think at present day he has broken the most RRA records ever, bettering Eileen Sheridan's total of 28.

The End to End obviously hasn't blunted Ralph's enthusiasm and the records broken since are:

His own Trike record 12 hrs 3 times 1995 251.6 miles 1995 257.5 miles 1996 266.3 miles

London - York	1995	8-42-20	Approx	23 mins off Duffields 1961 record
York - Edinburgh	1996	8-39-43	"	9 mins off J Arnolds 1963 "
London - Liverpool	1995	8-56-59	"	53 mins off J Arnolds 1952 "
Liverpool - Edinburgh	1994	9-54-29	"	26 mins off J.L.Kay 1986 "
Lands End - London	1996	13-16-13	"	48 mins off S Jacksons 1981 "
London-Pembroke	1995	11-33-58	"	54 mins off E Hargraves 1976 "
London-Cardiff	1996	6-45-59	"	2m 36 secs off D Pitt 1978 "
London - B'ham	1994	4-48-49	"	17 mins off D Pitt 1987 "
Pembroke-Great Yarmouth	1997	17-54-06	"	21 mins off J Hopper 1996 "
London-Brighton-London	1997	4-50-44	"	23 secs off D Pitt 1979 "

Tandem Trike records with D Johnson 1999 London to Brighton and back
2000 London to Portsmouth and back

Tandem Trike records with Marina Bloom in 2000, 2001, 2003/4 : No less than 10 in all, including one 'grand slam' where they broke 4 records in one ride:

London - York 12 hr with 264.2 miles London - Edinburgh 24 hr of 447.9 miles.

As you can see, Ralph certainly seemed to have 'lost the plot' at the end of his Lands End to John o Groats record . He is normally a very astute calculating rider and his account of the ride openly shows what over two days without sleep can do to a person. Even a very strong willed person like Ralph can be tricked almost into submission by tiredness. He had already 'imagined' taking a nights sleep at Edinburgh in readiness for the Grampians, but then realised he couldn't do that. I think a lot of credit must go to his team of helpers for their untiring persuasion over that last 12 hours to help him realise his most courageous record so far.

My thanks to Ralph for this very honest and witty description of his ride, with extra details and record data from myself.

No 34 JODI GROESBECK and ADRIAN HARRIS 5th AUGUST 1998 MIXED TANDEM

Mixed Tandem RRA Standard time to beat 72 hrs

Adrian and Jodi's build up for the mixed tandem End to End attempt started some three years prior to 1998. They were lucky in that they were naturally compatible on a tandem, although Jodi lived in New Hampshire USA and Adrian in New Jersey, which limited the amount of training they could fit in together.

Almost from the start of their successful tandem partnership, Jodi 'captained' the front of the tandem and Adrian was the 'stoker'. Adrian prefers the feeling of pushing a big gear which is the sensation one gets on the back of a tandem, purely due to the position of the saddle to the pedals, whereas Jodi preferred a normal position turning the gear easily. The second advantage with Adrian being English, navigating the End to End route on a map was easier on the back of a tandem where steering isn't a problem.

Adrian says Jodi is the more talented rider and she had many cycling accolades including twice winning the 'National Masters Cyclo-cross championship' which gives her brilliant bike

handling ability. Their tandem riding and training in the USA didn't include any set time trial distances but was composed mainly of 200, 400 and 600 K 'Brevets' or Audax style rides. Rowing and Kayaking gave Jodi her upper body strength to handle the tandem so well.
Both Jodi and Adrian have completed the RAAM (Race across America) 3000 miles from coast to coast on solo bikes. They hold the mixed tandem course record for the Michigan National 24 hr, but their greatest ride was Paris Brest Paris in 1999, completing the 1200 K in 49 hrs 16 mins, so sleep wasn't a problem for either of them

Adrians only other experience of RRA record attempting was with Gerry Tatrai in 1997 when they were attacking the 2 days 2 hrs 14 mins 25 secs record set by Swinden and Withers back in 1966, but Adrian said they hadn't got the right wind and they packed on Shap.

The tandems they used were 'Santana' both made in California, one made of aluminium with Shimano 105 8 sp triple gearing and the main one they used was made of titanium with Shimano Ultegra 27 speed gearing. Both tandems had Vredestein 700 x 25 Fortezza Tyres but in hindsight, Adrian thinks a 28mm section tyre would have been more comfortable and possibly faster over the rough sections of the road prior to Bristol and the A9 after Perth. Their food for the first few hundred miles was made up of American brand names such as 'GU' 'Powergel' 'Ensure' and 'Cytomax' all probably carbo and electrolyte products. Adrian admits to the dietary plans falling apart mid way and resorting to chicken sandwiches, crisps, chocolate, baked beans on toast. At the time of the ride, Jodi was 39, approximately 5ft 8" and weighed 9 stone. Adrian was 38, 5 ft 11" and 10 st 2 lbs.

They came over to England on a fortnight's holiday; Adrian's wife Tricia who had helped him on many rides was the only US member of the helping team. Other members of the team who Jodi and Adrian are indebted to are, Lee Bullock, Peter Davies, and Lynn & Mike McElheron. Apart from Lee who had helped on his RAAM, the rest of the team were new to it and didn't realise what they were letting themselves in for. The officials on the team comprised of Albert Ayton, Jean Bayliss, Alan Griffiths, Reg Randall and Dai Davies, the timekeeper.

When they arrived in the UK on the Saturday, Adrian phoned Phil Leigh for a weather report. Phil himself was an End to End aspirant and at the time was studying meteorology at Lancaster University. The beginning of the week gave west to north west winds for the first week with wet south west winds in Scotland. By Wednesday they would be over the jet-lag so decided to go with a westerly wind. On their drive down to Lands end on the A30, Jodi who was to steer the tandem had her first sight of busy holiday traffic on an English dual carriageway. She was horrified as to what they were letting themselves in for, plus this is one of the hilliest stretches of the course, nearly 7000 ft of climbing in the first 117 miles.

On August 5th 1998, they started their attack on the RRA standard set at 72 hours, or 3 days exactly. They departed Lands End Hotel south door at 9.00 am and headed for Penzance 10 miles away. The first RRA checker they saw was Elaine Hancock, who had seen Adrian the previous year on the men's attempt. Adrian said he couldn't hazard a guess at Elaine's age, but to see her with walking sticks and shouting encouragement brought a lump to his throat and tears to his eyes. He says there is no describing the lift you get as you pass checkers at all hours and locations during the ride, their encouragement and helpful directions are what makes record breaking in Britain so appealing.

The wind at this point was blowing lightly from the north west and so is against them although they still made good progress. Feeding a tandem pair can be quite a daunting affair for the helpers. Two lots of food and drink, the tandem quite often going faster than a solo.

Jodi and Adrian were using the camel-back drinks system instead of the usual bottles. This is a slim two or three litre bag with a drinking tube. The bag is held in a lightweight rucksack on one's back. The tube routes itself towards ones chin and has a valve at the end so that the liquid can be sucked through when needed. The only advantage of this system over a bottle is that one can take a drink without using ones hands. The helper either Tricia or Lynn would hand up a bag containing 2 camel backs and food items to Adrian on the back. The 'stoker' puts on his camel back first, fills both persons pockets with food and then puts the 'captains' camel back on for her.

The wind now swung and came from the west which enabled them to reach Exeter at an average of 21 mph. They had got here faster than scheduled and had beaten the marshalls and checkers, so had to negotiate the city alone with 6 sets of traffic lights and 8 roundabouts, not an easy job. Adrian was worried that Jodi wouldn't cope with the city traffic, but she handled it well. The next few towns Cullompton, Taunton, Bridgwater and Highbridge were all negotiated between 3pm and 6 pm amidst very heavy traffic.

They were both now being hampered by traffic fumes affecting their breathing. They had planned to switch tandems at 150 miles for Jodi to have a break on the back, but it was decided the advantages were much greater with Jodi on the front and they continued as they were, although shortly after Taunton the rough roads had loosened Jodi's tribars and they were forced onto the other tandem while the bars were being fixed. This meant Adrian had to negotiate Bristol from the front and remembers not doing a very good job, coming off the Long Ashton bypass too early and having to go round a roundabout several times while he thought fruitlessly of where he could possibly be. By now they were both nauseated and stopped to ask the helpers 'which way ?'

Back on track once more they were confronted by a bridge closure and massive traffic jams which caused another 15 mins lost before they went under the magnificent Clifton Suspension Bridge and onto more familiar territory. By the time they had rejoined the A38 north of Bristol at Filton 202 miles their speed had dropped to 20 mph and it was now 7pm, but at least its getting cooler and quieter on the roads.

They stop now for night clothes as Jodi feels the cold more than most. The A38 road runs through Gloucester, Tewkesbury and up to Worcester, and all of these towns were familiar to Adrian, who had lived with his wife Tricia for two and a half years at Stratford upon Avon. The road is fairly flat and they arrived at Worcester at 10 pm to see welcoming banners saying 'Good luck Adrian and Jodi'. It lifted their flagging spirits as they entered their first night of riding.

When they got to the other side of Wolverhampton they were meant to have a change of RRA personell and helpers, also swapping back to the original tandem for Jodi to steer again. After a bit of a mix up with liason positions the swap was completed. Reg Randall who had come up from Lands End with them asked if he could stay on as a helper and the team was more than happy to have his help and advice. Reg broke the solo bicycle record in 1958 and at the time of this tandem record he still held the 1000 miles record. Albert Ayton was to stay on to

Carlisle where Dai Davies would come on board. Alan Griffiths who himself held tandem records was to stay as Observer to Edinburgh where Reg would once again take over.

We are now entering one of the most densely populated areas of the country and if it was ridden in daylight hours, the progress would be slow, with massive peak hour traffic to contend with. There is no better way to view these northern towns than under darkness of night. But then this is the industrial heart of England, the Black Country, Staffordshire, Warrington, Wigan, Preston, with club folk out on route to see them through. Adrian said he felt most at home here.

He noticed his computer reading 15 mph under good street lighting and a full moon. This always seems to be the phenomena when you feel you should be doing 'evens'. It is nowadays only the solo bike riders who can produce over 20 mph for the first day, in fact, for them it's a case of having to, to beat the previous record holder.

By Warrington at 4.00 am, the absence of the feed van was starting to worry the riders. At Preston 5 am still no feed van, Adrian is very worried at this point and stopped to call his parents who were acting as phone info HQ. It turned out the van had broken down at Knutsford, but was now back in service and trying to catch up. So although not perfect, everything is fine and they continued their ride stopping periodically to get food from the following car which was easier said than done. The food appeared to be well hidden away beneath clothing etc, and the riders ended up eating the officials and helpers own sandwiches until the van caught up.

They were now taking more than regular toilet stops, I think due to too much liquid intake. This is quite a common thing in the night when its cooler and the rider hasn't cut down on liquid consumption, and isn't sweating out the liquid.

At about 7 am they enter Lancaster to be greeted by Phil and Janette Leigh. These are the last few miles leading up to the last major climb in England - Shap Summit, and then Shap village where the previous year the men's tandem attempt by Adrian and Gerry Tatrai terminated. Adrian was by now looking forward to showing Jodi one of the most beautiful areas of England ,'the Lake District' however it was not to be. In Kendal they hit a band of rain which accompanied them into low clouds onto Shap summit, where they changed into warm dry clothing ready for the descent. So that the riders could change in a nice warm vehicle, the helpers had to stand outside in the cold wind and rain, some of them were just in shorts and 'T' shirts. After a cold wet descent they rode back into dry warm weather again at the bottom calling for a change back into shorts and racing kit. Through Penrith and on to Carlisle where the feed vehicle had to wait at the station to pick up Dai Davies whose train was running late.

Adrian adds "The final six miles in England are on what I consider to be the worst road of the route. The A74 is just an extension of the M6 but without an adequate hard shoulder". He goes on to say "If you want to get the feeling of the A74, ride for 6 miles on the 'New Jersey Turnpike' at rush hour without using the breakdown lane or hard shoulder. Better still ride in the fast lane against the concrete barrier. Just for fun, throw in a stiff crosswind and have the drivers see how close they can get to you" !

An extract from RRA observer Alan Griffith's report says: "Caught riders on the A74 at a bridge over the river Esk, riders were just dismounting. Citroen help vehicle unable to stop due to very dense traffic and atrocious weather conditions. We were able to pull into a lay by half a mile further on and the riders having seen us pass, came to us. They were quite distressed due to the weather and severe buffeting and spray from a continual stream of HGV'S".

Adrian continues "By the time we left the A74 at Gretna the first village in Scotland on the B7076, I was mentally exhausted from our ordeal. I had just enough energy to give Jodi a brief history of Gretna Green before suggesting a few minutes break to regain my composure. Gretna Green is the famous town to which young lovers would elope and marry without permission of their parents., In 1753 a new law in England passed by Lord Hardwicke made runaway marriages illegal. It did not take long for the young couples to realise that as soon as they crossed the Scottish border, nothing could prevent their marriage. The Scottish law demanded only that the couple proclaim in front of two witnesses that they wanted to get married and a legal marriage from that moment on was recognised in all countries".

The riders stopped for a brief rest and a meal of baked beans on toast at a transport café at Kirkpatrick Flemming. The café was full of smoking truck drivers but Adrian said "The smoke filled air seemed pleasurable after the car exhausts we had inhaled during the previous 500 miles. Those beans on toast, tea and second hand smoke proved to be the highlight of the trip". On this section of the road they were heading into a westerly wind so it was a good job they had 'fuelled up' for this flat stretch of road through Lockerbie and onto Johnstone bridge where a quieter section of the A74 is rejoined to take us to Moffat at the base of the 'Devils Beeftub' which for Jodi and Adrian was a perfect climb into spectacular scenery for Jodi to appreciate. Up over the top and then a fast descent. After 33 hours into the ride Jodi suggests a sleep for an hour. After 40 minutes we wake her and tell her she's had an hour and that we should make the most of the remaining daylight hours to get beyond Edinburgh.

Shortly after they re-started, still following the A701 towards the Edinburgh ring road they were faced with a road closure and had to take a detour which put approximately another 5 miles onto the journey, as if it isn't long enough ! The traffic on the Edinburgh ring road at 7.00 pm was still heavy and large electronic signs across all three lanes proclaiming 'tiredness kills' greeted the riders. By 7.45 pm they were crossing the 'Firth of Forth'and on through Cowdenbeath towards Perth, the gateway to the Scottish Highlands.

A beautiful narrow winding tree-lined descent and then a flat 10 mile run took them into Perth where Adrian's navigational skills failed him once again, requiring a slight detour back onto the correct road and then onto the A9 and into the second night to Inverness. This part of the route contains some of the most depressing climbs, one never knowing whether the summit has been reached or not, tricks of the light and tiredness leaving the riders struggling with the effort.

Adrian recalls "This is a beautiful region of Britain, but we are unable to appreciate it being almost dark. The A9 by passes every town from Perth to Inverness and I wish we could detour through them to break the monotony". Along this stretch Adrian was happily pedalling along on the back looking down at the bottom bracket when he noticed out of the corner of his eye, Jodi's arms stretched out wide. He suggested she replaced both hands on the bars, and reassured her that she could practice no-handed tandem riding any amount she wanted as long as he wasn't 'stoking'.

A few miles further on towards the Drumochter Summit the wind had completely disappeared. The only thing slowing their progress was very tired legs and a very rough road surface. Every few yards they disturb a group of rabbits off to the side of the road, the bike lights disturbing their play.

Once over Drumochter a slow descent takes them to the bottom of Slochd ready for the next climb which is only marginally more difficult than the descent. The last 70 miles had been covered at approximately 10 mph leaving the riders frustrated with their progress. Dropping down from Slochd Summit to the Kessock Bridge was good, achieving a top speed of 45 mph although Adrian felt they should have topped 55 mph in the given conditions.

Over the Morray Firth with 120 miles to go with spirits uplifted they were no more than a Sunday club ride away from the finish. After crossing the Cromarty Firth they picked up a tailwind. The problem with thinking you're nearly there with 7 hours pedalling is that time can go very slowly. The anticipation of the climbs of Helmsdale and Berriedale was enough to keep them interested. Adrian said he would have quite happily walked the climbs but Jodi being a US National Ladies hill climb champion, made it clear that walking was not an option.

After Berriedale the road becomes a rolling coast road and the riders really wanted it to be over quickly, but it took them another three agonizing hours. By far the worst section being the last 17 miles from Wick. Maybe if they had an actual record time to beat rather than a standard of 72 hours there would have been more pressure to push hard those final miles. They arrived at the finish after **2 days 8 hrs 28 mins** at 5.28 pm, and nearly 850 miles after leaving Lands End due to the detours and extra miles while getting lost in towns.

Dai Davies greeted them both with a customary pint of beer. After congratulations and photos an early bed seemed like a good idea. They had broken the RRA standard by 15 hrs 31 mins and 10 secs. After a few days recovery and relaxation, they flew back to the States having left a very good record on the books to be beaten.

What a remarkable achievement in just a few days overcoming jet lag and negotiating roads and traffic the length and breadth of Britain.

I asked Adrian if the End to End record got any acclaim or publicity in American cycling circles and he replied ' even less than in England'. At least we appreciated it, but then it is part of our cycling history, being one of the first organised competitive rides to be chronicled as far back as 1885.

With regard to Jodi and Adrian's P.B.P. Audax result, Adrian says *"We rode the P.B.P in 1999. I recall our time being 49.16, but I see it listed in some places as 49.03. Supposedly, the previous mixed tandem record was 49.29 by Gillet and Seurin, established in 1951. However, there is some debate over this. We set this time as our target and were happy to beat it. At least on the day our time was recognised as a record. However, several months later there was an article in the French press saying that the 1951 record had been mis-recorded and we had actually missed the record by 3 minutes! I have never successfully clarified this issue. Neither Jodi or I are currently riding. Jodi is enjoying her new role as a mother (she adopted a Chinese girl a little over a year ago) and I have been messing around with a variety of events; long distance orienteering, the Sahara marathon, adventure racing etc. I miss the cycling though, so I may get back on the bike this coming year 2005".*

My thanks to Adrian Harris for his ride description and comments.

No 35 ANDY WILKINSON and LYNNE TAYLOR 13th MAY 2000
MIXED TANDEM END TO END

The one and only 24 hour race left on the calendar, the famous Mersey Road Club 24 hr has attracted many famous riders over the years. I would go as far as to say that since the 1950's and certainly the '60's' most of the successful End to End record breakers have ridden it. Even the failed attemptees have all used it to test their strength and endurance for the ultimate time trial, End to End and 1000 miles.

Lynne was no exception. She had followed where I left off. She started riding the Mersey 24 hr in the early 90's progressing to win the ladies 'Turner Cup' in 1995 with 441 miles. The same year as Andy Wilko won with 501 miles. I helped Lynne on many of these occasions and as the years went on I felt that she could possibly be the next 'End to Ender'.

Lynne had obviously noticed Wilko's performances especially his record 24 hr 525 miles in 1997, who could miss that ! I hadn't really paid much attention to mixed tandem or mixed tandem trike record breaking as it was in its infancy as such, but I had to admit that the performances put up over any of the record routes or distances seemed to be very respectable. A lot of them not falling far short of the men's tandem or tandem trike performances.

I felt that although Lynne was almost ready for a solo attack it would be helpful if she knew the route and what was involved with record breaking. I knew I hadn't got the expertise or time needed to organise an attempt but I knew there were a very selective band of men out there who were 'gifted' at organising events and records, and making things happen ! Two of the very best came to mind - John Williams and Jim Turner. John ended up being the back -room organizer and Jim became the 'on-road' director of the tandem attempt.

Andy was approached in 1999, a tandem was purchased, and from the start the partnership worked very well. They used the tandem during the winter to go to club dinners wherever they could to give speeches, or prize presentations. They had both become very popular 'after dinner' speakers and guests and enjoyed the social atmosphere. John Williams and Jim Turner would go on later to organise or direct between them, the next four successful End to Ends and 1000 miles twice, taking us to the year 2002.

On a very cold and frosty day in March, with no helpful winds, on the same route and at the same time breaking the Liverpool-Edinburgh record, Lynne and Andy also broke the Northern RRA 100 mile record, and this decided them to attack the mixed tandem End to End held by Adrian Harris and Jodie Groesbeck. Harris and Groesbeck were an Anglo-American partnership and Dai Davies told me that they literally flew in from the States, motored down to Cornwall and started all within 4 days. Dai had been their timekeeper and advisor and after they took the record they then motored back and flew home

The decision making for Lynne and Andy's record attempts are mostly made in our local Balti house, in warm comfortable surroundings, usually with sleet hammering on the windows. Andy at the time was not happy with their performance on the Liverpool-Edinburgh and 100 miles, and said he didn't feel altogether comfortable with the tandem. One or two modifications were made, i.e. Lynne's handlebars were narrowed to eliminate the sway and roll Andy was having to compensate for, and crank angles were altered slightly. They then tackled a few more training weekends, culminating with the Shenstone Audax 200k into the

Peak District and back. At the time of attacking the record Lynne was 31 years old and Andy 36 years.

The main back up team was comprised of Jim Turner and Paul Histon, who along with John Williams had helped and masterminded Andy's successful recumbent End to End record, plus numerous BAR rides and of course, Andy's 525 mile 24 hour record. Lynne McKie, one of Andy's Port Sunlight club mates had proved invaluable on the Liverpool/Edinburgh record as female support for Lynne at comfort stops, clothing changes, sorting out chamois cream etc, and generally keeping things, especially Jim and Paul, under control.

Jim and Paul are not just physical support for Andy, they are his motivators, both knowing how to get the best out of him and as can be seen, the pep talks from the Shap area onwards, proved invaluable. They must have gone something like "If you can raise the speed to 18 mph we'll let you have another 10 mins sleep at Inverness", that sort of thing ! Lynne on the other hand just says "Am I doing all right ?" and I just say "Absolutely fine".

Colin Baldwin and Bert Owen were to be travelling masseurs and helpers at various places. Bert had been on Andy's recumbent End to End. The Williams family, namely, Ruth, Bob and Jonathan, were to provide the back up to the helpers, plus official cover in observing etc, as were Christine and Frank Minto, Mike Johnson and Ron Sant, plus Pat Kenny timing the start to 12 hours, and Dai Davies timekeeping the rest of the journey to John o Groats. Frank Shepherd, Andy's club mate was to join at Mitre Oak. Alan Griffiths observed in the feed car to the Midlands. Telephone and Internet HQ was provided by Shelagh and Edwin Hargraves, and Andy's parents, Judith and Stan provided the comfort caravan stops for 600 miles.

A weather pattern had emerged and we were informed by Dai Davies that a high and low pressure sitting either side of the UK would draw a wind up the centre of the country. We drove down on Friday 12th May picking up Pat Kenny en route, Taunton way, on his bike of course. It was a warm day with a northerly breeze. The support car with the riders arrived after tea. We all had a late supper and went to bed.

13th May 5.30 am Time to get up ! Lynne and Andy both had very restless sleeps, not just from nerves, but from eating a large supper with lots of pasta too late at night, and not being able to have a ride to stretch their legs and unwind from the journey down. However, I doubt that anyone faced with a two day assault on the longest road in the UK would have got much sleep.

Thick fog and mist blotted the landscape from view and the fog horn bellowed eerily in the distance just off Sennen Cove. Breakfast was consumed, last minute ablutions performed, we went outside. It was gloomy, wet, misty and cold, but at least the tandem was ready and raring to go. It was an aluminium, long wheelbase Cannondale mountain bike tandem with narrow rims and Vredestein slick tyres. The only item added to it was tri-bars on the front. The extra length gave Lynne breathing space on the back and enabled Andy to lean back and stretch his limbs and lower back periodically. The tandem set off and we motored down to the start. **10 mins to go.** The mist was blowing in from the east. Had a quick chat to Roy and Iris, some friends from Penzance waiting patiently with their two lovely Labradors, very unlike the 'Helms' cartoon dogs. People staying at Lands End Hotel having breakfast, were craning their necks to see what was going on. Andy and Lynne popped in and signed the record book at the hotel.

13th May 8 am Started on time: Timekeeper, Pat Kenny counted down the seconds. Pat, a previous End to End record holder on trike is probably one of the most experienced long distance riders and timekeepers since the famed F.T. Bidlake. Alan Griffiths, the observer in the feed car, himself a record breaker on tandem in the 50's with Jim Blackhurst, was the second witness. Our driver was Hugh Canning, a club mate of Lynne's and myself, whose experience with 24 hr races held him in good stead for the driving ahead of us. The van was loaned to us by 'AVC Hydraulics' of Liverpool, courtesy of Chris Parker, obviously a good mate of Andy's, knowing there was likely to be 2000 miles added onto the clock in five days ! The riders started with leg warmers and Assos windstop jackets on top of full racing kit as it was quite cold in the swirling mist at sea level. It was a very sporting road to Penzance with a strong wind from the right coming straight off the sea in exposed places.

8.26 am Penzance - 10 miles They sped through the town milling with Saturday shoppers not the least bit interested in record attempters. By the time they had got beyond Redruth and on towards Bodmin, the mist has cleared and off came the extra clothing.

10.20 am Bodmin - 52 miles It was at this point that suntan cream should have been replenished, as by 11 o'clock the sun was very hot and they both got sunburned and sore on their right sides. This was to prove a costly mistake later in the attempt with sunstroke. We saw Elaine Hancock here in two or three places, giving encouragement. Years ago her husband Syd came out to see Pat Kenny and myself set off from Lands End on our three attempts at the tandem trike End to End record.

The riders were settling down now to a steady pace, eating and drinking well. Full bottle of carbo on the hour, plus 'power bars' and tea cakes on the half hour. The weather was getting very warm., everything was going well, up and down the long climbs on the dual carriageways on the A30. The van closing up to the tandem where the slip roads come in from the left with cars entering at high speeds.

12.20 pm Okehampton - 100 miles Now just 10 mins inside 'evens' (20 mph) with the wind not exactly helpful coming from their right as they rounded Dartmoor and on towards Exeter, its still hot with the sun overhead.

1.30 pm Exeter - 117 miles A very busy place with the tandem having to weave around Saturday shoppers clogging the roads up. Here we saw Brian Griffiths and Pete Luxton cheering the pair on their way. Pete's wife Jean regularly marshalled and checked record attempts, but sadly she is no longer with us. Soon we were out through Broadclyst past the cider factory to Cullompton and on fairly quiet roads now but still hot.

2.26 pm Waterloo Cross - 145 miles Andy was starting to have problems with his back along this stretch and stopped to have a massage. At this point they were approximately 45 mins down on schedule. On through Taunton, again a very busy town full of shoppers and lots of red traffic lights against them. Out onto the Bridgwater flats, the sun still beating down with not much shade anywhere. Bridgwater was also an obstacle, with queues of cars blocking their progress.

4.39 pm Churchill Traffic Lights - 180 miles Now still 21 mins inside evens and 51 mins down on schedule this was already having a negative effect on Andy who had imagined the tandem to be as fast as a solo. Also, throughout the ride, there was never a strong south westerly wind. The climb of Redhill was tackled with ease with a slight breeze behind them. They rode as one, either in or out of the saddle, and with the sun still hot they were glad of the sponges.

5.50 pm Bristol was reached - 197 miles Climbing well now, up the side of the gorge, past Bristol Zoo and out over the downs, helped on by numerous club folk marshalling for them. Geoff Lonsdale and his crew were out here and Ian Boon reported 'definitely on Henleaze Road now'. Filton was negotiated and a left turn was made back onto the A38. Once out of the suburbs and industrial parks the road became reasonably quiet now, most of the heavy traffic having joined the M5 motorway.

5.49 pm North of Rudgeway - 206 miles A quick 12 mins stop here. We saw Edwin Hargraves out to wish them well. He had left Shelagh at home to 'man/woman' the phones. They were to provide telephone HQ and an interactive web site for anyone who was 'logged on' and computer literate. That definitely rules me out. I've only just mastered the mobile phone, and that was only because I had to, for record attempts. Around the Taunton/Bridgwater stretch onwards, we had seen this fellow taking photos at various vantage points. It was Dennis Naylor, and he'd been hopping on and off the motorway, taking shots with his digital camera, and within an hour or so of the tandem going through there would be a photo on the Internet. How brilliant ! It's a pity he wasn't going all the way to Scotland. Dennis is the brother of one of Lynne's clubmates Roger, who had a terrible accident three years before when a truck did a 'U' turn on him in a time trial, and left him wheelchair bound.

Pauline and Judi, our friends from Mullion Cove in Cornwall had tried to get out to see Lynne and Andy around Redruth but couldn't get through the mist, so eventually, by ringing up HQ they managed to catch us in Gloucester. Thanks for their support.

7.10 pm Gloucester - 229 miles Safely through here, good marshalling and good directions from Ted Tedaldi, whose notes on roadworks in the old town by the docks proved useful. Out again onto very quiet roads, all the shoppers had gone home, and the 'pubber's' hadn't come out yet.

7.34 pm Tewkesbury - 230 miles The sun was cooling off now. The feeding car had picked up Dai Davies in Gloucester. He would take over from Pat Kenny at the Mitre Oak stop. We saw Lynne's Aunts Donny and Rosie just north of Tewkesbury - thanks to them. Andy jokingly said to Lynne that he was shattered because of having to go fast just to impress all her friends and relatives !

8.00pm 12 hour point - Severn Stoke - 247.5 miles Jim Turner wishes it to be known that his best 12 hour was 247.6 miles, but Jim, were not the courses measured in furlongs in those days ? !! It was around here that we saw my sister Margaret and her husband Les. Marg had encouraged me to ride long distances with her, when I was 12, and then introduced me to Birmingham St Christopher's Cycling Club through her friend Joan Knox. That was really the start of all this, with St Christopher's being a long distance time trialling club, eventually spawning 7 or 8 record breakers over the years, so Lynne just had to do it, didn't she?

8.26 pm Worcester - 257 miles We saw Phil Palmer just north of Worcester, also my other sister Barbara and her husband John. The 'Mitre Oak pub' was reached at 8.45pm where the riders had a 45 mins break. Andy's parents had driven down from the Wirral and parked the family caravan on the car park. This was to provide the comfort stops to John o Groats. The riders had a good wash down and a massage, with Colin and Bert doing the honours. Lynne noticed at this point that her right leg was very sore from sunburn, as were Wilko's head and ears. It was the first real opportunity for me to check the tandem over. We were surrounded by people we knew from local clubs. I had quite a difficult job not to stand and chat. There was Mick and Nora de Mouilpied, Norman and Sylvia Powell, Tony Shardlow etc, about 50 people in all. I had to fit the light set which was a 'Smart' 6v lead-acid battery, running 2 watt and 6 watt bulbs. A Cateye BSI L.e.d gave an excellent red light at the rear. They used the 2 watt beam on the front for most of the night, and occasionally the 6 watt to pinpoint potholes and dark patches. The lights were on for approximately 7 hours. I used a new battery pack on the second night just to be on the safe side, but on test afterwards, there was still another 5 hours left in the original battery. Frank Shepherd, Andy's clubmate, joined us here, to help to the end.

9.30 pm Back on the road towards Kidderminster fully refreshed. Just before the stop Andy had seen a bunch of his Port Sunlight clubmates, and it cheered him up no end. The riders were well over an hour down on a tight schedule, but were well ahead of the original record holders at this point.

9.42 pm Kidderminster 269 miles Saw Dave Poutney at the right turn. Lynne asked me if I had seen her Nan out before Mitre Oak, as she thought she had. I said that I hadn't; was Lynne hallucinating already! It later turned out to have been Elaine Hancock, who had travelled up the country to see the pair. What a supporter ! On through Wolverhampton. Phil Mason of 'Climb on Bikes' reported that the riders were moving well here. Out on the north side of the city, going towards Gailey, there was quite a crowd waiting. We saw Reg Randall here, he was a long way from home ! Lynne's mum Liz had phoned Lynne's Nan and told her that Lynne and Andy had stopped to put on their night clothes. Lynne's nan was under the impression they would be riding in pyjamas and nightie with hot water bottles etc. When we told Lynne about it, she and Andy chuckled for miles.

10.57 pm Gailey Island - 294 miles Phil Guy reported that they were 'going like a train'. Here we took on fresh help and drivers. Hugh Canning went off home to Penkridge taking Lynne McKie, Paul and Jim for a few hours kip, with plans to rejoin at Shap. Bob Williams took over driving the following van with Dai Davies, myself and the spare tandem etc. Lots of local club folk, friends and relatives were out along this stretch. Lynne's brother Mike had driven up from London just to see them come through Gailey before driving back down to London. Lynne was so surprised to see him. Also here were Liz, Pam, Mary Harvey, Richard and Hazel, Neil, my club mates etc. What a crowd, too many to mention everyone.

1.20 pm North of Stafford - 305 miles Pedalling smoothly on quite a warm night, Lynne remembers seeing Debbie Capewell and asking her if she wanted to do a few hours on the back.. Debbie is the same size as Lynne and I am sure no one would have noticed the swap. 'No chance' came the reply. Where is a friend when you need one ! Lynne also remembered that she was down to ride the Walsall Roads CC Open 25 on that same course in approximately 8 hours time. No doubt they would accept her apologies for her first DNS ever. At least it was a good excuse.

12.00 Midnight Stone - 315 miles - Sunday 14th May 2000 Only another 525 miles to go. We saw Margaret and Jim Hopper, Les Lowe and Greta, plus lots of club folk from this area and our thanks to them.

George Longstaff reported that the pair were 'looking good' even though they were not on a Longstaff tandem ! That was at Talke island. Holmes Chapel, Knutsford and Warrington were well marshalled by the faithfull club folk who turn out in all weathers and rarely miss an End to End attempt. On now, the riders sped through Latchfordbridge.

2.15 am Winwick Church - 360 miles Tom Greep was here as on all the End to Ends I've been involved in. I think he must camp out here during the End to End season. Thanks to him. The riders were still on a mainly liquid diet with the occasional carbo bar and butty on the half hour. It was a very dark night out in the countryside and Andy was looking forward to dawn breaking and seeing the 'A' team again. The only relief was the odd patch of street lighting. Andy's relative's Roger and Sally did a wonderful job on a motorbike over this lonely section, cutting through the side lanes and popping up at junctions to see them through. Alan Rogerson said that 'the birds are singing' at Preston.

3.40 am Preston was reached - 381 miles The tired riders were now looking forward to the comfort stop at Garstang, on the bypass.

4.10 am Garstang - Approx 390 miles Andy and Lynne stopped for 40 mins here with Colin and Bert administering a massage. Christine Minto was providing back up for Lynne, sorting out chamois cream and fresh clothes etc. Judy and Stan Wilkinson gave them sustenance and exhaustion gave them sleep. Andy was really feeling the cold and he found the best way to sleep was under about 20 blankets, and this is where the sunstroke from the previous day set in. He had lost his cotton cap early on the first day and got quite sunburned on his forehead. Lynne in her notes remembers looking around in the caravan trying to find Andy, thinking he was hiding, and there he was, under all the blankets and coats. She remembers getting started back on the tandem and Andy was shivering and shaking violently with the cold. Lynne was trying to warm him up as they went along by putting her warm hands on his back. She recalls that quite a few times Andy said he didn't want to let her down but didn't think he could carry on, to which Lynne reassured him saying that he would make it. It was daylight now as they set off again.

5.14 am Galgate Traffic Lights - 404 miles Past Edwin Hargraves birthplace - Lancaster Royal Infirmary - a useful snippet of information here - shades of Dave Duffield do I hear you say?

6.25 am Levens Bridge - 420 miles Andy feeling very sleepy now, two more short 'cat naps' taken here.

6.42 am Kendal - 426 miles Michael Bracken reports 'no wind' and that the riders are 'cheerful but very tired'.

6.55 am - Climbing Shap Jonathan Williams reports "Wilko falling asleep and that they plan to have a rest in the caravan on Shap summit". Lynne's notes recall that they climbed very well together even when tired, and that when the 'A' team returned at the top of Shap, they inspired Andy so much that he decided to go on past Shap village for the 24 hours.

8.00 am 24 hours 444 miles 2 miles north of Shap village.

A stop was taken 1 mile south of Penrith for a long sleep. They were now over 3 hours down on a schedule aimed to beat the men's record of 2 days 2 hrs held by my two clubmate's Pete

Swinden and John Withers. Sadly John passed away, but I am sure he was looking down approving of everything we were doing. If he were alive I am sure he would have been on board, helping or observing. Pete is to be on Lynne's solo End to End but that is in the future isn't it ? Lynne used to ask John if he had anything nice left to eat in his back pockets after a 12 hour or 24 hour. She was probably about 10 or 11 years old at the time and used to help on the Oldbury 12 hour handing up bananas and mars bars, with her brother Mike and mum Liz, along with Pete's wife Barbara and their children Judy and Phil.

9.35 am One mile south of Penrith - 450 miles After another one and a quarter hours break, the riders emerged into a gloriously sunny Sunday morning. The mood of the helpers who had been with them during the night was almost as low as the riders, with mythical bets being taken as to how far and how long the attempt would last. Luckily at this point, Shelagh and Edwin were working on a new schedule to beat just the mixed tandem record. On now into the sunshine through Penrith. Andy was so relieved to have Paul and Jim back with them and they were also glad to be back. The two Lynne's were really pleased to see each other and have a chat on the long climbs and when they had a break. In hindsight, and its easy to be wise after the event, if the 'A' team had kept with them they could have been 40 miles further on by now, but who knows !

10.18 am Carlisle - 470 miles Christine Reed saw them through Carlisle by the railway station. Bob Derbyshire and Jim Turner report that 'Wilko is coming round now - he's smiling at us'.

10.50 am on the A74 towards Gretna - 480 miles This was along a very fast and dangerous dual carriageway that is a continuation of the M6 and links it to the M74. Luckily, the turn through Gretna takes you onto a lovely quiet stretch of road running parallel for about 30 miles with the next motorway, through Kirkpatrick Fleming, Kirtlebridge, Ecclefechan, Lockerbie, to Beattock and Johnstone Bridge. We had said goodbye to Bob Williams and Christine Minto. They had stopped at Gretna and took Hugh Canning's car back to Cheshire with them. The feeding car took on Ron Sant as Observer. Hugh would take over as driver now until the end. It was along this quiet stretch of road with the riders in the doldrums with no foreseeable help from the wind, the pair stopped and had a pep talk with Paul. Andy was very worried about being 4 hrs down on schedule. At this point John Williams asked the 'A' team to implement the more realistic schedule based on actually slower times, just to beat the mixed tandem record, where the riders would be up on schedule straight away - a good positive approach.

12.51 pm Moffat was reached - 510 miles A lovely tourist town, nestling in a valley at the base of the 'Devils Beef Tub' a dreaded climb on a bike let alone a tandem. It gets its name from a huge chasm in the ground off to the right, surrounded by a ridge of ominous looking peaks and mounds. The climb winds its way up the left hand side of the Beef Tub and the road can be seen high up in the distance. From Moffat to the top is approximately 7 miles. Lynne and Andy climbed it magnificently and forcefully, and flew over the summit. Maybe it was the fact that the road is a major right turn or maybe its so high at this point, the riders picked up a strong following breeze that took them to be 48 mins up on the new shedule at :

2.03 pm Crook Inn - 530 miles. On now to Blyth Bridge where a 25 minute sleep stop was taken before dropping down to Ledburn at 3.34 pm and 550 miles. The wind was still behind them on this long 45 miles of gradual downhill to Edinburgh. The River Tweed sources at the summit of the climb and grows from a trickle to a wide raging torrent when in full spate, in just a matter of miles. At this point, Andy was still losing confidence even though they were now up on schedule. Paul and Jim had their work cut out to keep him motivated. Carol Dietman and friend Jane saw them through **Lothian Burn Junction at 3.57 pm** and **Barnton at 4.21 pm.** Our thanks to them. Edinburgh Sunday tea time was very busy, just like a weekday but Andy steered his way through.

4.41 pm Forth Road Bridge - 573 miles Jim Turner reports from the north side of the bridge 'stopped for warm clothing now, it was chilly across the water'. The caravan came in useful again, a quiet haven blocking the noise of the roaring traffic coming off the bridge at motorway speeds. It was at this comfort stop that Lynne remembers Paul coming into the caravan and saying "Come on, times up, back on in two minutes". Lynne replied "Fine, but can I please put some clothes on first ?" - she had stripped off for a rub down ! They all fell about laughing and that was one of the happier, more memorable parts of the ride.

5.06 pm North of the Forth Road Bridge Back on the road again with a new lease of life, although Andy was still secretly worrying about the climbs that lay ahead. Jim reports ' going very well now, only 3hrs 40 mins down on original schedule. E.t.a. Perth 7.00 pm- eating Jim's special honey and peanut butter sandwiches'.

6.21 pm Glenfarg Alan Hodgetts reports 'going well 18-20 mph, followed by support van and George Berwick on recumbent, all at correct distance'.

6.55 pm Perth - 610 miles It was here that John Williams meticulous details and preparation came into play. We were following the tandem through the town and Andy had just one last crucial left turn to take. We were able to follow the route on a street guide provided by John, and when the turn came, we indicated left for Andy. He glanced back and it re-assured him of his direction.

7.15 pm 6 Miles North of Perth - Night stop taken Approximately one hour was taken. Warm food was available but Andy was feeling very sick at this point, despite the assurances from the team that they would definitely make it. Lynne as usual was generally happy but was getting very sore in the saddle area and was worried about Wilko.

8.14 pm Back on the road. I reported in that the lights had been fitted to the machine and that they were fully spondoodled and raring to go. On now towards Pitlochry, lots of long dual carriageways and steady climbs into the Highlands. Not much wind and traffic was light.

9.46pm Blair Athol - 640 miles 200 miles to go and 19 hours to break the record. Brian Parkins reported 'the riders looking good and a 'thumbs up' from Lynne'. Jim Turner had a phone call from Pete Swinden who was holidaying in Oban on the west coast. He said 'there is a 20 mph southerly wind on this side' - hmmm thanks a lot Pete !

11.15 pm Nearing top of Drumochter Pass - 660 miles The riders stopped here for more warm clothing. It was a clear dry night, getting very chilly with long sweeps downhill for 10 mins at a time to chill them off. Andy had built up all of these climbs in his mind, to be more severe than they actually were. In fact following them in the van, their speed never dropped below 17 mph and it was quite difficult to tell when the actual summits were reached.

Monday May 15th

1.12 am Kingussie by pass on to Aviemore - 674 miles Andy was very sleepy at this point and I was trying to work out a contingency plan where Lynne could go on the front for a few hours. Lynne had tried to get Andy to wear clear glasses as we are sure this actually stops the eyelids becoming too stiff and dried out because of being battered by the wind. It certainly works for her. Lynne pointed out the snow caps on the mountain tops to Andy. They were eerily visible in the moonlight but Andy was busy trying to miss potholes thrown up by the ravages of the winter and the result of heavy lorry traffic, this being the only route on the east of the country. Lynne was getting extremely sore now, and both of them were anxious to get to Inverness for a comfort stop.

2.10 am Slochd Summit - 702 miles It was very touch and go now, Andy looked very weary and the team said the lights had gone out in his eyes, leaving a blank stare. With 140 miles still to go anything could happen.

There was not much help from the wind and indeed there hadn't been much all the way. Lynne needed dry shorts and fresh soothing chamois cream. The back of the tandem shielded her from the wind but creates a lot of heat for the rider, which in itself is uncomfortable, along with sitting directly over the back wheel, getting road shock. She was using an elastomer sprung seat post to try and alleviate some of the pain. She had been getting sore since the 400 mile point in the Lake District. This was the last long stretch to Inverness and neither of them wanted anymore unnecessary stops until they got there. In the following van I had got to know the tell tale signs of sleep deprivation and at one point I saw the tandem meander just a few inches. I said to Hugh "Just pip the horn gently" We were nowhere near civilisation so affecting no one with the noise. It was enough to concentrate their minds and Lynne gave a wave to acknowledge us. After the ride was over I asked her if she remembered the incident. She thought Andy had been a gentleman and swerved to avoid a pothole for her, however, Andy when asked, admitted that he had actually nodded off ! Lynne in her notes recalling the ride, said she really enjoyed this last section to Inverness with a very long three mile drop downhill, where at times the van had a job to keep its lights focussed on the riders doing just under 60 mph.

4.42 am Inverness at last - 720 miles The city is by passed nowadays so the caravan was parked on a large service area with the magnificent vista of lights across the water, visible from the car park. The riders had 20 mins sleep out of a total of 42 mins break with Andy as usual under a mountain of blankets to get warm. That sunburn on the first day hadn't done them any favours, although Jim and Paul told me that Andy goes ice cold and shivery during, and at the end of all his long distance conquests, as though the effort has consumed every last ounce of energy, leaving just skin and bone. A quick massage and hot rice pudding was taken here. Time to get going now and back on the road again.

4.50 pm Kessock Bridge Dawn is breaking now with 120 miles to do. Lynne commented to Andy that it would only be like riding the Shenstone Audax 200k but just a little hillier {for anyone who knows both routes1} She knew that Andy wanted to get inside 2 days 2 hrs 14 mins to beat the men's record and at this point it still seemed possible, however, one forgets the severity of the climbs of Helmsdale, Berriedale and Dunbeath, all ranging from 1 in 6 to 1 in 12 and very difficult on a tandem. It was at this point Lynne remembers saying to Andy 'look at that castle on the right'. All Andy heard was 'right' which when they are climbing was the signal to both get out of the saddle. Andy did, Lynne didn't, and she recalls that the tandem went a bit pear shaped. However, they soon recovered ! On through Invergordon with the coast on our right, and now we could see the oil platforms out to sea.

5.51 am Tain - 752 miles It was almost fully light now with a dusky orange glow to our right. Hugh Canning reports 'Lynne still amazingly fresh - Wilko 'man of steel' feeling dreadful, but still hopefully pushing on.' The phrase 'running on empty' is appropriate to use here I think.

8.11 am Helmsdale climbed Just over 48 hours The team were all out of the car running alongside up here as the tandem negotiated the tight hairpins. The riders breasted the summit, Andy was feeling and looking good now and thoroughly enjoying the prospect of getting there. Long testing downhill stretches with tight bends at the end were all accomplished expertly - a wonderful sight to witness. Lynne says she even managed to get Andy to glance at a castle on one side and a trio of red deer standing magnificently on a hill watching the entourage go past.

9.07 am Berriedale - 796 miles Another strenuous climb done with just Dunbeath to complete the hat trick. The team as ever, ecstatic, running alongside and giving 100 %. Now just Latheron and Lybster to pass through before Wick. Jim reported them going very strongly through the 'Ord of Caithness'. 800 miles done and just 40 miles to go. The support car went ahead to make sure the timekeeper got to John o Groats to record this epic ride. Hugh Canning reports 'everybody has got huge grins on their faces, even the riders !' I remember ringing Liz at the shop and also Lynne's two grans to say they would be finished in one hour. They all said they had hardly any sleep for thinking about the riders.

10.28 am Wick - 823 miles 17 miles to go, Lynne was very sore now and asked Andy to freewheel on the downhill sections to ease her backside, not that there is much downhill. At last the fairytale towers of John o Groats hotel came into view. The long swoop down the last mile was a touching moment - such relief.

11.19 am 840 miles - John o Groats - 2 days 3 hrs 19 mins 23 secs

A FIVE HOUR BEATING OF THE OLD RECORD

In all the emotion and commotion nobody remembered to inform Shelagh and Edwin Hargraves at HQ and for a whole hour or more people logged on or phoned in and couldn't get a result, so nail biting and frustrating it must have been, like watching a cup final on a draw in extra time and having a power cut. Our apologies go out to them. Although we were stretched looking after the riders, it was still no excuse.

We had seen a few members of the Caithness CC on this last section, although most people were probably at work, it being a Monday morning. Our relatives Phil and Stuart with Mindy their dog were at John o Groats to welcome us in. It seems very strange to see someone you knew who used to live in the Midlands and now live in a beautiful setting overlooking the most northerly tip of Scotland. They were absolutely amazed at the feat of endurance from Lynne and Andy. I was too wound up at the finish to have a sleep so I took a couple of hours off and visited their new home. The views are breathtaking, overlooking 280 degrees of coastline; the Orkneys, Pentland Firth and Scapa Flow. One of the good things about the attempt was that the weather, although not windy enough, was good and clear, giving lovely views throughout the journey.

Lynne's account of the last few moments of the ride were feelings of sheer relief as she was now very sore with broken skin over quite a large area. The thought of continuing for a further 170 miles for the 1000 mile record seemed remote. She remembered Andy putting his hand back and holding hers as they crossed the line outside the hotel. He was also so relieved it was over. The pair were whisked off to the hotel one mile south of John o Groats for a shower and sleep. The John o Groat's hotel is boarded up now and only the bar downstairs is open for locals.

Colin applied a light toning-down massage to Lynne and had a good chat to her as she drifted in and out of sleep. She remembered waking up with a jump thinking she was still riding. Later she awoke when Lynne Mckie came into the room and Lynne asked her if she had got to get back on yet ! The next interruption to sleep was Jim asking if she was up for the 1000 miles. She said although she was very sore that if Andy wanted to go on then yes she would. Luckily the answer from Andy was a definite 'no'.

Down in the dining room a fine meal was polished off, with a few glasses of wine. Andy's parent's Judy and Stan were delighted that we had all come through OK. They had now seen at first hand what Andy gets up to on his weekends away ! It was the longest journey they had ever undertaken with their caravan. Yet more was to come for Stan, as Judy went on to ride the end to end herself the following year for the 'Roy Castle Cancer Appeal', on a mountain bike, followed by Stan with the caravan, and that was their 'Summer Holiday'. What an epic in itself, 18 days and over 1000 miles on the scenic route.

Ron Sant, who holds the Audax Gold Medal for the End to End inside 80 hours of unaided riding, was our observer over the stretch from Gretna to the top. He said it was one of the most memorable events he had ever been part of and would love to do it again soon - please !

We rang John Williams and Shelagh and Edwin from the dinner table, thanked them for all their help., and toasted them down the phone with champagne. It was a very touching moment and we wished they were with us. They had kept the outside world informed of the ride and John had masterminded the whole plot.

Evening came and we all had a stroll down to the headland and stood by the mile post 'Lands End 860 miles' for photos, with the setting sun making patterns on the islands behind us.

What a lovely ending to an epic three days. I am sure the people who took part will look back and remember it forever - I know I will.

One of the most useful instruments to be employed on these events nowadays apart from bikes, tandems and cars, is the mobile phone, keeping people and vehicles in touch with each other, and also for people going out to marshal, and ringing into HQ. Another brilliant gadget is the Internet, keeping the world informed if necessary. I know of people in Canada and New Zealand who were following the ride, and even downloading photographs. This was only possible because of Shelagh and Edwin Hargraves loading and updating the web site brilliantly. Thank you so much to them. They even ran a virtual reality sweepstake as to when the tandem would reach John o Groats, and would you believe, it was won by John Williams! Insider information no doubt ! But of course, you do need a couple of very good riders and good back up teams as well. They do come in useful.

Next day before we motored back we had a photo session for Science in Sport (SIS) who had contributed free sports drinks, with Andy and Lynne standing by the tandem. Lynne told us an elderly lady walked past and wished them good luck and she was sure they would make it! She thought they were about to start.

Our immense thanks to our sponsors who helped with transport, drink products, hotel bills, fuel bills etc, and all the officials who gave up their time so willingly. Last but not least, sincere thanks to all the helpers who did an undying job to the end and beyond.

Sadly since this record, Bert Owens, our masseur, has passed away and will be missed by all.

No 36 LYNNE TAYLOR 26TH SEPTEMBER 2001
LANDS END TO JOHN O GROATS
LADIES SINGLE BICYCLE RECORD ATTEMPT

After successfully breaking the mixed tandem End to End with Andy Wilkinson in Millenium year Lynne felt she was now ready for a shot at the solo record held by Pauline Strong since 1990 with 2 days 6 hrs 49 mins 45 secs.

Pauline was a very consistent rider and riding as a professional for Raleigh, she had broken numerous place to place records including a 100 mile of 3 hr 49 min 42 secs, and a 12 hr record with 259.5 miles. I knew she was fast as well as strong, but had never got round to riding a 24 hr. I also knew she had struggled with adverse conditions on her second night with wind and rain, making her knees painful. So with this knowledge of the previous record holder, I reckoned Lynne was in a good position to attack the record, having ridden 10 or more 24 hr races, winning the Turner Cup six times, her best mileage being 441 in 1995, and having covered the route on the tandem End to End was also good preparation.

Lynne's build up for the solo End to End was a full season of racing, from an early season two up 25 in March with Neil Peart, which they won, nine 10 mile events with a best of 23.38, thirteen 25's best solo ride 59.26, five 50's best 2.01.15 secs, three 100's best and fastest lady of the year with 4.09.08. A personal best 12 hr winning a third place in the West Cheshire open 12 hr with 249 miles, a Mersey Roads 24 hr of 423 miles. 32 races in all, a total of 1,637 miles in competition , in temperatures ranging from below freezing to 83 F in the 24 hr; this mileage plus another 15,000 training and general mileage is a typical 'season' for Lynne.

She had just handed her number in to John Williams in exchange for a free cup of tea after her 249 mile 12 hour when he said "Right Lynne, I've got a form for you to sign"! John is a timekeeper and a computer man, having just worked out the final positions and mileages of the 12 hour race. He is also a prolific organizer, anything from open time trials, road races, three day races, road records, at all distances including End to End and 1000 miles. The form to be signed was of course the RRA notification form to attack the record. After waiting for a few weeks for the right wind and weather, it was fast approaching the end of September and the dark nights and colder weather was closing in. At last on Monday, 24th September, we got the call from John Williams, "its on for Wednesday 26th ". All Systems go !

25.9.01 Motored down to Senen with plenty of time to spare for Lynne to have a good ride to combat restless legs from the car journey. Two thirds of the team were here. Paul Histon, Andy Wilkinson and Frank and Christine Minto who were our Observer and Time keeper for the first stage. A last minute check over of the bikes and van and then off to have our last supper, at the 'First and Last Inn'. Lynne was looking fairly relaxed. It was now raining and blowing a gale as only Cornwall can muster. Gethin Butler and Gillian were staying at the same hotel and had a meal with us at the Inn. Gethin was in good spirits and seemed relaxed and confident, ready for his 10 am start on Thursday.

26.9.01 Wednesday arrived all too soon, up at 6 am. When I asked Lynne if she had had a good sleep, she replied 'no comment'. Lynne knows that as long as she has rested she will be okay. Before the tandem record attempt she had been too nervous to sleep properly so had been through it all before. The day dawned murky and mild with not much wind either way. The roaring south westerly blowing the previous night had blown itself out by 1.30 am. Roy and Iris were there to see us off with the two Labradors. They had been there at the successful tandem start, and seemed like a good omen. The time had come:

8.00 am Lynne was at the south door of the Lands End Hotel and Frank Minto despatched her promptly away. I couldn't help her anymore, she was on her own now, for two days plus. Unbeknown to us, Lynne took a wrong turn from the Hotel, and ended up in the car park, having to go over the grass to get back on the road. The first of many little detours !

Past the Hotel, Gethin and Gillian cheered her on and away now towards Penzance. A very bumpy undulating road with a light drizzle and mild. Lynne was on her Giant carbon fibre bike with Campag Shamal wheels which would each gain a cupful of rainwater by the end of the attempt. She was drinking a 10% solution of PSP22 carbo blackcurrant. The wind was three quarters behind from the south now onto the Penzance by-pass. There was Elaine Hancock and her son Syd. Syd senior had been at the start of most End to Ends over the last 50 years, and after his passing, Elaine had taken on the role, also regularly turning up on RRA records and at the Mersey 24 hr and Anfield 100. Lynne was moving steadily on now and took on a Maxim carbo bar. We saw our friend Pauline, who had dashed from her home at Mullion Cove against the rush hour traffic. Another good omen and thanks to her. On the hour a fresh bottle of carbo for Lynne. Heavy traffic now at Chiverton Cross, just 4 mins inside evens, and rain getting heavier. Next check was at 60 mile in 2.55 hrs. Lynne suggested 'wind unfavourable' in a questioning voice, still taking a full bottle every hour, plus Maxim bars and a honey butty. The weather was looking a bit brighter ahead.

12.25 pm Five mins for a toilet stop and putting on a gillet (sleeveless jacket) Jim Turner on his way down with Gethin's team reported by mobile phone that it was fine in Exeter. Okehampton by pass - **100 miles in 4hrs 56 mins.** On towards Exeter, a three quarter headwind as we rounded Dartmoor. On the A30 there are a lot of slip roads coming in from the left and I found it was necessary at virtually all of them to close up on the rider to protect her. One lorry driver was quite insistent on trying to cut in on us, however, I made it awkward for him and he was forced to stop. We saw Gethin's team on their way down on this stretch, comprising of Jim Turner, Dai Davies - timekeeper, Colin Baldwin - masseur, Ron Sant - Observer. They had stopped to cheer Lynne on. She took another 5 min toilet stop and as the rain was easing she removed her gillet.

2.00 pm 126 miles Butty, banana and bottle of PSP. Through Exeter now, very heavy traffic, lost touch with Lynne here. On now towards Taunton **151 miles,** Lynne, as in Exeter, keeps getting caught in very heavy traffic. Rain starting again.

4.00 pm 159 miles Just down on evens now. 10 mins stop here for dry shorts, upper kit, arm warmers and gillet as the rain is now getting to her and not much help with the wind. Bridgwater Flats, one hour down on schedule and 15 mins down on evens. On towards Bristol now.

5.15 pm 181 miles Nine and a quarter hours done, another 5 mins stop. Andy is now reducing bottles from 750 ml to 500 ml per hour.

5.45 pm The team cheered Lynne up Redhill, as by this point she was a bit cheesed off with the weather. On now to Churchill Traffic Lights towards Bristol. She even got caught at these lights and the rain was getting heavier now. The collapse of the road and a landslip on the usual route up the gorge into Bristol meant a detour had to be made up to Bristol Zoo over the Clifton Suspension Bridge. As you can imagine it was very steep to get to the bridge. A great team of marshalls led by Geoff Lonsdale, left nothing to chance. We saw Bridget Boon here and Lynne managed to get through Bristol without any problems. Heavy traffic and poor visibility made progress dangerous up through Filton.

6.40 pm On to the A38, its getting dark and murky now with spray off the road.

8.00 pm 12 hours - 225.4 miles. Rain easing, got to Gloucester and Lynne took a wrong turning. We chased her down when we realised, but lost about 5 mins with traffic lights as well. Marshalls helped us through the centre of Gloucester and it was on this stretch we saw Neville Channin. He wrote to Lynne afterwards and said he felt sorry seeing her emerging out of a wet gloom without any helping wind, and being down on schedule, but he also had great faith in her, having followed her racing exploits over the years, and knew she wouldn't give up. Tewkesbury now and Lynne's Aunts Rosie and Donny were here as on the tandem attempt in 2000. We had a quick word from the van window and thanked them. They were concerned that she was down on schedule.

9.55 pm 248 miles - a quick toilet stop and Lynne changed onto her night bike with better lights. On towards Worcester where we took a wrong turn on the approach. I took the schedule details as gospel and turned left along A44 with Lynne looking behind and taking my indicator as her direction. I quickly realised it was the A44 Evesham to Malvern bypass road and chased after Lynne. After another 5 mins lost we got her back onto the old road into Worcester, and through the town. It was well marshalled and the traffic was still busy. We were in a hurry now to catch Lynne and make sure she didn't go wrong again. Onto 'The Tything' round a sharp bend, and there she was going through heavy traffic. Luckily, Lynne took the correct left hand fork for Kidderminster. Martin Purser, an old tandem trike adversary of mine cheered Lynne through here.

10.15 pm 269 miles - arrived at 'Mitre Oak' the designated 12 hour stop a bit late as you can see. A small group had gathered here including Mick and Nora de Mouilpied. Mick not in very good health now; he was one of the prolific RRA and MRA organisers in the 60's to the 80's. I had a quick check on the equipment, tyres, lights etc. Lynne McKie came on board here as Lynne's female support. She is a lovely lass, same age as our Lynne and a very bubbly caring and positive helper. She had been on the tandem End to End and Liverpool to Edinburgh record as a help for Lynne when she needed to change clothes and on toilet stops (very important). We used Harry Wilkinson's van decked out with bunk beds, portaloo, stove, curtains etc. Harry had driven down from Oldham with John Arnold to provide four or more comfort stops en route. They were now going to drive towards Kendal, 435 miles, for her next stop at approximately 24 hours. Harry and John had both watched Lynne's racing performances for quite a few years, and were hoping to see history made, with Gethin following the next day. A unique double maybe; lets hope so. Away from the Mitre Oak now and saw Tony Shardlow. Lynne looking fairly cheerful but still the conditions were not helpful; damp, drizzly and still. Here we saw Lisa and Keeley, two more young lassies, again similar age to Lynne, who, inspired by Lynne and Andy's tandem End to End, did the ride themselves for charity, going from John o Groats to Lands End in atrocious conditions, over 10 days.

286 Miles Going into Wolverhampton, no traffic to worry about here, they are all in bed at this time of night. Lynne knows her way through here. Out now to the M54 junction with A449. Lynne's club mates from Walsall Roads CC and Wolverhampton Wheelers CC were out in force here, especially 'Uncle Gordon', who rang me after the ride and said he hoped I wasn't docking Lynne's wages for taking three days off ! He was only joking of course - as if I would!

12.30 am 297 miles Gailey Island, what a crowd ! We did an observer swap here. Lynne was going well, probably close to tears at seeing so many people she knew. My clubmates, Derek, Tony, Bob, Pete, Pat, Graham Dayman Richard Dickinson, Alan Richards, Dave Merriman, Pam, Phil and Pauline St John, Charlie Larkin and John Read; too many to name them all. Liz, Lynne's mum brought out fresh flasks of coffee and food for the helpers. She had as much to put up with as us, not getting much sleep and taking phone calls from people who could not get through to the HQ, and also running the shop while we were away for a week. She took Frank and Christine Minto back to our house where they had left their car. Our very sincere thanks to them for giving up their valuable time. I hope it's a success for them. Hazel Kenny bought out Pat, and Judi bought out Pete Swinden. These two were to be our next observers to Gretna Green. We loaded Pat's bike onto the roof rack and zoomed off after Lynne and caught her up just as she was going through Stafford. We saw Neil Peart here and he made sure Lynne got through Stafford OK. Lynne had got a slight tailwind at this point. Hugh Canning also came out here before his telephone stint through the night. Our thanks to him. On now to Stone and Newcastle under Lyme. Lynne had a quick toilet stop.

1.06 am 27.9.01 - 309 miles We saw Jim and Margaret Hopper, Les Lowe, Neil again, and Karl Austin. Quite a lot of steady climbing now towards Congleton, saw Pete Hambley, out into the country towards Holmes Chapel. The roads are drying and we've seen some flags flying in the right direction.. Lynne had been taking regular bottles and feeds and was using herbal peppermint tea as a hot drink.

2.37 am 333 miles - Lynne had a little stop at **3.06 am**, a bit sleepy. She went 'off course' going into Warrington at **4.06** am. Luckily, a very helpful police car spotted her and went ahead at all the danger spots such as traffic lights and islands and put their blue light on. Our many thanks to them. At Winwick church we saw Dave Brabbin and Tom Greep.

4.20 am 357 miles Its started raining heavily again and Lynne has another stop and puts on dry shorts. She had peppermint tea and teacake, still taking regular PSP, Maxim and Rego drinks in between. Must keep that base of carbo going into the system so as not to get any very low points, or the 'knock'. 368 miles now and Pat reckoned Lynne was now 2.5 hours down on schedule at Warrington swing bridge.

5.37 am 384 miles - very wet now but Pat reckoned she could still do a possible 420 for 24 hours.

5.56 am 389 miles. Toilet stop, 6 mins, Lynne puts on Altura jacket on top of her Assos thermal top. The cold and wet is getting to her now. She has had approximately 20 out of 24 hours of rain, varying from drizzle to heavy.

6.29 am 395 miles Rain stopping - dawn breaking.

7.13 am 408 miles Just south of Lancaster. The team told Lynne they planned a stop at Kendal for 30mins.

7.58 am 419 miles so approximately **420 miles for 24 hours**. Now very wet again and no wind.

9.00 am 435 miles Kendal was reached. Lynne had a 35 min stop at the bottom of the Shap climb. Pete Swinden reckons that Shap is the hardest climb on the route. John Arnold noticed that Lynne was looking very pale and drawn, not her usual radiant self, but then she'd had a very hard 25 hours and what lay ahead ?
The support team were very enthusiastic, but Andy was looking at me with eyes that reflected what I was secretly thinking. How long can she go on in these conditions without any help from the weather ? John Williams's internet report at this time after a mobile phone conversation with Wilko says "on the second day, after another stop for a short sleep the time slip down on schedule was nearly 4.5 hours, and the attempt was at a very crucial point. Having failed to get the first two records, 12 hr and 24 hr, it was apparent that she would fail to reach John o Groats in time if she slipped any further. Crossing Shap Fells in torrential rain and with no help from the wind, Attempt Director, Andy Wilkinson, began to contemplate the possibility of abandoning". John went on to say that "fortunately, Lynne had other ideas and knuckled down to holding up her speed and defying the elements !" Although we didn't know at the time, a band of rain had travelled up the country just in front of Lynne for the first 30 hours, whereas Gethin who was just about to start at Lands End, had got perfect winds, and warm dry conditions leaving with him. Lynne hadn't been allowed to go on the same day as Gethin due to RRA rules. Just before Lynne started away on the climb up Shap, I had made a comment to her that if she carried on at this speed, approximately 14 mph, she could still get the record. Lynne replied 'you are not doubting my ability are you ?' I am afraid everyone except Paul was feeling a bit negative knowing what lay ahead in the next 400 miles and with no help from the weather it seemed a cruel task we were sending her on. She pedalled gamely on up Shap. Usually magnificent views are seen, but now only mist and rain coming down in 'stair rods' which reminded me of a 'Patterson' Lake District sketch.

10.25 am 444 miles Shap Summit, lots of encouragement from the team and unbeknown to me, Liz had phoned Wilko on the mobile and told him that Lynne's Uncle 'Inky' Stephen Moss had travelled up from Birmingham on the train and was waiting for her outside Carlisle railway station. When Wilko told Lynne she reacted positively using this as a stepping stone, and pedalled even harder. There was now a headwind and driving rain. She stopped halfway down Shap for new glasses. The old ones had broken due to constantly wiping them with her gloves!

11.01 am 455 miles Five miles south of Penrith - still very wet.

12.04 pm 471 miles Toilet and food stop taken just before Carlisle. Incidentally, we found out later that one of the local clubmen who never missed an End to End and sees the riders on Shap on his way to work, waited over two hours, but with the worsening conditions and Lynne being a long way down, didn't think she would come, let alone break the record, so he carried on to work. Pat reckoned at this point that Lynne was about 4 hrs 22 mins down, but if she didn't take the scheduled hour break at Gretna Green she could regain quite a lot of her losses.

2.11 pm 473 miles Carlisle was reached. Lynne's Uncle Inky popped up at the side of the road to give a shout before getting on the train back to Birmingham. If she had scheduled for a weekend, he would have gone up to Inverness and got a taxi to do the same again. Inky is a grandson of the late Charlie Moss of MC and AC fame at the turn of the last century. He was one of the first winners of the Bath Road 100 and Speedwell 100 winning the Anfield 100 three times, riding against others such as Tom Peck, G.A.Olley and Leon Meredith. Back to present day with lots of heavy traffic at dinnertime in Carlisle, and despite Lynne getting delayed at various lights and junctions, it took a long while to catch her. We managed to stay behind her on the A74 to shield her from the heavy fast traffic continuing off the M6. Thank god its only a short stretch to Gretna where she carried on without a break. The two vehicles exchanged Observers here. We said goodbye and thanks to Pat Kenny who cycled back to Carlisle and the train home, and to Pete Swinden who had arranged a walking holiday with Ken Sutton, starting from Gretna. We took on Bob Williams as Observer in the following car, and Mike Johnson who'd been a passenger and helper in the feed car since Arclid Lights, now became Observer. Mike had provided the feed car for the attempt and mentioned at the end that he had never got to drive it. Many thanks to him. Meanwhile Lynne had picked up a tailwind along this very straight, boring, long stretch, which runs parallel for miles alongside the M74.

1.55 pm 504 miles Lockerbie was reached, drizzle had set in again.

2.20 pm Lynne was suffering with wet shorts and tiredness. An eleven minute break for dry shorts and peppermint tea, and away again to Beattock Summit, then right off this long stretch of road, to Moffat, a lovely town for tourists, but no such fun for Lynne as the climb of the 'Devils Beeftub' was looming ahead. It's a long and winding climb that you can see for miles ahead of you, and it goes over and along Tweedsdale. It is where the source of the River Tweed is, and the river goes from a few feet wide to a huge wide torrent within a few miles as it runs downhill towards Edinburgh.

3.55 pm 534 miles On the descent from the Beeftub,. Lynne stopped for 10 mins to ease her eyes and take a hot drink. Back on now and the long 20 mile descent to Penicuik, but Lynne was still cheerful and eating and drinking well.

Now for the rush hour in Edinburgh and I'm not looking forward to this. The route through Edinburgh used to be much easier if a little dangerous on the bypass, but Police will not allow a cyclist on this road now. Approaching Edinburgh Lynne took a wrong turn. It happened to be the road she and Andy had used on the Liverpool-Edinburgh record, which ends up in the centre of the capital on Princes Street. The feeding car who were ahead but on an adjacent road could see her. They blew horns and shouted her and luckily she saw them but the traffic was so heavy it took minutes to correct the mistake. Back on the correct route she took another little detour up a side road which with all the traffic lights and congestion cost about 12 mins in total. A lot more time would have been lost here but for the great help from Carol Dietman, Jane and her helpers. How they got through the traffic to pop up at strategic turning points I do not know. Their help was immense. Carol also took turns on the telephone help line for the attempt, so once again, our many thanks to them all. Out of the suburbs and now the road became a horrible, dangerous, 8 lane highway which led directly to the Forth Road Bridge. Night was closing in now and we tried to protect Lynne as much as we could. She made it safely to the bridge and then had to divert round the queues for the toll booths to join a thin walkway strip that runs along the side of the bridge. Lynne Mckie in the feed car said our Lynne looked very small in the scale of things on this huge bridge that loomed up in an arc over the vast expanse of water. Jonathan Williams was on this bridge just in case help was needed, but all was fine. We stopped and waited for her to come off the bridge to put her on her night bike with fresh lights here, for this next busy stretch to Cowdenbeath.

7.15 pm 586 miles We are hoping to get Lynne beyond Perth for her next big stop at the comfort van. She said she could feel a help from the wind and the roads were drying out, and yes, she would like to get beyond Perth ! How's that for positive thinking. Wilko says it's the best news he'd heard for a long time.

8.30 pm 592 miles I think everybody was feeling there was an 'even chance' now, but so much depended on her keeping warm, well, and not too sleepy. The feeding team along this stretch, were seen hiding behind a wall eating fish and chips out of sight in case Lynne saw them and demanded her share. Perth was entered and much as we tried to follow Lynne and keep to the scheduled route, we still got lost. By the time we got through Perth and onto the A9, we didn't know whether she had got safely through, but there, up ahead in the lay by was the comfort stop van, with Lynne getting all the necessary attention.

9.30 pm 607 miles Harry Wilkinson and John Arnold have done a wonderful job again, with hot drinks etc. Lynne stopped for 32 mins here. She had a massage on her back and legs and a change to dry clothing. Paul sent her on her way saying she had had a good 40 mins stop with a sleep. In 24 hour events, if Lynne needs a sleep I usually let her have about 5 mins, just to relax her eyelid muscles. That is actually all you need. Lynne knows just what she has to do now. Just over 230 miles in 16.5 hours. Paul had omitted the odd 49 mins so it acted like a safety barrier of time to break the record by. Lynne knows she has to average 14.5 miles per hour, still not an easy job after all these hours. Anyone who watches Lynne ride knows that her style is steady pedalling, and I've never seen her struggle or take a 'bad patch' in all the years I've helped her , covering thousands of miles. I almost felt confident that it was just possible now. On into the second night, it was now virtually A9 all the way. She still had the route card on her handlebars, so she could relate to where she was and what lay head. She couldn't possibly get lost now. Harry and John motored on ahead to Inverness, over 100 miles away, to get another comfort stop ready, hopefully her last. She was still taking regular drinks of carbo, peppermint, and Psp rego a recovery drink that Lynne says is like a milk shake. Andy was now going to reduce her liquid intake from here to cut down on the toilet stops.

11 pm 635 miles Pitlochry bypass. All the towns were now bypassed which is faster but a little boring if you are a tired rider. Lynne stops for 8 mins sleep and warm up. Andy deliberated about giving her coffee or tea but decided against it, not wanting to cause highs and lows at this late stage. It was dry now with a slight tail wind. On to Blair Atholl by pass, Lynne moving well with a very smooth style. The team took a detour here to get ahead of her, to give extra encouragement, and to beat the 30 mins 'unwritten' passing rule.

29.09.01 2.00 am 685 miles. Just 12 hours and 49 mins (12 hours to Lynne) to do 155 miles.

3.05 am Lynne had to have 10 mins sleep here as she's worried about falling asleep on the bike. Back on the bike now and Andy told Lynne that she must hurry to Inverness if she wanted to have a comfort break there. Its cold now and for the first time we can see stars. The traffic was very light, just the odd articulated lorry putting lots of lights on the road for Lynne, and the friendly toot of the horn as they pass, as if they knew exactly what was going on. Along the A9 to Inverness there were onlookers and observers popping up at odd locations. Jonathan and Ruth Williams had motored all the way up and saw Lynne regularly along here. An ideal situation if there had been a problem with any of the cars or helpers. Our thanks to them. Lynne afterwards said she had been hallucinating, seeing purple glittering laybys and hedgerows looking like white plastic figures. A trick of the headlights and tiredness. I told her that on Pat Kenny's and my tandem trike attempt, I had said 'good morning' and had a conversation with a chap in a red sweater near Golspie. It turned out to be a red post box on a pole.

Lynne is now on the long descent into Inverness and its very cold. On Lynne and Andy's tandem record the following car had a job to keep up with the tandem touching nearly 60 mph. Lynne could only manage about 35 mph against the wind. The town at Inverness is bypassed so Harry and John had the comfort van parked on a services area. Lynne had a massage to her lower back by Andy and dry shorts fitted by Lynne Mckie. 12 mins sleep, what a luxury, plus honey sweetened black coffee and hot rice pudding , what a treat, served up by master chef John Arnold. Total stop time was 22 mins.

5.25 am 720 miles Just over 9 hours to do 120 miles, and still three or four very tortuous climbs to come, and every time the road bore to the right, Lynne was into an almost block headwind off the sea.

Although she was very tired she was doing her own mental arithmetic and was trying to break the remaining ride down into 50 mile segments. She found it was much easier to think about 50 miles in 4.5 hours. I was thinking that people who do charity rides would split this 100 mile section into two days with a YHA stop. She had to do it before 2.49 pm the same day. It was still dark when she went onto the Kessock Bridge over the Morray Firth with the lights of Inverness twinkling away below on our left. Over the Cromarty Firth now and the start of the Tain by pass.

752 miles now covered. Day had broken but it is a very dull grey orangy dawn and quite cool. Along the coast road early morning traffic now coming to life. Both vehicles took on diesel now. The first garage we had seen open since Perth.

8.40 am 782 miles Golspie was reached. Lynne was pressing on with great determination into a grey beige daylight and a stiff headwind off the sea.

10.00 am She has a 6 min toilet stop and some more food, muesli bars, butties and banana, five miles before she climbed Helmsdale. The team planned to get ahead now and run in turn alongside Lynne on the steep bends. She climbed Helmsdale in thick mist, very aggressively, although she almost came to a standstill a couple of times as she turned into a headwind on

42/23 gearing. Andy Wilko's report states that she climbed more stylishly than you could expect any rider to do even after 100 miles, let alone after 800.

10.50 am Lynne is now at the foot of the Berriedale climb. I'd forgotten just how steep these climbs are. On a road race they would be 1st category climb classification I'm sure. Again the team ran alongside her. Lynne Mckie chatted until she was out of breath. Paul Histon had done most of the running, or was it just his gazelle like stature I noticed more ? His voice had almost disappeared now with a cold and sore throat imminent.

11.20 am Lynne took on a teacake with jam in the rain, one mile before the Dunbeath climb. 38 miles to go in 2hrs 35 mins for a 2.00 pm finish which gives a 49 minute beating of the record. Its still raining and its quite cool. She is still riding with great determination but the headwind is getting to her.

11.45 am Lynne has just 28 miles to do and we can say its almost in the bag !

12.36 pm Now with stone faced determination just south of Wick. All the way through the 'Ord of Caithness' the half light and mist made the surrounding countryside very drab.

12.55 pm 2 miles north of Wick 15 miles to go. Heavy rain and very strong side winds from the right. Hoping for a 2 o'clock finish, everyone thinking about a bath or shower and sleep before going on for the 1000 mile attempt. John o Groats loomed out of the mist and gloom, everywhere, looking grey and bleak. One mile to go and Lynne was storming down the road. The team had gone ahead to see her in safely. Nobby Clarke did the timekeeping honours and recorded

A new record of 2 days 5 hrs 48 mins 21 secs.

Lynne had broken Pauline Strong's 11 year old record by 1 hour 10 mins.

We all felt very emotional at this point. Obviously Lynne's state of health would have to be assessed prior to the continuation for the 1000 mile record. Another 160 miles in atrocious conditions with 19 hours to do it. It doesn't sound all that hard, but when you work it out, after a stop for a sleep and shower plus probably a sleep later on going into the third cold night, it meant doing approx 12 mph at least. Out of 53 hours of riding, Lynne had had at least 45 hours of rain. She left the decision making up to us -the people who had helped her.

I was quite concerned about how she looked. Her skin and eyes were looking 'puffy' and she was stiffening up. Her ankles were troubling her and she had to be helped off her bike at the end, not surprising you might say, but I have seen Lynne at the end of virtually all of her long distance rides, and even after the tandem End to End she still looked 100% better than she did now. Her face was ashen and she seemed to have shrunk. Most people who have seen Lynne finish a hard 12 or 24 hr race would say she looks as though she's just finished a hard club run. She's always got a good colour and she never has any trouble walking, in fact, she has been known to do a cartwheel and take a ride on a 'Penny Farthing' after riding one of the Mersey Road 24 hr races. I based my decision on how she now looked, and luckily, the rest of the team felt the same. Knowing that if we put her back on her bike at 5 pm, she would soon be going into darkness and it could take her up to 9 am the next day. Based on these facts, I think we all made the right decision not to carry on. Even Lynne looked relieved. At the end of the tandem record she had been very saddle sore but was still ready to go for the 1000 if we wanted her to.

John Arnold and Harry had followed us up all of the way and now wanted to know if their services were still required for the 1000. As it was not, they were going to motor back down and see Gethin coming through the Highlands. What a fantastic pair; I hope I have as much energy as them when I am their age. The timekeeper, Nobby Clarke, asked if his services were required and after we declined his offer and thanked him for travelling up from Aberdeen, he went back to be with his wife who was ill.

Lynne was now at the Hotel and in the shower awaiting our decision. She had to have an electric fan heater on her for about three hours to bring her back up to temperature. That last 12 hours had taken a lot out of her and left her hypothermic, but what an achievement Obviously Telephone HQ had been informed, unlike last year, when everybody, including myself, had failed to tell Edwin and Shelagh Hargraves manning the phone and the internet, that Lynne and Andy had finished.

I had telephoned John Williams, who had masterminded both of these successful End to Ends, just before Wick to say that barring accidents, Lynne would break the record. His voice was monotone in response, He sounded drained, he had worked so hard for weeks to try and get the attempt off the ground. His telephone bill must have cost a fortune and the Met Office updates at £17 a time beggar belief. Everytime we spoke on the phone prior to the attempt John sounded as though he was knee deep in paperwork and computer paper. He must have taken the strain of this organisation very heavily and our immense thanks go out to him for guiding us through it all, and believing it could be done as late as September/October.

It was nail biting right from the previous weekend where the winds were looking right and they did come right, but about 12-15 hours too late for Lynne. Not John's fault at all; if he could have had his way the attempt would have started on the Thursday, the day Gethin went, however, the RRA when pressed on this matter, would only allow attempts on separate days. In hindsight the wind got even stronger on the Friday and blew at gale force for quite a number of days after that.

A good sleep was had by all, but despite the downing of several glasses of red wine before bed, courtesy of Andy Wilkinson's parents, the team and Lynne were up and ready by 5 am the next day, 29th September, to cheer Gethin in at 6.00 am. Our team had been told of his progress up through Scotland by mobile phones. Gethin put up a new 24 hour record, and despite taking a packet and blowing after Edinburgh, he continued to be one hour up on his schedule for most of the second day. When he came down the road from Wick the wind was gusting very strongly and he went with such speed over the finish line at John o Groats that we thought he would plough into the hotel wall. However he stopped OK and said within a few minutes that he would take a short break and go for the 1000 mile record. What bravery, going back into that wind for a further 170 miles. Gethin had broken Andy Wilkinson's End to End record of 1 day 21 hours 2 mins 18 secs, by 58 mins and it now stands at **1 day 20 hours 4 mins 20 secs.** Gethin then went on to break Reg Randall's 1000 mile record in a time of **2 days 7 hrs 59 mins.**

"WHAT A DIFFERENCE A DAY MAKES" - AND TO HAVE A HELPFUL WIND

We had witnessed history being made by two of the Country's top long distance riders within 24 hours. The last time anything like this happened was in 1954, nearly 50 years ago, when Eileen Sheridan broke the End to End and 1000 miles, and the following day, Albert Crimes and John Arnold broke the 12hr, 24 hr End to End and 1000 mile Tandem trike record. That must have been something to see. The John o Groats hotel is boarded up now and sadly not in use, but one could imagine all the riders and support crews staying there and celebrating - What a do !

That is my story, which only leaves Lynne and myself to thank everybody involved. The magnificent team, those who waited on the cold wet roadside for hours; the people who rang in or logged on to the web site from the comfort of their homes; all the people who donated their time; people who assisted with hotel bills, meals, and donations to help Lynne with her expenses; Marshalls, Observers, and especially, John Williams, who organised it perfectly.

Many thanks, and dare I say it "see you next year". We know that with the right winds, Lynne could get close to 2 days and those were her own words as soon as she got off her bike, however, that will be her decision, and for me, another story.

Song Title for Lynne "What a difference a day makes"

Song Title for Gethin "Oh, what a perfect day"

In August 2004 Harry Wilkinson passed peacefully away aged 86 years.

No 37 GETHIN BUTLER 27TH SEPTEMBER 2001 SOLO BICYCLE

LANDS END TO JOHN O GROATS - 1 DAY 20 HRS 4 MINS 20 SECS
1000 MILES - 2 DAYS 7 HRS 59 MINS 24 HRS - 505. 8 MILES

When Gethin read about John Woodburn's End to End, he had been riding for only two years. After a diet of road racing coming into the Elite class, then winning lots of time trials and the BBAR twice, plus the second greatest distance at 24 hrs with 509 miles, Gethin felt he was as ready as he ever would be for the End to End. His style of riding, again very smooth in the tuck position. He is what I would class 'a mile eater', an avid Audax enthusiast riding all distances up to Paris-Brest-Paris, the fastest Englishman ever to do so in 49 hrs in 2003.

Jim Turner was to be the organizer, Dai Davies the overall timekeeper, Gillian his wife looked after his feeding along with Gethins dad, Keith. Mike Speight was to prove very useful as the mechanic and mentor as Gethin had 4 punctures throughout the ride. Colin Baldwin again a seasoned masseur and source of encouragement on previous records, was to prove good for Gethin's very tired limbs. Anne Turner provided telephone back up along with brother Roger back at the base in Cheshire. George and Brenda Jackson drove the journey from the Midlands to provide a warm camper van for Gethin to recuperate en route. Ron Sant provided his services as an observer. Malcolm Firth kept the country informed through his internet website and Paul Hewitt provided the bike and backing for the attempt.

Gethin's bike weighed about 17 lbs. It was a 'Paul Hewitt'made with 'Columbus Foco' tubing with 'Time' carbon forks and a mix of Campag and Shimano components. His main foods were 'Extran' (a carbo-hydrate polymer drink), sausages, Maxim bars, hot Bovril and cheese and ham rolls when stopped. He used the Liverpool-Edinburgh as a good pointer to what record breaking was about as it covered 170 miles of the End to End course. He took 35 mins off Ken Joys 1954 record and it helped Gethin to bond with his team over some difficult terrain.

Gethin waited like Lynne for a decent forecast and chose the 27th September for two reasons (a) the wind and weather was to be more favourable on the Thursday. Hence the saying 'what a difference a day makes' and (b) Gethin is a mathematician and superstitious to boot, so he wanted a number that could be divided by nine, thus it had to be the 27th.

10 am 27th September 2001 Lands End Hotel, dry, cold, winds west south west and gusting from 16-28 mph. The first 25 miles through Penzance and Redruth in under the hour. The 100 was covered in 3 hrs 58 mins. Gethin was pushing large gears at this point. He was relieved to be getting off the A30 at Exeter but after a few miles he wished he was back on it as the road surfaces leave a lot to be desired between here and Bristol.

Neville Channin was to be seen regularly along here to cheer Gethin on; to Bristol now and a very steep climb up to and over the Clifton Suspension Bridge due to a landslide collapse on the usual road. Again, as had been the previous day for Lynne, Bristol was so well marshalled by Ian and Bridget Boon, and Geoff Lonsdales large band of helpers and marshalls right through to **Filton at 18.24 pm - 199 miles** and 54 mins up on schedule. Lights had been donned just after Bristol . The website reported Gethin going through Gloucester marshalled by Ann Woolridge and the Gloucester City CC. Neville Channin says "We felt really honoured to have witnessed two record attempts in 2 days" - Lynne had been through 24 hrs earlier.

Gethin put up **279.5 miles for his first 12 hours**, a cracking mileage considering what lay ahead. He stopped just south of Wolverhampton to change his clothing and put more lights on, still a good following wind for him on this stretch. A slight 'off course' at Wombourne in Wolverhampton, and missing a short cut in the city, lost him probably 2 mins here. Gethin says the ride through the Midlands, Cheshire, Warrington, Wigan, Preston, Lancashire through the border to the top of the Beeftub will remain in his memory forever, for the amount of people out on route cheering him on. He says he realised it wouldn't be just himself that he would let down if he didn't finish !

On now through his home town of **Preston 4.25 am - approx 404 miles**, slight drizzle and stops to don legwarmers. At Lancaster he is an hour up on schedule, could the 24 hr record go ? Thick mist and fog on Shap make it a tortuous 9 mile climb for Gethin and a dangerous one as the steep descents cannot be used to their full extent to get any speed up. The scene at the top more than made up for the climb as it was crowded with cyclists from all over, at 6 am on a Friday morning. He says that he has no recollections of the next 15 miles to Penrith although he says he's seen the photos so he must have done it ! I think it's the fact that the course from Shap to Carlisle and beyond is pretty flat with no really outstanding features. Negotiating heavy traffic in Carlisle soon brought him back to normality. Gethin now reaches **Gretna Green 481 miles at 8.35 am** so the 24 hr record is about to go. He was hoping to get to the summit of the Devils Beeftub approximately 517 miles for the 24 hr, could he do it ? He pressed on along the old main road to Beattock, but tiredness was now taking its toll. Beattock bypass was reached and the **24 hr point yielded 505. 8 miles - a new RRA record**, adding just over 11 miles onto John Woodburn's record in 1982, also put up on the End to End.

Still 50 mins up on schedule he was now 'riding into the unknown' never having raced beyond 24 hrs. What would the next few hours yield ? Off right through Moffat and then the long arduous climb of the 'Beeftub' riding it in swirling low cloud, Gethin said it gave him a depressive feeling as normally the views from here are magnificent, looking back right over England at the Borders. He eventually made it to the top, cold and soaked through. The high from getting the 24 hr record now turned to a 'low'. He stopped for hot Bovril and a rest and change of clothing, which surprisingly took up the best part of an hour. Jim Turner being the good organizer, was hovering around anxiously trying to get Gethin back on his bike, knowing that his 50 minute gain was now virtually 'wiped out'.

Gethin reluctantly got back on, having lost interest even though it's a long 45 miles or so drop down to Edinburgh. He said his morale was low, he'd been working it out in his head that there was still over a third of the journey left to do and if he went on for the 1000 miles he was only just halfway. His legs felt very tired 'full of ache' was how he described it. He needed another 10 min sleep which he took in a bus shelter at Penicuik, just south of Edinburgh - it did the trick - he got back on refreshed. Over the Forth Road Bridge its now 2pm warmish with a little wind, still the right way. Showers and drizzle accompanied him to Perth. Although Gethin remembers, around the Kinross area, just pulling up by the helpers for a quick chat, and recalls "If anyone had offered me a shower and a bed I would have stopped". But the only answer he got from Gillian was "If you think we've all come this far just for you to climb off, you've got another think coming up". For Gethin it was a very low point, not just a physical thing, more a 'what the hell am I doing here?' feeling. After one or two minor detours for temporary traffic lights etc, he left Perth with 600 miles done, and now the long slog up the A9. Remembering the last words Jim Turner had given him at Lands End "No one who has got past Perth on one of my attempts has packed or failed".

As you go onto the A9, the first sign is for Inverness 108 miles. 20 miles on he passes through Dunkeld now 14 mins down on schedule. He can't afford to lose anymore time now with nightfall coming up, although the wind and weather is in his favour, Jim Turner is getting worried. Gethin cannot afford to slip back anymore. He stopped for lights just after Pitlochry and then amazingly he started to pick up speed. Gillian said afterwards that it was as if he had been in 'tourist mode' for about 6 or 7 hours, and was now back onto the job of racing. Through Blair Atholl then the 'Pass of Drumochter' - a short stop for more night clothing now - 8.30 pm - second night. An internet message from Alasdair Maclennan shows the more positive mood Gethin was in 'Just returned from seeing Gethin on the leg from Drumochter to Inverness, spoke to him when he was putting on his night clothes and having a massage from Colin. He was in great form, cracking jokes etc. I passed on the good news that the wind would pick up from the South East - mainly dry.' Gethin continued to claw back time, on through Dalwhinnie, Kingussie, Aviemore, surrounded by the Cairngorms, Carrbridge, then the long climb to the Slochd Summit, Tomatin, then one final 'kick' of a hill at Daviot before a 60 mph drop to Inverness, which brought Gethin almost back on schedule. Two of his friends, Alastair and Roddy, had started to walk up from opposite sides of the Kessock Bridge which prompted the local police to give the bridge a visit - a passing local had raised the alarm thinking they were 'jumpers'. Gethins happier mood says he thought of them not as 'jumpers' more 'anoraks'.

Once the Kessock Bridge is crossed you start seeing signs for John o Groats - 120 miles. Gethin thought of this mentally as his last section, a seventh of the journey, or more than Lands End to Exeter. He wanted to get it down to double figures. On to the Black Isle now to cross the Cromarty Firth, 2 mins up on schedule now but every time the road turned right he found himself flogging into a block headwind off the sea. There was also thick sea fog which erased any landmarks. Gethin felt this next 80 miles in the dark and the fog was going to be his most challenging ride ever with three big climbs to come.

2.40 am just passing Helmsdale YHA now the start of a tortuous 4 mile climb with back breaking hairpins. A puncture here was quickly sorted by 'Mike the mechanic'. With the fog and mist, the hairpins going down became treacherous braking areas, Gethin trying to claw the bike onto the road, as in many places there was a 200 ft drop to the rocks and sea below.

Gethin says he only knew he'd finished climbing Helmsdale when he started the kamikaze 1 in 7 drop into Berriedale another 10 miles on. He is now over 15 mins down on schedule and couldn't engage his 21 tooth sprocket due to the last wheel change which meant he had to dance on the pedals instead of sitting down up the hills. Latheron was reached so he departed from the A9 to join the A99 to Wick, where still the fog and headwind were troubling him greatly, now only 17 miles to go, and a very strong wind from the right off the sea made him lean into the wind to stay upright.

5.35 am - 10 miles to go Soon Gethin is in Freswick, the last village before John o Groats. He recalls "Suddenly a car came the other way and there was a squeal of brakes. Three people got out and I climbed the last hill, with the yells of Paul Histon, Lynne Taylor and Wilko ringing in my ears". Then the long last drop to John o Groats.

I was actually there when Gethin powered down the road to the Hotel. I thought 'crikey' he's going to smash straight into the wall at that speed, but even after **1 day 20 hrs 4 mins 20 secs** his reactions were good. He was cheerful as one would be after that. I was absolutely amazed as he just stood there and said "I'm going for the 1000". The weather was bleak and atrocious. Okay, we had been up since 5.30 am after Lynne's End to End and we hadn't really recuperated from the day before, so it probably seemed worse, but wild horses wouldn't have got me on a bike at that particular time. In the battle he had over those last few hours he'd managed to claw back enough time to beat Wilko's record by 57 mins 59 secs. What a feat ! What a fight ! As he walked back to the motor home to have a change of clothes, we stood sheltering behind a wall, listening to the wind 'wailing' in the telephone wires in that remote spot. It was now daybreak into a greyish dawn as we waited to see Gethin off to start his remaining 160 miles. His helpers were dashing around. Gillian was trying to keep all but essential people out of the motor home so that Gethin could have a decent massage off Colin. Its easy to waste valuable time chatting at these crucial stages.

Gethin later reflected on how well he felt. He said to give you some idea of the conditions, "Imagine sitting in a camper van in a barren place. The van is rocking violently in the wind, which is also coming through every nook and cranny it can find, all you can hear is the wind whistling, its still dark and misty. If I had been at home that morning and anybody had said to me would I like to go on a 160 mile bike ride in those conditions, I would have said they were stupid - and anyway, Jim hadn't got a hotel booked till teatime, so I had to carry on"! Another reason to continue was that no-one had successfully carried on to take the solo gents

1000 mile record at the end of an End to End attempt for 64 years, Sid Ferris being the last one, so it seemed the right thing to do.

7.30 am - Gethin restarted his ride and by 8.35 had covered approximately 22 miles of his first lap of 50 miles to be covered three times taking in Thurso, Wick and Castletown. After about 50 miles the drizzle, mist and rain clouds lifted only to come back with a vengeance at about the 950 mile mark. At that point he was soaked through and freezing again. He stopped when he reached the van and took a 40 min break for dry clothes and food.

He left the van hoping to complete the last 65 miles (the extra miles as guarantee he had done 1000) without stopping but it wasn't to be. The rain lashed into him and after 20 miles he climbed back into the camper for a sleep. Gillian said he looked like an old man at that point. After a short sleep he climbs back out for the last 45 miles up to Wick, now against a very tough wind on 'heavy' roads; then the final turn to Thurso and Castletown to finish down by Dunnet at just before 6 pm with **2 days 7 hrs 59 mins.** What a ride, taking 2hrs 41mins off Reg Randalls 1960 1000 mile record.

Alasdair Washington and Malcolm Gray who were both involved, along with other Caithness CC clubmen, with organizing the final 170 miles course for the 1000 miles, were acknowledged by Jim Turner in an article in the 'Caithness Courier'. Jim went on to say he was very impressed by the 'co-operation, help and friendliness of the local club folk'.

Malcolm Gray who was involved in supporting both Lynne and Gethin said **"In Caithness we are accustomed to meritorious End to End rides, but these were outstanding athletic performances and in a totally different ballpark. It was a tremendous weekend for British long distance cycle racing".** Apart from nearly 'blowing' at the top of the 'Beeftub' and worrying everyone, and then going into 'tourist' mode, (i.e. slightly less than 20 mph until he got to Pitlochry) Gethin had a trouble free ride. Don't forget, riders of Gethins callibre normally race at 28-29 mph, so it is difficult coming to terms with cruising along at 17 to 20 mph, so it is all praise to his ability to adapt.

Gethins speed was a bit blunted in 2002 but by 2003 it had come back and he went on to retain his 24 hrs championship crown with 475 miles, a real glutton for punishment, even the arrival on the scene of his lovely baby daughter, hadn't affected his speed. He had also completed the Paris Brest Paris as I mentioned at the beginning of the article.

Early in 2004 he was winning Hilly early season classic time trials. Gethin comes from a famous cycling family background, his father Keith, won many famous classic road race titles in the 60's and 70's and went on to become a very respected official and organizer of our sport in the Southern Counties. Gethins grandad, Stan Butler, won the 24 hr championship in 1950 with 458 miles, creating a new competition record. Stan Butler was also on Eileen Sheridan's 1954 End to End, so it has all turned full circle and one wonders what other challenges are there for Gethin to tackle ?

In an interview with Ken Mathews for Cycling Magazine in 1990, Andy Wilkinson modestly said "If I could do it, anyone could". I think he must realise that he, and Gethin who took 57 mins 59 secs off in 2001, were **the top men** and it will be very hard now to find somebody to beat them.

The next rider must be capable of 500 miles in a 24 hr, but not slow down below 17 mph for the next 20 hrs. I can only think of one man - Kevin Dawson.

GETHINS END TO END AND 1000 MILE ACCOUNT CAME MAINLY FROM HIS OWN ARTICLE:

THE PREFACE BEING: "THIS BOOK IS DEDICATED TO THOSE MEN AND WOMEN, BOTH NAMED AND UNNAMED WHO GAVE THEIR TIME FREELY AND WILLINGLY IN ORDER THAT I COULD PROVE TO THE CYCLING WORLD THAT I AM NUTS"

This story begins, like all good stories, a long time ago. In fact I probably would find it extremely difficult to recall when I first had a conscious thought about doing the End to End. Obviously I had heard stories of past endeavours but when John Woodburn went and got the record in 1982, I had only been riding for two years.

The next successful attempt wasn't until 1990 when Wilko set the current record of 1 day 21 hours 2 minutes 18 seconds. By this time I was a bit more knowledgeable as far as riding and racing went. This year was what I class as my first successful season. I managed 2nd in the BBAR and 2nd in the National 100 as well as finishing my Maths degree at Lancaster. When Wilko went I was just recovering from my first bout of tonsillitis and so it did not register straight away. I soon learnt that he had got it by the skin of his teeth and had suffered fairly badly towards the end.

At this point in my career I had no inkling that one day I too would be wending my merry way across England and Scotland in an attempt to prove that I too am a compete nutter ! I'd only just managed to do a decent 12 hour on my third try.

Not much happened over the next few years except that I gradually became more and more mental as my enthusiasm for 100's gradually turned into enthusiasm for 12's . Then the unimaginable occurred! Despite hints and warnings to keep away from the jolly looking big man who was always laughing, smiling and dipping his hand into his jacket pocket, we met. It was at the Lancashire Road Club dinner in January 1997. His name was Jim Turner and the reason his hands were always disappearing from sight was to produce entry forms for the Mersey Roads 24 Hour, of which he was the organiser. These he would give to unsuspecting victims with promises of much enjoyment and self satisfaction. There would be a myriad of reasons given for why you should ride, afterwards forgotten of course, and then like a poor fly you are gradually enticed into the spiders web. Gotcha !

I agreed. When I told my mum she told me that I was far too young and shouldn't be thinking of 24's until I was older. I did point out that I'd won the BBAR twice, I was 28 and that if Kevin Dawson had said he was doing it she wouldn't have batted an eyelid and he was younger than me. That was the only barrier of note.

I prepared meticulously and went into the event with some of the best form I've ever had. Despite this I suffered like nothing on Earth. I made the mistake of using Low Profile bikes and managed to get sores from damp clothing. I finished but I knew I wasn't actually tired from the event but I was just unable to sit on my bike properly.

In support of this I rode round the Trough of Bowland the next day and followed this up with a 3 hr 40 min 100 on the Sunday (course record by 11 mins and is still my personal best on Brock).

Of course this didn't actually make me feel any more inclined towards doing any more. However, exactly a year after I had met Jim at the Lancs RC Dinner, we again met at the same venue and as we left at the end of the night I turned to Jim and said those ill-fated words, "Could you send me a schedule for the End to End ? Although I won't go before 2001." Almost the next day a schedule arrived through the post with my name printed in the relative spaces where once had stood Wilko's. I looked at it then filed it away with my list of things to contemplate for the future, where it remained for many months.

The next brick in the wall came from a sometime training and racing partner Phil Leigh, who had decided to have a go at the End to End himself. Unfortunately Phil had been unsuccessful in his two attempts but had decided to make a video of the second attempt and the planning behind it. The video and talk were at Lancaster University and were very emotive which led to a resurgence of interest on my side.

With this new burst of enthusiasm I entered the Mersey Road 24 Hour in 2000. This proved to be a good day and a very good morale booster as far as riding 24's goes. I was fortunate to finish with the second furthest distance ever (509 miles) and actually felt that I still had a lot left in my legs. Fear of the consequences if I overdid it were still ripe in my mind from '97. After I had finished my mind began to compute: 509 miles in 24 hours

leaves 330 miles in 21 hours for the End to End - average 15.75 mph

leaves 160 miles in 13.75 hours for the 1000 miles - average 11.65 mph

It sounds so easy doesn't it? Only having to average under 16 mph for 330 miles and then a mere 12 mph for 160 miles. A piece of cake ! I was hooked.

I think I decided fairly quickly that I would have a go the following year although I don't know to whom I mentioned it first. The problem with telling people daft things like this is that it goes through the cycling grapevine quicker than Queally can do the kilometre. I kept it fairly quiet for a while then finally mentioned it to Jim. Jim was ecstatic and instantly started coming up with plans and a new schedule for the attempt. He was determined to be involved and believe me I was glad to let him arrange it. The downside of telling Jim was that suddenly everyone knew, which meant the pressure was on.

My sincere thanks to Gethin for allowing me to use extracts and information from an article written by him about his experiences during the ride. You will have seen from the light-hearted and amusing comments he makes, he doesn't take himself too seriously - just serious enough to be 100 % focused on the day.

No 38 LYNNE TAYLOR 1ST OCTOBER 2002
'THREE DAYS OF SLEEPLESS NIGHTS'

LYNNE'S SECOND SOLO END TO END (AND 1000 MILES)
6 AM 1ST OCTOBER 2002

It had all started at John o Groats Hotel after the end of Lynne's 2001 record. The first thing she said to me as she was helped off the bike was "I've got to go again haven't I Dad?" This was such a positive thing to say after just suffering over 48 hrs of rain on the hardest ride of her life. I said to her "You could put it inside two days, with the right wind".

We had asked **Jim Turner** as far back as November 2001 if he would organize her 2002 attempt and he was happy to do so. A schedule was submitted to the RRA in May to run from June onwards and although it incorporated Christine Roberts 24 hr record of 467.30 miles, Lynne's own End to End record of 2 days 5 hrs 48 mins 21 secs, the main aim was to beat **Eileen Sheridan's** 1000 mile record of 3 days 1 hr that had stood since 1954.

Lynne's training and racing throughout the year (2002) had gone well, her 5th place BBAR position was made up of a 59-42 for '25', a 2hr-00-26 '50' and a 4-12-47 '100'. More importantly for her mental and physical state, she had ridden a good 12 hr 244 miles and a very good 438miles for 24 hr.

People have criticised the decision for Lynne to keep attacking the record year after year, not allowing for recovery, however in my opinion, so many other things can get in the way and prevent an attempt taking place. Lack of motivation, finances, family, work commitments, lack lustre results, joint stiffness, digestive disorders, women's ailments (not that I know much about those), and most important of all, is the body starting to wear out ? In Lynne's case only two of these problems existed. She had slight bouts of sickness in all the long distances i.e.100's, 12hrs and 24 hrs, enough to rethink her feeding regime. The other problem was Achilles tendon soreness in certain footwear.

Lynne never questions our decisions, Jims and mine, the only thing she would ask while waiting is "You wouldn't send me without a decent wind would you ?", to which a lump would appear in my throat and I would say "Hmm of course not!"

It was to be a new helping team and officials for this year as with the long wait for the wind and conditions, peoples lives had changed the plans. **Yvonne Unsworth** along with **Colin Baldwin** were to be Lynne's main support and masseur. **Neil Peart** who had helped and fed Lynne over the last five years, along with **Mike Taylor**, Lynne's brother were to be the mainstays of the driving team. **Christine Minto** was to time her from Lands End to Gretna, and **Tony Shardlow** was to complete the End to End and 1000 miles. **Pete Swinden** and **Ron Sant** were again to be observers in the feed car. **Mike Johnson** provided extra cover with a Landrover and as a spare observer he played a crucial role later on in the record.

Last but not least **Jim and Anne Turner**. Anne was to again provide telephone cover along with Jim who was the overall organiser. Jim was to stay at home 'on call' on this one. The effort of being on the road throughout **Gethin's** End to End and 1000 miles the previous year had taken its toll on Jim and it took him weeks to recover. **Malcolm Firth** was to provide an active website for people to 'log on' and 'look in' from all over the country, indeed the world, also providing digital pictures of the attempt en route.

After picking up Gethin's bike at John o Groats in 2001, I decided to make Lynne a lighter bike using an 'Orbea' frame and fork. The frame was Columbus alloy tubing bonded into carbon wishbone seat stays, the forks were also carbon. The wheels were Shimano Dura-ace with 16 spokes in each. The transmission was a mix of Shimano Ultegra and Dura-ace with gears ranging from 42" to 119", plus the weight was down to approx 18 lbs. The 16 spoke wheels were a godsend with the notorious crosswinds in Cornwall and Scotland.

We waited months for the right wind and conditions and the best forecast we could get was for 4 days of southerly 12-15 mph winds and fairly warm at the beginning of October. Again we stayed at the 'Old Manor House Hotel' at Sennen Cove. Peter, the owner, now does evening meals so no time is wasted eating out. He caters for 'End to Enders' getting up as early as 4.00 am to get breakfast. There has now been seven successful records from there in the last 3 years What a good omen.

Morning comes all too soon, Lynne looking a little more relaxed this year, admitting to having had at least two hours sleep. After a light breakfast it was out into the cold black misty gloom with a fog horn bellowing out to sea, like a stricken dinosaur. **Roy and Iris** with the two white Labradors were again there to see us off for the third year running. Our second good omen in place.

It was a very eerie place to be, at the Southern most tip of England in almost pitch dark, with a swirling mist and just one light on at the Hotel entrance. We have to illuminate large boulders with torches in the car park which looks like an obstacle course. A small fishing boat chugged away from the cliffs below us into the inky blackness, rather them than me I thought. **Christine Minto** counts Lynne's last few seconds as her husband Frank had done the year before.

October lst - 6 am The road through 'Drift' just past Sennen had its surface 'scarified' leaving large raised manhole covers and ramps for about 2 miles, which gave us concern as to whether Lynne would get through unscathed.

6.30 am Penzance - 10 miles Commuting traffic on the move now between Hayle and Redruth. We were checked through and cheered by **Elaine Hancock**, another good omen over the last few years for us. She is one of Lynne's and Gethin's biggest supporters.

7.07 am Redruth By pass - 22 miles The weather is damp and misty. The traffic is getting heavier by the minute, where on earth are they all going to at this time of day? Pauline appears in the lay by after having to get up at an ungodly hour to see Lynne. She was 'spooked' by a black jeep driving up very close to her car so she locked the doors and windows. In the poor light and swirling mist, four big unshaven fellows got out and started clapping and jumping up and down. It was then that she realised it was Mike and the team. What a relief, and thanks for the hug, it goes a long way. That's another good omen in place.

8.35 am Bodmin By pass - 52 miles Just inside 'evens' and looking quite comfortable, only 950 miles to go. We are keeping our eye on Lynne with very heavy rush hour traffic on these dual carriageways with cars swooping in from the left on the slip roads, we have to protect her at all of these danger spots. She is drinking a 750 ml bottle of 'PSP' per hour.

9.48 am Launceston Bypass - 77 miles Sun breaking through patchy mist pockets.

10.36 am Okehampton Bypass - 92 miles After some very long stiff climbs Lynne stops to change into dry clothes after 4.5 hours of mist had soaked the fibres. She was riding very strongly. just on 20 mph, but without any wind at all she knew she would reach the Midlands well down on schedule. At least there was one saving grace - it wasn't raining was it ? With a lump back in my throat, I hid back in the van. She has a hot peppermint tea and is away again.

11.51 am Just south of Exeter - 117 miles Lynne is looking forward to narrow quieter roads now. She is just on schedule but the roads through the town are greasy with the drizzle.

12.26 pm Cullompton - 132 miles Just on 'evens' and schedule now but still no wind. The surfaces of these narrow back roads leave a lot to be desired.

1.42 pm Taunton - 151 miles What a bottleneck; Lynne is baulked by heavy dinnertime traffic here and has to weave through the traffic in heavy rain. She is now 8 mins down on schedule but is still happy.

2.17 pm Bridgwater - 160 miles Torrential rain now, Lynne has to put on waterproof clothing and is taking 'Rennies' for an upset stomach. All along the Bridgwater Flats the rain was relentless with spray from huge lorries and surface water. **Shelagh Hargraves** gave us an apprehensive look on this stretch, she knew what Lynne had suffered on last years record. Lynne has to have two or three changes of clothing to stay comfortable, her main aim is the 1000 and knows she must have no soreness for this. Christine Minto takes the precaution of drying·Lynne's wet clothing out over the van heater along this stretch of road, so as to have plenty of reserves for later on. The aroma of olbus oil helped immensely.

3.43 pm Churchill Traffic Lights - 180 miles Very steep hills and very lumpy roads now all the way to Bristol. Again all the way up from the South we were told the warm sunny weather was just ahead of us and that we would ride into it. Mike Taylor rang the Bike Shop in Cannock and said "What's it like there?" and Lynne's mum answered "Its fine and sunny with a light breeze". Lynne is now 40 mins down, I was starting to feel very guilty now, sitting in a nice warm van watching the spray coming up from Lynne's back wheel. She had a spare race bike specially kitted out with full mudguards on, but when do you make the decision to change bikes? On into Bristol now and the grovelling climb up to the Clifton Suspension Bridge, where she was very ably marshalled through by **Ian and Bridget Boon** and the **Geoff Lonsdale team.** All done in pouring rain.

5.04pm Filton - 199 miles Over an hour down on schedule, Lynne met very heavy going home traffic here and couldn't afford to take risks with the slow moving traffic in heavy rain. All the traffic lights seemed to be red, another loss of 12 minutes here. Her approximate **12 hour distance was 213 miles.** Along this stretch to Gloucester Lynne was combating sickness with peppermint tea and dry toast and she had a problem with 'the runs'. Another 7 mins lost on this stretch.

6.43pm Gloucester - 227 miles The rain was easing now just as nightfall approached, through Tewkesbury now for a stop under a bridge holding up the M50, for a massage, a bike check, full night lights and dry clothing. Lynne was still very cheerful and positive and said the main aim was the 1000 miles, of which there were still 750 to do.

8.49 pm Worcester - 257 miles She is 1 hr 40 mins down, the road is slightly simpler as a detour down by the river is now omitted.

9.35 pm Kidderminster - 269 miles. Now 1 hr 53 mins down. From here onwards Lynne knows the roads very well; through to Stone and beyond she started to see well wishers she knew and this helped a lot. We picked up **Tony Shardlow** at the 'Mitre Oak' hotel who was to be an Observer for a while and then Timekeeper from Gretna.

10.34 Wolverhampton - 286 miles 2 hrs down now where beyond the town there are crowds of club folk she knows well and rides and races with. Through Gailey Island where various personnel were coming on board. Lynne gives everyone the thumbs up and I know she's probably fighting back the tears again. In the lay by there were some poor lorry drivers trying to have a 'kip'. They had no chance with the crowds shouting Lynne on. She starts to pick up some time now between here and Stone to have gained back another 18 mins by Newcastle under Lyme. We saw **George and Beverley Longstaff** here. Sadly this was to be the last successful End to End George would see as he passed away in 2003. He's been seeing End to Enders through for at least 40 years to my knowledge.

1.48am Knutsford - 341 miles Another stop for dry clothes, Lynne is consciously making every effort to stay comfortable so as not to have too many chaffed or raw patches later on for the 1000 miles. She knew at this point she would barely scrape 400 miles for the 24 hr leaving a lot to do later on. She was now having recurring bouts of sickness, she could be seen 'heaving' while still travelling at 20 mph. **Ruth, Bob and Jonathan Williams** were out to see her over the A556 and on towards Warrington. The sky was becoming lighter now, not from daylight, but from the motorway lights and conurbations we were passing through.

Cartoonist, Johnny Helms and his wife were out to marshall her through another junction in Warrington. **Mike Johnson** started to appear from Holmes Chapel onwards, he marshalled Lynne through lots of tricky junctions and turns by 'by-passing' the rider. His years spent in transport and his knowledge of roads in the UK is unsurpassed. On now to Winwick Church, again Tom Greep, saw us through here as on other years, with **Joan and John Kershaw, Carol and John Pardoe.**

4.25 am Preston - 382 miles 2 hrs 22mins down but still battling away, the roads are dry. **Gethin Butler and Gillian** saw us through here and on for about 50 miles knowing all the back routes to by-pass Lynne, she was very pleased to have someone to chat to. They handed us a three day fax forecast issued by the Met Office which was in hindsight, absolutely 'smack on' but we had started to disbelieve anything about weather forecasts as we had become very pessimistic.

6 am - 24 hours - Carnforth - 410 miles Lynne is still 10 miles below her 2001 distance at this time.

6.45 am Just south of Kendal 416 miles 2 hrs 30 mins down she stops in a lay by looking down on a shallow fast flowing beck with the mist just hovering above. We gave her a quick 'make-over' and took off lights etc and prepared her for the daunting climb of Shap Fell. This year she could see the climb and attacked it like a club hill climb, to reach Shap summit at 8.34 am. She should have been here at 5.11 am so technically she is 3 hrs 23 mins down, but there is an hours rest built in at 450 miles and everyone hopes she will be strong enough not to take it. Over the top now and reaching speeds of up to 40 mph, we pass **Len and Lucinda Leavesley** who have seen most rides go through here over the last 50 years. Lynne reached

Stoney Beck Island 9.50 am North of Penrith - 454 miles Lynne is foregoing her break and ploughs on towards Carlisle after donning 'shades' and sun tan crème. Not much wind but certainly getting hotter, the light breeze was just lifting the smoke from some large chimney stacks at the concrete works off to the right.

10.42 am Carlisle - 471 miles. 2 hrs 20 mins down, the traffic is a bit easier this year. Eileen Sheridan, the current 1000 mile record holder, sends Lynne a message of encouragement to a mobile phone in the van. Lynne puts her thumbs up. That will give her a boost along this next bit of flat dual carriageway that runs up to Gretna. The traffic is horrendous on here, the noise of the lorry tyres on concrete could get to you after 30 hours. At Gretna, **Tony Shardlow** took over the role as Timekeeper from **Christine Minto**, so many thanks to her. **Ron Sant** takes over the role of Observer in the support car. The last four End to Ends have all been successful for him. I hope this one is also. Les Brown waves her through at Lockerbie; Lynne dropped a bottle he was handing up.

12.35 pm Johnstone Bridge - 503 miles Lynne is halfway for the 1000 miles and 340 to go for the End to End. Approximately thirty and a half hours to here and she had reduced her deficit to 2 hrs 5 mins. Its still sunny with a bit of a tailwind, freshening all the while. The road swings off now to pass through Moffat, a picturesque market town, nestling in lush green pastures, but all the rider wants to do now is to get the gruesome climb of the 'Devils Beeftub' out of the way. It has been looming in the distance on our right for the last 25 miles or more. The lush green meadows soon give way to coarse moorland, tors and fells. The road can be seen way up high in the distance snaking round a ridge to the right, it climbs for about 8 miles twisting and turning. Off to the right the earth drops away to a huge deep chasm known as the 'Beeftub'. The climb is so severe in places, the following car has to pull in off the road for the rider to get ahead, Lynne battles on with a slight tailwind which helps.

1.40 pm Beeftub Summit - 517 miles only 2hrs 15 mins down, she takes a short break to rest her legs and back. She looks at me and says "I'm sure someone's put more air in my tyres without telling me!" Little things were starting to get to her now and after 37 hours in the saddle its not surprising. From here there is approximately 36 miles of gentle downhill with breathtaking views of the Tweed valley on our right. The road winds on to

3.39 pm Penicuik - 553 miles The strengthening tailwind has helped Lynne claw back nearly 30 mins along here. This is getting exciting for us but with Edinburgh looming on a Wednesday teatime, anything could happen. Rush hour traffic is building up at the junctions, Lynne is helped through to the 'Drum-brae' turning and the A90 by a couple of regular marshalls over the years, **Carol Dietman** and her friend **Jane.**

4.46 pm Forth Road Bridge - 572.8 miles now only 1 hr 39 mins down, Lynne's Uncle **'Inky' Moss** has once again travelled up to Scotland via train and taxi to see her across the Bridge. Again, she's amazed to see him so far from home. This huge bridge, with a lone cyclist going over what looks like an ocean, was crossed. - not for the 'faint hearted' ! The temperature has dropped now as the sun has sunk low in the sky. Lynne puts on night clothes and goes off left to Cowdenbeath. **Mike Johnson** and I had gone on ahead to check the directions and make sure we were on the right route when luckily we came onto a diversion because a bridge over a railway line was collapsing. We were able to stop and marshall Lynne along a path which saved her a costly detour. Kinross and Glenfarg were reached and down came the rain in a muddy deluge. Time to put on lights now. Lynne has a short break but says she's again looking forward to getting to Perth.

7.21pm Perth - 607 miles 1 hr 47 mins down but still looking strong and eating well. We've lowered her carbo drink intake and she's responding well. Again Mike and I go ahead while she is stopped, to check out Perth, as last year I had got completely lost, looking for road names in poorly lit streets. It was lucky we did because Glenearn road was dug up with 4 way temporary lights taking about 7 mins to get through. We managed to marshal Lynne through a muddy pedestrian walkway with ropes and debris everywhere. She got through Perth and we picked her up just as she went into a second dark night out on to the A9 and northward.

8.20 pm Dunkeld - 622 miles Now holding a steady deficit of 1 hr 42 mins, Lynne is pulling it back along here, riding at 'evens'. Its drizzling again ' sleep deprivation' is now the main worry here as Lynne struggles to see the surface of a wet black road. I also think the headlights of the following vehicle caused her to see the road as blood red, probably the blood vessels behind the retina. This was just one of her hallucinations on this long dark 100 mile stretch through the Highlands. Passing lorries on this stretch were giving a 'toot' and lighting the road up with their headlights. Unbeknown to us, Jim Turner had phoned the Perth local radio station and told them what was happening, and for drivers to look out for her in the dark on the A9.

9.40 pm North of Blair Atholl - 640 miles Drizzle is now sleet and rain, this is such a slog in the dark, the only good thing is that you cant see the road climbing away in the distance, the height and severity is only given away when you see snow markers along the edges to guide the snowploughs after a bad storm. At 650 miles Lynne has a short stop to rest her backside, she again accused us of putting more air in her tyres at the last stop. It was all in the imagination, we hadn't touched them since Lands End. They had actually lost pressure slightly as latex tubes always do after about 30 hours. The wind had dropped completely but she was still averaging 16-18 mph. She wanted to rest her eyelids but didn't want to lose anymore time. We told her she only had 180 miles to get to John o Groats, and most of the climbs were done. She climbs to Drumochter Summit and reaches

12.17 am Kingussie - 674 miles through Aviemore where 10 days after the record, the road was blocked with a snowfall. Lynne's hallucinations were becoming more vivid now. Spruce trees and bracken moving around like huge toys, the black lay-bys now appear like purple velvet. At one stage she saw rows of penguins watching her go by (I think they were probably black and white striped marker posts) Around here we picked up a very favourable shipping forecast on the radio It gave southerly winds backing west for northern coastal waters. **Alan Richards** rang from France and was, like us, concerned for her progress. He had always taken an interest in Lynne, having known her since she was about 12 years old and supplied her first racer, a 24" wheel 'Viking Warlord'. He was pleased that the forecast was good from here onwards. Soon we were to be looking out to sea after Inverness.

2.00 am Slochd Summit - 702 miles Approximately 1hr 40 mins down, Lynne climbs well here knowing it is the last long drag before Inverness. She appears to hesitate on the pedals every now and then. At first I thought it was her gears playing up, but when I asked her about the problem she said she was easing back for the traffic lights. She was hallucinating again. At last we drop down to the Beauly Firth and on to the :

Kessock Bridge - 720 miles at 3.25 am. The lights of Inverness twinkling in the waters of the Beauly Firth. Her eyes are tired but she wants to see the sign John o Groats 120 miles before she sleeps. **Roger Sewell** of the North Roads CC is out to see her in his slippers - he lives in Dingwall and its past his bedtime! Lynne says hello to him, she knows its Roger, but the name keeps coming out wrong: she calls him George. He was probably glad she could still speak at this stage, again tiredness takes its toll on the brain. Over the Cromarty Firth now she picks up a good tail wind as she turns right to the:

Tain bypass 752 miles at 5.31am. She has gained back 23 mins to be only 1 hr 17mins down. Day has dawned, the oil rigs out on the horizon to the right clearly visible. Over the Dornoch Firth, the last stretch of water to be crossed.

6.30 am Golspie - 770 miles Another 15 mins gained, only 1 hr 2 mins down. This is hold your breath time, for us anyway, can she do it ? She's got much better conditions here than last year, its dry, not too cold, and she has a tailwind and a beautiful dawn to look at over on the right out to sea. The rising sun giving a gold lining to a long thin cloud. The only cloud in a clear blue sky, only 70 miles to go now and there is a real urgency in her riding, she is really fighting back against the clock. She now reaches

Helmsdale YHA - 787 miles 7.41 am Less than an hour down now. **Tony Shardlow** says he's never seen a woman climb hills like that before, she had obviously realized she could break her own record and get the 1000 miles. Her speed was averaging 15 mph all along here. The sun was starting to give a bit of warmth and the wind was getting stronger.

8.22 am Berriedale - 796 miles now only 44 mins off schedule, I was forced out of the van here by Colin and Tony, to run behind her and shout her on - NO CHANCE - the legs didn't work, the lungs and brain didn't function, and I was limping and gasping. Lynne looked to one side of her and powered away. She said afterwards that she heard these fumbling footsteps and heavy breathing and though it was someone trying to steal her new bike !

9.10 am Lybster - 810 miles The lads from the Caithness cc are starting to appear now, they hadn't expected her quite so soon, knowing how far she had been 'down' in the Highlands. **Jim** had informed **Alasdair Washington** so that they could put the details for the 1000 miles into motion as they had done so well for **Gethin** last year. Along this stretch we nearly all got taken out by a huge Tesco lorry which overtook us and tried to get in the gap between us and Lynne. He was doing about 50 mph and with wheels locked and smoke coming off his tyres he nearly ploughed into three cars coming the opposite way. Everyone was forced to brake and stop. In hindsight, we should have been closer to her to protect her on this very narrow road.

9.50 am Wick - 823 miles only 2 mins down with 17 miles left to cover. To equal her existing record she has got 1 hr 58 mins to do it. At the right turn at Reiss, **Mike Johnson** takes the timekeeper to organize the finish. One green horizon is followed by another and then the sea comes into view. Now we can see the Orkneys, surely John o Groats is next - no just a few crofters cottages on the edge of a peat bog. Then at last the conical towered roofs of the hotel are in sight. She's flown from Wick in 55 minutes.

A new record of 2 days 4 hrs 45 mins 11 secs

Lynne has made it, taking 1 hr 3 mins off her own record. She's finished so fast that nobody but the Timekeeper **Tony** and **Mike** plus Liz's cousins, **Phil and Stuart** are here. They are our last good omen having been here at the finish for the last three years running.

Lynne has a quick hug and a kiss and then turns and retraces to the guest house up the road as she is now on route for the 1000 miles and the clock is ticking !. No-one in the history of the RRA has taken their **own** End to End record, paced or un-paced, on consecutive years on the same machine. Lynne is also the first person since G.P. Mills in 1895 to break an End to End record on three consecutive years.

Lynne got out of her tights and warm clothing now and has a shower, soup and a bit to eat, a 5 mins sleep and gets into racing strip. **Tony** played **Eileen Sheridan's** message of support in which she said she hoped Lynne would break the 1000 mile record. Good gadgets these mobile phones. Lynne was overwhelmed at this point as we all were. I opted to stay out in the fresh air and clean Lynne's bike and check it over. I could also tidy the van a bit and get lights and spares ready for the third night. I felt surprisingly fresh at this point, unlike the two previous records where I've suffered the 'collywobbles' and 'forward movement' Approximately an hour and a quarter were taken here for a break. **Yvonne and Colin** were doing a magnificent job. Colin couldn't do too much to the muscles because of the tenderness in the legs and the deep ache. Just a light rub. **Yvonne** helped Lynne in and out of the shower. Lynne didn't collapse this year but she did see very vivid colours in the shower and bright red flowers, but when she checked the next day, the tiles were white and the curtains plain. Lynne emerged at midday looking as if she was just going to start a 25 mile. She hadn't realised the clock was still ticking towards the final total and said "How long have I had?" When we said 1 hr 17 mins, she said "I would have been out half an hour ago if I'd realised". As she is being re-started by **Tony**, Lynne says "Oooh Dad, you've cleaned my bike !"

12.02 pm Lynne restarts - 160 miles to go plus extra miles for safety. Along the road that runs along the very tip of Scotland towards Thurso now, with magnificent views to the right over the Orkneys. Lynne was in very good spirits and so were we. She now has until 7 am the next morning to complete the 1000 miles, but we all hope she doesn't take that long because beef stew and potatoes are on the menu up until midnight courtesy of **Ian and his wife** at the **Caber Feidh Guest House** at John o Groats.

1.22 pm Thurso - 859 miles Lynne was now 12 mins down on a schedule that only allowed for a half hour stop at John o Groats and it was quite a moderate mph which aimed to complete the 1000 miles at half past midnight,. We went left now to the traffic lights at:

Wick 2.28 pm - 879 miles Just over the hour to complete that last 20 miles against the wind, now she's 20 mins up on that schedule so we may get our beef stew after all. Quite a few squally showers and sunshine around here, a bit like April. Luckily Lynne manages to miss most of the rain. Lovely rainbows were to be seen across the islands. Lynne stops for warmer clothing now in the late afternoon. She presses on : **4.15 pm Castletown 904 miles** Now nearly 40 mins up, a good tailwind on that section has really helped her reach ;

5.15 pm Wick second time - 929 miles now 53 mins up. A broken down bus blocked the dead turn here and we panicked when we saw the road closed sign, however, **Phil and Stuart** were there to point out the sign and marshal Lynne through to turn a few yards short around **Mike Johnson.** By heck, he gets everywhere that chap ! Lynne is still very positive and cheerful, although she complained about the road surfaces from time to time. She still occasionally hesitates on the pedals so she is still imagining red traffic lights that aren't there. She stops now to put on full kit of warm clothing for the last 80 miles. When you think about it, when was the last time you ventured out to do 80 miles. A daunting task for most people but coming after 930 miles non stop, the brain cannot perceive what she had done. There were virtually no signs of weariness at all and when she stopped for any reason she got back on and rode off at 18 mph almost mechanically. Apart from the imaginary red traffic lights, Lynne keeps seeing the front of her helmet and ducking thinking she is going under a very low bridge. Full lights have been fitted now for the last time as she returns to :

7.33 pm Castletown 954 miles 1 hr 35 mins up. Fantastic, she now returns through Thurso towards Wick for the last time. All along here we can see the Northern Lights or 'Aurora Borealis' for the clever ones. A fantastic sight, a crescent shaped band of light lying horizontally over the islands out to sea, with vertical fingers of shimmering silvery light playing into the sky pulsing and changing shape from one minute to the next. Are we dreaming? It is the third night! Lynne points at it out to sea.; I think it was a first time experience for most of us. Even the locals from the **Wick Wheelers** and the **Caithness CC** said it was the best they had seen.

They were such a positive part of the last day from Helmsdale onwards and were gathering force in numbers as the mileage increased until in the end they were lining all the turns and road junctions. The helpers in the feed car were magnificent all the way through her ride and on this last stretch **our Mike** had bought flashing devils horns headgear for all to wear like Halloween characters, just to keep her spirits up. Lynne really appreciated all this, but after the Northern Lights, what other natural phenomena could succeed it. How about a meteor shower, just to see her through the last bit of darkness !

9.18 pm Wick turn - last time - 979 miles 1 hr 31 mins up. A good gathering here to send her back to Thurso for the last time.

10.35 pm Thurso traffic lights - 999.7 miles

10.37 pm 1000 miles Total Time 2 DAYS 16 HOURS 38 MINUTES

But its not over yet. Lynne has to carry on back towards John o Groats. **Tony Shardlow** is taking all intermediate time checks now and its deadly serious in the van. Just another 12 miles to do as a precaution to falling short on the distance when the End to End is re-measured.

Remembering what happened to **Dick Poole's** 1000 mile attempt which fell short by just over one mile back in 1965. From this point the club lads of the Caithness cc had put 1 mile marker points along the route, adding to this, **Tony** had noted lots of intermediate check points to identify features such as road signs, house entrances, 30 mph signs etc. We now had to check Lynne through all of these places as accurately as possible. I shouted 'now' Tony split the time and recorded it, and **Colin** read the trip meter. Deadly serious stuff. All three of us had had such a laugh earlier on when preparing for this. **Colin** trying to boost his job title to 'odometer operative'. For the next twelve miles we carried out this procedure right through to the Castle of Mey. By this time the convoy of cars had grown a little, this normally being a very quiet stretch of road at this time of night. The last two miles were all uphill and considering the fact that Lynne probably didn't need to do them anyway, she attacked them at 18-23 mph, until the last lay by.

THAT'S IT - NOW IT'S ALL OVER !!

Tears of joy, it seemed like a dream, all of the cycling fraternity were out. We were so pleased Lynne had done it at last. It seems that what the God's had taken away from her on the first day, they had repaid on the second and third day. Lynne had done the first 500 miles to Johnstone Bridge in 30 hours, and the last 500 in 34 hrs. What a recovery. She had done the remaining 160 miles as fast as Gethin. There were handshakes and hugs all round. Many thanks to **Alasdair Washington** and **Malcolm Gray** of the **Caithness cc** and the members of the **Wick Wheelers** for their welcoming help and support over the remaining miles. **Phil and Stuart** who saw Lynne in lots of different locations, and as was mentioned before, its been the highlight of the season up there for the last three years running. Four successful End to Ends and two successful 1000 mile records.

Its all over too quickly and back at the accommodation Lynne phones **Liz,** has a shower, has a bit of beef stew, opens a bottle of champagne from **our Mike**, and chats until about 2 am. Apart from her eyes looking a little bloodshot, she looks quite normal and is so relieved its all over. She said apart from being a little bit weary and sleepy, she felt good. She thanked everybody for making it possible, and went off to bed.

October 4th - Friday Up at 8.30 for a decent breakfast, vehicles loaded, postcards sent, yes, **Jim** said he couldn't believe it when he got a postcard off Lynne thanking him, from John o Groats. I said "Lynne's got to have something to think about as she's climbing Drumochter, making herself a mental list of who to send a card to 'there's my **Nan**, my **Gran**, my **Mum**, **Jim and Anne**, the **lads at the shop** etc etc' **That's Lynne"**.

Lynne had received a call from **Eileen Sheridan** congratulating her on breaking both records, especially the 1000 mile record which Eileen had held for 48 years. She so wanted Lynne to get it and I think it will have stirred up lots of painful but happy memories for her. I know she can recall it as if it were yesterday, walking up Helmsdale with her manager, **Frank Southall** and **Harry H England**, the then Editor of **The Cycling Magazine,** who kept his journal informed hour by hour of her progress with text and photo's. Nowadays, you have to be a continental professional with a stubble, dressed as a 'Lion King' or someone caught up in a drug scandal, to warrant any attention, let alone a photograph.

If anyone out there in the 'media' world could see what a story there is, and we've informed enough influential people over the last few years. The hundreds of phone calls Jim had, the

7000 or more hits of the web site over 5 days from all over the world. There is a story to be told, not just to the people who know Lynne and go out to see her go through, but for anyone with an imagination and ambition to do something themselves, maybe it would inspire future youngsters to embark on a physical achievement. How many people outside the cycling fraternity know about **Lynne** and **Gethin's** epic rides. I am afraid if its any longer than about one and a half hours effort with no reward, you can forget it. An 'E' mail on the web site from strangers to the cycling world who were driving back from Cornwall, **Wendy and Dave Lambert**, said 'little did we guess what we saw when our car passed a lone cyclist plodding up a steep hill in Cornwall two mornings ago. Back home in Kent that evening thanks to the internet, we found out and we have tracked Lynne's progress ever since. What an unbelievable achievement. We feel privileged to have seen a bit of cycling history in the making . Many many congratulations from us both"!

Another web comment from **Geoff Lonsdale**, Clevedon and District cc, who has seen most End to Enders through and has with a team, marshalled Lynne through Bristol two years running in pouring rain "Saw Lynne north of Bristol in pouring rain, got soaked but worth it; sent a message to **Jim Turner** when I saw the End to End had been broken, I sit here with tears in my eyes after reading the latest update! Fantastic, can't say any more". **Geoff** isn't the only one. This is how everyone feels, seeing an End to Ender riding through their patch, a lone figure disappearing into the dark or into the rain, or in the early stages with a few hundred miles left to go, with the odds' against them. It leaves you tearful when you've found out they have done it two days later. Another message from **Margaret and Jim Hopper** "Congratulations Lynne on beating your own End to End, what a ride, she is truly wonderful - now for the 1000 miles, we wish you all the best and are with you all the way. When you reach your goal you will be the perfect successor to a great lady, Eileen Sheridan."

A small piece on the web site from **Phil** sums her up "Saw you at John o Groats, such an amazing feat. Such an amazing time, just wonderful. Saw you outside Thurso - going so strong. Saw you at Wick - cool and strong, so determined. Lynne- you're a star and there are many in the Caithness sky tonight, however you are the brightest - all our love, Phil and Stuart". Lynne had gone from being my little girl to my hero ever since her first 24 hr taking her place amongst the 'greats' of the past. **Eileen Sheridan, Joan Kershaw, Beryl Burton, John Arnold, Dick Poole, John Woodburn , Pete Swinden, John Withers, Pat Kenny**, and current day, **Andy Wilkinson** and **Gethin Butler**, to name but a few.

Lynne has been actively riding long distance time trials for about 14 years, culminating in the End to End the last three years and 1000 miles. When I help or drive the following car and she's going very well and conditions are good, I say to myself, 'that's our Lynne up there' but when the weather is bad and she's down on schedule or in the Highlands, climbing Drumochter, and her eyes are tired, I think 'that's my little girl'.

An amusing incident that happened in the Johnstonbridge area, was that Lynne had mentioned to Mike Johnson that her eyes were sore. By the time the message got relayed back to the feed car, it had become that her a-se was sore. The team pulled Lynne in, chamois creme at the ready. Lynne was rather puzzled at first and then everyone had a good laugh when they realised their mistake.

Finally, a dedication to **Liz**, never knowing when her life would be turned upside down again. Three years running, never knowing when to book a holiday, always watching the weather forecasts and making contingency plans for staffing the Bike Shop while Lynne and I are away, coping with the emotion as the drama unfolds. The stress of being at home and worrying about it is probably greater than being on the road. Putting up with the little outbursts leading up to the attempt - and that's just from me - and always trying to appear calm. All this has provided a harmonious environment during these years.

After a 14 hour drive home, we unloaded the van with the clothes, bikes and bottles, and then its back to work on the Monday. Lynne serves her first customer " Yes, I can recommend these shorts, very hardwearing and comfortable, especially if you are doing a long ride" !

DID THE LAST FIVE DAYS REALLY HAPPEN
OR WERE WE ALL HALLUCINATING ?

No. 39 UNORTHODOX RIDES

ANDY WILKINSON RECUMBENT "FAIRED" TRICYCLE END TO END - 2ND APRIL 1996

Courtesy of John Williams the author of the original description of Andy's ride - my many thanks to him for allowing me to re-write certain sections for my book and make additions to the text.

At 6.00 am with low cloud cover and a slight south west wind, Andy Wilkinson 'Wilko' rode away from the Lands End Hotel on the first ever 'faired' recumbent tricycle attempt. It was not an official RRA attempt, but was authenticated by RRA officials who witnessed and timed the ride. The machine Andy was riding was a tricycle with the two wheels at the front. It stood waist high, and the rider sat low down in a shaped seat in a semi-lying position with his legs out in front of him. The whole machine was enclosed in a composite casing with a Perspex cockpit to look out of. It was made by Bob Dixon of 'The Seat of the Pants Company Ltd', with design input from Mike Burrows.

Andy was always keen to break with tradition, after all, a lot of his rides in long distance events were done on a mountain bike, with slick tyred wheels and tri-bars. He found this a more comfy position for his back which regularly played him up.

The intention was to observe the RRA rules as far as possible as in 1995 when Andy had ridden the same machine over the Liverpool to Edinburgh course in 7 hrs 48 minutes, beating Ken Joy's existing RRA bicycle record by 1 hr 17 mins. Andy had a lot of support from RRA observers on that attempt who were sympathetic to what he was trying to achieve, while keeping in mind the possibility that if the RRA does get round to amending its rules, retrospective recognition of the performance might be possible.

The official timekeepers were Pat Kenny, Rod Goodfellow and Nobby Clarke, who were also to act as official observers along with Bob Williams, Alan Griffiths and Ken Mathews. Pat Kenny and Bob Williams covered the South, Rod Goodfellow and Alan Griffiths covered the

Midlands to Scotland and Nobby Clarke would time the finish. Bob McNamee was drafted in as a reserve timekeeper and observer to act in either zones. Paul Histon and Jim Turner were the main on-the-road helpers throughout the ride.

Back to the start now, which had been delayed by 10 mins due to absolute chaos. Andy was witnessed going through Penzance on the by pass by Elaine Hancock. The first 25 miles were completed in 58 mins. At the Bodmin bypass (50 miles) in 1 hr 51 mins he was over 5 mins up on schedule. After climbing Bodmin Moor, Andy reached Okehampton 12 minutes down on schedule, but was still going very well. Don't forget, the sun was well up in the sky and it must have been very hot on these long climbs, on a recumbent you can only sit back and push, you can't ease yourself out of the saddle and stand on the pedals as with a standard bike, or trike. Jim Turner, one of the main helpers, reported Andy had reached Whiddon Down at 10.14 am - **100 miles in 4 hrs 4 mins.** Now starts the long descent to Exeter.

Jean Luxton had devised a special diversion for Andy at Exeter and he was soon through the town. By Cullompton Andy was exactly on schedule at 11.09. At 11.54 he was through Taunton, but was reported to be having trouble with the "water tube", now I'm not too sure whether this was a tube putting water into Andy, or taking it away ! I know there was an elaborate set up to save him having to stop for a 'pee'. 12.42 Pat Kenny reports horrendous traffic congestion at 'Rooks Bridge' junction A38/M5. By 3.35, Andy had reached Bristol, seen here by Janet Tebbutt. Calamity as Andy climbed Bridge Valley road up the Gorge, the back axle snapped, leaving him stationary, unable to move. To make matters worse, the spare 'standard' recumbent trike was in a van stuck in traffic some 20 mins behind.

Andy by this stage would have been absolutely saturated with sweat in the enclosed 'pod'., The minute he got out he was rapidly chilled and Jim Turner was getting quite worried as to how to keep him warm. 25 mins later the mechanic rode up on the spare machine as it was the quickest way to get past the traffic hold ups. Just after 2.00 pm Andy rode off onto the Westbury Road shivering violently and wearing Bob Jumps anorak and cloth cap. At Filton, where he joined the A38, Andy was now 29 mins behind schedule. The wind cheetah machine had been repaired with a new axle and was on its way in a van in 'hot pursuit' of its rider. By 3 o'clock, machine and rider had been re-united. Heavy traffic flow was baulking Andy along this three lane stretch of the A38 due to cars overtaking riders in a 10 mile time trial. At Whitminster Andy was reported to be 'going like a train' ! At Gloucester, both the observer car and the rider went off course, but at different places and in different directions but luckily not too much time was lost. (I'm glad Lynne and myself are not the only ones who get lost in these towns).

By 4.10 pm, Pat was back following Andy on the A38 towards Worcester. Andy went off course again in Worcester, but was witnessed on route by three people. By 4.51pm he was well along the A449 at the 'Mitre Oak', seen by Les Lowe and Therese Mason. It was now drizzling. At Kidderminster, Andy was having trouble with smears on the windscreen and went off course again towards the town centre. Pat Kenny marshalled him back on course after realising what had happened. He was now 12 mins down on schedule.

By 6.00 pm Andy had passed through Wolverhampton after getting stuck in road works. Pete Swinden saw him through Coven, and at Gailey Island one minute before his 12 hours was up, Lynne and Tony Wiggin witnessed him flashing past. Pat was stuck in the same road works worried that he wouldn't catch Andy up to time his 12 hr point. He made it with seconds to spare. 6.10pm at Rodbaston Agricultural College, which when measured gave a **12 hour distance of 295.5 miles** What a tremendous ride in itself. When one adds up the minutes lost through mechanical problems and time lost off course plus traffic jams, one realises probably another 20 miles at least could be added onto this total.

Alan Griffiths took over as observer now that Pat had timed the 12 hours. Andy was moving so well along here, that the following van didn't catch up with him until he was north of Stafford on the A34. The rain had cleared, there was a strong breeze behind the rider and his speed was high. Margaret Hopper saw Andy through Eccleshall Island at 6.44. During this time the telephone HQ was absolutely buzzing with people wanting to know of Andy's progress. Also there was a lot of work involved for Jim, arranging with John Williams as to whether Andy would be taking the full scheduled 60 mins stop at the caravan at Grapenhall. John Williams was also very busy making sure the marshalling teams would be in position in the Warrington and Preston area. Edwin Hargraves had played quite an important role for the last 200 miles or so, especially when the official observers were struggling to either get through towns or traffic jams.

At Holmes Chapel, Andy was 8 minutes up on schedule - John Arnold was out taking photos. On the descent from Talke towards the traffic lights, Andy's speed was over 50 mph. By 8.00 pm he was through 'Mere' traffic lights, witnessed by Ruth Williams. A couple of minutes later, Andy took a break at the caravan, which was well south of the original location.

He restarted at 8.33 pm, now well ahead of schedule by 30 mins. The only problem was that many of the marshalls and checkers wouldn't be in place. Andy was witnessed by Stan Jones at Latchford Bridge after being diverted onto the 'ring road'. At 8.54 pm Tom Greep saw Andy through at Winwick Church and reported back that Andy's lights were working. Lots of faithful supporters were out on this populated stretch to Bamber Bridge, Jack Tottie, C. Millington, Carol and Keith Boardman, A.J.Mathews, Bob Harrison, Norman Maggs, and D.E.Jackson. Andy took a slight detour before Bamber Bridge to cut out the awful road surface there. This put some of the observers into a panic as to where he'd got to. Rod Goodfellow had now joined the team to time the 24 hrs, although he had got a long time to go yet.

At 10.33, Andy was nearly at Garstang on the A6. He was making rapid progress and the forecasted thunder storm had moved into the Lake District. Austin Bridge, a gentleman who had been a helper on the Cowsill and Denton tandem record in 1952, saw Andy at Bolton le Sands and commented "what a rider".

By midnight, Andy had passed through Kendal some 435 miles in 18 hours with 6 hrs to go for his 24 hr. But he was now experiencing problems with his windscreen misting up due to the temperature dropping outside. A small hole was drilled and the screen was sprayed with de-mister. 40 mins later Jim Turner phoned in to say that Andy had climbed Shap and was on the summit with the same problem of 'misting'. Faced with a fast winding descent to Shap village in even cooler air, Jim was getting worried for Andy's safety. He was now 1 hr 18 mins up on schedule.

Next came the problem of guessing where Andy's 24 hrs would get him to, and where to park the caravan for a break. By Penrith he was 1 hr 32 mins up. He stopped to have more holes drilled in the screen and more de-mister applied. The shaped screen was at such an aerodynamic angle, that Andy wasn't so much looking through it, but along its length. At 2 am, fog was causing problems just south of Carlisle which lasted through until Andy turned off the A74. A decision had to be made soon to park the 'rest' caravan somewhere before the mobile phones got into a 'dead-spot' area and all communication was lost between the teams, and also the HQ.

Andy was now feeling drowsy, this stretch of road through Lockerbie is fairly flat, straight and quiet. It had been decided to stop him at the caravan parked in Moffat town centre. Edwin Hargraves and Les Brown saw Andy turn off for Moffat . At the caravan he had a much needed massage, shower, some soup and a quick sleep.

He left to climb the 'Devils Beeftub' at 5.13 am. Andy attacked it vigorously and was cheered on over the summit in patchy fog at 5.45 by Edwin Hargraves, Rod Goodfellow and Ken Mathews. He was now 8 minutes up on schedule with nearly 50 miles of virtual downhill all the way to Edinburgh. Rod Goodfellow was now following closely to time the **24 hr** which ran out 1.6 miles beyond 'Crook Inn', estimated distance **530 miles**.

This is the greatest 24 hr mileage ever ridden by a cyclist unpaced in history. It represents an average speed in excess of 22 mph. From here on towards Penicuik, Andy suffered a 'bad patch' made worse by trying to clear his misting windscreen. He omitted the original post 24 hr stop of 90 minutes which immediately made him 1 hr 48 mins ahead of schedule.

Being in the phone 'dead spot' area of the Tweed Valley, it was now feared that any marshalls or helpers wanting to see Andy through Edinburgh would miss him, due to him being so far ahead of time. John Murdoch going out to Penicuik from Edinburgh saw Andy just outside Edinburgh, doing approximately 30 mph going in the opposite direction.

Thick fog was back again, making the notorious ring road, a dangerous place to be at 7.30 am. Carol Dietman and her friend Jane were at Maybury roundabout at 7.50 am. Andy was now almost clear of the city and 20 mins later was just starting to cross the Forth Road Bridge on the main carriageway, not the cycle path.

At 9.13am Margaret and George Berwick witnessed Andy pass through Milnathort. By 10.00 he had passed through Perth, some two hours ahead of schedule now. He stopped just south of Pitlochry to have a massage from Gavin, the Physio, hoping to get some more speed out of his legs. Andy felt that he was struggling; Paul Histon was re-assuring him there was nothing to worry about. It was here with Andy having a massage in the van, that the party of helpers were subjected to an harangue by an angry Policeman. The intervention of a friendly local person whom Ken Mathews though was a local government official, induced him to go away. Apparently he objected to the following car and was unsure about the safety of a 'faired ' recumbent.

By looking at the times and places Andy is reaching i.e. Perth in 28 hours, one realises that most of the recent solo male record breakers, including Andy in 1990, would have been in Perth in 31 hours. By 11.16am he was back on the road again feeling refreshed. Its now hotting up in the enclosed capsule of the 'wind cheetah'. Andy stops to take off his jersey and hat.

By 11.50 he was struggling on the Pass of Killiecrankie. A small tape recorder was passed to him through the food hatch. There were messages from Ken Mathews, Jim Turner and Paul Histon. Don't forget the recumbent trike is fully enclosed, so a lot of drumming noise would be experienced by the rider from road vibrations. Andy had his food and drink passed through a side window hatch, so wouldn't be able to hear what people were saying. At 12.30 Andy started the climb of Drumochter pass, it was now raining, on the summit there was snow on the roadside, but at least the rain had stopped, leaving the air misty and damp. A planned 50 mins break on this section was missed so as to put him 2 hrs 25 mins ahead of schedule.

John Williams was now making arrangement for the team when they reached John o Groats. He called Brian Johnstone at the John o Groats House hotel, confirmed bookings for 17 people at approximately 10 pm. The menu should be hot soup, rolls, sandwiches and **champagne**. Andy had now picked up his speed again and between 2.00pm and 4.00pm had ridden through the remainder of the Grampians, Kingussie, Aviemore, Slochd Summit, Moy, and was now crossing the Kessock Bridge after a hair raising drop into Inverness. I'd love to know what speed he reached.

He stopped for an extensive massage to his legs, mainly his left one. Gavin the Physio expressed his concern as to the state of Andy's left leg, leaving Jim and Bob with the opinion that his leg was 'dodgy' and that plans to attempt the 1000 miles should be abandoned. After 33 minutes, Andy restarted. Nobby Clarke, the Scottish timekeeper joined the team and quipped "Only 120 miles to the door" By 5.15 Andy had crossed the 'Black Isle'. At 6.00pm he put his lights on and expressed the wish to forego a 50 minutes scheduled stop, so that he could get to John o Groats by 10 pm and so be inside 40 hours.

Brian Johnstone, from the Hotel, phoned to say that there had been some work done on the car park and that there were two hazards for Andy to negotiate, neither of them were lit. He was worried that if he came in at the same speed as in 1990, he would slam into a large hole. Hopefully we could get members of the team to safeguard his finish.

At 6.20 pm Andy passed the John o Groats 82 miles sign in thick fog. Golspie, Brora and then Helmsdale YHA were reached, over three hours 20 mins ahead of time. Bob Dixon, owner of 'The Seat of the Pants' Company had travelled with the team. He must have been very proud of Andy's ride and the machine he had produced for him. Bob McNamee, the reserve timekeeper was unwell at this point and arrangements were made for Bob Jump to assist Nobby Clarke as the back up timekeeper.

At 7.46 pm, from a call box in Berriedale, Edwin Hargraves reported to HQ that a nasty north easterly wind had sprung up and was bringing in a cold mist from the North sea, causing serious visibility problems on the climbs and hill tops. At 8.10 John Arnold who had been travelling with Harry Wilkinson in Harry's van, reported that Andy had reached the summit of the 'Ord of Caithness' in thick mist and was facing a strong headwind. John is an excellent photographer and had been out on course from the Midlands, taking some wonderful photos of the ride.

These last tortuous climbs had taken their toll on Andy putting even more of a strain on that left leg. He was cheered by the helpers who ran alongside him on these foggy headlands. He reached Wick at 10.16 pm and Reiss at 10.27. Edwin went past to make sure everything was in place at John o Groats. When he got there he realised the obstructions on the 'run in' weren't lit up, so pointed his headlights at the spot hoping Andy would avoid the holes. Andy sped down the last slope, and after making an abrupt stop to avoid the danger he got going again to reach the finish at **11.14 pm** with a time of **1 day 17 hrs 4 mins 22 secs.**

After scoffing the very welcome soup, rolls, sandwiches and champagne, the landlord left them to drink the bar dry. Andy's leg recovered quickly, the journey home was safely completed, Bob McNamee's illness was short lived and that was the end of a hectic weekend, which saw no less that 3 records set for the future. **A 295.5 miles 12 hour; a 530 miles 24 hr and a 41 hr 4 minute End to End.** It gives a **22 mph average speed up to 24 hr,** and just over **20 mph average** for the whole journey. It also took just under 4 hours off his own solo bicycle End to End ridden in 1990.

Andy went on to thank the many helpers and officials and indeed all who came out to see him and marshall him through on his ride. He concluded by saying **"I continue to dream that one day the efforts of all involved will be rewarded by official recognition of the ride"**

The reason for a record ride so early in the year was two fold. The first was so that Andy didn't get 'cooked' in the enclosed machine and the second reason was that he still had time to recover physically and mentally enough to compete with the countries best time triallists in the BBAR Competition. Two months later he produced **Competition Record for 50 miles in 1 hr 37 mins 26 secs; Comp record 100 miles in 3 hrs 27 mins 39 secs,** and to top it off **Comp Record 12 hours with 300.27 miles.** With these performances he put up a new **Competition record BBAR speed of 28.236 mph.**

A year later in 1997, Andy improved Roy Cromack's **24 hr Competition Record** distance to **525 miles** in the Mersey RC 24 hr. **WHAT A REMARKABLE MAN !**

Andy, at a later date, told me that he put a lot of his successes of 1996 down to one man, **Alan Roberts.** He advised Andy as to a training and feeding programme for his recumbent End to End and then a recovery programme which allowed Andy to regain his speed in two months ready to tackle the BBAR competition. Alan knew all the fast courses and how to tackle them having ridden most of them himself or when helping his wife Christine. Andy won the BBAR with just three fast rides.

HUGH CULVERHOUSE - ONE LEGGED END TO ENDER - SEPTEMBER 1987

One of the most amazing and heroic End to End performances was in September 1987 by Hugh Culverhouse; having the use of only one leg made the task even more formidable. He had already produced a 78 hour record ride but knew he could reduce that time if given the right conditions.

Hugh didn't get the right weather and wind until well into the Grampians. He started off against a headwind that had the flag poles bending, nevertheless, he reached Exeter only 33 minutes down on a 72 hour schedule. Despite taking a sleep on the roadside bench at Wigan and getting lost at Lancaster, Hugh was maintaining a 1 hr 7 minute deficit on his schedule.

Shap Fell was a testing time for this 'gutsy' rider, it required patience, low gears and a slow steady rhythm. I had seen him as he came through the Midlands and I was impressed by his

35
VISCOUNT

TRUMANNS STEEL
MANCHESTER WHEELERS
36

38
RADFORD

37
50

39

42

41

40

43
A9
Dunbeath 8
Latheron 12
Wick 30
Thurso 36
John o' Groats 47

44

46

45

SUNLIGHT
cannondale
47
BED & BREAKFAST
FROM £15
EN SUITE ROOMS
FULLY LICENSED
HOME COOKING
OPEN TO NON RESIDENTS
SUNLIGHT
cannondale
48
49

50
51
52

53

54

55

56
57
58

59
GROATS INN
60
61

speed To get maximum effort from his one leg, he pulled hard against the handlebars and slid along his saddle to get a circular pedalling action. His left leg was held immobile and straight at the knee, resting on a left crank and pedal.

His leg was giving him pain as he climbed over the top of Shap, but the agony was eased slightly by club folk appearing out of the darkness to cheer him on. His next big challenge came in the form of the Devils Beeftub climb. Once he had conquered this section of the ride, the temperature dropped rapidly with swirling mist and damp clothing that lasted until the Forth Road Bridge. He had a welcome massage to his painful leg but despite all this time lost, he was still only 1 hr and 12 mins down on schedule.

Hugh declined a 1 hour break at Pitlochry so as to reduce his deficit. As he climbed the Grampians he picked up a rising tail wind, the first real help from the weather since he'd started. This put him 28 mins ahead of schedule for the first time. Lack of sleep was now posing a real problem but an eyewash in the cold waters of a stream and a couple of caffeine tablets perked him up enough to carry on.

The third night was entered as he tackled the climb from Aviemore to Inverness. By the time he'd reached Helmsdale and Berriedale, Hugh had increased his gain on time to be 2.5 hours ahead of schedule. The wind was still a good help along here and he realised that a sub 70 hour ride was possible.

Hugh averaged 18 mph for the last 30 miles, he sprinted down to the John o Groats hotel finish line to record 69 hours 5 mins 4 secs. What a plucky ride by a man who normally used a crutch and a walking stick when not riding his bike. He had a wonderful back up crew consisting of Peter Hartt, Jeanette Bent (the maker of jam and banana sandwiches), Wayne Stewart, Cedric Ellingworth (masseur) Dave Houston and Justin Oakley.

His average speed was 12.35 mph over the 853 mile journey, including 6 miles 'off course'. His feeding was mainly by a liquid diet using 'Ultra-Energy', a formula he had used on his R.A.A.M. (Race across America) the previous year.

Although Hugh Culverhouse's ride isn't ratified or recognised by the RRA, and there isn't a category for a one legged rider, I felt it was well witnessed, timed and documented enough for me to include in this book which is written as a tribute to brave record breakers over this strenuous journey.

Information courtesy of 'Cycling Weekly', written by Justin Oakley, with comments from myself.

ALEX BAXTER - END TO END 1999 - PENNY FARTHING

Just one other unorthodox Lands End to John o Groats ride I feel I must mention was performed on an original 'Penny Farthing' or 'High Ordinary' cycle, by Alex Baxter, in **5 days, 8 hrs, 15 mins.**

He wasn't a clubman or racing man, but a retired farmer, who had always been fascinated by the Penny Farthing bicycle and its romantic links with the Lands End to John o Groats journey. The record wasn't authenticated by officials but it was witnessed and timed.

I met Alex at John Woodburn's End to End film show in Hammersmith a couple of years ago. He stood in the foyer dressed resplendently in 'turn of the century' clothing, beside his ancient machine.

I'm glad I met him, as it reminded me of how it all started some 100 years ago.

SECTION FIVE

SEPARATE 1000 MILE RECORDS FROM 1930

JACK ROSSITER - SUNDAY AUGUST 3RD 1930 - SOLO BICYCLE

One year on from his End to End victory Jack Rossiter started his 1000 miles attempt using a similar version of the course that Olley, Fisher and Welsh had used, some 20 or more years previously. He started at the top of Marlborough Hill in heavy rain and reached London some 72 miles later in 4 hours. He turned and headed north through Welwyn, Hitchin to Girtford at 120 miles in 6hrs 55 mins. The wind had dropped but it was now a heavy drizzly atmosphere.

In his first 12 hours he had covered 205 miles. At York, some 269 miles had taken him 15 hrs 40 mins and it was now dark as he pressed on even further north on the A1, through Northallerton at 301 miles, to reach the turn at Croft at half past midnight. He'd changed to a lower gear but was still struggling against a strong wind as he headed south.

He reached the 24 hr point at Bentley just north of Doncaster. As well as the troublesome wind the dawn had brought more rain but Rossiter was still cheerful, even though he'd failed to improve the 24 hr record he'd still covered a very creditable 382 miles.

He took his first break at Frank Thorley's café on Barnby Moor. He had his gear reduced once again to 72" on which he rode till the end. After an hours rest he resumed his ride. He was wearing yellow waterproof clothing, probably 'oil skins' which kept him dry but must have encroached upon his speed. Oilskins are the same type of garment that north sea fishermen wear in bad weather.

He rode steadily on over Great Gonerby Hill and the next 21 hills between Grantham and Stamford. He eventually reached Norman's Cross some 479 miles in 1 day 8 hrs 40 mins. By taking only a short break here he cut his loss on time to just over two hours. It was dry when he restarted from here in the afternoon, but by the time Peterborough was reached, the rain was back again making the tramlines through the town very slippery and dangerous. Rossiter skidded on a tramline and fell heavily, bending a crank and straining a muscle. The crank was replaced but the muscle was to prove very painful towards the end of the ride.

He fought the wind back to Kimbolton at 529 miles getting there in 1 day 13 hrs 10 mins. By the time he entered the Fen District through Cambridge, Ely, Chatteris, and to Wisbech, his leg muscle was really giving him trouble. 660 miles was reached in 48 hours and he had a change of clothes and a sleep here. He left at 8 am Tuesday, and travelled over these flat boring roads at a speed much slower than his normal racing speed. As he went into the dark on Tuesday night he suffered a succession of punctures. On one of his detours back to Cambridge at 802 miles, the helpers estimated him to be nearly six hours down on schedule but still considerably ahead of Welsh's record at this time.

Jack Rossiter was now suffering muscle pains in his legs and as he went into the dawn of Wednesday morning, drowsiness overcame him. This was staved off by rain showers. After another 50 mile circuit of Fenland roads were covered he detoured onto the Cambridge to

Royston road and took an unscheduled stop at Fowlmere. He stayed there for over two hours, the helpers were worried as to the state he was in and the pain he was suffering in his legs and they feared the worse at this late stage in the ride.

But mind over matter must have prevailed enough for Rossiter to make a remarkable recovery. He awoke after a while, cheerful and chirpy, ran to his bike and rode off without anymore pain. At Biggleswade there were 20 miles left to cover and although heavy rain was now falling on the surrounding cabbage fields, turning an autumn day more like a winter's one, Jack Rossiter turned on the pressure to speed over these last few miles of the record, which he took with **3 days 11 hrs 58 mins**, a beating of Welsh's 21 year old record by almost six hours.

He rode a Curry's cycle with 'Ambra-Superga' tyres, a Sturmer Archer three speed gear, Resillion brakes and saddle top, Coventry chain, Brampton pedals. His lights were made by Powell and Hanmer using 'Chemico Carbide and Oils'. He wore F.W. Holdsworth clothing and drank 'Virol' and milk throughout the ride. The Curry's cycle he used was on display later at their Peckham Depot.

The next two 1000 miles records by **Hubert Opperman** first of all with **3 days 1 hr 52 mins** and then **Sid Ferris** with **2 days 22 hrs 40 mins,** were both done as additions to their successful End to Ends in **1934 and 1937**.

Information courtesy of Cycling

G.E. (GEORGE) LAWRIE - 1000 MILES TRICYCLE - 1938

The next 1000 miles to be broken on a timescale of years was by George Lawrie on a tricycle in 1938. He had an RRA standard of 4 days 12 hrs to attack and beat. George, a member of the Viking Wheelers had almost continuous rain for four days. He again used a course based simply on the A1 and went as far north as Newcastle upon Tyne and over to Ipswich in the east.

Lawrie rode 175 miles in the first 12 hours and 145 miles in the second 12 hrs. The second 24 hrs brought 230 miles but this included a considerable delay due to an accident to the following car in torrential rain. In the car was the timekeeper Mr J.T. Wells who suffered facial injuries and a passenger who was also slightly injured. A reserve car was used as the original following car had been badly damaged when it slid into the ditch in a blinding rainstorm. Lawrie endured severe flooding at York but although he was riding on tubular tyres, he only suffered two punctures.

He had a total of 10 hours sleep in the four days and when he fell asleep climbing a hill on the last night and started to roll backwards, he was forced to take a 2 hrs break. He finished back at the same 33rd milestone from London as he had started at, in a time of **4 days 6 hrs 32 mins.**

By the end of 1942, George Lawrie had taken a total of seven RRA records, five of them on Tandem Tricycle, either with R. Morford or B.F.C. Gough.

Information courtesy of Cycling and RRA archives.

WYNNE WRIGHTSON - THE FIRST LADIES AMATEUR 1000 MILES BICYCLE RECORD JUNE 1953

Starting on a Tuesday and finishing on the Friday, using a 'star' shaped course, Wynne Wrightson of the Cheltenham Phoenix Cycling Club, set a new amateur record for the Women's Roads Record Association 1000 miles. This 'star' shaped course consisted of 'out and home' journeys using a different route each day.

The plan was ingenious and simple Every morning at 5 o'clock she would set out on a carefully arranged route of about 260 miles which would bring her back to home about midnight, where she would sleep and then resume her ride again at 5 am the next day. If Wynne fell behind schedule, she would have a shorter sleep.

Wynne had to start at 5 am due to a network of club folk and helpers, checkers and observers, being in position throughout the day, based upon that 5 am start. All went well, and where club checkers were missing, Wynne obtained signatures from other people to verify her time and place.

A 14 mph schedule was maintained throughout the ride except for the last day where a 1 hr 5 mins loss was incurred. The only mechanical problem Wynne sustained was when her tyre blew off the rim, but husband Jack's bicycle was close at hand as a spare machine, luckily they both had the same riding positions and soon Wynne was back on her own bike.

Her patient tireless style changed to a burst of speed on Friday night as she reached her estimated 1000 mile point at Whitminster Cross, where she then set about riding her 'reserve' mileage of about 9 miles which took her to 'Westgate' at the start of the Gloucester by pass. This finishing point is only a stone's throw from Woottons Island where she set out from on the previous Tuesday.

Wynne looked fit and contented, with limbs tanned to a deep colour. At the finish she stood and chatted about her ride as though she had just finished a '25'. The areas she travelled through took her to Hereford in the west to Aylesbury in the east. A brisk wind, which constantly changed direction, blew for most of the time but at least it was behind her on the final run from Filton to Gloucester.

The record attempt took a lot of planning. A job taken on by husband Jack, it was done using Wynne's annual works holiday week, not exactly restful but it made a change ! The actual time taken for Wynne's **1000 miles,** was **3 days 15 hrs 53 min,** which was only 4 hrs 9 mins slower than the ladies professional record held by Marguerite Wilson at that time.

As far as I know, this was the first 1000 miles ride where the rider returned home to their own bed every night.

Mrs Wrightson is the Western Counties RRA 24 hour record holder. Her timekeeper B.W. (Bill) Best started her on the Tuesday, then returned on the Friday to follow her for the last 3 hours and take times at 17 different locations for the 1000 miles. In between times Bill Best had travelled down to Lands End and then returned behind Ken Joy, to time his successful Lands End to London record - so, someone else was enjoying a 'holiday'.

This article is courtesy of Cycling with additional text from myself.

DAVE DUFFIELD - TRICYCLE - 1000 MILES - MAY 1956

Over the May Whitsun holiday, this tall classy trike rider took 18 hrs 17 mins off George Lawrie's 18 year old record. He started his epic ride from Yardley, a suburb of Birmingham at 4 am on Saturday. The previous year he'd taken the RRA 12 hr record, narrowly improving Syd Parkers record with 230.75 miles. He'd now got over 4 times this distance to ride in one long effort.

He rode a specially built 26" framed trike with reinforced rear stays, using 8 gears from 55" to 90" and high pressure wired on tyres which proved very reliable. His only mechanical problem on the attempt was a broken front hub spindle at St Albans with 82 miles covered. He was soon on his way with a spare wheel courtesy of the Arnold Brothers John and Alf. The cause of the breakage was a stretch of very roughly surfaced road. Stan Miles cycle shop in St Albans supplied the wheel repair.

At Thetford after 157 miles he was 45 mins ahead of schedule but a bout of stomach trouble saw him start to lose most of his advantage, so that by the time he'd returned to Birmingham at 316 miles he was level with his schedule. He took just over four hours rest and sleep here before riding to Fazeley near Tamworth on the Sunday morning. At the 490 miles point he was half an hour down on schedule but by Shrewsbury he'd pulled back time to be almost on target.

David suffered with the cold for the next few hours and was behind schedule at Worcester with 603 miles covered. He took another rest here in the early hours of Monday morning and by the time he'd detoured to Bridgnorth at 700 miles he was one and a half hours down but he had stopped for food along here. Back at Worcester with 865 miles completed he was still holding his loss on time to one and a half hours. He took a scheduled break going into Tuesday morning and started on the last part of his epic ride at 6.30 am.

He was soon moving well now with the end of his ride in sight. At Longdon 918 miles he was less than half an hour down. The last part of the journey was in the Worcestershire lanes which is home territory for David. He clocked 20 mph over those last remaining miles to Bidford on Avon. He took a 30 minute break and then resumed riding for his safety margin of an extra 35 miles to make allowances for mileage discrepancies.

David rode past a crowd of club girls gathered by the roadside who sang "Happy Birthday to You". He was 25 years of age that day. What a wonderful present to have just broken the 1000 mile record surrounded by club girls. This Beacon Roads CC rider really hadn't wasted his bank holiday.

This was to be only the second of a total of twelve RRA records David went on to beat, between 1955 and 1971, including two End to End rides. His 1000 mile trike record now stood at 3 days 12 hrs 15 mins.

Information courtesy of Cycling and John Arnold

ARTHUR RENDER FRIDAY 20TH JUNE 1956
1000 MILE SOLO BICYCLE
(THIS IS ARTHURS OWN STORY)

"It is now eight years since I rode the 1000 and I wonder as I write if the readers will find this of interest, but as Ian has asked me to give an account of it, I will do my best to give him some copy for our journal. It must be borne in mind that I was never a good racing man, but on long runs I had always shown a peculiarity of being able to ride extremely long distances without apparent fatigue. Racing, however, after years of trying, I had only managed a l.3 for a 25, a 2.11 for a 50, 4.45 for a 100, when I joined the Oldbury in 1954 and I had (or so I thought) packed in racing. That winter I rode a lot with Ken Pitchford, then Worcestershire's B.A.R. and in 1955 I was persuaded to have a last try at racing. The result was a ride of 439 miles in the Mersey 24 hr; this was completely unexpected by most people. I had no car to assist, but many of our club had ridden up to help me. It was a chance remark of Ken Pitchford's that made me think of the 1000 miles. He said I looked fresh enough on the ciruit to do another. Perhaps he exaggerated, but the idea was in my mind, and I kept thinking it over.

Like most of us, I had always wanted to do some ride out of the ordinary, and I though Sid Ferris's ride of 2 days 22 hours should be able to be broken, especially on a star shaped course centred on the Midlands. Perhaps you belong to those who think the 1000 should be on the End to End route; I know one long distance rider who said he thought it wasn't sporting to separate them, but the End to End sets many problems for helpers so I had no qualms about separating them.

When it was broached to the club, and they recovered from the shock, everyone took up the idea with enthusiasm, all the organisation was taken out of my hands, and all I had to do was train for the ride. This involved very long weekends, several exceeding 350 miles, on a 62" gear, and in the year 1955 I had ridden a total of 23,000 miles. By the Spring of 1956 a large number of Midland clubs were enthusiastically assisting, and our club found a new side of the game that we'd never before been in. By the time of the event, clubs and officials all along the route were brought in; all appeared keen to marshal, feed, check, or assist in any way possible. It seems incredible that so many would so willingly assist one man to achieve the record. Cyril Underhill undertook the chief task as organiser with Frank Taylor the enormous task of feeding. Apart from my own club-men, Gerry Tromans of the North Worcesters', Sid Mountford, Doug Osmonde, Bill Perrett and Sid Genders all did a marvellous job.

Then to the morning of the start; I had stayed the night before at Cyril Underhill's and I rode the bike to the start about a mile away. At the start we were a little bit early and I sat in the car by myself; it was still a bit dark and the headlights were on. Everyone else gathered in a group, I think they were all a little overawed at the thought of the ride.

As I sat alone, and a little nervous, I watched a rat sitting on its back legs, in the pool of light cast by the car headlights, he was washing himself so industriously. It is strange that of all the events of that weekend, it stands out so clear in my memory. The darkness, the subdued group of officials and well wishers, and so unconcerned, a rat washing himself.

Soon it was time to be away. Alan Tomkins sent me off, and with encouraging calls from my friends I started. The route was like a large letter Y with the chief turns at Lincoln, Bristol and Prestatyn, with numerous legs branching off. The first spell was to Gailey, down the A5 to Cross in Hands, to Leicester, and on to Saxondale Crossroads. Left to West Bridgford, retrace to Saxondale Crossroads, left via Newark to Lincoln, twice round a ciruit recommended by the Lincoln people, and then over to Leadenham Crossroads and back, eventually retracing down via Leicester and Lutterworth, and so to Teddington Hands.

We had prepared for most eventualities, but a broken crank at 30 miles was not on the list of expected mishaps. However, I had a spare machine on to which I changed. After 70 miles I was enabled to return to my favourite cycle.

All along the road, helpers kept giving encouragement. Some I knew, some I didn't. A bout of sickness at Saxondale was a new experience, but I still felt O.K. The cheeriness of the helpers impressed me. I hoped I'd do the record for their sakes. It is so much better to have been marshalling a man who takes a record than one who fails.

So I proceeded, holding tight to my schedule, but riding well within myself. Down to the lovely Cotswold country and it was lovely. A beautiful stretch down to Broadway remains a vivid memory. In the following van they were debating whether I was noticing the countryside I was passing. If I am riding easily, I not only notice it, but retain a vivid recollection of the same. I have only to close my eyes to see again the exquisite shading of the hills near Lower Quinton and the full moon just rising, and later the beautiful Cotswold villages with their stonework, all at peace with the world and unmarred by the terrible tourists who usually despoil the beauty of them. A fair at Broadway struck a jarring note, and then the sight of Duffield and his men recalled me to the record. Sometimes I get into a seemingly effortless riding style, and although my body is maintaining an excellent speed, my mind appears to be detached, as if its two people on the machine, a racing man driving the machine on, whilst the tourist admires the scenery and dreams of pleasant weekends and lazy days to come.

At Teddington it was with misgiving that I ate the chicken specially prepared. My misgivings were justified, it proved far too rich, and before I left Teddington I was violently sick and restarted in terrible pain. My stomach felt dreadfully upset, and as I rode along it was impossible to stop my thoughts from wondering if I had twisted a muscle or ruptured myself. All along the front of my stomach was swollen, and at each end of the swelling was a huge protrusion the size of a cricket ball. Occasional twinges of pain made it impossible to forget this.

I persevered down to Gloucester, up to Cheltenham and back to Gloucester, and so down to Patchway, falling slowly behind schedule. The road back from Patchway will always remain as the crucial stage. My speed dropped alarmingly; the darkness, bright lights and record began to fade. Eventually I was compelled to stop and rest for a short while and eventually reached Gloucester well down on schedule. Of that Friday night I have little or no recollection; evidently I rode automatically at a greatly reduced pace, but fortunately I don't remember it. After a light meal at Lew Morris's I retired to bed just as I was. My chief helpers were discussing in another room whether a wash or a bath was best before I went to bed. When they'd made their minds up, they came out to find me fast asleep, so that problem was solved.

Leaving Gloucester at 6.25 am I was pleased to see Frank and Ethel with Alan Tomkins and Dr Hamley at Tewkesbury. The course continued via Worcester to the Mitre Oak and back. Then up to the caravan site at Bromsgrove and back to Droitwich, and so following the W.C.A. 12 hour course.

I was feeling a bit grim, but now I was right back in my own area, friends were bobbing up all over, and it was found that I could eat porridge without any undue pain resulting. I was now two hours down on my schedule, but I was not losing any more, so it continued all day Saturday and into the night. My stomach was still causing terrific pain, and for over 24 hours I hadn't been to the toilet.

At Spetchley I had a feed from Alan and Val, Jimmy Sutton and Sid Payne, who kept bobbing up in their car to feed me. The café at Droitwich made me some lovely gruel and for several hours I rode mainly on this. Dave and Heather Duffield were also out again on this stretch. After riding for hours with double vision I thought "Ferris didn't have this trouble". Ferris was handicapped by only having one eye and always wore an eye-shade. Suddenly I though that if I had an eye shade I'd be better, and after requesting one I was soon showered with them. I had about four offered me.

So eventually we reached Warwick where Arthur Millest appeared. How active he was, like a Jack-in the-box, I thought. (I hope he doesn't mind if he reads this, but thats what I thought). He gave me a thorough and very refreshing sponge down, and I had some fruit. It was easier to take the fruit than to argue with him. I noticed that he had a book with him to read. I think it was about horticulture, but can't be sure. I remember thinking "what a queer taste in reading". Feeling very much better, I continued. Shortly afterwards I saw Cyril Underhill and then one of my friends from work, Harry Stacey, who is deaf and almost totally blind. I thought of stopping to give him a message, but contented myself with shouting to his wife "tell him I'm going much better, and am OK now", and I saw her lift his hand and start touching out my message to him. He called "Good luck Arthur", and I carried on with renewed vigour. Round Tyburn and Dunton, on to Lichfield and up to Burton and back.

At Alrewas I turned left and pressed onwards. The railway signal chap shouted "what's on?" but I'd no time to answer. That was a long leg, but coming back I was picking up very well and feeling much better. By now I was eating fruit a lot and cream cracker biscuits and feeling much better. Back to Alrewas and a feed. I refused the lovely chicken as I was sure it would upset me again. Then I though, "now for the last leg", and set off via Gailey Island, Newport Island, Chester, to the Nant Hall turn. I had a spot of trouble before many miles when my nose started to bleed badly. We had to plug it, and then I carried on.

I cut the stops to a minimum, (only twenty eight minutes sleep that night). The breeze was against me on the Nant Hall leg, but after the turn the wind was dead behind me. Eventually at this, the Prestatyn turn, I was able to go to the toilet, and from there on with

a slight tail wind, I gained back lost time. My stomach trouble had completely disappeared and I really started moving, cramming all the food I could get down me, and thumping my 90" gear round, and now confident of getting the record.

Once again my thoughts were not of the event. Whilst retaining perfect control of the machine without any trouble at all, it seemed as if I were a dual personality. My body was riding along, but my mind was no longer worried. I was thinking of friends of my younger days when I first started cycling. Of how I went for a weekend to Malham, only about 35 miles from home. The club, called the Leeds Hostellers CC left at 2.30 pm to be there by 7.00 pm. With about eight mile to go, I was holding the club up so much that I was ignominiously transferred to the back of Don Watson's tandem, whilst his girl friend rode my bike. We made it by 7.00 pm.

Then the weekend to Rosedale, 50 miles away. "Too hard for you to try Arthur". I grinned as I thought of it. Yes, that club caused me some pain. Some of them were keen on the White Rose Ladies, and what hammerings I took as they hastened back to Otley to meet them. Edythe Pickering, Madge, Dot and Olive were the chief stalwarts that I remember, and Mrs Woods. In those days I was very small. At 18 I was only 5ft 3" and weighted 7 stone 8 lbs when I went in the Forces.

When I was 14 I was like a lad of 10. Of all the old club, I wondered if any cycle now. I know Edythe Pickering is still interested. I saw her in London about two years ago. I wonder if she knows that the lad who had the huge home made cake at The Falcon, was one day to ride a 1000 miles, and what she'd think as she read "Cycling".

So my thoughts ran on as the bike sped along past Chester and then past Mrs Booth's at Tarvin, and back again. "Get me some salted cream crackers" I cried. They got them. Bill Perrett it was who dashed into the pub for them and brought out the whole sheet that hung up. So on to Whitchurch, left to Nantwich, back again, down to battlefield Corner and Tern Hill, Newport and Newport Island. Around here my throat started to swell and I had great difficulty breathing. By Gailey I had picked up again, and then the last few miles.

With the record safe and huge quantities of ice-cream easing my throat, or at least, so I believed, I was riding it out strongly, encouraged by hosts of spectators and friends. Up the long grind (I dropped a gear), left to Stone and Trentham and back, and the final wind assisted miles past the 1,000 mile mark. But where was everyone ? They were all behind me in a huge crocodile. So down to Alrewas and the final few extra miles to make sure, and then the end of it all - *in 2 days 16 hrs 50 mins.*

An unforgettable experience, and to all who helped and to all who sent best wishes and later congratulations, my sincere thanks. It was wonderful the way everyone encouraged me and cheered me in every possible way. The weather - almost perfect. It turned out that I beat the record by just under six hours. As a matter of interest, after the first 100 miles, I had ridden in top gear, 90, most of the way. Since then Reg Randall has lowered the record another six hours in a most magnificent ride; who, I wonder, will be the next?"

This article by Arthur Render is reproduced courtesy of the 24 hr Fellowship Journal, and Ian Shaw

Alf Arnold recalled *"Our team took over helping and observing from Alrewas. When we found out he'd been sick and had stomach pains, Peter and Tommy Barlow were very concerned. Tommy, being a qualified chemist, made up a drink of very strong peppermint and when Arthur was given it, Alf said you could hear him 'burping' half a mile away. Tommy said Arthur had been taking too much rubbish and too many fruit drinks and that he now needed some good food such as rice pudding, steak, chops, and soup etc."*

What a remarkable ride by this Oldbury and District CC clubman, who never thought of himself as a racing man. After a Friday 4.00 am start, he rode to Lincolnshire and back, his 12 hours gave 223 miles and after a bout of sickness at 300 miles, he rode through Gloucester, Warwick, Chadwick End - 581 miles, where he was still down on schedule by nearly three hours.

His next checkpoint at Alrewas 669 miles still gave him over 2.5 hours down. After a 30 mins break he pushed on to Prestatyn where double vision was affecting his judgement of distance. He had now completed 788 miles and had the wind behind him. At Acton he saw Peter Barlow on route and jokingly asked for a Mersey 24hr entry form ! At 856 miles he'd cut his losses to 2 hrs and at Battlefield corner, Shrewsbury, he was calculated at having done 'evens' for quite a few hours. He cut out all the pre-arranged stops and at 951 miles he was told 'you're seven minutes up'. His 1000 mile journey finished just outside Rugeley. Later that night he was checked out by a doctor who said all he'd got wrong was a slight gum infection and some nervous strain.

He rode on high pressure tyres and used a 5 speed gear ranging from 70" to 90". His training consisted of 24,000 miles in 1955 including two 24 hr rides 440 miles and 427 miles and prior to his record in 1956 he'd put lots of long weekend rides in of over 400 miles. Arthur Render is the brother in law of 'Lol' Innes, the famous tandem End to Ender of 1938

This information courtesy of Cycling and Alf Arnold

ALBERT CRIMES TRICYCLE 1000 MILES 14-17 AUGUST 1958

Timekeeper, Bill Bailey, started Albert Crimes at 10 am Thursday 14th August, one mile from Middlewich on the Nantwich Road. The course had been devised by that mathematical genius Tommy Barlow. It ran to Grange-over-Sands, North of Morecambe Bay to Onibury in Shropshire with detours to Warrington, Whitchurch, Shrewsbury, Nantwich, Wem, Bangor-on-Dee, Prestatyn, Chester, Warrington, Wigan, Preston, starting and finishing near Middlewich.

Each 200 mile section of the course was manned by a fresh team of helpers and observers. In overall charge of operations was that other genius, Alf Arnold, John's brother. The record Albert was striving to beat belonged to David Duffield at 3 days 12 hrs 15 mins, put up in 1956. Dave was out helping Albert in one of the teams as was John Arnold, Albert's tandem trike partner. Such is the camaraderie that exists amongst long distance record breaking clubmen and their helpers and supporters.

Conditions were favourable as Albert started on his epic journey through his favourite counties of Cheshire, Lancashire, Staffordshire and Shropshire. He made good progress through

Nantwich, Chester, Whitchurch, Warrington to Preston at 107 miles, reached at just below evens. Through Levensbridge to Grange-over-sands at 154 miles he was now over 1.5 hours up on schedule here. Alf Arnold reflected his thoughts on Albert's ride as it progressed.

"Albert set off as usual, very fast and upset plans very early on in the attempt, and went like hell from the start. I detoured through Ashton-in-Makerfield to get ahead of Albert to see him safely through the road repairs in Wigan. We had asked the local police to help him through the obstruction which they excelled at, also seeing him safely through traffic lights in the town.

Ed Green who was president of the Tricycle Association was to be the official observer at the turn but unbeknown to me he'd suffered an accident on his way there. Luckily I'd sent our motorbike marshall Don Grieves ahead to check. Don saved the day checking Albert turned at the right place. Albert sped on his way back to Warrington, where Bill Davies of the Mersey RC took over observing duties for the RRA all the way to Stafford where Richard Hulse was the turn observer."

Albert had completed 223 miles in the first 12 hours and was now 2 hrs up on schedule. Rain started around this time and Albert suffered a bout of sickness which soon passed. A feed was taken at Goosetree, put on by Mrs Bates, before pressing on to Warrington, Chester and Marford at 375 miles. At 'Nant Hall', Prestatyn, he'd covered 407 miles in 23 hrs 17 mins. He stopped for a quick sleep, a massage and a wash.

Alf recalls **"I had warned Rex Austin, the observer in the following car, to have blankets ready in case Albert was feeling tired, and I was right. At Prestatyn he had to have a lie down wrapped in blankets for a 40 mins sleep. After a tidy up he got going again and rode well to Stockton Heath at 449 miles where Les Brown and his wife were waiting to follow him down to 'The Harp Inn' at Quina Brook, where he stopped for a 3 hour sleep."**

The weather was warm and the wind was a helpful one as he rode towards his first major stop at Quina Brook, near Wem, which was at 486 miles. He'd averaged 17 mph up to this point and was well ahead of schedule which from here onwards was made out at 14 mph until the last 120 miles when it slowed again to 12 mph.

"Mr and Mrs Edwards had kindly consented to let us use the 'Harp Inn' as Headquarters from 5.00 pm Friday until the finish on Sunday morning, also allowing us to use the telephone as the communication point for the Staffordshire and Shropshire area without charge. The telephone engineer had put a direct line through to the Inn. Albert left the 'Harp Inn' at just after 6 pm on the Friday, fully refreshed and rode through Wem towards Redbrook Pump and the Bangor on Dee turn."

Albert retraced via Wem to the 'Raven' at Prees Heath, where Peter Barlow took over the role as observer. Albert was still 1 hr 40 mins up at this point although a stiff breeze was worrying him as he went into the second night.

He travelled south via Newport to Stafford. Somewhere along this dark stretch he must have hit a pot-hole and wrecked his front rim. A spare wheel was quickly fitted and he turned at the Royal Oak at Stafford at one minute past midnight, nearly two hours up on time. Back through Newport to Shrewsbury at 2.55 am and then a sit down feed at the Acorn Café near Prees Heath.

Tommy Barlow now took over as following observer. The scheduled report shows Albert doing virtually 'evens' all night in between feed stops. At 618 miles he had a massage and changed both lights. Various detours all turning at Shewsbury, bought him to mid-morning 10.12 am, still 1 hr 50 mins up on time. He was still happy and just after noon on Saturday he'd topped 750 miles and sat down to a late breakfast of bacon and eggs, before facing a 40 mile slog into the wind through Gobowen and Oswestry to turn at Cawrsws at 4.29 pm, still 1.5 hours inside schedule. He was now feeling very tired but was still cheerful and moving well. The weather was still kind to him but he kept asking for ice-cream which the team soon got for him.

After a fifteen minute stop to rest his eyes, he wanted to carry on and make use of the breeze blowing him home. Arrangements were then made by telephone for the helpers to organise a sleep stop at Bicton with 858 miles covered. He left at 9.00 pm with an hour in hand over his schedule and got to Battlefield **'going like a bomb'** said Alf Arnold.; back to Hodnet at 11 pm. Detours through the lanes bought Albert back to Hodnet at 12.50 am Sunday, where a heavy ground mist made things difficult for the rider and the following car.

"After Battlefield, Nr. Shrewsbury, Albert started to make his way northwards to Whitchurch. I can remember seeing him going up to the Nantwich turn. We waited for him to come back in the square at Whitchurch During that time a policeman came up staggering all over the place, drunk, at that time of the morning. Jack Ducker's told me later, he was one of the old ones who they didn't bother about ! Albert came back from Nantwich like a two year old, after 946 miles, done at an average speed of 16 mph. He carried on route to Tarvin where Bill Bailey, the timekeeper, was waiting to follow him to the finish."

Albert remained 98 minutes up from here until the end of his ride back through Tarporley, to finish near Middlewich at 7.37 am, with a record time of **2 days 21 hrs 37 mins.** The old record had been smashed by 14 hrs 38 mins.

The Barlow's telephone HQ had taken nearly 200 calls in the first two days and 'The Harp' at Quina had taken nearly 500.

Any old Mersey Road Club 24 hr contestants will instantly recognise most of the places Albert passed through on his record, such as 'The Harp' at Quina Brook which used to be a sit down feed at dinnertime on the Sunday, with lots of custard and trifle to eat, also the Wem, Welshampton to 'Redbrook Pump' optional detour. 'Nant Hall' was a favourite of mine because it was dark and very flat and I enjoyed riding at night.

So Albert chose his route well, or was it all down to Tommy Barlow who knew all the distances on this famous course. This tremendous ride was the pinnacle of Albert Crimes's road record breaking career.

The passages in heavy type are Alf Arnolds recollection of the ride as it unfolded. The rest of the information I've gleaned from the Cycling Magazine having put my own slant and thoughts into it.

REG RANDALL   1000 MILE RECORD   AUGUST 19TH 1960 SOLO BICYCLE

At 6 am on Friday August 19th, Reg started on his mammoth journey which took him south west through Guildford, Reading, Marlborough, Langport and Taunton. At the 50 miles point he was 10 minutes up on a modest schedule aimed to beat his predecessor, Arthur Render's record by 50 mins.

He rattled off his first 100 miles in 4 hrs 44 mins into the teeth of a very strong south westerly wind. Over the next few hours the wind played a cruel trick and veered from south west to north west. This left Reg 14 mins down on schedule at Frome with 197 miles covered. The 12 hr's produced 231 miles which was 8 miles more than Arthur Render had done, but Render had suffered a broken crank and a puncture in that time.

At Pinhoe, 278 miles, Reg was 22 mins down and stopped for night clothes. From here the wind turned favourable for him, enough to reach Bristol at 351 miles only 3 mins behind time. It was midnight now and raining but Reg battled on into the darkness to reach Gloucester in the early hours with 400 miles covered. He'd suffered a bout of sickness at Cambridge but he recovered well as he rode through a cold grey dawn at Worcester. A tour of the villages here, Martin Hussingtree, Spetchley, Evesham, Alcester and Broadway, took him past the 24 hr point with 448 miles covered. He took two short stops to change clothing to stay comfortable for the second 500 miles. He was 25 mins up at the halfway mark, but instead of decreasing his speed as the schedule was written, he accelerated towards the 600 miles point at Gloucester in just over 33 hours, now 38 mins up. Reg rode out of Worcestershire, eastwards through the Cotswolds - Chipping Sodbury, Chippenham, Calne, Newbury and Pangbourne. All beautiful cycling countryside but it didn't distract Reg's attention from the task that still confronted him.

At 700 miles he'd gained an hour on schedule, as he went into his second long night. He was now fighting tiredness and even large drops of icy cold rain failed to stave off drooping eyelids, but he pulled through and resisted the temptation to sleep and lose his time advantage.

At 800 miles dawn was breaking through again He'd been in the saddle for 46 hours and had gained 1 hr 44 mins up on schedule. At 900 miles he'd taken 51 hours 42 mins and due to a slowing schedule, he was now over three and a half hours up.

The final 100 miles through Bicester, Aylesbury, Thame to Little-Kimble crossroads took just 6 hours 37 mins giving a new 1000 mile record time of **2 days 10 hours 40 mins** - a six hour 10 mins improvement of Arthur Render's 1956 time.

This sturdy 35 year old 'mile-eater' had put himself into a class above ordinary mortals at long distance racing. He was at the peak of his fitness after 18 years of riding, including being the holder of the Lands End to John o Groat's record. He lived on his bike, which is useful considering he trained specifically for this attempt over 8 months, covering each section of the course, but as Reg said **"it's a bit different when the sections are linked together".**

It would be 41 years before this record is broken by Gethin Butler, taking 1 hr 37 mins off the time. This shows the tremendous quality of Reg's ride all those years ago.

A trophy that all the 1000 mile record breakers get to hold is a shield that was presented to the RRA by G.A. Olley in 1925. Five years after Reg broke the 1000 miles, when he found out that Dick Poole's record had been disallowed for being 1.5 miles short, he turned the shield round to face the wall in respect to Dick. Such was the measure of a true sportsman. He knew Dick could have walked the last mile and a half and still taken 2 hours off his record.

This article is courtesy of The Cycling Magazine - the report was by Phillip Bevan, and has been re-worked with my own additional information.

PETE SWINDEN - JOHN WITHERS - 1000 MILE TANDEM RECORD 17TH JULY 1964

As reported by Pat Kenny - Birmingham St Christopher's CCC

When members of my club and myself first heard that there was to be a long distance RRA record attempt during 1964, they pounced on the idea eagerly, offering to give as much help and assistance as possible.

The original idea was for a tandem attempt on the 24 hr record standing at 492 miles; the 'guinea pigs' to be long standing club members Pete Swinden and John Withers. They had done a fair amount of tandem riding in the past, and amongst their competitive achievements was the successful beating of the Midland RRA tandem 24 hour record with 454 miles in 1961, in very unfavourable conditions.

It was on the suggestion of our good friend Mick de Mouilpied of the Beacon Roads, that the 1000 miles record was first considered as possible. An argument in its favour was arrived at (not that these mile-thirsty lads needed any excuse) which ran roughly on the lines that if 500 miles were covered in the first 24 hours, the remaining 500 would only have to be ridden at a mere 9 mph average to beat Cowsill and Denton's existing 3 days 7 hours 41 mins record, allowing plenty of resting time.

Early in the preparation the help and advice of Doctor Hamley of Loughborough College was enlisted and a series of visits were arranged for the riders. He was able to advise them on the best time of the year to attempt the ride, dieting before and feeding during, rest when and where most necessary and the best schedule to work to, etc, etc.

My role in the organising was not that of the normal organiser, due to inexperience and the lack of a great deal of spare time, so that preparatory work was shared between the riders and myself. The course was chosen by the riders themselves, their choice being to utilise roads well known to them, with start and finish in the Midlands (so that both riders could sleep in their own beds the night before) and base the bulk of the course in East Anglia. These flat roads are very necessary to tandem riding due to the lifelessness of this type of machine on hills.

A telephone centre was made available to us in the Cambridge area, thanks to the generosity of club member John Newman and his wife, and therefore it was decided to base more of the course in this area, which would facilitate easy change-over of helpers.

Whilst a fair amount of the course measurements were known, there were big gaps that were not, so during the ride the tandem was to be equipped with a mileometer, from which we were to base our calculations and final claim.

A great deal of training was put in during the early part of the year by the riders on both solo's and tandem, and a series of three Midland RRA middle and long distance records were ridden as a test of their mounting fitness. All were successful, the most encouraging of which was their third one, the 304 miles mountainous Birmingham to Holyhead and Back, which they had held for three years, and the 45 minute bettering of the time showed their great overall improvements since that time, their previous best season.

With the riders thus prepared, the major task remaining was that of seeking the help and guidance of many long distance record experts within reach of the course.

I've now been associated with many record attempts, but it never ceases to amaze me at the number of stalwarts of the cycling game, who are prepared to give up their valuable time for this specialised and unusual side of the game. This occasion was no exception and many contacts were made and friendships cemented during the pre-attempt months of preparation, all of whom were prepared to go to great lengths to give the riders encouragement and help at every opportunity before and during their ride.

The RRA officials numbered six in all. Alan Tomkins was the timekeeper, whilst the official observers were Cyril Underhill, Jack Spackman, Mick de Mouilpied, Jack Clements and Richard Hulse, all of whom had been associated with at least one successful "1000" attempt previously.

When the great day (Friday 17th July) dawned, the weather conditions weren't the wind-free and warm ones we had hoped for. Timekeeper Tomkins, quite a weather forecast expert, was able to tell us to expect fair to strong Northerly winds which, for the 8 am start were already beginning to make themselves felt.

Although we had scheduled for an early start, there was a fair gathering of our club members and other keen cyclists to give the riders a rousing send off from Alrewas on their first leg to Coventry and back. This first 50 miles was handled by the Coventry Road Club, and helping cars had an early chance of resting whilst awaiting the rider's return some 3.5 minutes up on their schedule, which was made out for 495 miles in 24 hours.

This early gain was, however, soon lost with their rural ride up to Nottingham, which had a mainly northern trend to it. With 15 minutes lost up to here, they then set off to link up the well known fast time trial courses A.12 and A.23, before arriving at Newark - 129 miles in 5.75 hours.

Newark was the start of one of the many circuits which, covered twice, were to form the basis of the course. It was on the first of these circuits that the riders decided to abandon the 24 hour target and concentrate of the much "easier" one of the 1000. Now there were many of us pleased with this decision because we have visions of the riders tiring themselves in a desperate bid to get 492 miles plus in their first day, and a consequent inability to continue towards their overall aim, rendering failure in both attempts. This decision was punctuated by the first rest, totalling 25 minutes. It was also on the first circuit near Sleaford that Jack

Spackman, the doyen of long distance unpaced riders, first popped up, and , I'm sure that his friendly shouts were a source of new energy, for he has long been admired by both riders alike. Back at Newark, they were 58 minutes down, but, with the new overall schedule to beat the "1000" by 16 hours being introduced, the helpers early pessimism had turned to optimistic horizons.

Forty seven miles later, again saw us at Newark, at the completion of the second circuit, this time 1 hour 10 minutes down on schedule. The time now being 6.40 pm; the riders were happy in the knowledge that the helping strength was to be supplemented by some 'fresh' faces, making a change from our uninspiring haggard looks. The first of these arrivals was Ian Shaw who joined the caravan at Grantham, at 9.20 pm, whilst the night clothing was being donned. Here Brian Kent joined Ian after a hurried introduction. Brian had taken a few days of his holiday off, cycled up to the Midlands to join us for the entire ride, and what a bundle of energy he proved to be !

Meanwhile we were having a change of official observers, Jack Spackman taking over from Cyril Underhill, who had been following for the entire first thirteen hours. We wished the riders good luck as they headed off down 'Biddy's' beloved North Road, heading into their first night.

Stamford 300 miles, was reached in 14.75 hours, no time to stop though, they were expected further down the road by the Peterborough CC, who were to see them away from the noise of the A.1 to the quiet of well known Fen Roads around Ely, Kings Lynn and Wisbech. Interest in the ride was now mounting, with the telephone headquarters handling many more enquiries than at any time earlier. And this interest wasn't confined to cyclists. Whilst phoning one of my regular progress reports through, I asked for a reverse charge call to Harston 726 from a small rural exchange. "What name is it? Oh yes! How are the riders going ? Norman Bird's just been calling as well".

Wisbech at 410 miles was reached after 21.5 hours, with a new day just dawning. This dawn brought the inevitable drop in temperature, and on the short leg of 11 miles to Guyhirn Island and back, the riders took a 35 minute rest, mainly to get away from the cold. Another lap of the 51 miles Wisbech - Downham Market - Kings Lynn loop saw them gain 20 minutes, and on the way South to Cambridge, the 24 hour point was passed with 448 miles ridden.

At Cambridge we had our first change over of helpers with the Stafford contingent returning home, to be succeeded by more club members from both our London and Birmingham sections. It was also here at Cambridge that the riders encountered some very heavy rain, and some hail thrown in to make things even more unpleasant. None the less, little time was lost here, with just the short stop to take on waterproofs. *(The Stafford contingent comprised of lots of Pete's work colleagues from English Electric).*

On the circuit linking Cambridge - Godmanchester and Caxton Gibbet, the riders were overcome by tiredness, and, as the rain had then ceased, they had a short rest on blankets at the side of the road. Time here for late breakfast, which was of a pattern now familiar to them and helpers; cereal and milk; the latter being their staple diet throughout the ride.

Back at Cambridge gave me my first and only chance of a rest; this, of four hours, was spent back at H.Q. in bed. This also brought a chance of relief to our very busy telephonist, Barbara who had been beside the phone for 20 of the last 24 hours. A quick perusal of the telephone list during my period of rest shows that at Cambridge again they had lost a further 16 minutes on the second 30 mile lap, but as they'd had another short rest, this was nothing to worry about. It is interesting to note here that Dr Hamley had emphasised that the periods of sleep should never exceed 30 minutes and that 25 was even better.

The rain was again falling as the riders headed off to cover the roads in the Newmarket and Barton Mills area, with night again drawing in. On again joining the helpers, I found that stoker John had been suffering with acute saddle-soreness and when the stop was made for the night clothing near Ely, he was able to change into a fresh pair of shorts, heavily coated with talcum powder. Psychologically, this felt better, but it wasn't long before John was off again, feeling worse. The only thing to do was to contact Dr Hamley for his advice, even though it was now 10.30 pm on Saturday. He prescribed hourly treatment with surgical spirit followed by lanolin covered by paper tissues.

I must explain that this wasn't saddle-soreness as we mere 24 hour riders know it, but a breaking of the skin on top of each leg due to chafing on the saddle, and with his position being over the back wheel, directly taking all the bumps, the wound had gone from bad to worse. With lanolin in our kit, we had the problem of getting the surgical spirit. At the next village, after much fruitless searching, Brian suddenly produced the elusive liquid like a rabbit out of a hat. John responded very well to the treatment, and with foam rubber now attached to the saddle, time losses were cut to a minimum.

Checks around this time revealed a slight slowing relative to the schedule, but the hourly stops were enough to throw anyone out of their stride. Retracing our outward journey through Chatteris and Guyhirn Island, the A.1 was reached at Glatton with 695 miles ridden in 40.5 hours, registering 4.5 hours down on schedule, but some 11.5 hrs inside the existing record. The route then took us South to cover the North Road course in the Baldock and Royston area. The feeding on this section was being supplemented most efficiently by Bill Sargeant, who had covered almost as much road as the riders for their stay in East Anglia - on his trike !

The second dawn this time saw the rising of a very strong nagging northerly wind, into which the riders had to ride for 50 of the next 100 miles round the two circuits based on Royston. The North Road was reached at last, near St Neots for the final run up into the, now, near gale-force wind. It was therefore, encouraging for us to be able to convey to the riders that at the 870 miles point near Brampton Hut, the elapsed time was 2 days 6 hours exactly, over two hours faster than Cowsill and Denton had taken for their End to End record in 1952. The riders greeted this news with increased effort and instead of losing time into the wind, they had actually pulled back 15 minutes by the time they turned for home at Grantham.

When they arrived at Nottingham, quite a few club folk had gathered there, and were able to marshal the riders round every turn, following an earlier complaint that their minds were blank regarding this route. This was hardly surprising considering that they had now been going for exactly 2.5 days and ridden 945 miles.

Dr Hamley was out to see the riders at Sawley Cross Road, some 10 miles beyond Nottingham, and was very surprised to find that the riders weren't in a state of near collapse. During their 25 minute stop, he was able to make a close examination of the state of John's saddle soreness which hadn't deteriorated since treatment had started. It was also here that we had our last change of following observer - timekeeper Alan Tomkins taking over from Richard Hulse, and he was to take time checks in and around the 1000 mile point.

With the riders now progressing on to really local roads their spirits, and consequently ours, were very high and when they reached Alrewas and passed John's house at 980 miles, the huge cheer from his many relatives gathered there, must have had the same effect as a gale force wind behind them.

We were now into our third night and there was a tremendous feeling of success amongst the helpers, as we all headed for our timing stations. Those stations were well known landmarks around the 1000 mile point, and time checks were taken from the following car when we flashed a light simultaneous with the riders passing.

A further 30 miles were covered beyond the 1000 just in case our calculations were short, and on the suggestion of Alan Tomkins we claimed the time at our calculated distance of 1012 miles, with a time of **2 days 17 hours 18 minutes.** When re-measured later, the exact record time was **2 days 18 hours 9 minutes,** beating Cowsill and Denton's record by 13 hours 32 minutes.

In conclusion, the riders have asked that they be associated with a message of gratitude - "To **all** our helpers, known and unknown, our most sincere and deepest thanks, and, I hope that you're as pleased as I to have been associated with a truly magnificent achievement, carried out in a most sporting manner".

JANET TEBBUTT - 1000 MILE LADIES AMATEUR BICYCLE ROAD RECORD AUGUST 1974

Incredible - Janet's 1000 mile record - was how the 'Cycling' magazine's headlines described her ride in galeforce winds to beat Wynne Wrightson's 1953 amateur record by 6 hrs 24 mins.

Janet's ride started at 5 am on Thursday 8th August at Congresbury near Weston Super Mare. She had fair conditions until midday, then a very strong south west wind and heavy showers buffeted her for the first 19 hours.

On her first day Janet had ridden through Bridgwater, Taunton, Wellington, Cullompton, Ilchester, Highbridge, Glastonbury, Wells, Cheddar, Axbridge, Bristol. She took a 4 hours sleep and then resumed her battle against time and the elements.
Fridays mileage took her through Bath, Warminster, Wilton, Salisbury, Ringwood, where the first 500 miles had been completed. The weather was so bad Janet had to battle against gale force winds and flooded roads at Salisbury. She retraced through Ringwood, Lyndhurst, Warminster, Bath and back towards Chippenham. Her 48 hours of riding had produced 571 miles.

Saturday was dry but very strong winds affected her speed as she pressed on through Calne, Marlborough, Newbury, Oxford, Cirencester, Fairford, Lechlade, Faringdon, Chipping Sodbury. At 2.30 am on Sunday morning Janet was 4 hours down on schedule, but gambled on taking an hours sleep to refresh her. It did the trick and she sped on through Bath and Yate, and by the time 3 days had elapsed she had covered 860 miles.

On the fourth day, with just over 140 miles to cover, Janet headed through Almondsbury, Gloucester, Tewkesbury, Teddington-Hands, then returned back towards Bristol where she lived. For safety sake she rode another 26 miles over the 1000 on a 13 miles circuit, based on Upper Norton, Lower Stone, and Oldbury. The record was broken by mid afternoon giving a time of 3 days 9 hours 29 mins.

The timekeeper was Eric Wilkinson, with Reg Randall an observer, who knew the roads well, having used a similar course when he broke the 1000 miles record himself in 1960. John Ford manned the phone HQ, and Alan, Janet's husband, had organised and scheduled this epic ride which must have taken months to prepare.

Janet told me recently she did a lot of the typing and paperwork involved in the record attempt, but she still managed to amass over 6,000 training miles before the record.

Janet, a member of the Clevedon and District RC for 21 years up till the date of the record, produced moderate performances at the shorter distances, but excelled at the long distances of a 100 miles plus, including 12 hrs and 24 hrs. She has time trialled since the late 1950's up until present day, some 45 years or more. In recent years, along with her husband Alan, she has organised time trials in her local Bristol area, and has worked hard for the sport.

Two years later in 1976, at 40 years of age, Janet went on to take the Ladies Amateur End to End. In 1979 the Ladies Amateur status was no longer recognised and records from then onwards were taken purely on the fastest speed, irrespective of status.

Information courtesy of Cycling with additional comments from Janet and myself.

I've changed my mind – I'd prefer to start from John O'Groats.

SECTION SIX

GLORIOUS ABANDONMENTS

I've headed this section 'Glorious Abandonments' because I feel that these riders were at the peak of their careers, and on paper they could have been worthy successors to the title. Abandonment in most cases has been caused by either an underlying illness, heat stroke, sleep deprivation, painful swollen joints, but most commonly, adverse weather conditions have played a major role.

Where riders have broken the record, after a previous abandonment, I've included the details with their record ride.

KEN JOY JULY 1954

After a successful time trialling career riding for The Medway Wheelers in the late 1940's, Ken broke his first RRA record in 1949, the London to Brighton and back. He won the BBAR 4 years running from 1949 leading the Medway Wheelers to the same BBAR team success's. In 1952 he won the Anfield 100 with 4 hrs 15 mins 57 secs setting a new course and event record by eleven minutes.

Ken Joy turned professional for 'Hercules Cycles' in 1953. The other rival professional team in those days were the 'BSA' Cycles squad. Bob Maitland and Ken Joy, over the next two years, attacked each others records for their companies prestige. Records, such as Lands End to London, Pembroke to London, London to Bath and back, and Liverpool to Edinburgh. Both of these riders were evenly matched. In all, Ken Joy took a total of 12 RRA records. The greatest distance Ken had completed was 288 miles on the Lands End to London in 1953.

At the very end of July 1954 at 7 am on a Wednesday morning, Ken left Lands End hoping to be the natural successor to Sid Ferris, the Raleigh professional who held the 17 years old End to end record. He started very fast, completed his first 50 miles in 2 hours amidst freak showers and sunshine. He crashed after sliding on a hairpin bend at Launceston, as in those days all of the towns on route had to be negotiated.

The first 100 miles was covered in 4 hrs 18 mins. He reached Bristol in 8 hrs 36 mins. He was now 30 mins up on schedule here and two and a half hours up on Ferris at this point. Ken's second 100 produced 4 hrs 32 mins. He went off course at Kidderminster losing a minute or two, but despite the losses so far incurred, he ran out his first 12 hours somewhere in the Bridgnorth area with 271 miles.

He was now 61 miles ahead of Ferris's performance at this point. From now on the temperature dropped rapidly to be a very cold night through the Potteries and into Lancashire and the Lake District. 300 miles went by in 14 hours 1 min, so still 59 mins inside 'evens'. His earlier exertions had made him even more susceptible to the cold and wet conditions to come. 400 miles just before Lancaster had taken him 19 hrs 32 mins, so still an inside 'evens' ride so far. Ken found it hard now to maintain his speed. He suffered two bouts of sickness and was reduced to drinking mainly water. The cold squally showers and a north westerly wind were taking their toll.

The day dawned wet and cold, but in spite of all this, he put up a tremendous 475.75 miles for the 24 hours, reaching well beyond Carlisle to Gretna Green. He'd added 8 miles onto Cyril Hepplestone's fifteen year old RRA record.

There was now only 395 miles left to complete this epic journey to John o Groats, to be done in 30.5 hours. The roads in this area had been wet and flooded for the past fortnight and the prospects of sunshine were very slim. Ken took an hours rest in the 'Hercules' caravan that had followed him for most of the journey. His helpers managed to get some food into him and thaw him out. His feet were so cold that on Shap he'd had to walk the last steep rise just to get the circulation back. These conditions were very different to those experienced by Eileen Sheridan and probably the same team of helpers, only three weeks prior to Ken's ride. He now had to ride at a slower pace than he was used to. Ken showed a 'glint' of cheerfulness when he asked his helpers "am I on the right road for London?"

When climbing to the Beattock Summit, the wind knocked him back to 10 mph. After a few tantalizing periods of sunshine, which barely warmed him at all, he finally climbed off between Dunblane and Stirling. I think its fair to say that the weather conditions had played a big part in the outcome of this ride.

Ken Joy's 24 hour record taken 'en route' was to stand for 28 years.

RON COUKHAM   JULY 1960

Ron Coukham's attempt on the End to End finally drew to a close along Glen Annan, after nearly 500 miles. Coukham had battled against sickness, cold, wind and rain, with a grim determination.

From Warrington onwards the teeming rain had lashed the rider and when the wind finally turned to howl down on him from due north, he bowed to his powerful foe - the weather. Rutland CC's national 24 hour champion had taken over 27 hours for the 500 miles to this bleak part of Dumfriesshire.

NIM CARLINE - 1966

Nim started very well with just a little help from a side breeze. The temperature was in the high 70's and during the day Nim tried to keep himself cool by pouring water over his head. Four weeks previously he'd won the Wessex 24 hr with 496 miles, which was a new Competition Record.

This tough 38 year old Market Gardener lost contact with his helpers due to very heavy traffic in the West Country so perhaps missed out on regular drinks to keep him hydrated. He had scheduled to attack both the 12 hr and 24 hr records on route, but then everyone who attacks the End to End would include these records just in cast the wind is gale force enough to achieve them.

Nim failed to get the 12 hr record after battling through the heat of the afternoon. He reached just beyond Worcester some 16 miles short of 'Shake' Earnshaw's 1939 record. As he went into the night the temperature became cooler and more bearable, but he was now feeling very sleepy. He was still riding strongly enough to maybe beat Ken Joy's 1954 record of 475.75 miles, but tiredness was getting the better of him. He passed through Whitchurch still 'up' on Dick Poole's ride and at Wigan he was still up on 'evens', but slowed from here on.

Nim crossed the border into Scotland but eventually succumbed to sleep and climbed off at Ecclefechan. In hindsight, having seen the effects of mild heatstroke on riders, I don't think anything could have resurrected his ride. He was one of the hardest, most focussed riders I have ever seen riding a 24 hr. His trademark 'flat cap' he donned at nightfall was generally all the extra clothing he resorted to wearing although I have seen him in a sweater and trousers on a really cold night.

His physical job as a Market Gardener kept him outdoors in all weathers, an ideal preparation for long distance racing, but he was fair haired and what I would class, fair skinned, so would be more susceptible to heat stroke, which one could perhaps get away with on a 24 hr knowing you would be finished in just a few hours.

Frank Fischer who timed Dick Poole's ride made some very interesting comparisons in the 'Sporting Cyclist' of October 1966, saying that he felt Nim had gone off too fast, much faster than Keeler, Randall or Poole, but that's the way he rides.
Interestingly enough in the same magazine, Roy Green interviews Nim on his rhubarb farm at Morley in the West Riding of Yorkshire. Nim described his way of doing things, like not bothering with a schedule on his 'record 24' he just hammered right from the start. 4.17 for first 100 miles, 262 miles for the 12 hrs, at 350 miles he just needed to do 'evens' for the last 7.5 hours to break 500 miles. He pushed gears of 100" and 110"all through the ride feeling that he would be wasting his strength using lower gears.

He drank, hot tea, soup, and some of John Arnold's famous peppermint. Nim thanked John for rustling him up two lamb cutlets straight from the frying pan in the night. That's the way he rode his 24's.

Norrie Ward who organised Nims End to End sent out an instruction sheet for helpers on route. It said "Nim is omnivorous, endowed by nature with a powerful capacity to convert anything edible into energy" Although Norrie had written Nim a schedule for his attempt, he said he would probably tackle it like a 24 hr. His average mileage through that summer was 600 miles a week, having checked out most of the End to End route before starting it.

At 38 years of age, Nim felt he needed to tackle the End to End sooner rather than later, stating "I cant go on forever and I want it before Eric Mathews puts it on the shelf ! I think he's the next bloke to get it".

Information courtesy of the 24hr Fellowship Journal, Frank Fischer, Sporting Cyclist, with comments from myself.

JOHN BAINES - JULY/AUGUST 1971

John 'Bomber' Baines of The Icknield Road Club at 31 years of age, after winning the Wessex National Championship 24 hr in 1970, felt the time was right to attack Dick Poole's End to End record. He had won the 24 hr with 473 miles, which is a high enough mileage to base a decision on, especially if you fancy tackling the End to End. John had fared well in time trials at all distances, but like all the other End to End aspirants, he favoured the longer distances, i.e. 100 miles, 12 hrs, and 24 hrs.

On his first scheduled attempt in June 1971, the wind was totally wrong and the attempt was called off. Later, at the end of July, after waiting for a full moon and the right wind, he started from Lands End with high hopes, but by Bristol the wind had turned 180 degrees and was blowing from the north. As the course actually turns more directly into the north at this point, it became a headwind and John soon dropped below schedule. At this point, he climbed off and abandoned.

In all he rode 12 twenty four hour races, mainly 'North Road' events, and in all events barring two, he was always in the first five riders at the finish. He went on to contest the 'VTTA Long Distance Championship' winning it three times.

ROY CROMACK 1974

Five years after breaking Competition Record for 24 hours with 507 miles, a record that stood for 28 years, Roy Cromack started out from Lands end to attack Dick Poole's sub two day record.

He had a very good start keeping to schedule, but a bad fall at 123 miles in the Exeter area while taking food, damaged his knee. The pain increased over the next 200 miles to be bad enough to abandon his ride at Whitchurch at 325 miles.

GEORGE BERWICK - 1975

In my mind, the most 'glorious abandonment' on the men's solo bicycle End to End, was by George Berwick in 1975. He was attempting to beat Dick Poole's record.

From the start, George was 'up' on Poole's record; his attacking style of riding seemed favourable on the hills in Cornwall and Devon. At Exeter he was 11 mins up on Dick, Taunton 8 mins up, Worcester 25 mins up, Bridgnorth 23 mins up. By Kendal he was 11 mins down on Poole's ride.

At the 24 hr point he'd just got the edge on Dick by about a mile, with 455 miles just beyond Penrith. George was a member of the Edinburgh RC and knew the network of roads around the Beattock area very well. He opted to go right to Edinburgh and across the Forth Road Bridge, and so diverted away from the route Dick Poole had used in 1965 which went through Stirling to Perth. George emerged at Perth 54 mins up on Dick, so the route was obviously quicker and shorter. At Dunkeld with 618 miles covered, George had a wash down but didn't re-oil his legs as it was still warm. When he restarted he was still over 30 mins up on Poole at this point. Don Spraggett who was a helper on George's attempt recalls what went wrong from here on in an article he wrote for the 24 hr Fellowship Journal. I've used just relevant details from the article to describe George's plight.

"Heavy rain on the 'Pass of Killiecrankie', George put on his nylon jacket and tracksuit bottoms but nobody knew his legs weren't oiled. On the descents there was a considerable chilling effect, and waterproof trousers would have been more effective to keep the wet and cold off his legs.

George had obviously suffered over the 'Grampians' on this cold second night and by Inverness he was only 11 mins up on Poole. I got back on the road after Inverness having taken a 1.5 hrs rest break. I was very surprised to catch George up so quickly, he had suffered acute knee trouble which came on after Dingwall. He was now in severe pain and retired 3 miles beyond Evanton after covering 748 miles".

Ironically, the wind that was forecasted to help through the Grampians, didn't arrive until George had abandoned. What a cruel twist of fate. What a heroic effort ! The furthest attempt before abandoning until our tandem trike 'climb off' at Bonar Bridge in 1979. I hadn't realised until I began to research all of the details for this book, just how far George had gone, with just over 100 miles to cover and time-wise still in with a chance of the record.

George had at least another three attempts after that. In 1976 he got to Gretna, 478 miles; in 1977 to Carlisle 469 miles and in 1980, Lancaster 410 miles. The weather being the main reasons for the abandonments.

Over the years, George Berwick has been a regular competitor in 24 hr time trials and to my knowledge has ridden at least forty two, winning 3 of them. His best mileage being in the Mersey 24 hr of 1974 - 454.92 miles which won the event. He has broken many Scottish RRA records and still holds the RRA-York to Edinburgh tandem record in 8 hrs 2 mins with John Murdoch, done in 1986. His last RRA record was also on the tandem with John in 1988, breaking the London to Edinburgh with 18 hrs 42 mins. George isn't your average time trial list, he tends to ride mainly long distances and spends his life virtually 'in the saddle'. He's never happier than when he's riding long audax's or camping out or 'roughing it' on a remote route miles from anywhere. At 63 years of age, I wish him many more years on the road.

Don Spraggett died in 2004. He achieved high mileages and placings in 24 hr races. He would help anybody on a long distance event, even when he had 'packed' in a race, rather than go home, he would stay out and help other riders. He was a gentleman who will be sadly missed.

Information courtesy of 24 hr Fellowship Journal, Don Spraggett, and Frank Fischer - re-worked by myself

TOM FINNEY 1977

Tom Finney was a team mate of Mick Coupe's and rode with him and John Cahill for the North Staffs St Christophers CCC. He was in the winning 24 hr Championship team for the North Staffs St Christophers CCC team three times from 1975 and later at least another three times when the lads changed clubs to join the Horwich CC.

Tom Finney, when he attempted the End to End, actually rode for the Army C.U. and his back up team were all army personnel. He was attacking Dick Poole's record and when he got to Bridgnorth the drizzle had already settled in and he was already down on schedule. I was out with Pete Swinden and John Withers to see him through, and it seemed strange to see men in uniform in army Landrovers following a racing cyclist. The attempt got to Shap, but by then he was well behind time.

JOE PILLING JUNE 1978

Joe was attacking Dick Poole's record of 1 day 23 hrs 46 mins which at the least required a helpful wind through Cornwall, that he didn't get. He started at the very unorthodox time of 2 am and after a puncture and spoke problems he battled against a wind, that took a lot out of him. He finally retired at Kidderminster, 270 miles, after being 1.5 hours down on schedule.

IAN MARSHALL 1979

Thirty four year old Ian Marshall of the Leicestershie RC - Kirkby and West, started his End to End attempt in poor conditions. He was an all round rider with a 4-00-13 100 and 252 mile 12 hour to his credit. He held 'evens' for 8 hours but by Bristol he was already nearly two hours behind schedule. By Worcester he'd lost almost another hour and at Warrington, after battling a northerly wind, he finally retired.

PAT KENNY AND JOHN TAYLOR TANDEM TRIKE 1979 (x THREE)

After breaking numerous tandem trike MRRA records and 3 RRA records between 1977 and 1978, Pat thought there was a chance of getting the End to End. I put aside all of my feelings of inadequacy brought about by hero worship and listened as to what the plan was to be.

Pat had worked it out on paper, that Albert Crimes and John Arnold had lost a lot of time through illness and scheduled stops. After all, in those days, it was deemed necessary to have sit down feeds, sleeps in a bed, and take a bath, plus their route was longer and hillier. Pat felt that all of this worked out to be worth, probably, four hours.

Provided we had very similar weather, with the same strength winds, and that we managed to keep going rather than take long stops we stood just a slim chance of pulling it off. After all, this is what all record breakers face when the time comes.

Don't get me wrong, we knew that when Crimes and Arnold were riding well, it was an 'evens' plus pace, but with all the stops it reduced the average speed of the journey to less than 17 mph. So looking at it logically, if we could average 19 mph for 24 hrs, giving 456 miles, we only had to do 414 miles in the remaining 28 hours, which is approximately 14 mph. So you could see the logic in Pat's thinking, and one has to admit it nearly worked. We broke a few MRRA place to place records in the spring for our build up.

We started our End to End attempt in May 1979, Roy Moss was our timekeeper, Pete Swinden, Ivy Mitton, Graham Dayman, Alan Richard's and Tony Shardlow, were our helpers and observers. We had a good start with a fair wind that got us to Exeter and Bristol. We knew our way through these towns as we had broken some local records such as Lands End to Bristol etc, in the previous years.

Our 12 hour mileage got us to beyond Tewkesbury, we had a short break at Worcester, but I was having a struggle to pass water, and was getting uncomfortable. On a racing tandem one of the problems I found was not knowing the limits of my strength or stamina. I could literally ride myself almost into oblivion on the back. I could close my eyes and ride till I was virtually hyperventilating, then I knew I was at my limit. Needless to say it gave me a terrific thirst.

Another problem with being a 'stoker' on any tandem type is one of excess heat, even on a cold day, the steersman shields you from the cooling wind. In turn you sweat buckets and so drink probably double your normal requirement. Pat Kenny is one of the 'old school' of racing men, a big breakfast before the start and then one standard size bottle would last him three to four hours, even on a hot day. He very rarely 'snacked' even when racing, whereas I would have been drinking inside the first hour, and eating little bits all the while. Don't forget, this was in the days before polymer feeding.

In the first 100 miles I would have drunk my two bottles on the frame and asked if I could have some of his. Pat only ever got peckish at proper meal times, even on record attempts, whereas my body clock would go haywire inside 5 hours.

We carried on through the Midlands reaching Gailey Island still on 'evens'. The smoke from the tar distillery chimneys at Four Ashes was directly with us. All of our friends and families were out along here. My wife Liz reminded me, we were well up on time at Gailey, she was decorating at the time and had to leave a piece of wallpaper half stuck to the wall, so as to get herself, Lynne and Mike, there on time. Hazel, Pat's wife, who was running the phone HQ had rung Liz to say we were well ahead of schedule.

Out through the Potteries, the speed dropped on the drags and we now knew we'd got a fight on our hands not to drop below our schedule. The Cheshire lanes gave way to the Industrial towns of Warrington, Wigan and Preston. One lasting memory of riding through these towns was dropping downhill with rows of 'Coronation Street' type houses off either side. At the bottom of the hill was a set of traffic lights. We seemed to be gathering speed instead of slowing, on the back of the tandem trike you have no brakes and no control. It was in the small hours, virtually no traffic at all, even in these dense suburbs. I think Pat misjudged the distance to the lights, which were on red, the brakes went on at the very last minute - too late - cant stop.

Just at that second a taxi whose right of way it was shot across the lights and missed our back end by about a foot - giving him a fright and raising our heart rates at the same time.

Out through Lancashire the night became calmer. We climbed Shap, which I think, was a first time experience for me. I was out of the saddle a lot and can remember Pat trying to get the gears lower and me looking down to realise we were already on the lowest gear ! Ed Green was at the top, you could hear him from miles away. He was a 'larger than life' character you never forgot. Once over the top, the descent is great to a tired body, but we had now realised that the wind had dropped, and it remained calm and unhelpful for the rest of the ride. 448 miles was covered in the first 24 hours.

After Carlisle came the notorious stretch up the A74 which was coned down to one lane for miles. There was no alternative route so all we could do was go as fast as we could, and try to ignore what was behind us. When we got to the end of the restriction there was quite a way to go on dual carriageway. Luckily I could turn my head to the left so as to ignore the abuse from the passing irate motorists. Eric Tremaine in his article thought they were waves of admiration when traversing that same stretch of road, but I'm not so sure !

The next memory I have of our ride is climbing the 'Devils Beeftub' and thinking it was almost a rerun of Shap, only hotter now. By the time we had dropped down almost to Edinburgh, my left knee was feeling stiff and swollen. I thought that was the last of our worries really, the fact that we were down on schedule and still had no wind to help us was more important than my knee.

I remembered us going over lots of rough roads earlier in the ride, where my knees had taken a real battering, especially my left one, such as, dropping down road edge drains while still pushing down on the pedals, the top tube smacks into the knee.

By the time we reached Kinross, it had blown up to twice its normal size and I was having to ride lopsided to stop it catching the top tube. Alan Richards and Tony Shardlow who had helped us from the start were hatching a plan to get one pedal welded up onto another to ease my problems. Alan used a local blacksmith on route to effect the repair. He knew he had to get the job done before we got into the Grampians at nightfall, due to nowhere else being open. He fitted the pedal while we changed into fresh dry clothes for this next part of the journey. My knee didn't seem to get any worse as we rode through the Grampians on this second night. Pat was getting exasperated due to the lack of wind and progress, but we were still in with a chance. The consensus of opinion from our helpers and officials was that we should carry on until it became an impossibility time wise to get the record.

On the long drop down to Inverness, Pat got very cold and this had a drastic effect on our speed, as mild hypothermia had set in making him sleepy - was this the end ? No, a decision was made for us to stop after the town and swap over onto Alan's spare machine, so I could steer, and Pat could get warm and have a rest on the back. This is the first time I had ever steered a tandem trike - what a sharp learning curve this would be, with the climb and descent of Aultnamain in darkness still to come, at least it took my mind off the pain in my knee. Pat didn't quite fit on the back but he knew it was the only solution, even if it was only short term. Ten minutes later he was humming to himself on the back. I knew this meant he was quite close to sleep, but he was still pedalling quite strongly as we climbed Aultnamain.

Now came the tricky bit, getting down the other side without running out of road on this 'Cresta Run'. It was a white knuckle ride all the way down to the bottom. Pat had gone unusually quiet, I thought perhaps he was speechless with fear, with badly cambered bends, and me trying to brake with just two cantilever centre pull brakes on one front wheel, with over 35 stone of men and machine to stop ! We reached the bottom and got onto the flat road. Pat's head was now bumping the middle of my back - he was asleep, but still pedalling. A mile or two later he was refreshed enough to swap back onto our original machine.

The wind was now coming in, straight off the sea, and we realised now, we hadn't got a chance. The helpers said carry on a bit longer until its irretrievable, just in case the wind turns. At Bonar Bridge with 4 hours left, we climbed off, with 80 miles to go and three major climbs, it was now an impossibility.

Everyone said how close we were to getting it. I felt quite elated just to get close to a Crimes and Arnold record. After driving back home I had my knee problem sorted by a 'physio' in Grantham, apparently he was the one who did Les West's legs so he must have been good. I was busy at my work as a Crypton Engine Tuner, tuning car engines; being in a partnership meant feeling guilty taking time off for record breaking, but then, winds didn't just blow in the right direction on Sundays and Bank Holidays.

Two months later while on holiday in Devon, I rang Pat to see how the winds were shaping up. His reply was "looking good for two days time - I'll pick you up en route !" I'd already bumped into Brenda and Keith Robins on the beach at Croyde and told them we were waiting to go again, but I didn't expect it to be that soon !

The weather and wind didn't turn out to be as good as the forecasters predicted. The sea at Lands End was like a mill pond, dead calm, no wind and very hot, even early in the morning. When we started, it was oppressive heat and was like breathing the contents of a hot oven. We struggled through Cornwall in heavy traffic, had a few drinks and sponges from Brenda and Keith which was lucky because our car was stuck in jams. By the time we got through Devon and onto the Bridgwater Flats, the heat was about 80 degrees F, and still no helpful wind. We were dropping behind schedule already.

Then calamity struck - the top tube on the tandem trike had broken. I thought, Oh Well, that's it, ride over. But the team got us onto a spare machine quickly. Alan Richards dashed back up the motorway to his Cycle shop in Erdington 'Tower Cycles' and brazed a new top tube into the stricken machine.

By this time we had limped up through Bristol, Gloucester, Worcester, Wolverhampton and were reunited with our No 1 machine at Gailey. Now that's good service, but still the writing was on the wall. After being way down on schedule, we finally climbed off at Trentham Gardens - slightly cooler but still no wind.

This still didn't blunt Pat's enthusiasm. We had already reconnoitred the route through Glasgow the previous year, and although it was longer, it wasn't as hilly as the Edinburgh route. The helping team and officials were prepared to give it one last try, so one month later, we went again.

The route was to be identical to the first two attempts until you get to the turn for Edinburgh, and here you carry straight on through Glasgow and alongside Loch Lomond on the A82 to Crianlarich, Glen Coe, Ballachulish, Fort William, Fort Agustus and along Loch Ness to Inverness to rejoin the usual route.

So another couple of months later we set off on our last attempt which again didn't get the right wind, and by the borders we were down on schedule but still in with a chance.

By Glasgow it was raining and by the time we got alongside Loch Lomond we were soaked. The thirty mile run alongside the Loch was like a chinese water torture, with water cascading off the hillsides on our left and gushing through gulleys under the road and into the cold wet loch. The overhanging trees added to the dilemma and by the end of the loch we'd had enough.

It was now getting dark and we were going into our second night. Soon we would be into the Grampians and on to Rannoch Moor. With local hotels and inns about to close for the night we decided to pack. We were soaked and cold and so were the helpers. We had got to the end of Loch Lomond at the point of no return.

It wasn't all doom and gloom though. I have a lasting memory of the hotel that we stayed in. Even though we were absolutely shattered and very tired, we had a few amusing incidents. I noticed first of all that the 'fire doors' which in 1979 would have been a fairly new regulation, were being held open all night with sand buckets ! As we were the last guests in, we didn't have much choice as to which rooms we could have. I ended up sharing a bed with Alan Richards who by the time he came to bed, had consumed a fair drop of 'pop' in the bar. Our bedroom was looking out over the length of the loch and it was freezing. After a lot of noise and cursing as he fell over things, Alan said "I've shut the 'bloody' window". He also pulled the curtain. Dawn rose and we awoke still absolutely freezing. When we looked hard we noticed there was **no glass** in two of the windows !

In the morning I've got to admit the breakfast was good, but then it was our first proper food for 48 hours. It was then I noticed the large lampshade was ripped and held together with sticky tape, and when I looked around the dining room, the heavy flock wallpaper was held onto the wall by sellotape on its edges.

I think these funny moments for me almost made up for my disappointment of another failure. The rest of the team weren't too down hearted, at least Alan and Tony, could see the funny side of it.

PHILIP BARLOW 1994

The Kiveton Park CC rider started in ideal conditions and the South Westerly wind helped him to be 33 mins ahead of schedule at 100 miles. A diversion at Bristol and the onset of pleurisy whittled his time advantage down to just 12 minutes at Worcester.

Barlow rode on through the night, but after snatching twenty minutes sleep which put him even further behind schedule, he finally climbed off, exhausted and shivering, just north of Lancaster, at 5 am the next morning. The pleurisy was apparently a complication of a chest infection after a heavy cold in weeks prior to the attempt.

At the time of the attempt, Phil Barlow was the current 24 hour champion.

CHRISTINE ROBERTS - JUNE 1997

Christine, after fifteen years or more of dominating the ladies long distance time trialling scene and after getting regular top six BBAR placements, came to 1997 in excellent form. She already held **Competition Record at 24 hours of 461.45 miles**, produced in the Mersey RC 24 hr in 1993.

I was out on that weekend helping Lynne; it wasn't easy riding conditions, with a very tough high pressure wind and terrific heat for the first 6 or 7 hours. Every time I saw Christine she was pushing a big gear so determinedly. At all the checking points there was a 'buzz' in the air, that she was on for Competition Record and was being challenged by Bridget Boon. It ended up being a battle-royal with Christine coming out on top with 461.45 miles, on what was a very tough weekend. She had pushed Ann Mann's ten year old record up by 23 miles. Christine won the 24 hr again in 1994 with 442 miles. I always felt that she was a natural contender for the End to End title.

Christine had actually scheduled to go for the End to End in 1996, but weather conditions were never promising enough all year, so it was 1997 when she finally got away from Lands End with a very good wind to help her, she reached the Midlands well up on schedule. The main aim was Eileen Sheridan's 24 hr record of 446.25 miles, Pauline Strong's 2 days 6 hrs 49 mins End to End, and Eileen's 1000 mile record of 3 days 1 hr.

I saw Christine come through Fordhouses just north of Wolverhampton with 290 miles covered at just after 10 pm. She was now 45 mins up on a schedule to beat the 24 hr record by 5 miles. There was still a firm helping wind along this section, she'd already got night clothes on and was pedalling smoothly. She looked confident and acknowledged Liz and myself.

Pete Swinden, who was an observer in the feed car, said that as they got up towards Shap, early morning , the wind had become almost gale force. Christine broke the 24 hours record with 467.30 miles, getting almost to Carlisle, but the helpers had noticed that during the night she had been freewheeling down a lot of the hills and not taking full advantage of the conditions; so would 480 miles have been a possibility ?

The helpers could do no more than watch and hope that Christine gained more confidence as the day warmed up, but it wasn't to be. On every stretch of decent downhill, when her speed went up to 'evens', she braked, unable to take advantage of the wind. After stopping many times, and having words with her new helping team that included Andy Wilkinson, she eventually abandoned the attempt just before Edinburgh.

In 1987 Christine had been the victim of a serious collision with a car while riding her bike. She was badly injured, lost consciousness and needed intensive hospital care. Physically she healed well, and as you will have read, she went on to produce some marvellous rides in the 90's, but the traumas and flashbacks left Christine with a sense of insecurity on the road, especially busy main roads with fast passing traffic.

So ended what I consider to be one of the bravest attempts ever on this tough route. Christine's husband Alan Roberts has been the main driving force behind her successful racing career. He himself has been a prolific winner of time trials for the last thirty years, with distances from 10 miles to 12 hours. A regular BAR contender and 'Anfield 100' winner in 1977.

Alan has also been a vital source of knowledge on training methods and diet to a lot of riders including Lynne and Andy. He has set many a training plan for an up-and-coming time triallist over the years.

Alan suffered terrible injuries early in 2004 when he was hit by a 4x4 vehicle whilst riding locally in the lanes. He has been left paralysed with major spinal injuries and has been bed-ridden for quite a long period. But in spite of all this, his friends and family who have been visiting him in hospital, say he is surprisingly cheerful. I'm sure all our thoughts go to Alan and Christine at this very difficult time.

PHILIP LEIGH - 17th SEPTEMBER 1999

Information taken from his own account

Phillip Leigh of the Kent Valley RC in 1999 attacked Andy Wilkinson's End to End figures of 45 hrs 2 mins 18 secs.

After 25 years in cycling, going from a tourist to a 1st Category road man, also time trialling at all distances from 10 miles to 24 hrs with 461.85 miles, Phil felt the time was right for an End to End.

At 9 am on Friday 17th September 1999, the wind and weather looked about right as Phil started from Lands End . He averaged 23 mph to Exeter, and reached there some 20 mins up on schedule. From Exeter through to Kendal the wind was to be spasmodic. After a soaking at Bristol due to an horrendous cloudburst, Phil experienced a very sore backside, possibly some sort of contamination sprayed up off the road, had covered his nether regions in a rash, to which he had to have regular attention throughout his journey. It soon became agony to sit on the saddle, very worrying, so early in the ride.

There was not much help from the wind as he travelled through the Midlands, it was blowing a gale out in the Irish Sea, some 100 miles or more to the left. Warrington, Shap and Carlisle were reached but Phil was down on schedule now, without any help from the wind.

He crossed over the border into Scotland, by the time he reached the Forth Road Bridge, he realised he'd got to average 20 mph to the finish, another 270 miles.

Thirty one hours after starting at Lands End, he abandoned the ride. This was the first End to End attempt to my knowledge that used the internet so that people could communicate 'on line' as to the riders progress. A film was made of Phil's attempt and put onto video which, like John Woodburn's' was a good insight into long distance record breaking.

JOHN WOODBURN - AUGUST 1987 - 1000 MILE ABANDONMENT

Five years after John Woodburn broke the End to End, he tried to better Reg Randall's 1000 mile record of 2 days 10 hours 40 mins put up in 1960.

From the 9 am start on the Saturday, John never really looked to be in control of the ride. After a few hours he was down on his schedule. At Oxford after 180 miles he was 20 mins down, although that loss included a puncture.

By Milton Keynes at 280 miles, after a feed and change of clothes, he'd lost another 20 minutes. At Stamford with 343 miles covered he still hadn't recovered any of his losses. On his long leg northward on the A1 in the dead of night, he had to stop for a 45 minute sleep before he reached the Blyth turn. He lacked his usual rhythm and tenacity and it seemed that his heart wasn't on the job in hand. His helper, Keith Robins, said "John never got to grips with the task".

After nearly 23 hours of riding, John finally climbed off at Newark with 434 miles covered. It was estimated that he would have done around 450 miles for the 24 hours but he had been pushing into a strong south westerly wind on his return trip.

"I've had enough" he called to timekeeper Joe Summerlin, and later confessed that he may have been pushing his luck to tackle such a tough record at 50 years of age. "That's definitely the end of my long distance career, except perhaps the odd 12 hour for the VTTA BAR" said Woodburn.

This information courtesy of Cycling Weekly.

Congratulations Lynne, Johnny HELMS

SECTION SEVEN

"WHERE ARE THEY NOW?"

I was at the Anfield 100 in 2004 and was pleased to be able to re-unite Lynne with Elaine Hancock and introduce Andy Wilkinson and Gethin Butler to this elderly lady who has seen most End to Enders through Penzance and Redruth over the last 25 years at least. She tries to get up to the Anfield every year and on this occasion it was touching to see them all chatting away. Lynne had ridden the 100, Andy had been out with his club helping, and Gethin was presenting prizes, so as you can see, they are all still very much involved with club life.

Andy said a couple of years ago how nice it was to be able to meet and go out with his club, the Port Sunlight Wheelers, and not have to dash around the country chasing records, or 'BAR' courses. Gethin is still racing every weekend for the Preston Wheelers, but after all he is a bit younger. He is another rider who couldn't wait to get the End to End over and done with so he could concentrate on his long distance audaxing and touring, and training rides in his favourite 'Trough of Bowland'. Lynne, like Gethin hasn't stopped racing or training for over 15 years or more. She enjoys all aspects of club life with the Walsall Roads CC, being their President, keeping the lads in check on winter club runs, and giving them a 'run for their money' in local time trials.

Ralph Dadswell still races and attacks records. I last saw him at the Burton DCA 100 held on a very windy cold Saturday in June. He rode tandem trike with Dave Johnson and did a very creditable ride, with 4 hrs 17 mins 14 secs, on what was a very hard day. I chatted to him afterwards and he was telling me he hasn't lost any enthusiasm since his End to End and still enjoys a 'good thrash' for a few hours - his sense of humour still showing through.

John Woodburn still time trials and has had a full season most years since breaking the End to End in 1982 winning many events since then and taking veteran awards and veteran BAR places. Dick Poole still rides regularly and in 2002 set a local vets record at 10 miles of 24-36, at 72 years of age ! Pete Swinden still rides with Birmingham St Christopher's CCC, Northern Section, riding most Sundays and a couple of days during the week with the 'lads'. He's helped or observed on numerous record attempts including at least ten End to End attempts.

Pat Kenny, also Birmingham St Christopher's and the Tricycle Association, still rides everyday. His main love nowadays, when not timekeeping or observing, is riding long distance audaxes all over the country. He holds the second highest mileage ever with nearly 800,000 miles. All this and Pat still works a full week as a Civil Engineer, so as you can see, the End to End hasn't done him any harm, or blunted his enthusiasm. Apart from Eric Tremaine, who I've already mentioned, the only other one I know who is still riding and competing at over 75 years of age is Jim Bailey. Like Pete Swinden he was the steersman on the tandem End to End prior to Pete's. Both of their 'stokers' suffered fairly premature deaths.

John Arnold who supported many End to Ends and was on Lynne's first solo ride, is still active and keeps in touch with all of his old friends. He doesn't ride his bike much, mainly due to traffic volume, but prefers to let the 'train take the strain'. I last saw him at the North West Tricycle Association Dinner at Preston in November 2004, where he was once again rightfully acknowledged for his wonderful achievements.

Reg Randall is, I am glad to say, still active, but mainly goes walking with friends. Like John he manages to pop up to observe riders attacking records, sometimes a long way from his West Country home. I last saw him at the RRA Dinner at Hatfield along with Syd Parker, the 'stoker' on the 1949 tandem trike End to End. Both men looked remarkably well and were chattering away with the younger record breakers. Reg and Syd have both written to me with details for this book, and have both stressed the important role their helpers played all those years ago, although sadly most of them have passed away.

Ethel Brambleby, a lady in her late eighties was at this same RRA dinner. She has links with riders in the late 1930's, riders such as Jack Rossiter, Lilian Dredge, and Marguerite Wilson. Ethel has raced at all distances up to 24 hours over at least a 50 year period of time. Living closer to London, she remembers various record attempts by the professional stars of the 30's, 40's and 50's, either from marshalling them on their routes or providing cups of tea or lodgings for them at her home. At 87 years of age she chats about them as if it were yesterday.

One other very famous lady is, of course, Eileen Sheridan, who I have had the pleasure of knowing and speaking to at various functions, either RRA or CTT meetings or dinners. She is still as sparkling and vivacious as ever, some fifty years on from her famous records. Her links to the sport must go back to the early 1940's, along with Lilian Dredge and Marguerite Wilson, they were the high profile women riders who made female participation acceptable to what had been up until then a virtually all male sport. Eileen's regular appearances in magazines, radio interviews, news films, documentaries, cycle shows and public functions, made her the female figurehead of all that was good in women's cycling.

Lynne and I still keep in regular contact with Eileen mainly by letter and telephone and she is so supportive of cycling issues and keeps up to date on current news and views. Her artistic talents are still in evidence with cards, coloured cartoons and drawings with witty, up to date comments, adorning them.

Andy Wilkinson popped down to see us in November 2004, having just returned from a three month holiday touring America on a motorbike. (his other hobby). He still looked lean and very fit. When I asked him what his plans were and could we expect a 'RAAM' (race across America) of some 3000 miles, coast to coast in the near future, he replied 'no comment'. He still loves his club riding and 'rough stuff' exploits, and has a huge circle of friends to keep in touch with.

Andy, prior to going to America, had with Bob Williams and Mike Bloom, finished measuring the two sections of the End to End route that the RRA were unsure about, so as to get a very accurate measurement and time for the 1000 miles record belonging to Gethin and Lynne, and of course, for future record aspirants. The outcome was to reduce Gethin's 24 hr record to 505.8 miles and his 1000 miles now stands at 2 days 7 hrs 59 mins. Lynnes 1000 is now 2 days 16 hours 38 mins, another rewarding job well done.

Gethin, since his epic ride has, like Lynne, had three very successful seasons, winning many events at all distances and getting BBAR placings in the top twelve. His love of the sport is immense and when he isn't racing he can be found just riding his bike for the love of it. He now has a lovely daughter named Annwin, who he takes on the back of his bike in a kiddy seat. So could she be a fourth generation future cycling star from the Butler family ?

Lynne, like Andy and Gethin, loves the social side of cycling and the all round club scene. After three successful End to Ends and 1000 miles, she is still as keen as ever. Lynne has had two very full seasons after being joined by Marina Bloom, Tracey Maund, Ann Wooldridge and Claire Ashton. Recently she asked me if she should be attempting any of the shorter distance records and my advice was that unless it was a burning desire, then no, only do it if you really want to. It really messes your life about. She has a full time job working 9 hours a day, 5 days a week at our bike shop, tackling virtually all types of work involved, from selling bikes, clothing and accessories, to building new bikes from the box and carrying out quite a lot of basic repairs. Handling the heavy boxes and storing them has given her very good upper body strength. Standing for nine hours every day has given her terrific stamina. Also swimming 1.5 miles three times a week before work, keeps her supple. Record breaking is all about getting the right conditions and dropping everything at a days notice, a bit different to time trialling where its all pre-organised and takes place at the given time, except in extreme circumstances. At least you can organise your life around time trials.

I found records, such as Edinburgh to London, required being driven up to Edinburgh after work and through the night to get to the head post office in Princes Street just in time for a 6 am start. Feeling quite jaded from the car journey it took a lot of enthusiasm and soul-searching to get going.

I remember our tandem trike Pembroke to London record. Roy Moss timed us on our way with a fair wind behind us up through Wales. Eventually getting to Cheltenham over an hour up on schedule. We approached the Heathrow area still way up on time but after about the fiftieth set of traffic lights in an hour, and as many junctions, I had almost lost interest. By the time we reached Marble Arch after about 130 traffic lights and weaving in and out of Sunday afternoon traffic in the Capital, risking life and limb, I really didn't care any more about getting the record. It wasn't about speed and athleticism by then, it was a case of either 'self destruct' or 'self preservation'. We broke Twedell and Stotts 1951 record by 1 hour and 6 mins, and that was in 1977, so that by now I would imagine conditions are much worse. Some riders will revel in their fierce tussle with heavy traffic, but I found it just a dangerous lottery.

As long ago as the 1940's, riders attempting a record that either started, terminated, or turned in London, would aim to be in and out of the Capital, no later that 3 am, such was the traffic even in those days. I think the failure rate would be at least 40%.

I based my answer to Lynne's question about tackling shorter place to place records on this basis. I've tried to be honest with my views, even if they do come across as negative. But then record breaking is all about taking that slim chance at victory !

This year, apart from winning the Turner Cup for the ninth time with 443 miles for the 24 hr, another P.B, Lynne has again been part of a Competition Record breaking team for the fourth time, also winning the Championship 24 team prize from the men.

Lynne, Marina and Tracey broke their own 24 hour team Comp record with 1295 miles. Three weeks later in the Essex 12 hour, Lynne scored another PB with 251 miles. Marina produced 247 miles, followed closely by Tracey on 244, giving them another Competition record of 742 miles. The reason given why both records got just a few lines covering them in the media was either 'The Tour' coverage or the 'Giro' taking preference. Oh well, there's always next year! Being part of a team, a truly amateur club team, has given all the girls a new lease of life and has probably extended their racing careers. At 50miles, 100 miles and 12 hours, they are so evenly matched, its difficult to pick a winner right up to the line.

That just about covers everyone I've managed to track down to present day. My only exasperation these last few years, with Gethin's and Lynne's multi-record breaking exploits over this awesome journey, is that they haven't been given the coverage they deserve, either at the time or with a 'later' article. I along with many many others have written and E-mailed the 'powers that be', to no avail, not even a reply.

When I've spoken to other club folk in various parts of the Country and it amounts to hundreds of people, plus the customers at the bike shop who all read the various magazines, they cannot believe the scant coverage of these purely amateur club riders, whose heroic deeds are eclipsed by reports of mainly continental professional performances by riders who may or may not be on drugs. Pages are devoted to our own one or two 'star' continental and international performers, although one has been banned, he seems to get even more coverage.

Time trialling, unless it's a Rudy Project series event, gets very little in the way of text or pictures and even in midsummer covers as little as two pages, including results; record breaking gets even less.

I hope the chapters of this book help redress the situation !

"ONLY ANOTHER 790 MILES TO GO."

SECTION EIGHT

MANAGERS, ORGANISERS, RIDE DIRECTORS, ADVISORS, TIMEKEEPERS & OBSERVERS

In the olden days, riders of any note, be it professional or amateur, if they were in any doubt of their abilities they would have spoken to F.T.Bidlake, a prolific record breaker himself, who had timed numerous End to Enders over the years. He would have suggested certain criteria required for a successful ride. Their 12 and 24 hour performances would have been an important pedigree required even in those days. George Herbert Stancer was another who looked after riders careers.

Charlie Davey, a top rider and record breaker of his time became a trainer and manager to mainly vegetarian riders such as Sid Ferris in 1937 up to Dave Keeler in 1958. All of the Hercules professionals were managed by the famous **Frank Southall**, along with his brother **'Monty'**, they successfully saw Marguerite Wilson and Eileen Sheridan to their destinations at John o Groats. Reg Randall himself was advised by Frank Southall, that he stood a good chance. **George Dixon** and **Jack Spencer** were his team organisers, each overseeing Reg through half the distance; George to the border, and Jack from there onwards.

The riders from Cheshire and Lancashire were all helped by **Peter and Tommy Barlow** and **Alf Arnold**, John's brother. Riders such as Bert Parkes on trike twice, Albert Crimes on trike, Crimes and Arnold on tandem trike and in between, a 'Brummie' on a trike riding the wrong way - David Duffield.

A lot of riders came from the Midlands, quite a number from the Birmingham/Coventry area. Eileen Sheridan, Edith Atkins, Lynne Taylor, Paul Carbutt, Dave Duffield, Pat Kenny, Pete Swinden, John Withers and Eric Tremaine.

Swinden, Withers and Kenny were all from the same club, The Birmingham St Christophers CCC, whose members broke no less than 16 RRA records between them. Pat Kenny being the main recipient with 9 records to his credit. When looking for a common denominator between Duffield, Swinden, Withers and Kenny, it has to be one man, **Mick de Mouilpied.** Originally from Guernsey, but lived most of his life at Selly Oak in Birmingham, Mick was a member of the Beacon Roads CC, the same club as Dave Duffield.

Mick, in his earlier days, had ridden a few long distance time trials, his best performance was the Mersey RC 24 hr in 1957, producing 390 miles, and he only considered himself to be a tourist. He rode his own Club's Birmingham to Weston and back 200 mile reliability trial quite a few times, done in the middle of winter every year. He was the organiser for a lot of Duffield's records and orchestrated his successful End to Ends and separate 1000 miles.

Many of Pat Kenny's successful records were supervised and scheduled by Mick. He had quite an input into Swinden and Withers tandem records, the 1000 and separate End to End, plus many Midland RRA records the lads attacked on a regular basis, as training for the big rides. So in the 50's, 60's and 70's, he was the man to see if you were a Midlander aspiring to a record. Mick's house just off the Bristol Road was perfectly located for him to start and finish many Midland RRA records terminating at Birmingham. His wife Nora helped with the details, making everyone welcome to use their home as a base. He was a tireless RTTC timekeeper with scores of Midland open and club time trials to his credit over the years. Sadly, by the year 2000, Mick had fallen prey to Alzheimer's and that once brilliant organising mind has gone. The last time he was out on a record was Lynne's solo attempt in 2001. By that time he had faded quite badly.

In the 80's and 90's the man to ask for advice was **Pat Kenny** himself. Already a competent timekeeper for quite a few years officiating at many open time trials in the Midlands. What Pat doesn't know about record breaking isn't worth knowing. He's advised many riders over the last 20 years; he's timed or observed numerous MRRA and RRA records in that time, including Mick Coupe's, John Woodburn's Ralph Dadswell's, Swinden and Withers, Andy Wilkinson and Lynne's tandem and Lynne's first solo, being his last one.

He organised his own End to End and also had quite an input into the Swinden and Withers rides. His knowledge of the End to End and conditions needed to be a success is a gift that comes with experience.

It was Pat Kenny who looked at the old End to End route which until the 70's went through Kidderminster to Bridgnorth. It was a dark undulating road coming just when the rider is getting weary on the first night. After Bridgnorth the road doesn't improve much going through what was Wellington to Whitchurch - Wellington is now Telford. Many riders have suffered badly on this stretch giving them a soul searching time.

When Pat was looking for a better route for a tandem trike attempt with me, he suddenly realised that it is actually much flatter going through Wolverhampton. There's lots of well lit dual carriageways right the way through Stafford, Stone, Congleton and back out into the flatter roads of Cheshire. Pat will tell you he hates hills, so the flatter the course the better.

The stretch between Wolverhampton and Warrington is tackled anytime between 9 pm till 3 am and that is the time and the area most club folk come out to cheer the riders on. Gailey Island where the A5 crosses the A449 is probably one of the most popular places on the route where helpers swap cars, fresh officials come on board, and anyone wanting to by pass the rider has ample opportunities with the motorway nearby. There are no problems with traffic due to the time of day and who knows, this route may have been the saviour of one or two riders in the past. The boost and encouragement playing a big part. I think Mick Coupe was the first solo bike rider to use this route in 1982, though apparently Dave Duffield used a version of it as far back as 1960.

As the Eighties raced into the 90's two other major organisers rose to prominence, **John Williams,** President of the Mersey Roads CC, and **Jim Turner**. Jim is better known as the Organiser of the famous Mersey RC 24 hr race held annually, an event he ran for 13 consecutive years until 2000. In the last 5 years he's helped or organised numerous successful RRA records. He was 'on road' Director of the mixed tandem record's, Lynne and Andy's Liverpool-Edinburgh followed by the End to End. He organised and directed Gethin's Liverpool-Edinburgh RRA record and organised and directed his End to End and 1000 miles, going all the way which in hindsight put a terrific strain on him physically, so that when we requested his help on Lynne's End to End and 1000 he said 'Yes, I'll gladly do it, but I will organise it from home'. This left my son Mike to co-ordinate the on road teams. This was his 'baptism of fire' and he came through it well having never been on a record attempt previously.

Jim's generosity knows no bounds, if he thinks he can help somebody achieve a goal in cycling terms he will help all he can. You've only got to mention to Jim that you fancy a trip to Cornwall or Scotland in the near future and you get an End to End Schedule in the post next day ! He is as passionate as anyone about the End to End, and when we reminisce about either Lynne's, Andy's or Gethin's records, like me, he gets very nostalgic and gets a lump in his throat at the thought of it all. I know for a fact that when he had overseen Gethin's struggle through Scotland and then was sorting out the details for the 1000 as the team got there, he was close to exhaustion. I saw him just before Gethin started his 1000 and he looked tired and tense, but then he had been on the road for over 48 hours, with all the timing, marshalling, hotel and transport to sort out, its not surprising at the strain put on him.

The other main man of the 90's taking us to 2001 as I've mentioned is **John Williams**. A most meticulous organiser who's directive skills know no bounds. Once he has a team together, nobody is left in any doubt as to what their job is, its actually written down minute to minute, hour by hour, day by day ! The system works like clockwork, leaving nothing to chance, even having reserve helpers ready to step in at a phone call from John. The whole Williams family, from John Williams senior back in the 30's, 40's and 50's, through to the 70's to his sons Bob and John . Bob's wife, Ruth and sons David and Jonathan, all have played a big part in organised cycling in the Cheshire, Shropshire and Liverpool area. Each giving many hours of their time each week, either marshalling, observing, organising or timing events for other people to enjoy. I have known their family for many years and appreciate all of the help they've given all of us over the years.

Keith Boardman organised Andy's solo bike record of 1990 and John Williams was the 'on road director'. The drama of the last few hours of the ride where Andy almost succumbed to sleep must have been a worrying time for him.

In the year 2000 John went on to organise the mixed tandem record of Lynne and Andy's Liverpool to Edinburgh. That was to be a test ride before their End to End. All went according to plan for him and then in May that same year he successfully organised their End to End which again for John and all of us on the team had nail biting moments as Andy started to suffer towards Shap. I think it was only the fact that Andy didn't want to let Lynne down that kept him going. In hindsight this was probably one End to End too many for Andy who had 'come out of retirement' for this one last big ride.

John had to make a decision at 24 hrs to disregard what was an ambitious schedule, aimed at being inside two days and to implement a new schedule that Shelagh and Edwin had produced, just to keep them going and break the Groesbeck-Harris record. This became the turning point for the riders, although there were more hitches later in the ride. John was rewarded with another successful result.

Lynne's first solo attempt over a year later was his last involvement in organising an End to End, by this time John had suffered an arrhythmia and was struggling to maintain a steady heart rate. He agreed to help us and the next few weeks till she finally started were spent waiting for a weather slot and trying to choose a day that Gethin wouldn't use. As Gethin had got his 'notice' of intention in before Lynne, the RRA rules allow only one ride per day thus giving him first choice. Three weeks of waiting were as anxious a time for him as they were for Lynne and the team. As is written in Lynne's episode, No 36, John must have been under terrific strain during her ride until the last few miles were completed, giving him yet again another success, but probably his toughest mission of all time.

With either Jim or John organising, all you had to do was sign the RRA form and turn up to ride on the day. They did the rest, but stresses like these take their toll, both men being in their 60's and neither of them are still in 'mint' condition. Having both given their all for others sporting achievements, we owe them both a debt of gratitude.

Whilst on the subject of people who have organised records, I feel it is equally important to profile the Timekeepers, Observers and Officials over the last 50 years. Without them there would be no Road Records Association. I can only go back memory wise with the RRA to about 1970. I already knew a lot of timekeepers from my time trialling days; Tommy Barlow, **Ron McQueen,** who timed numerous End to Ends. Ron was principal timekeeper at the Mersey RC 24 hr for 35 consecutive years, earning a gold badge at 76 years of age. There were two or three timekeepers since 1947 who I have only read about in End to End reports, the first being **F.W. (Robby) Robinson** who successfully timed Jim Letts and Syd Parker on their End to End and 1000, and then two years later was present on Jim Letts successful End to End on trike. **Alan Gordon** timed Edie Atkins successful End to End in 1953 and then the following year he timed Eileen Sheridan's successful rides. **Ted Bricknell** was the man who timed David Duffields trike End to End in 1960.

Tom Anderton was the timekeeper on the famous four records in one ride in 1954, of Crimes and Arnold. What a reward for a timekeeper, some never get to time a successful road record at all, let alone four.

I can well recall **Tommy Barlow** who was the timekeeper responsible for the 'optional' detours on the Mersey RC 24 hr. He would be stood at the side of the road just before the junction with his cap on, puffing on his cigarette, looking at his stopwatch, surrounded by clubmen waiting to see which riders he was going to send on those extra miles. I can only remember being sent down the 'Saltney to Marford and back' leg once; I must have been fit that year. Tom's son **Peter Barlow**, apart from being a record organiser and observer was also an RTTC official. I recall being ticked off by him in the middle of the night in the Mersey 24 hr for 'company riding' (having a chat more likely !)

Eric Wilkinson, the timekeeper on the successful Swinden and Withers tandem End to End in 1966, was himself a long distance champion having won the North Road CC 24 hr plus breaking competition record on trike in 1938 at 100 miles and 12 hours. He went on to be the principal timekeeper at the North Road 24 hrs for quite a few years. A very prestigious role for a timekeeper, I well remember being started by him on that famous course.

Whilst on the subject of Mersey RC 24 hr timekeepers, **Rod Goodfellow** has taken over the role of principal timekeeper along with his wife Margaret who also times. Rod has also done interim timing on the End to End and has been instrumental on many records in the North West. He was also a prolific 24 hr man winning the event on solo bike four times - 1967 with 475 miles, 1975 with 478 miles, 1976 with 476 miles and 1982 with 456 miles. Then in 1991 he rode tandem with his son Peter and put up Comp Record with 501 miles which still stands to this day. When I spoke to him recently I asked him why he hadn't been contender for the End to End as I'm sure he had the right aptitude and stamina. He replied that he'd seriously considered it but had chosen to pursue his career by working abroad so relinquishing his chances at this coveted record.

Dick Poole's timekeeper was a man who came from Stafford - **Frank Fischer**. He went on to write lots of interesting articles for the 24 hr Fellowship Journal, comparing various End to End rides. I have used some of his material in this book.

Al Harper was one of our local timekeepers on Midland courses. He timed all distances from 10 miles to 12 hrs. He could be found most weekends administering his services on the 'K' courses. He was one of my first timekeepers when I started time trialling in the late 50's and he was still timing when Lynne started in the 80's. If there was a Midland RRA record such as the Birmingham to Shrewsbury and back, or Manchester and back, we used to start virtually on Al's doorstep as he lived just off the Chester Road at Streetly.

Roy Moss was the man for timing record attempts between the mid 70's to the 90's, culminating in Pauline Strong's successful End to End in 1990. Roy had timed lots of Midland RRA and Welsh RRA records over a 30 year career. He was a meticulous and well organised man who was always ready to help riders, virtually at the drop of a hat. He timed mine and Pat's tandem trike End to end attempts in 79. There was no reproach from him when we failed. He knew it would be a tightly run ride right to the point of impossibility, but his first remarks when we packed at Bonar Bridge were 'if you had a decent wind on the second day you could have got it' which gave us the incentive to try again, twice.

Roy was an avid tourist and photographer and enjoyed nothing more than showing us his latest collections of holiday or tour photos. They were of a professional standard. We used to meet up once a year with him until he passed away in 2001. He had been suffering with Alzheimer's and for the last few months of his life was in a nursing home. Shelagh and Edwin Hargraves had been a regular help and comfort for him and visited him regularly. Roy accepted his illness quite calmly. The last time Peter Swinden and I went out with him to a local pub near his home, Roy got out of the car, stood for a few moments and then proceeded to get back in. When we said 'hang on Roy, we haven't eaten yet', he chuckled and said "that's the problem with Alzheimer's, you don't know if you're coming or going".

Apart from timing road records, Roy had given over 40 years valuable service to the Welsh time trialling scene. Needless to say, he is missed by all of his friends.

Audrey Hughes was in 1992 as far as I'm aware, the first woman timekeeper to time an End to End record. Ralph Dadswell's. Audrey was better known to me and probably lots of other cyclists as being the C.T.C Tourist and Map Reading Champion in the 70's and 80's, winning many competitions around that time. She scolded Ralph in the last few hours, saying she hadn't gone without sleep for two days for him to mess things up now !

Edwin Hargraves who along with Stuart Jackson in the late 70's, early 80's, took no less than 6 tandem trike records together. Edwin broke a solo trike record taking the Pembroke to London in 1976 with 12 hrs 28 mins. Edwin won the Mersey RC 24 in 1998 at the ripe old age of 48, with 462 miles, probably the oldest man ever to win this event. Along with **Shelagh**, his wife, they have both given a big part of their lives as organisers and officials for the RRA and the Welsh time trial scene, either as timekeepers, event organisers, or as secretaries of the

Welsh RTTC Edwin was the secretary of the RRA for 11 years from 1986 to 1997. Shelagh since the year 2000 has with Edwin, provided telephone and internet information on all three of Lynne's records - two solo and one mixed tandem with Andy.

I feel sure that if Edwin and Stuart had attacked the Crimes and Arnold End to End record in the early 80's they would have stood a very good chance. Stuart had ridden some prolific 24 hrs on solo bike and trike. He won the North Road 24 hr in 1982 with 496 miles and won again in 1983 with 488 miles, and again in 1984 with 494, all on solo bike, so ranks as one of the top distance riders ever, and in fact in the 80's he would have stood an equal chance of the End to End against Coupe or Woodburn. I think ed:

Edwin and Jim Hopper had planned to attack the tandem trike End to End the year after Edwin's Mersey success, but a deadly stomach bug put Edwin in hospital for much of that summer. The consequences of which effectively ended his racing career.

Joe Summerlin Along with **Ivy Mitton** were the officials on Eric Tremaine's trike record in 1982, Joe being the timekeeper, this was probably one of his most notable assignments as an RRA timekeeper. I know Joe more recently from helping his wife Gail in time trials up to 24 hrs in length, regularly riding the same events I go out to with Lynne.

Ivy Mitton along with her husband Pete, has been a timekeeper or Observer on many MRRA and RRA records. She gave a lot of help to Pat and myself when we were attacking Midland records week after week, as a build up to our End to End attempt.

Fred Allcoat also gave his timekeeping services to many Midland record breakers in the 70's and 80's. Like **Alan Tomkins** who timed the Swinden and Withers 1000 mile record he was also a revered 'Amateur Athletics Association' timekeeper. Arthur Renders 1000 mile record was another of Alan's successes.

When **Jim 'Nobby' Clarke,** the timekeeper from Aberdeen came to our rescue on Lynne's End to End and motored up to John o Groats, we didn't realise he had had to leave his wife who was very ill, so that was a great sacrifice from him, for which we are all grateful. I'm only glad it was a success, after a near 300 mile round trip for him. Whilst on the subject of Scottish Time Keeping, I must mention **David Harris**, who was the timekeeper on Wilko's bike End to End in 1990.

Our next providers of help over the years, either observing, timekeeping or helping on record attempts or long distance time trials are **Brenda and George Jackson**. It was they who provided the comfort of a motor home for Gethin on his End to End and 1000 miles in 2001. Out at all hours, in all weathers, no job too big or too small for them. Brenda has suffered some health problems in recent months including a road accident, but makes light of it. Such a positive couple and long standing stalwarts at the Mersey 24 hr, helping in many ways.

Christine and Frank Minto known more in recent years as RTTC and RRA timekeepers hailing from Barnsley in Yorkshire. They have between them timed the start of at least two of the last successful End to Ends, going to either Gailey Island or Gretna as observers or timekeepers but never getting the opportunity to time the finish at John o Groats. Always willing, even at short notice, to help wherever they can. Regularly timing local time trials on the Yorkshire courses.

Christine is still very fit either on trike or tandem. She beats 'girls' half her age. She is a past ladies 24 hr champion beating comp record in three consecutive years with 409 miles, 420 miles and 427 miles between 1967 and 1969. When I asked her if she had ever thought about the End to End, Christine said she hadn't really considered it; with family commitments and finances it would have been very difficult for her. She also mentioned that living in Yorkshire on the east side of the country, folks didn't go to see the End to Enders through on the western side of the country so there wasn't the 'following' interest.

Frank Minto was possibly better known as the organiser of the British Best All Round or BBAR competition, a job previously done by Tommy Barlow. He was the man who checked and collated everybody's times in 'BAR' qualifying events. A duty he carried out cheerfully for nigh on 25 years or more. Our thanks to them for years of dedication to the sport, again, nothing too big or too small, as I recall Christine drying Lynne's wet clothes out over the van heater on her second solo ride, going towards Bristol.

Dai Davies came to prominence as a timekeeper for the RRA on the mixed tandem End to End record of Jodi Groesbeck and Adrian Harris in 1998. Although he had been a regular RTTC timekeeper for quite a few years, he is more famous for his End to End exploits. He actually advised and helped prepare the Groesbeck Harris team as to what would be involved in an RRA record. As they lived in America it was a steep learning curve all round. The record was a success for everyone involved. Dai's next End to End assignment was the mixed tandem record of Lynne and Andy in the year 2000. He had given me some background history on the previous holders and the way they went about securing the record. He mentioned how Jodi had spent much of the ride on the front of the tandem. I thought what a good idea that either rider could take the battering at the front and set a plan in motion to make Lynne and Andy's tandem so it could be steered by Lynne if Andy was very tired. The record was another success for Dai and them with a five hour beating. His next success was undoubtedly one of the biggest ever in 2001 - Gethin's End to End and 1000 taking the 24 hr record on the way.

That was to be probably his last timing duty as a recurring digestive illness now prevents him from travelling too far. He now performs a phone round service from home, informing everybody as to when a record is imminent, so taking a lot of pressure off other RRA officials - officials such as :

Eddie Mundy who has done many jobs as an RRA official from President for 7 years, 1994-2001, to being the current records secretary at 80 years of age. His third place ride of 448 miles in the Mersey 24 hr of 1953 behind Nick Carter and John Arnold was probably one of his best performances, and this is the same E. Mundy who won the North Road 24 hrs in 1952 with 467 miles, a new competition record. I seem to have been getting RRA post and notices from Eddie for at least 30 years.

Richard Hulse - to see him either stood by his cycle or better still riding it, was like looking back into time to the 1920's. The way he dressed was immaculate, with a stiff starched white collar, his hair parted in the middle and slicked back. He always wore a smartly tailored jacket, usually grey, and 'plus fours' with knee length socks, finished off with black leather cycling shoes, with a large leather flap over the laces. His cycle was a black 'Raleigh Record Ace' complete with mudguards and saddlebag. On his handlebars was a large 'chime' bell and an acetylene lamp.

I well remember him turning up on many of our Midland RRA records and our RRA Edinburgh-York on tandem trike in 1978. He usually stood well back from the road, smoking a pipe, not a hair out of place. I attended quite a few Midlands RRA meetings in Birmingham when record breaking was in its heyday and Richard would be there - always a staunch supporter.

My record's show that he rode at least two 24 hr time trials, riding for his native Speedwell Bicycle Club, one of the oldest cycling clubs in our history. Richard produced 358 miles in 1948's Mersey RC event and 362 miles in the 1949 event. I can only imagine he was riding in Alpaca jacket and tights as befitting a rider of a bygone age. What a good mileage by someone who was more of a steady tourist and an onlooker, and supporter of our sport.

Another long serving RRA committee man is **Keith Robbins** who with his wife Brenda has been actively involved in record attempts over the years. Probably their most famous one being John Woodburn's in 1982 where they appear on film helping the great man to his record. The film in question is described in John's article Episode No 30. They played a big part in the organising and 'behind the scenes' work for the RRA over the last 30 or more years, organising most of the functions put on by the organisation.

George Hunton was the Honorable Secretary of the RRA from 1978 to 1986. I recognise him more as a timekeeper on many occasions. He also appeared in the film '2 days and 2 nights' and was the timekeeper on John's record. George passed away in 2001 having served the sport well over many years.

Les Lowe Observer and course measurer, long distance record breaker on all forms of cycle, also a Speedwell Bicycle Club member, and prolific 12 and 24 hr rider for more years than I can dare to remember, he seems to have been 'observing' on all of the ones I've missed. Les's knowledge of the rules of the RRA is immense, his memory of events, not only End to Ends but also other place to place records and long distance time trialling over the years could fill a book, so come on Les, the next time we have a rainy day, start writing.

Pete Swinden I've already chronicled Pete's main record breaking rides with John Withers. He's been a clubmate and family friend for 47 years. He still goes out on his bike with the lads three times a week, but is quite happy to stop and admire the scenery or to potter along his favourite lanes in Shropshire and Staffordshire. He's been a constant source of help as an observer for the last 25 years or more, putting back into the sport far more than he took out. If you counted the unsuccessful attempts on the End to End he's observed on as well as the successful ones, I would say its at least twelve, maybe more. He also helped on numerous occasions on this famous route.

A fixed wheel was his favourite as well as a Sturmey Archer in his earlier years. He encouraged me in the days when Birmingham to Llangollen and back or Birmingham to Weston and back were accepted as 'reliability' trials in the middle of winter. The latter one being some 200 miles riding through the night. Pete's helped Lynne and myself on End to Ends and Mersey 24 hrs, weekends almost too numerous to remember.

Pete said after the last End to End which was an unsuccessful attempt by Chris Hopkinson, that he'd almost had enough of sitting in a car staying awake for 24 hrs. Words that were echoed by another staunch record observer over the last few years;

Ron Sant - himself a record breaker with Jim Hopper on tandem trike at 12 and 24 hrs, gaining MRRA and NRRA records in 1991 with 436.75 miles. Ron had also gained the Audax gold medal for completing the End to End inside 80 hours in 1995, so he knew what 'staying awake' was all about. He observed on Lynne and Andy's mixed tandem record in 2000, Gethin's End to End and 1000 in 2001, and finally Lynne's End to End and 1000 in 2002. He was an avid collector of antique cycles and his knowledge of the subject was immense. Ron had an underlying heart problem over the last few years that not many people knew about. I last saw him at the end of the Mersey RC 24 hr in July at Farndon in 2004 looking tired, but then I thought maybe he'd been out all night helping. The next thing I knew was that he'd suffered a heart attack while leading a procession of antique bikes through Telford. He'd fallen from his machine, a wooden bike, and never regained consciousness, finally passing away in September 2004, having reached 70 years of age. Ron we will miss you !

Tony Shardlow himself an RRA record breaker at 25 miles on tandem bike with Alan Richards 44 mins 07 secs in 1977. Primarily a short distance speed man but over the years has produced many MRRA place to place and fixed distance records on solo bike, solo trike, tandem and tandem trike with Alan Richards. His first services as a helper on an End to End were in 1979 helping Pat and myself on our three unsuccessful attempts that year along with **Alan Richards.** They formed a formidable partnership, always ready to see the funnier side of things. Tony says people are so serious nowadays when they're racing. No one smiles or has a laugh anymore.

I well remember riding the Oldbury 12hr and stopping at the toilets in Rugeley and taking my bike inside. I came out of the cubicle - bike had gone, my heart sank - on top of the theft I would probably have to walk home having no motorised helpers. On leaving the toilets I hear voices and 'chuckling' behind the hedge. Yes, you've guessed, Richards and Shardlow, playing tricks, luckily I did see the funny side of it after about 10 miles of cursing them, while riding along.

Alan who owned Tower Cycles in Erdington was a great source of help to Pat Kenny and myself over our years of record breaking going as far as Bonar Bridge on our first attempt. On the second attempt the tandem trike top tube broke at Bridgwater, and Alan motored back to Erdington leaving us on his spare machine. He brazed a new top tube into place and by the time we had got to Gailey we were reunited with our machine. We did complain that he'd only undercoated it and it didn't match the rest of the machine ! You can imagine the reply. That attempt was doomed to failure and we climbed off at Trentham Gardens. The next attempt Alan and Tony helped on terminated at Loch Lomond, but I have already written about these attempts in 'Glorious Abandomnents'. Tony became an RTTC and RRA Timekeeper, timing many Midland events over the last few years. His last big 'stint' at timing was Lynne's solo End to End and 1000 miles in 2002. All through Scotland he was working out what she needed to do to get the record, and then when the breeze became helpful with a 100 miles to go, like us all, he found it difficult to contain his feelings, being part of history being made.

Paul Histon wasn't just a helper, he was such a positive 'mentor'. He'd been on a lot of Andy Wilkinson's successful rides starting with his recumbent End to End in 1996. Paul was present on all of Andy's big rides, and with Jim Turner, he made an incredible team helping Andy in his successful 'BAR' bid in 1996 where he broke competition records at 50 miles, 100 miles and 12 hrs also putting up the fastest ever average BAR speed of 28.236 mph at that time. Paul knew all of Andy's weak points and knew how to get the best out of him, and how to perk him up when he was having a bad patch. I watched him in amazement on the mixed tandem attempt in 2000, when we felt that it was nearly all over on Shap. Paul managed to sweet talk Andy into carrying on for Lynne's sake, and then after another bad patch around the Lockerbie area, he succeeded in motivating Andy to try another few hours. And so it went on, all through the second night, to its final conclusion. Paul's energy at keeping 'chipper' for all those two days left me amazed. Probably Paul's finest achievement with Andy was pushing him to his 525 miles Competition record 24 hr in 1997.

He showed the same enthusiastic skills on Lynne's first solo record carried out for most of the time in heavy rain. I don't think Lynne would have 'packed' but all of us, except Paul, thought she was on a 'hiding to nothing' right from Bristol onwards. He obviously could see that as long as she didn't have a gale turn against her and as long as she didn't slow as much as the schedule allowed for at the end, she could just make it. Paul kept us all cheerful including Lynne. Being a rally driver, his skills with the stopwatch were a useful asset and so were his navigational skills. That record was another success for him.

In 2002 his job didn't allow him any time off when Lynne went again. The conditions again were similar, the weather that had been forecasted didn't materialise and by the Midlands Lynne was well down on schedule again. When she rode through Gailey, Paul was there and was still there all through Cheshire cheering her on. Funnily enough he had a worried look on his face when we greeted each other, seeing how far she was down on schedule and knowing exactly what she had to do, he wasn't very optimistic as to the outcome, although we felt exactly the same as him, we were keeping enthusiastic for Lynne's sake. I told him what Lynne had said at Tewkesbury about concentrating on the 1000 mile record and Paul said 'That's confidence for you', but when he left us to go home to bed in the wee small hours, I bet there were doubts in his mind as well as ours.

In 2003 Paul went on to help Andy as his mentor, trainer and advisor on the 'HERCULES' challenge on BBC TV. It was a challenge to test 12 athletes over 12 days, competing against each other on a time 'knock out' basis. Each day a different task was performed using a different set of muscles in the body. Paul's motivational skills shone through to keep Andy active and in control. Again, Paul wasn't just helping Andy,
he was in there pleading and cajoling him to carry on through the pain.

Andy came third in a test of strength that made most sports and athletics events look like 'kids stuff'. It had strong men in tears and a lot of them packed in with muscular injuries, and these were men who were 'top of the tree' in their particular sport. Paul was definitely 'the' mentor on that programme, knowing his man's mind and body inside out. So thank you Paul, for giving us all confidence.

Mike Johnson has either helped or officiated as a travelling observer over the last few years from 2000 onwards, although I'm sure he'd been involved in many more before I met him,. I've enjoyed his company and have had great support from him over the last 3 or 4 records. His vast knowledge of the road network being a godsend. As an ex-lorry driver his skills are superb, knowing lots of alternative routes and back streets in the towns to get ahead of the rider to marshal or feed. Mike's father, Phil Johnson, lived on the A49 at 'Newton le Willows'. His house is the one used by riders from the 1920's to 1960's where they were fed and washed and were assured of a sleep at any time of the day or night. Mike remembers as a 'nipper' being turfed out of bed so that an 'End to Ender' could have a 'kip', and he recalls being given treats of sweets and chocolates, fruit and cakes, from the helpers when food rationing was on after the war.

Mike is a staunch Tricycle Association man and has ridden at all distances up to 24 hours He's an ex-rugby player and an ex-merchant seaman. He sports a large beard, and his burly appearance and gruff manner hides a soft heart of gold. Lynne nicknamed him 'teddy bear' on her End to End. I remember at breakfast the day after Lynne's record and Lynne was chattering away nineteen to the dozen, as one would do after being deprived of company for over two days. Mike looked over his glasses and said "Stop your wittering lass and eat your breakfast - it'll get cold".

In recent years he has provided a comfort caravan on the Mersey RC 24 hr in the Hodnet area helped by Yvonne, they have dispensed food, drink, warmth, sleep and advice to many a weary rider. His ribald quips giving them something to chuckle about over the next hour or so. I remember this year (2004) stopping at the caravan just as George Berwick and George Shepherd went past on the tandem, and Mike bellowed out "Come on you ugly couple of b . . . . . s, stop slacking !"

"THEY'VE ABANDONED."

SECTION NINE

THE ROUTE FROM 1929 TO PRESENT DAY

To help drive home a picture of the severity of the route and the endurance the rider must have, I suggest that using a road map of England and Scotland will help you appreciate these journeys as they unfold. Remember the next holiday you take in Devon, Cornwall, the lake District, the Borders, or right up into Scotland, try and imagine their plight.

If you are on the M6 going north, drop off in the Kendal area and have a look at Shap. It will give you some indication of what confronts the rider as dawn is breaking. It is a severe 9 mile stomach wrencher of a climb, being on the old A6 which used to be the main road linking England to Scotland on the west side of the country.

The climb of Shap Fell was so severe for lorry drivers in years gone by with the road being regularly blocked with snow and ice. I can well remember the BBC news bulletins on the radio years ago back in the 50's and 60's, where the first falls of snow claimed the lives of lorry drivers going either up or down Shap. Nowadays of course the traffic is all on the M6 running parallel only 2 miles away, and the gradients are so slight most people wouldn't even know they were climbing to over a 1000 ft.

Once you are into Scotland and on your way past Gretna, why not drop off the M74 and go through Moffat towards Edinburgh by climbing 'The Devils Beeftub' another very tough climb very similar in severity as 'Shap', and similar in length. It is usually climbed late morning or midday onwards on the second day, with the rider fighting against drowsiness.

Years ago up until the 1960's before the Forth Road Bridge became widely used by 'End to Enders', the riders used to climb the long severe climb of Beattock to its summit, usually taking a break at the transport café at Abington to recover from the climb, before continuing on to Stirling. Eileen Sheridan told me she suffered very badly on Beattock with not only an adverse wind, but also the exhaust fumes from the passing lorries, not to mention the stinging cold rain battering her from the side.

If you get the chance to either cycle or walk across the Forth Road Bridge on the separate walkway, take the opportunity and see how it feels when you look over the edge or through the mesh barrier at the 2 mile expanse of water that is hundreds of feet below you. Imagine the tired rider going over in adverse conditions or 'side winds' after 30 hours of riding.

Once you have got to Perth, and don't forget the saying 'any fool can get to Perth' (a saying that must have been uttered originally by a non-record breaker)(it was in fact Tommy Barlow who said it); stop and have a look at the map (a contoured one is best) at the journey still left to do. There is no alternative flat 240 miles route; you must tackle the Grampians, which means climbing for hours, albeit not so severe as Shap. The road is soul-destroying, luckily, most of it is done under the cover of darkness.

The drop to Inverness is wonderful, even in a car, but by then the rider is usually past caring, only thinking about sleep and keeping their bodies going for another few hours to tackle the climbs ahead. The Kessock Bridge, the drags up to Tain, then the tortuous 100 miles of coast road with 3 major climbs 'Helmsdale' 'Berriedale' and 'Dunbeath' still to come. And finally, that last 17 miles across a featureless tract of land, jutting out into the North Sea, exposed and often windswept at any time of the year, with its fair share of uphill gradients.

The roads have changed quite drastically over the years. I can only give you my thoughts on the subject. I remember as a youth of 17 or 18, riding down overnight along the old Bristol Road through Worcester, Gloucester, Bristol and as far as Exeter, where I would get a meal at the 'Blue Boar' transport café, open all night, and then sleep in a bus shelter for a couple of hours, before I turned and rode home. This sort of journey was obviously done in the summer months of 1960 onwards, and apart from the fact there were transport cafes every 30 or 40 miles, nothing much has changed in 40 years. The End to Ender still goes through these towns and along these same roads.

The M5 has taken most of the 'through' traffic, leaving these roads for the local traffic. The places where there has been quite a remarkable difference made to the route is in the West Country where towns such as Bodmin, Launceston, and Okehampton, have now been by-passed completely by swathes of dual carriageway.

Pete Swinden always reminds me of how, on their tandem record in 1966, they had to go through all these towns, usually with a hill to climb out of them all, and generally losing time with traffic. Nowadays from Penzance to Exeter, its nearly all dual carriageway which saves considerable time , but there are still four or five severe drops and climbs of 300 or 400 ft in places.

From Exeter, the road through Taunton and across the Bridgwater Flats and past Brent Knoll is pretty much the same for today's riders all the way to Bristol and as far as Kidderminster, where as I've mentioned the rider now uses the route through Wolverhampton and doesn't rejoin the old route until just south of Warrington is reached.

The swing bridge at Warrington over the Manchester Ship Canal is the same one that's been used by all of the riders up until present day. The route through Wigan, Preston, Lancaster, Kendal, Shap, Penrith, Carlisle, Gretna Green, Ecclefechan, and Lockerbie, is virtually the same except for one or two stretches of dual carriageway. Its here where riders up until the 60's went over the Beattock Summit, through Stirling to Perth. The riders nowadays all use the Forth Road Bridge which is a much shorter route, but the roads are what I would call rural 'A' roads, mainly single carriageway.

Around the Perth area, more dual carriageway is evident and from there onwards its virtually all dual carriageway or fast three lane highway to Inverness. This is all new road put down over the last 30 years to take traffic to and from the oil terminals at Invergordon. All the riders prior to that had to go through the towns and villages on route, Dunkeld, Pitlochry, Blair Atholl, Dalwhinnie, Kingussie, Carrbridge, Tomatin to Inverness. The old roads are still there running through the towns and linking up with the main A9 bypass road. A lot of them are still the same width and as bendy and bumpy as in years gone by.

The Kessock Bridge over the Beauly Firth makes it unnecessary for the rider to go through Inverness nowadays, also cutting out the trip through Beauly. This must save 30 mins here.

The next big saving in time and mileage is by missing out the climb to 'Aultnamain Inn' from Alness. There is a new road over the Black Isle and another over the Dornoch Firth, all of these improvements in Scotland have reduced the End to End route by over 25 miles in the last 30 or more years. Although the carriageways have been improved from Golspie onwards, there is no reduction in mileage from here to John O Groats, and its exactly the same road as G.P. Mills would have ridden over 100 years ago.

The modern scheduled route that Lynne and Gethin took in 2001, was approximately 840 miles.

SECTION TEN

EQUIPMENT

In this book I have written much about the riders, but not a lot about their bikes, equipment and clothing. In the 1930's 40's and 50's there was not really much variation. I would go as far as to say that for time trialling purposes and general club riding, a single speed fixed wheel bicycle was very popular. The variable continental derailleur gear was in its infancy and not really trusted by club folk. If multi gearing was required it was generally provided by a Sturmey Archer 3 or 4 speed hub gear with the trigger gear changer on the handlebars or on the top tube.

Raleigh's contribution to the End to End was through three professional male riders who all used Sturmey Archer hub gears of one type or another. **Harry Green** in 1908 - 2 days 19 hours 50 mins. **Jack Rossiter** 1929 - 2 days 13 hours 22 mins and **Sid Ferris's** 1937 - 2 days 6 hrs 33 mins. The frames would have been of lightweight steel tubing held together by brazing the ends of the tubes into 'lugs' or joints. The wheel rims were possibly aluminium. The Conloy 'ASP' rim being popular for quite a number of years. The tyres were probably 'John Bull', 'Dunlop' or 'Constrictor'. The weight of these cycles would have been approximately 23-25 lbs.

Hubert Opperman in 1934 took Jack Rossiter's record riding a 'BSA' Malvern Star. The letters stand for Birmingham Small Arms and they also had a professional team headed by Bob Maitland in the '50's. As well as manufacturing cycles and motorcycles at their factory in Small Heath, they also made guns and rifles in fact, the BSA head badge emblem is 3 rifles stood upright. Opperman broke from tradition and used an early Cyclo 3 speed rear derailleur gear operated by a lever on the top tube. Looking at the photograph reproduced from Alan J Ray's book, Opperman is riding with 'Catos' toe clips. Made in Aston- Birmingham where a lot of cycle components were made in the 50's and 60's and exported worldwide. My sisters both rode gents BSA 'Tour of Britain' racers in the 50's and one was passed down to me and on it I started my club riding and time trialling. The model I had was equipped with a 5 speed Cyclo Benelux rear derailleur and 'GB' aluminium brakes. The BSA factory was only two miles from the house I lived in as a boy.

The one thing I can well remember in the 60's is having poor brakes and breaking cables regularly. The nipples would literally shear off causing me to spend many a Saturday night trying to solder nipples back on for a race or club ride on the Sunday. Nowadays I'm glad to say, this problem is a thing of the past, partially due to cables being hidden under handlebar tape and more importantly, better quality inner cables, pulling a more efficient dual pivot brake on, requiring much less pressure to be applied.

The first woman professional, Lilian Dredge, rode for Claud Butler Cycles. Claud Butler, famous for his hand built frames, some of them lugless at a later date, was the only cycle manufacturer to support a woman rider at that time. The wheels were 26" Conloy aluminium rims with Constrictor tyres, Resilion cantilever brakes, Catos toe clips on probably Brampton pedals. She had a double chain ring, giving her effectively 6 gears. The chain had to be shifted physically by hand from one ring to another; the inside chain ring being used probably in Cornwall up to Bristol, then for climbing Shap, and finally for the Grampians to the finish.

The rear Cyclo derailleur gear operated on a three sprocket freewheel, pulling a lever on the top tube would pull one cable and shift the chain inwards and pushing the lever forwards would shift the chain outwards.

The Claud Butler was built for speed and comfort with a wheelbase long enough for mudguards and a generous fork rake to give a smooth ride from the front wheel. The photo also shows Lilian wearing the customary dress of the day; an all black 'Alpaca' Jacket and black tights so as not to draw attention to oneself when on the road. Marguerite Wilson also had to wear the same restrictive attire, although she did roll her sleeves up occasionally. It wasn't until the late 40's that shorts and short sleeved vests were allowed in competition on the road. Edith Atkins, Eileen Sheridan and Dave Keeler being amongst the first riders to take advantage of the new ruling. Eileen on many of her professional records rode in very short shorts ! setting a new fashion for that era.

Another common factor up until probably the late 60's is that most riders had aluminium drinking bottles mounted in cages on the handlebars. Some had two, some even had flexible plastic 'straw' tubes so that they could just bend forwards and suck whatever was their favourite drink. Even the continental professionals in the 'Tour de France' had their 'bidons' mounted on the handlebars. Nowadays of course the modern frames have bottle cage bosses brazed into the down tube or the seat tube or both, leaving the handlebars free to fit computers, heart monitors, GPS systems, lights, and tri-bars.

Another system of hydration on the move is the 'Camel-Back' and is described in the Groesbeck-Harris mixed tandem End to End in 1998, Chapter 34, In the last two years this system has become quite common in time trials, the camel back being worn under one's skin suit making the rider look like Quasimodo. I'm not too sure what happens in a 12 hour when one needs a refill, but then maybe I'm old fashioned and a bit biased towards a plastic bottle. In triathlons, a common position for bottles on the bike is mounted behind the saddle, so as to become more aerodynamic, although I've seen many riders come to grief at the end, trying to lift their leg to dismount and catching the bottles, giving a less than graceful performance.

Going back to racing clothing, up until the 70's riders shorts were made of an acrylic material or wool, with a genuine 'chamois' leather patch for the groin and undercarriage area. This system was fine until it rained and then the woollen shorts got heavier and wetter and would start to hang low and sag, making out-of-the saddle hill climbing a risky business. Racing vests were of the same material and suffered from the same problems, and if you were riding a long distance event with food or a spare tubular in your back pocket, you could end up with your vest hanging on the back wheel - not a pretty sight. Reg Randall, in 1958, is probably one of the last to wear a racing vest with pockets at the front as well as the back. When much food was stuffed in the front pockets it made male riders the same sort of shape as Marilyn Monroe, but somehow different, and not so eye catching.

It wasn't until the mid 70's that Lycra was introduced, mainly for shorts and tights, and what a godsend that was, so comfortable - like a second skin In fact the first time I rode in Lycra shorts I had to keep looking down to make sure I was wearing anything at all. They were so cool, pliable and lightweight, no flapping, no sagging. It was around this time that the material for racing vests altered to become more 'user friendly' with 'moisture wicking' cellular properties, so useful for long distance riding, also under vests with 'wicking' fibres to stop that cold wet feeling when descending. I can remember in the late fifties, being on club runs in the winter and getting to the tea time stop on the way home. Being young, you never thought to put a dry vest in your saddlebag, so when it was time to go home and the temperature had dropped below freezing, your damp top suddenly went icy cold. I can remember shivering for miles with chattering teeth. Modern materials have virtually eliminated that. So our End to End riders since the eighties have never had it so good, have they ?

Alan Richards who owned 'Tower Cycles' in Erdington, Birmingham gave Pat Kenny and myself lots of help, along with Tony Shardlow. He supported a lot of our record attempts, and for our End to End he made me wear an under vest knowing how the sweat pours out of you if you are the 'stoker' and that is when I first became aware of modern materials. We failed to break the record, I had to pay for the vest, its gone a bit yellow recently, I think its time for a new one !

A few items I've failed to mention as being almost everyday wear for racing and leisure club cyclists are track mitts, Roubaix or Thermal tights, sunglasses or clear glasses, overshoes and race capes, and in the extreme cold in Scotland over the last few attempts, technical thermal jackets.

Years ago back in the late 20's to the 50's riders made use of whatever the materials of the day were. Rossiter made his own waterproof jacket, and looking at the old photos, Eileen Sheridan is clad in a huge thick white woollen jumper, possibly a cricket type sweater, belonging to Frank Southall. Dick Poole resorted to wearing a woollen sweater at night. Ferris wore a boiler suit at night in Scotland; he was so cold.

As I've mentioned earlier, Pat Kenny in the 80's was probably the first to wear overshoes on the End to End. These were constructed of waterproof padded nylon with a zip fastening running vertically from the heel at the back. They provided a bit of warmth but were made mainly to stop the spray off the front wheel getting you soaked too quickly. In later attempts in the 90's these overshoes were made mainly of neoprene, the same material diving suits are made of. The purpose of this material isn't to stop the wet getting to you, but to turn the wet into an insulative layer. The material is very pliable and fairly tough, again zipped or in recent years, Velcro has been used to fasten the rear opening. The overshoes all have a hole in the sole for shoe plates to protrude through and locate the pedals. I can recall trying all sorts of things to keep my feet warm cycling to and fro from work in the winters in the snow. Cutting out liners from polystyrene tiles was one, and also using bread bags another. Not too successful !

Track mitts are a must for riders, whatever the duration or type of riding they are doing. Years ago, in the 50's, I remember cutting the fingers off a pair of my Moms Kid gloves to use. I thought they looked the part but Mom wasn't too pleased ! Proper track mitts as worn by track riders were made of sturdy leather with leather or crochet string backs. The palms were padded not just for comfort but to stop abrasions or 'gravel rash' as the rider slid along the wooden or tarmac track after coming off. The modern day track mitts are similar but made of 'skay' stretch leather with padded or 'gel' filled patches on the palms and lycra material on the back. Nowadays they are worn skin tight for grip. Full winter cycling gloves are now constructed of a mixture of materials. Lycra and neoprene for stretch, zorbothane and gel for padding and insulative properties.

Its very rare for an End to Ender, whatever the month of the year, to get through the second night in the Highlands without the use of full gloves. When reading the accounts of various records you realise that its not only the cold, but the extra padding that's needed for sore and blistered hands, such as Eric Tremaine wearing skiing gloves in 1982.

Roubaix or thermal tights have now taken over from the old 'plus two's or plus four's, trousers of the past. Plus four's were big baggy trousers that finished just below the knees and were gathered in either by an elastic cuff or welt, or buttoned strap. The materials ranged from Cavalry twill, Hebden cord, and Tweed, to a wool and gaberdine mix. They were worn with long woollen socks up to the knee, and by the 50's and 60's the socks took on a brighter mode and were quite often harlequin patterned or striped with shapes in overlapping colours.

This attire was superceded in the late 60's, by fleecy track suit bottoms and knee length pantalons, which were semi tight with a double seat. They got heavy when wet and sagged at the crotch. By the 90's, tights were now made of 'Roubaix' material. I think the origins of the material arose from being worn by riders in the 'Paris-Roubaix' classic race, where extreme types of weather I.e. cold wet rain, hail and snow, are experienced. The Roubaix material has various grades of thermal 'flocking' for warmth. It has a lycra mix surface for 'cling' and can even be provided with a Teflon waterproof surface. The beauty of this material is that it fits like a second skin and if its very cold rain, it doesn't let you get cold. Two more worthwhile properties are (a) it doesn't get heavy and water logged, and (b) it dries out very quickly leaving the surface of your skin warm; so, as you can see, its ideal for End to Enders. If a rider doesn't want to stop for a top or a pair of tights, they can take on board, a pair of arm, leg or knee warmers which are just a tube of material made of either lycra or roubaix material, pulled on over the bare arms, knees or legs. Sometimes just enough to cover cool, moist skin with, as they ride along.

The next item of clothing is a race cape. In the early years cyclists wore big touring capes made either of oilskin or PVC, usually yellow or black. In the very light traffic conditions of years gone by they were ideal, but by the 70's they were dying out. The younger generations of club cyclist and racing men wanted something lighter, more sleek, than a tent shaped covering which can be a hazard on a windy day with passing lorries. The continentals were already riding in race capes and in the 'Tour de France' as the riders climbed over the summits of the mountains they not only stuffed newspapers down the front of their jerseys, they also were putting on a zip fronted lightweight plastic jacket, quite often in transparent material to show their trade team colours underneath.

By the 90's the race capes were even lighter and more compact with 'breathing vents' down the sides and a longer 'tail' piece at the back to stop the spray from the back wheel soaking your backside, and with Velcro fastening at the front you could easily put them on whilst 'on the move'. Whereas Eileen Sheridan and Dick Poole had donned thick sweaters and Sid Ferris had put on a thick twill boiler suit to keep out the cold, the modern day End to Ender uses a lightweight, thermal, windproof , waterproof, breathable, fairly figure hugging 'technical jacket' costing anything from £60 to £120. It is now fairly common attire for club riders of today, whether training in the cold or just 'pottering'. Most of these materials were developed on the Continent either in Belgium, Switzerland or France, where riders are subjected to extremes of temperatures when climbing or descending alpine passes in dry, wet, windy or cold conditions going from sunshine through mist and into snow.

Another useful item to mention; sunglasses or clear 'shades'. You may not think this item is very important, in fact you may think it's a 'posers' accessory, to be seen at the end of a race with your 'Bolle's' or 'Oakley's' on, but actually to most cyclists, it's a very important piece of kit. The development about ten years, or more, ago, of the wrap around sunglasses which stopped draughts creeping around the sides and over the tops of the lenses preventing your eyes from watering and also gave complete protection for your eyes, against dust, hail, rain, flies, insects etc. You can now buy very modestly priced wrap around glasses with interchangeable 'snap in' lenses for about £30.00, clear or yellow tinge are ideal for dawn and dusk and night riding and reactalite or silvered lenses are good for bright sunlight or for going through contrasting degrees of shade and brightness.

Again this piece of kit is worn by a high percentage of regular cyclists whether 'on' or 'off' road. On the End to End the last few riders have all used 'wrap around' glasses to some degree. Lynne found that they stopped her eyes from getting tired, shielding the soft tissue around the eyes and stopping the eyelids from drying out and becoming stiff. She wears her glasses permanently on the bike and attributes her alertness for so may hours to the protection given by them. She experimented back as far as 1994 in some of her early 24 hr races with clear shades, and found it helped her get through the night and early dawn without getting 'heavy' eyes. Going back to Victorian times and up to as late as 1950, bike riders in extreme mud or dust would use clear goggles to protect their eyes, a bit like a motorcyclist or aviators in an open cockpit would use. I don't know what the riders from the '50's to the 80's wore, maybe they didn't bother and maybe this is why a lot of them suffered with sleep deprivation, or very tired eyes - who knows ?

The tandems and tandem trikes used until the 80's were generally either touring machines with faster wheels put in, or short distance racing machines, much too short in length to allow a decent position for the 'stoker' at the back, in fact on Pat's tandem trike, a Rensch, made from an ultra short wheelbase tandem, having a 'Holdsworth' trike conversion back end brazed on. I used to get a very stiff neck from bending my head to one side of Pat's waist or a sore nose from burying my head into his back pocket. I was sitting more than 6 inches behind my normal saddle position in relation to the pedals. A lot of tricycles prior to George Longstaff's era were made by Higgins, although I stand to be corrected by the T.A. on this subject. James was another manufacturer and Holdsworth made a conversion kit to fit onto a standard frame. Claud Butler tandems feature once or twice on this famous record.

Marguerite Wilson who was a professional for Hercules Cycles rode her End to End in 1939, on a three speed derailleur equipped bike with a single chain ring and the gear lever on what was to become the conventional place for it, the down tube. Her handlebars were similar in shape to 'Maes' bars and she rode a leather saddle, probably a 'Brooks'. Her handlebar mounted bottle cages had a sprung loaded clasp at the top to stop the bottles rattling and shooting out if she rode over a pot hole.

Eileen Sheridan looked a bit stretched lengthwise on her Hercules, with only an inch of seat post showing. The handlebars were very deeply curved to allow Eileen to attain a flat back position for her races using cyclo gears, from 72 to 92 inches, G.B. brakes and handlebar stem, Dunlop Tyres, Renolds Chain. Most components were made in the Midlands, many of them in the Birmingham area. How times have changed ! Eileen was, to my knowledge, one of the first riders to have a caravan following the attempt, used to sleep, rest, eat and change clothing etc.

Pictures of her support cars also show racks on the back of the cars to hook spare machines onto, rather like primitive versions of today's modern boot racks which strap onto most cars. On checking Marguerite Wilson's ride details, she also used a specially equipped caravan in 1939.

Reg Randall, in 1958, rode a lightweight steel tubed bike made by 'Mal Rees' with Reynolds '531' tubes with 'Nervex Professional' lugs, G.B. brakes with rubber brake hoods, a Brooks saddle, Campag 'Gran Sport' rear gear, 'wing nuts' on his front wheel, lots of padding under the cloth tape on his handlebars and a plastic drinks bottle on the handlebars in a thin steel bottle cage. Reg was probably the last rider to use steel cotter pin cranks, probably 'Milremo' with 'TA' alloy chainring. He used the same bike for the 1000 mile record.

Dave Keeler, two months prior to Reg's record had succeeded using a new method of gear changing produced by Campagnolo. It was operated by a long lever on the seat stay which unlocked the back wheel and a quick back pedal action swapped the chain onto another sprocket. The rear wheel was then re-locked into position via the long lever. It was an unconventional method of gear changing requiring a lot of skill and concentration by the rider. It was the constant leaning back to change gear that reputedly caused Dave to have a bad back when well into the ride. I am glad to say this method of gear shift died a natural death, and was soon forgotten.

Dick Poole, in 1965, was the first to use a double ring chainset and a front gear shifter to push the chain from one ring to another, operated from a handlebar end lever. Quite good for changing gear when riding on the 'drops'. The rear Campagnolo gears were also operated this way, from the handlebars. His wheels had got large flange aluminium quick release hubs. His chainset was made of aluminium and was 'cotterless', as compared to all the other previous End to Enders who had used steel chainsets held onto an axle with cotter pins. His frame was made by 'Mercian' of Derby and was made probably from Reynolds butted chrome-moly steel tubing. His bottle cage was now mounted on the down tube and his brakes were 'Mafac' centre pulls.

So he is the first man inside two days, riding a modern bike, with all up to date 1960's equipment. In just 7 years, the bikes had seen numerous changes. At least 8 gears instead of 4; bar end controlled gear levers; quick release wheels making punctures easier to fix, or faster wheel changes. A lighter aluminium chainset and cranks; a very efficient rear and front derailleur; a down tube bottle cage and bigger more comfortable Mafac brake levers, with contoured rubber hoods on for climbing or gripping. The bikes would now be around 20 lbs in weight.

Dick had also used 'Complan' for some of his feeding. It is a powdered food to which you add hot water or milk. It has lots of nutrients and minerals as well as carbohydrates and you drink it. This saves having to digest solid food, leaving more blood for the limbs, the lungs and the brain, while still riding at speed. I still think he would have broken two days without all this, but who knows ?

The next 14 year gap until Paul Carbutt's ride in 1979 sees more significant changes to the bike. Paul was a professional riding for 'Viking' cycles of Warrington, formerly made in Wolverhampton. They had produced a bike especially for the record attempt. The frameset was made from T.I.Reynolds 753 tubing, Campagnolo super record 14 speed gears and groupset. 24 spoke wheels with Campag super record hubs into Mavic 'blue' rims Specially made Clement tubulars with a wider section for the rough roads. These 'tubs' had only been produced for two other riders before Paul. Fausto Coppi and Eddy Mercks. Titanium and Dural sprockets made up the 7 speed Regina freewheel, finished off with a Regina chain.. By now a lot of components were produced in France or Italy.

The handlebars and stem were made by Cinelli and the saddle was an Isca. The Campagnolo 'Picolo' brakes were the first to use allen keys to bolt them to the frame. We now really did have a vastly improved bike with an estimated cost £ 1000. He used 42/54 tooth chain rings making this gearing the highest ever used on the End to End. The weight - sub 20 lbs.
Mick Coupe, 3 years later, rode a 'Viscount' cycle. The frame was made by a small manufacturer with some innovative ideas mechanically. He patented a new sealed bottom bracket that fitted into a threadless shell, but I think that the frame Mick used was of standard design, probably using Reynolds tubing with Prugnat lugs. The group set was top of the range Campagnolo on 28 spoke wheels. He used lights designed by his brother Roger, who was an electronics engineer. Mick pushed a top gear of 108 " (52 x 13) and climbed the hills in (42 x 19)

John Woodburn's bike is much the same design with similar equipment as the previous two riders, Coupe and Carbutt. John's bike was made by 'Stan Pike' and was a Reynolds 753 butted tubed frame with Campagnolo 'Record' equipment with 14 speeds, weighing in at around 19 lbs.

The last three riders have all been big gear pushers, but only big in comparison to their predecessors. To maintain 'evens' for 30 or more hours the riders must now use time trialling sized gearing, to beat the previous record holder.

Its interesting to note at this point that John Woodburn was the only one of this last trio to turn out regular 25, 50, 100 wins on a regular weekly basis prior to his ride. I know Carbutt couldn't do this, being a professional, so it must have been difficult for him to measure his fitness for such a task. M ick Coupe relied more on his training, plus riding the 24 hr races which were available to measure his fitness, riding the odd 25, 50, 100 but not on a weekly basis.

After an eight year gap now to Andy Wilkinson's ride in 1990. A few subtle innovations had come into the bike game. One was 'indexed' gearing by a Japanese company called Shimano, where one pulls the gear lever one click back and changes one sprocket, so making for more positive gearing, but not absolutely necessary as riders using Campagnolo gears were already using Simplex 'ratchet' gear levers in conjunction with a Campagnolo rear and front derailleur This made almost as good a change without gear lever 'slip' which 'dumps' the rider into a big gear. Most of the professionals on the Continent were using this system prior to Shimano Gears. Clipless pedals had arrived from the Continent made by 'Look', a French company, famous for their ski-binding mechanism for the skiing fraternity. A method where the rider uses a special wedge shaped plastic plate bolted onto the stiff plastic sole of the shoe. The pedal which is 'weighted' to hang at an angle prior to engagement, has a sprung loaded rear clamp. The rider simply pushes his shoeplate against the nose of the pedal and then presses down against the rear clamp, thereby 'clicking' into place. The shoes at this time started to see a revolution in style. Gone was the old fashioned black leather sole and uppers, taken over by sometimes garishly coloured skay or kangaroo skin uppers on a hard resin plastic-sole, fastened now by a large Velcro flap.

Andy's bike was supplied by 'K' Cycles of The Wirral. It was a Peugeot Carbon Fibre frame on Shimano Dura-ace and Mavic open four wheels, 28 spoked with Michelin Hi-lite comps. The frame was a spin-off from ones tested and used by Pro's such as Robert Millar, on the Continent in 1988/89. The group set was Dura-ace 8/16 speed, with profile aero tri-bars, a revelation at the time, not yet recognised or allowed by the RTTC as at 1990, so a first for an End to End. He rode a Rolls saddle which Andy reckoned was definitely 'second hand' by the finish. He rode in a 'Bell' hardshell helmet with a lycra cover for most of the ride until nearing the end when he put on his favourite balaclava. He had a constant supply of the latest gloves which were made from Lycra covered thermal foam. Don't forget his ride came very late in the year with hours of very heavy cold rain. As I have already mentioned in Andy's attempt write up, he got through dozens of pairs of shorts due to getting soaked, and obviously towards the end, his orange balaclava was used to stave off hypothermia.

Andy was eager to use all the modern scientific methods that were at his disposal. Peter Keen suggested that to succeed with the 'steadier state' riding, he needed to use a pulse meter which gives an indication as to when you are tired or overdoing it. Your pulse doesn't recover back to a lower rate quickly enough when you are 'cruising' or on a rest period, or if you are tired or have an underlying illness. Hydration is linked with pulse rate and if you don't drink regularly, before, during, and after exercise you will tire yourself much too soon and it will also take a longer time for your pulse rate to recover.

Andy at this time was advised as to the use of 'Polymer feeding' and technically was the first to use the new regime of specially produced sports drinks, although other End to Enders had taken 'Complan' in the past, it wasn't done in a scientific manner. Complan is fine for a person who has a problem digesting proper solid food such as a patient recovering from an illness or surgery, but it really isn't suitable for total feeding of 'high endurance' athletes, in my opinion.

There are nowadays, lots of different trade names producing 'polymer' drink products; names such as S.I.S. (Science in Sport) 'Maxim' 'High 5', 'Allsports' to name but a few. They all produce a carbohydrate drink which some riders prefer flavoured. Also necessary is a mineral supplement drink to help avoid muscle cramp and to replace the bodies natural salts and minerals that are evaporated through the pores of the skin when sweating. Finally there is a recovery drink which contains all of these carbohydrates and electrolytes and chemicals needed for muscle recovery. The carbohydrate generally is of a 'rice' derivative.

Andy trained religiously with all of the scientific aids and in his own words "I was surprised that a liquid could keep me going, because having cycled for quite a few years now, it is drummed into you right from the start that you can't cycle for more than about 3 hours without food, without getting the knock". It is a feeling somewhat akin to drunkeness, loss of balance, a feeling of nausea , almost total loss of control in the worst case. The 'knock' state can be ridden through but only very gently and with a need to replenish the body as soon as possible with carbo-hydrate and liquid. I have regularly gone through this state, it can happen whether fit or unfit, more often unfit ! The worst case for me was having to stagger up the road where I live, pushing my bike, with a feverish sweat coming on, getting to the door, then once I'd gathered up the energy to find my keys, I had to lift my right arm up, supported by my left hand, to locate the key into the lock. Once inside the house, I'd eat and eat till the feeling subsided. So you can see the reason for Andy's delight at this new wonderful way of taking food. The products he used were 'Maxi-Joule' and 'Dyna Carb'. Although he did supplement his liquid feeding with beans on toast before Penrith at about 450 miles, and then after that, from Moffat onwards , a small bun in between bottles. This method of feeding is now widely used for all types of sporting events, even just leisure riding and most record breakers since Andy have benefited from its use.

Lynne was introduced to liquid feeding by Christine and Alan Roberts who had originally been in at the start of this new concept, along with Andy. They were very meticulous with it, mixing the drinks up to the correct consistency for the riders body weight per fluid ounce. Handing up a new full bottle on the hour, the rider being instructed to drink every drop.

For Lynne, Alan and Christine it worked very well. Alan was already, like Andy, a top time trialling man in the North West, and Christine went on to produce Competition Record at 24 hrs and also the straight out RRA 24 hour record, also winning the BAR and getting top placings for many years. The first time Lynne strictly used polymer feeding in 1996, she produced a 4 hr 7 min 43 sec 100 mile time on the F1 and got within a few minutes of Christine. After ten or more years of using, almost exclusively, polymer feeding, Lynne has recently suffered sickness bouts in her last 2 or 3 long distance 12 hr and 24 hr events and has had to reduce the strength of the solution and also take interim feeds of liquid rice pudding which luckily has overcome the problems.

From Cycling - August 23rd 1905 - by G.A. Olley:

"Being an abstainer from meat, fish or fowl, my feeding arrangements will not perhaps harmonize with those of most riders, but it is interesting to note that, however fond of the "fleshpots" a rider may be, when on the actual ride, and presumably feeding with the set purpose of obtaining the best possible results, he lives almost exclusively on milk, eggs, cereals, fresh and dried nuts. In the basket on my handlebar I could often humour my appetite with selections from the following: Rice pudding, Mellin's food biscuits, sandwiches of cheese, "Olley paste" (comprising cheese, eggs etc. butter, or jam, grapes, bananas, muscatels, and I had no desire to mix therewith pieces of dead chicken and other 'delicacies'

In the drink line milk and egg, soda and milk, tea (weak) and egg, lemonade and egg, ginger ale and milk, and often in the heat I was pleased to stop at the many mountain streams passed on the route and drink the refreshingly cold "Adams ale"

Aluminium and carbon fibre is now playing a prominent part in the manufacture of cycles and components. Carbon fibre wheels with 3 or 4 pear shaped or oval carbon blades radiating from an aluminium hub out to a carbon deep section rim. The hub being bonded to the carbon with epoxy-resin. The only down side to this type of wheel on the End to End route is side winds that tend to blow a larger mass surface area all over the road, plus a ceramic braking surface at the rim isn't ideal, given the steep descents involved.

Andy, Lynne and Gethin all rode with Tri-bars, as did both the mixed tandems, an innovation originally introduced from America where the sport of Triathlon allowed their use. Tri-bars are either a simple inverted 'U' shape bend made of aluminium or lightweight alloy, bolted to the riders own handlebars with two arm rests, or 'cups' to lean on. The rider reaches forward and tucks his arms inwards with the elbows only about 4 inches apart, rests his forearms on the cups and pulls against the tri bars so making for a more aerodynamic position, again, a position similar to downhill skiing. Other forms of tri bars are also used such as an 'all in one' flat topped 'air wing', with two separate forward pointed bars, mounted on an adjustable centre clamp. Gear levers are mounted separately at the forward end of these two protrusions so that the only time a rider comes out of the 'tuck' aerodynamic position is to apply the brakes.

Tri bars were allowed in time trials around 1991 and also quite common at this time was 'hidden' brake cables, a trend originated by a Company called 'Modolo' and soon snapped up by Shimano and Campagnolo. This system at first didn't improve the efficiency of the brakes but did eliminate cable 'snag' and broken inner cables. Things didn't improve anymore until Shimano developed a 'dual pivot' calliper which to my mind increased braking.power a 100%. This is the system now used by all brake manufacturers for road bikes. Gethin Butler and Lynne Taylor are the only ones to have used the modern dual pivot brakes on an End to End

Although helmets are mandatory for road racing and track, the time trial and record aspirants are not governed by this rule, although time triallists tend to favour Aero helmets, an aerodynamic carbon shell with a tear drop shape - the point going to the rear, with virtually no air venting at all and no safety standard. This cooks the riders head on a hot day, rendering it absolutely useless after about 3 hours, thereby not much use on a 24 hr or End to End. The modern lightweight multi -vented hard shell helmet weighting about 4 oz (100 grams) is a good safety device summer or winter, racing or leisure. That is my own personal opinion. Lynne uses one all the while and has never found it a problem, but I do know lots of other riders who are biased against them, but there I will leave the subject alone.

On Andy's first End to End on solo bike he used a heart rate monitor but for some reason it failed to function after a short while on the road. A lot of riders from the late 80's onwards trained with this method, using it as a guide to their fitness and recovery rates giving them an insight as to whether they were over training. Heart rate levels can also be monitored to show up an underlying illness. Andy, Gethin and Lynne all use heart rate monitors either for training or racing. Combined with use on a static home cycle trainer, it can be a useful alternative on a cold wet night.

Another innovation that came in at the same time was the electronic computer, which mounts onto the handlebars. A small magnet attached to a spoke goes past a sensor mounted on the front forks when the wheel is rotated. It sends a signal, either through a wire, or a radio signal, up to the computer head which displays the speed either in kilometres or miles. Most modern computers give, time of day, trip distance, overall distance, time elapsed, current speed and average speed. Andy used one as did Ralph Dadswell and Gethin Butler. Gethin, on his attempt, said that the computer is fine when you are going well, but when you are struggling to keep up an average speed that you need to maintain, it can become a negative measure. Lynne on the other hand uses one for training and club riding, but when time trialling or End to Ending she relies upon instinct and details her helpers tell her as to how she is performing.

One very good innovation brought about by Shimano in the mid 80's was the use of a cassette rear hub, taking, in those days, six or seven cogs slipped onto splines sideways onto the hub, and then locked into position. The new Shimano hub instead of having an exposed length of unsupported axle on the freewheel side, which regularly broke going over a sharp pot hole, has quarter inch bearings supporting almost the complete length of the axle to the edges. The ratchet freewheel body is built onto the end of the hub body and houses one of the quarter ball races on its outer edges. I would go as far as to say that its use on bikes has virtually eliminated axle breakage and also has helped to cut down spoke breakage with its flanges being slightly wider apart.

We have now in 2004 gone from 7 speed to 10 speed on the latest Dura-ace and Ultegra systems and 9 and 10 speeds for all of the Campagnolo gears. The more expensive systems using dural and titanium components are encased in aluminium or carbon shells. Lance Armstrong's Trek carbon 'tour de france' bike is now weighing 15 lbs. Gethin's 'Paul Hewitt' bike was approximately 17.5 lbs and Lynne's 'Orbea' just under 19 lbs. Both riders using carbon forks and aero wheels with approximately 16 flat blade spokes cutting down wind resistance from front and sides. The saddles nowadays are generally very narrow with gel inserts at strategic points for comfort, and titanium hollow rails for lightness. All fitted onto a thin aerodynamic carbon or aluminium seat post.

In the very late 80's Shimano developed a method of changing gear from the brake levers. It was developed in the Tour de France, ranging at the time from 8 speeds to 16 speeds. The gears are indexed and a gear change is made by swinging the brake lever over towards the centre of the bike till it clicks. Two or three sprockets can be jumped if you push the lever far enough enabling a rapid gear change. The one vast advantage with this method, also copied by Campagnolo, is that it allows the rider to stay in complete control of the handlebars with both hands while gear changing and even applying the brakes at the same time. Lynne used the Shimano version of the gearing and Gethin used the Campagnolo type.

One innovation I've failed to mention in all of this is the sealed bearing bottom bracket which has made maintenance in this area a thing of the past. Using neoprene seals round a roller bearing at each end all encapsulated in an aluminium shell, it also saves a lot of weight.

Finally, the latest modern introduction to technology that Lynne and Gethin both used - the A'head clamp on the handlebar stem allowing quick assembly and attachment to the forks, plus very easy headset bearing adjustment, all done using allen keys, also changing one's handlebars by just releasing the stem end cap, means various different positions can be tried without too much work involved.

I would estimate the cost of a bike using all of the popular lightweight components I've mentioned, to be in the region of £ 2,500. So compared with Paul Carbutt's 'Viking' made especially for that one purpose and costing £ 1000, today's bike which will withstand a lot of punishment appears to be excellent value. A clubman's bike with all these features and even with a triple chainset giving 27 speeds weighing in at just 20 lbs can cost as little as £ 800.

The only sad thing is the demise of the cycle making industry in England. I lived in Tyseley and worked in Birmingham and on my daily travels either to school or work on my BSA Tour of Britain racer, I would pass the Dawes Cycle factory in Tyseley with a few doors away from it Reynolds Tubing. Going through Small Heath to work I would pass the BSA factory where Oppermans 'Malvern Star' and Bob Maitlands 'Tour of Britain' and 'Tour de France' bikes were manufactured. I have just looked through a 1949 'Cycling' magazine and counted six adverts for saddles, all made in Birmingham: Brooks, Lycett, Mansfield, Wilby, Terry's and Wrights. The last three named were generally more utility saddles with lots of padding and springs. In the same magazine there were six cycle manufacturers all in the Birmingham area, four of them only a mile or two from my home: B.S.A., Dawes, James, Hercules, Armstrong and phillips. Component manufacturers were almost too numerous to mention: Cyclo Benelux, Bayliss-Wiley, T.D.Cross, Reynolds Tubes, Victree Bells, Monitor brakes, Ashby toe clips, TI Tubing, Oldbury, Midland Gearcase, Apex Pumps, Webbs Pedals, Brampton hubs and pedals, Miller Dynamos and Dunlop Tyres.

When I worked in Hockley, I would pass Cyclo Gears in Aston and surrounding Cyclo were lots of small plating and 'metal bashing' firms producing small parts for the bike, motor bike and car trade. Coventry and Nottingham were the other two large manufacturing towns in the industry. Now we have nothing at all.

The Raleigh factory has gone, everything is produced in either Vietnam, the Phillipines, China, Taiwan, Japan or India. Whether it be a cheap and cheerful bike, or a top end lightweight marketed by any of the major and specialist bike companies, you can bet that apart from Campagnolo which is purely Italian, and Mavic rims which are French, the rest of the products come from 'Pacific Rim' countries. Italy, France and Spain do actually produce their own, mainly racing bikes.

I even know of British companies who send out Reynolds tube sets to be tig welded in Poland and Czeckoslovakia and then get sent back here, painted and ready for assembly. There are of course exceptions to the rule. You still have small companies and individual frame makers such as 'Mercian' who produced Dick Poole's bike, and George Longstaff, who produced Eric Tremaine's trike and also Ralph Dadswell's machine. But all of these small Companies combined probably only supply about 5% of just the lightweight road bike market in the UK. I would say that since the 60's the continental road race scene including obviously 'The Tour' has had a great impact on what we determine as lightweight in England. End to Enders from the '60's onwards started to use Campagnolo gears and components; Carbutt, Coupe, Woodburn, up to Butler present day.

When the Americans started to become prominent on the European racing scene, more and more Japanese components got tried and tested and eventually more popular to club riders, for racing and leisure riding alike. Lynne's two solo rides along with both the mixed tandem rides of 1998 and 2000 were done on machines equipped with Shimano.

Saddles over the years have played a very important role in long distance racing. In the 40's, 50's and 60's, Brooks, Wrights or Lycett saddles would have been fitted to most lightweight road bikes. These saddles were made of leather, shaped and riveted onto a stiff wire frame. I rode a Lycett cut-away saddle which was a very thin strip of leather to sit on. Later when it was all the fashion, I switched to a Brooks 'Professional'. In the mid 60's plastic saddles had started to appear. Tradenames such as 'Unica' and 'Unicanitor' were two I used. They were made in Europe, and other club folks snubbed them preferring their leather ones.

By the 70's there was quite a range of 'leather skin' covered plastic saddles on the market, and by that time the micro-adjust seat post had also become available. It was called micro-adjust because you could do literally that; adjust angles and position with one or two allen keys or hexagon head metric bolts, making minute alterations, whereas the old steel brooks clips tended to flatten and distort after a while, leaving the saddle to shift if you went over a pothole. Dick Poole in 1965 looks to be using a plastic based saddle, the beauty was the fact that they didn't go out of shape when they were wet.

Nowadays, probably 95% of racing cycles are sold with a plastic based saddle with leather covered gel padding , all mounted on aluminium or titanium rails. 'Touring' cycles in the more expensive 'hand-built' section, tend to have Brooks saddles fitted. For the very lightest in weight, a carbon weave sheet is layered, shaped and moulded onto titanium rails, but it is generally used only over short distances due to its rigidity.

There have been many new innovations from the saddle companies. Gel padding has been introduced to some success. Pneumatic cushions at the rear of the saddle have also been tried. Oblong holes in the centre of the saddle, running long ways, have been introduced but any of these saddles can now cost up to £70. Lynne has experimented with various types of saddle over the years, including the ones mentioned above, but generally she does most of her miles on a basic, slim, 'San Marco' costing about £ 20. No one knows how comfortable a saddle will be until you've ridden a 12 hr or 24 hr on it, or even a 1000 miles !

One statistic I have overlooked is tyres, and I don't profess to know all the answers. I will however give details of the ones I do know. Marguerite Wilson and Lilian Dredge used Constrictor tyres on Conloy rims. Letts and Parker on tandem trike and Swinden and Withers on tandem all used standard sports tyres of the day. Reg Randall and John Woodburn were on tubulars. Mick Coupe and Andy Wilkinson were on Michelin 'Hi Lite' 700 x 23 slick tyres. Pat Kenny, Eric Tremaine and Paul Carbutt were on Clement tubulars. Ralph Dadswell rode Vittoria Corsa CX tyres on his trike. Jodi Groesbeck and Adrian Harris rode on Vredestein Fortezza 700 x 25 tyres on the mixed tandem. Lynne and Andy rode on Vredestein 26 x 1.3 slick mountain bike tyres on their mixed tandem record. Lynne on her first solo record rode Continental Grand Prix 700 x 23 tyres and the second time Veloflex Corsa 700 x 20 tyres. Finally Gethin Butler rode Continental Olympic 'B' tubulars but suffered punctures.

Lighting is a very important issue for End to Enders. Not much is known prior to 1929 about the lighting they used, but I learnt from Syd Parker that on his tandem trike record, he described the lights as being 'bobby dodgers'. Probably an Ever Ready front twin cell battery light and a small Pifco light at the rear, using a single U2 battery. Syd recalls how the lights used to flicker on and off on rough roads, a situation that hadn't improved even on Eric Tremaine's ride in 1982, some 35 years later. The main problems were the flimsy brass contacts soldered into the battery, and the spring contacts inside the lamp getting compressed. Tom Hughes in 1929 (Trike) was seen to be using a front hub dynamo, but rides done at the turn of the centurry would have used either oil, acetylene or carbide lamps.

The problem of poor lighting was the 'bane' of most cyclists. With dynamo's, one regularly 'blew' the bulbs going downhill, and the drag of the drive pulley on the side of the tyre made them impractical for fast night riding or racing. For a lot of End to Enders, that first night through Worcestershire and then the West Midlands, Staffordshire, Cheshire and Lancashire was difficult enough without worrying about having poor lights and incurring the wrath of motorists and police. Dick Poole, Pat Kenny, Eric Tremaine, and I'm sure many more, all had problems. I recall having to change Pat's front light on a regular basis on his trike record. In the end, a clip on French-made 'Wonder Lamp' was used with more success. I used this type of light, front and rear for 24 hr rides, and general night riding up until the late 90's when the vast improvement in rear lamps through the invention of 'l.e.d's or light emitting diodes, completely revolutionised the bike light industry.

The second night is just as important, except that there are fewer large towns to go through nowadays, so the rider isn't constantly worried about being stopped by police if a light failed. In recent years with the A9 by passing most villages and towns there really is only Perth to worry about. Most riders since the 30's have had following vehicles helping them with an observer or timekeeper on board. The headlights from these vehicles play a big part on this second night; obviously the time of the year one tackles this record affects visibility. Mid June would see a semi twilight the further north the rider managed to get, with virtual daylight returning at about 4 am or earlier in good weather. Both Lynne and Gethin's last solo rides 2001 and 2002 were done very late September into October and so required lights on as early as 6.30 pm, and staying on as long as 12 hours per night.

At about the same time as rear l.e.d. lights took over, the manufacturers came good with rechargeable front lights, using a 6 volt lead acid sealed battery which either fitted into a bottle cage or hung in a tough Velcro'ed pouch off the top tube of the bike. The lamps either single or double, could have a 2.5 watt bulb to give about 8 hrs of light, or 5 watt to give about 4 hours. Later, they introduced 10 and 20 watt bulbs which give fantastic light output, but would require at least 6 battery changes on just one night of the End to End. Apart from the 6 volt battery being relatively heavy, it proved to give a very reliable performance. Standard 'bulb using' front lamps running on small 'D' cell batteries had also improved by the late 90's, so by the time the frenzy of 'End to Ending' started in the year 2000, we had lots of well tested and well used light systems available. The Lynne and Andy mixed tandem used a 6 volt rechargeable system made by 'Smart' Lighting Co, and a 'Cateye' rear l.e.d, now built to British Standard. Both lights, front and rear, took only seconds to remove, and the same time to replace, for the second night. Lynne, on both her solo rides, used the very same lights in 2001 and 2002. Gethin used clip on compact front lamps on his ride, plus an l.e.d on the rear.

There is now a plethora of absolutely 'brilliant' lights and lighting systems on the market ranging from £ 15 for a front and rear compact set, to £ 300 plus for a specially developed system using a lightweight 'stick' shaped battery supplying a 10 or 20 watt bulb, with an incredible run time of 5 to 8 hrs, depending on bulb size and cost of battery.

I helped Lynne on the Mersey 24 hour race this year, 2004, and I've never seen such a high percentage of riders all with excellent lights. The system Lynne used was a very micro compact lightweight lamp, using 5 white 'l.e.d.'s and run on 3 x AAA batteries. The whole lamp weighing approximately 150 grams, and Cateye rear BSI approved l.e.d., weighing the same. The new front white l.e.d. lamps have revolutionised the cycle lighting forever. Being safe, very bright, in fact dazzling, and very reliable with very long run times from the batteries, all very light in weight and very affordable at £ 30 in total for front and rear. These new front lights have now been developed to throw a beam of light on the road. At last, cyclist's lighting has almost caught up with the car and motor bike industries, and its only taken 70 or 80 years to do it !

That just about 'sums up' the equipment , machines, clothing and training methods used by our End to End Heroes over the last 75 years. I've tried to list everything historically as it evolved, but I've also tried to include how it affected riders as they progressed to even greater average speeds over the distance. If I've repeated myself or jumped from subject to subject, it is for this reason.

I hope this gives the reader an insight as to the ever changing technology that has helped cyclists and particularly racing cyclist to keep ahead of their game. From the early steel tubed diamond shaped single speed bikes in Victorian times, to the modern aluminium and carbon fibre 20 and 30 speed models in the year 2004.

It enabled a man, G.P.Mills, in 1891 to cover the End to End route in 4 days 11 hrs 17 mins, using a heavy steel 'Ordinary' with solid tyres. By 1929 where this book starts, Jack Rossiter had reduced the time by nearly 2 days, with 2 days 13 hrs 22 mins without the use of ferries and riding a 3 speed steel framed, pneumatic tyred lightweight bicycle of the day. Now some 70 years after Rossiter, Gethin Butler has reduced it by the staggering amount of 16 hrs 18 mins to give a time of 1 day 20 hrs 4 mins 20 secs.

As I sit here at 10 o'clock at night putting the finishing touches to my pages on equipment etc, I learn that Marina Bloom, one of Lynne's team mates, has just established a new Womens RRA record from Pembroke to Great Yarmouth, a distance of some 347 miles, in 16 hrs 51 mins 56 secs, giving an average speed of over 20 mph. it's the middle of September 04, its been dark now for 3 hrs and raining heavily. Its been cold and windy enough for sweaters and long trousers in the house, so not exactly an 'Indian Summer' day. The wind was good for her from about Abergavenny onwards, but then turned into a crosswind in the latter half when it turned to a south westerly. She started at 5 am in the dark and finished just before 10 pm in the dark again. With this performance she has beaten the time standard set by the RRA by over 3 hours, and has also beaten the men's record put up last year by Chris Hopkinson, by over 6 minutes.

What a tremendous achievement so late in the season. This finishes off a successful season for Marina, having gained a PB in the Mersey 24 hr with 434 miles and also being part of the Walsall RCC Women's Competition Record Team again this year, for the 24 hrs and also the 12 hrs. At the shorter distances its been a mixed year for all of the team, Marina, Tracy and Lynne , having to chase events as late as September, trying to find a decent time trial course still in use, to get good BAR results. The bearer of this good news of the record was of course, Jim Turner who along with his wife Anne, has again managed the telephone HQ since before 5 am. Jim was over the moon, that's another successful RRA record he's organised. Tony Shardlow was the timekeeper who went all the way with them again, another successful record he has timed. He's now timed the End to End and the Coast to Coast. Mike Bloom, Marina's husband drove and helped in the main support vehicle. So a good day all round. I bet Eileen Sheridan will be proud of them all once again.

SECTION ELEVEN

WHAT MAKES A GOOD END TO END RIDER ?

I was asked recently "what makes a good End to Ender ?" and I've got to admit, there is no standard of ideal shape, size, age or height to be.

The women have ranged in height from Eileen Sheridan at 4ft 11" and nicknamed 'The Pocket Hercules' and Edith Atkins both ladies being 4ft 11" and 7 Stone, to Pauline Strong who is bordering on 5ft 10". The men have a similar height difference, from Reg Randall at 5ft 2" to Messrs Keeler and Duffield who were rated 'too tall' at 6ft 2" and 6ft 3" respectively.

So, your average woman is approximately 5ft 4" and man is 5ft 10". Lynne Taylor is 5ft 6" and has a racing weight of 8.5 stone. I would think the lightest man was probably Gethin Butler or Mick Coupe at about 10.5 stone and 5ft 10". The heaviest man would be Dave Keeler at 13 stone and 6ft 2". As long as they all have the ability to hoist their bodies up the hills, and their arms, shoulders and wrists are strong enough to support them for up to two days, that's all that matters.

I'm pretty sure in saying there's only one woman and one man on solo bikes who hadn't ridden above 12 hours in competition. In the case of Pauline Strong, a broken collar bone 6 weeks prior to the record prevented her riding a 24 hr before her attempt, and so she went into the 'unknown', what a brave endeavour. Paul Carbutt, although a winner of the Oldbury 12 hour and 'BAR' hero of the same year, turning professional for Viking, I would imagine prevented him from riding a 24 hr. I know he was also working regular hours as a pattern maker as well as being a professional at the weekends. He must, like Pauline, have gone into that first night not knowing what lay in store after midnight and beyond, not being used to sleep deprivation or losing the urge to eat and drink on the bike.

I think one of the qualities required for an 'End to Ender' is to be happy with your own company for hours on end. Don't forget, no radio, no music, no television, just your own thoughts. One or two riders have been known to sing out loud, whistle or even talk to themselves. Also the ability to carry on when the odds are against you; when a rider has dropped behind the actual times set by the previous record holder at a certain town along the route, or when you alter direction on course at say Bristol, where you veer almost north, or Carlisle where the road goes close to a left hand coast. The road from Inverness along that top north east coast can produce difficulties with a north east wind battering you for that last 120 mile section. Its where Gethin and I'm sure many others have suffered over the years. All these things must make you even more determined. I've seen riders in tears and that's not just the ladies, and riders being sick and still riding so as to save time.

So, if you're the sort of person who regularly climbs off when the weather gets rough, or when your opponent is two minutes up on you, or you can't stand a 'bad hair day' then I think the End to End is not for you. Another important quality you must possess is to be able to overcome sleep deprivation; it's a quality one must have, now that the men's and ladies records are so tight. If anyone said to me I need my regular 8 hours sleep at night, I would question their ability as a helper, let alone a rider. Obviously, adrenalin plays a large part in driving people on.

Wind exposure on the head should be avoided as much as possible, and people don't realise just how much energy they lose through heat going out of the top of their head without a cap or helmet on. Over exposure to the sun can have a similar effect, causing minor sun stroke. That's definitely affected riders in the last 5 years. In both cases they have to work harder to overcome the problem. So listen to your helper's advice, they may be able to see a problem arising that you, the rider, are not aware of.

Eyes need protection on these long distance records, and it makes sense to protect them with 'wrap around' clear or shaded glasses. I've had first hand experience with riders on the front of tandems or tandem trikes where a hat or helmet and definitely glasses would have improved their well being. Ideally, riders must be used to riding through the night.
Lynne experimented early on in her 24 hr races, wearing both helmet and glasses. If she has to take a quick shut-eye, its literally just enough to relax the eyelid muscles for approximately three to five minutes, then it's a quick wash and back on the road before her body shuts down. There is nowadays no margin of time on the men's or ladies record to take a proper sleep, only the odd 3 to 5 mins can be taken.

The worst time on the End to End is usually on the second night on the A9 over The Grampians. If its wet and the road is pitch black and doesn't reflect any light back to the eyes, it causes the rider to peer very hard at the surface or risk hitting a pot hole or the edge of the road. Even with the car's healights shining up the road the rider is quite often riding in their own shadow.

The first question a rider must ask themselves is "do I think I can do this, or am I kidding myself and everyone else ?" You must think in your own mind that you have a damn good chance and that you can let your body and mind take what can only be described as a self-inflicted flogging for two days and nights plus.

One common denominator to most of the riders of both sexes is a very smooth, almost effortless, economical pedalling style. I've seen either personally, or on film, at least 10 of the record breakers since the 1960's and they all have this wonderfully fluid style, gliding along at 20 to 25 mph for hour after hour. Maybe this is their secret. Two exceptions to this in the past have been Hubert Opperman and Reg Randall, both of whom had very 'punchy' aggressive styles of riding.

For the ladies, the only way to beat Lynne is to have a very good wind for the first 24 hours and produce say a 440 mile 24 hour, then hope to have similar conditions for the second 24 hrs, and hang on to a reasonable speed. Lynne had virtually no help from the weather in the first 24 hrs of both rides, plus hours of relentless rain on both. The turning point on her last record in 2002 was around the Inverness area after being hours down up to that point in the ride. She suddenly picked up a breeze that instead of being against her, actually helped her for the first time. She went from being nearly 1.5 hours down on schedule, to breaking her own record by over an hour. That's the difference between fighting the elements and having the elements with you. Then of course, there's the small detail of riding another 170 miles to get the 1000 miles record, which took another 11 hours 52 minutes to complete, including a 1 hr 17 mins break at John o Groats.

For the men, they must be capable of beating Gethin in a 24 hr race, capable of doing 510 miles for 24 hours even with a very good wind, and then they must be capable of hanging on at 17 mph for the last 330 miles. Then there is the 1000 to finish off at 14 mph. I'm sure there's someone out there who can do it, but only time will tell.

I know most record breakers are very 'headstrong' people, that's why they think they can do this, but if you are attempting it and the team of helpers are mainly people you know and trust for their decisions; listen to them; take heed of their suggestions, especially if they've helped on an End to End before. If they tell you to lower your gears, because they can see you are struggling, give it a try. Don't battle on if its going chilly and they say 'your skin feels cold, put your tights and long sleeve top on'.

After the first 12 hours you start feeling tired and from then on you are in the hands of the helpers. Don't tax your brain working out how fast you've got to go to get the record. Let the helpers work that out, and trust in them.

Although it isn't essential, try and find helpers who have been on a 12 hr or 24 hr with you so that there is a mutual bond already.

And finally, good luck !

I hope I haven't made it sound too impossible a task !

"I THOUGHT YOU WOULD HAVE HAD SOMEBODY IN THE CAR WHO CAN CHANGE A WHEEL."

SECTION TWELVE

THOSE WHO COULD/MIGHT HAVE MADE IT - WOMEN

When looking for women riders who could have challenged Eileen's record End to End, I have only got past records of Championship 24 hrs, Mersey RC result sheets and RTTC Comp record tables for my source of information.

My first contender would have been **Christine Minto - nee Moody**. She improved the 24 hours Competition record three years running with a best ride of 427 miles in 1969. I didn't know Christine at that time, but I must have ridden in the same events as her on those occasions.

I knew **Joan Kershaw** who won the ladies Mersey event with 422 miles in 1970. Joan was a very smooth fixed wheel rider and beat lots of men, including myself, in 100's, 12hrs, and 24 hrs. I remember her catching me in the Oldbury 12 hour, out at Burton on Trent in about 1960. In those days the A38 was a single carriageway road and her encouragement as she passed meant a lot to me.

Ann Mann in 1983 produced the next Competition record with 438 miles. When you consider their 24 hr performances, compared with Lynne's, and the fact that they would have been trying to beat 2 days 11 hours 7 mins and not Pauline Strong's 2 days 6 hrs 49 mins, I think they would all have stood a very good chance of either the amateur or professional record at that time. It would be interesting to see the results. After all, Lynne's first 24 hours in her first solo End to End was 420 miles and on her second solo End to End it was 410 miles.

Of course, I've forgotten one very famous lady who dominated the women's time trial scene from 1958 to 1986 **Beryl Burton** of the Morley CC. Beryl won the Women's BBAR for 25 years running and in that time produced sub four hour 100 mile rides and 277 miles for a 12 hour, beating all of the men in a Championship event in 1967.

Beryl did ride one 24 hr and that was in 1969, the year Roy Cromack produced 507 miles and set a new Competition record. Beryl rode the same event as Roy which was the Mersey RC 24 hr. She went virtually flat out from the start, probably the only way she knew to produce a winning result. She passed the 12 hour point way out in front of the field, but in the middle of the night at about the 300 miles mark, she suffered terrible pains in her knees, and retired while still ahead of the field. Cromack taking the ride at a steadier pace won the event and the rest, as they say, is history.

Beryl 'on paper' could have got the End to End, but would she have been able to have contained her speed in the earlier stages so as not to blow up later in the ride ? **Alas, we shall never know.**

Towards the end of the 80's, two women riders emerged **Bridget Boon** and **Christine Roberts.** Starting with Bridget who rode her first 24 hour races on a tandem in the 80's with her husband Ian, she went on to become a very tough solo competitor in long distance events. 1993 in particular was a very good year.

One month after taking second place to Christine Roberts in the Mersey RC 24 hr with 446.88 miles, Bridget won the North Road CC 24 hr beating all of the men, in an outright victory with 457.16 miles. Some eleven years later in 2004, this mileage is still the second greatest distance ever by a woman, after Christine's 461.45 miles.

Bridget beat the male runner up by nearly 40 miles to become the first and only woman to win an RTTC 24 hr time trial Now here is someone who in my estimation could have got the RRA 24 hr, End to End, and 1000 mile records around that time. Her performance wasn't just a 'one off' ride. It was a culmination of club riding, touring, long distances on the tandem, in fact, Bridget and Ian would have been ideal for the mixed tandem End to End.

Bridget was 34 years old at the time, an ideal age for an attempt. She was not only a time triallist, but also helped and marshalled in local events and was always in the Bristol area when an End to End went through. In an earlier Mersey 24 hr I remember my lights failing on the Shawbirch detour. Bridget and Ian came to help and lent me a set of lights which lasted all night. Such sportsmanship !

Christine Roberts, I have written about in Glorious Abandonments.

THOSE WHO COULD/MIGHT HAVE MADE IT - MEN

When looking through the results of the men's 24 hour races from the late 50's there are the names of many riders who either produced high mileages or regular wins, sometimes both. Some winning rides were done in atrocious conditions and weren't particularly high mileages, but never the less, all of these competitors I am about to mention would have been possible 'End to End' candidates.

At one time there were as many as four '24 hr' races in a year, possibly more. The Mersey RC, The North Road CC, Catford CC, Wessex RC, special promotions for the RTTC and regional events such as the 'Scottish 24 hr'. The importance of riding a 24 hr event I think is paramount, not just for the riders state of mind, but also for the support crew and officials to know that they are not wasting their time. In the history of the 'End to End' there are not many successful riders, male or female on various machines, who have not completed a 24 hr race of one type or another. i.e. Either a fast randonee-audax such ås Paris-Brest-Paris, RRA or regional RRA 24 hr record, or RTTC 24 hr. I can only think of two or three at the most.

The main event I either rode in or helped in from 1960 onwards, was the Mersey RC 24 hr, and occasionally the North Road CC event. I've actually seen most of these rider's I'm about to mention, in action, in these events. Prior to this date (1960) I've either had first hand knowledge passed onto me by club folk or by avidly reading 24 hr fellowship journals.

Starting with the 50's into the 60's - **P.E.A. (Nick) Carter** had four Mersey RC 24 hr wins with a best mileage of 464 miles. **Eddie Mundy** won the North Road 24 hr in 1952 with 467 miles. **John Arnold** on bike 466 miles, trike 457 miles. **Ron Coukham** 24 hr champion in 1959 with

468 miles. **Stuart Thompson** broke comp record twice with 469 miles and 474 miles in 1954 and 1955. **Ken Usher** who won two Mersey events, his best being 474 miles in 1962. **Arch. Harding** and **Fred Burell** were both older team mates of Dick Poole's. They both won 24 hr championship titles. Arch won the 'Mersey' in 1961 with 470 miles, and Fred did two almost identical rides of 477 miles to win two championships, usually on a single speed gear bike. **Dennis White**, Swindon Wheelers, the first man to beat 'evens' (480 miles) for a 24 hr race, broke comp record twice with 484.64 miles in 1956 and 484.75 miles in 1958.

Cliff Smith was nicknamed 'Smiler' and was a prolific 24 hr man, riding 38 events in all winning many races with rides over 470 miles. He always rode a Raleigh 'Record Ace' with a 3 speed hub gear. It didn't matter how much he was suffering he had always got a smile on his face. Cliff was a lot older than most of his adversaries, having spent a long time after his war service, with his back encased in a cumbersome body support, unable to move much at all. He was an Artillery man and his spine had suffered damage from the heavy 'pounding' while working with the big guns. In fact when you looked at him ride, you wondered just how he managed to go so fast for so long. Cliff Smith broke the London to Edinburgh record in 1965 in atrocious conditions, including snow blizzards. He was what I would describe as an 'iron man' almost indestructible.

Another superb rider at the time was **Eric Mathews** of the Altrincham RC. He won the Mersey RC 24 hr in 1963 with 473 miles, and then broke comp record the following year with a massive 490 miles. The same year that Roy Cromack pushed Comp record up to 507 miles, Eric turned out a 492 mile ride. His last Mersey win was in 1968 with 486 miles followed by winning the championship with 489 miles. From this you can see his mileages were consistently high enough to have a shot at the 'Blue Riband' of all records. He was such a smooth rider, although he did turn fairly high gears, being tall he made it look so easy. We will never know what Eric was fully capable of or what his views were on the End to End. Eric died after a long illness in 1989 from Septicaemia. To us all, he was a very respected rider.

Another hard man at that time was **Howard Bailey** of the Solihull CC. He rode mainly on a trike and was a big 'mile-eater'. He won the Mersey 24 hr in 1966 with 462 miles on a bike. His only weak point was his eyesight and when nightfall came in the Mersey he slowed slightly. Stan Bray, his team mate from the Solihull CC told me about the colossal training rides Howard used to do. Living out in the country, his club night round trip was 80 miles plus.

A rider I didn't see much of, due to his living closer to the North Road CC course, was **George Bettis.** His best mileage being 493miles in 1973. He was always a 'top five' rider and was a keen advocate of rice pudding made to his own recipe. Apparently that was his main food in a 24 hr event. George was another high training mileage enthusiast. He won the Championship 24 hr in 1972 with 470 miles and in 1976 with 482 miles.

John Cahill, Mick Coupe's cousin and club mate would have been another serious contender in the 1980's. He won the Championship three times with 469 miles, 477 miles and 482 miles, also getting team comp record in 1979 and 1980 and nine championship team wins between 1975 and 1987. His massive training mileages would have been ideal for the job. His top 24 hr mileage was 497 miles in 1980. Like Eric Mathews, John died relatively early.

Stuart Jackson won the Championship 24 hr medal three years running in 1982, 83 and 84, and once again in 1988. His mileages were all high ones, 496, 488 494 and 481. Stuart was a very confident rider who broke no less that 5 solo tricycle records and 6 tandem tricycle records with Edwin Hargraves. He could have contested the End to End on either the bike, trike or tandem trike.

Ian Dow of the Oxford City RC with three consecutive 24 hr championship wins of 480 miles in 1985, 488 miles in 1986 and 500 miles in 1987, would have been on the favourites list in the late '80's. He was such a smooth pedaller often riding a fixed wheel bike and looking comfortable and confident.

There were obviously other riders at the time who were good long distance men, winning events and performing good mileages such as **Stan Turner,** 480 miles, **Mick Potts** 486 miles, **Ian Butcher** 493 miles, **'Ticker' Mullins** 485 miles, **Rod Goodfellow** with a string of high mileages and wins. **Robin Buchan** 483 miles, **Glen Longland** who actually submitted an 'End to End' schedule in 1998 after winning the 24 hr Championship in 1994 with 475 miles, and won the 12 hour championship no less than 5 times, his best mileage being 291 miles. He also produced 12 hour Comp Record three times, his best being 300.08 in 1991.

My apologies for any omissions from this illustrious list of contenders, no doubt there will be somebody you think was worthy of a mention, but I feel that given the right wind and conditions, any of these riders I've mentioned, stood as much chance as anyone else of breaking the record, at the 'peak' of their careers.

My guess is that quite a high percentage of these riders I've mentioned would have asked themselves 'I wonder if I could have got the End to End record' ?

"NO, JOHN O' GROATS IS THAT WAY."

SECTION THIRTEEN

RECOLLECTIONS

I recently received a couple of letters sent to me by Margaret Ray, the widow of Alan J Ray, the author of 'Cycling Lands End to John o Groats'.

The first letter was dated **6th January 1970** from Eileen Sheridan with some last minute details for Alan's book that was published in 1971. In the letter Eileen answers Alan's question of why she went for the End to End, and this went as follows:

"As an amateur I couldn't afford to do many records, but it was always an ambition to go for place to place records and the End to End was a great challenge even though I was paid for it. The money doesn't help when the wind conditions are wrong, believe me, in fact it is a greater strain when you have a big company expecting results !

I was extremely lucky in having a jolly manager to look after me, if I had been mentally unhappy I couldn't have gone through some of the tough times. The elements were so changeable on the John o Groats ride, I don't think I shall ever forget the great pain I suffered from the cold going down the Grampians. Record breaking is such a lonely sport that one must have a very happy personality to keep going. It is so entirely different from time trialling, that it is always difficult to say how anyone would do (you asked me about Beryl Burton). One just can't say how anyone will react on such a journey. Tommy Barlow once said "any fool can get to Perth!". I felt sure that Ken Joy would easily manage it, he had the power and the backing.

You know I always rode with very little to eat (London to Edinburgh, solid food was one chicken leg only), and just hot soups and fruit drinks such as 'Ribena'. On the End to End I realise now I should have taken much more solid food, it would have made a great difference to my performance, it was my fault, and I didn't realise it at the time. After I stopped during the '1000' and had bacon and eggs, I rode strongly at the end - a bit too late !

It was the most wonderful feeling to be fit - effortless riding, being a complete part of my machine, I loved every moment. The hard times were a challenge it was simply fulfilling - a very satisfying feeling! Sometimes my hard rides and slower performances were more thrilling, I suppose one knew when one had given their best.

Time trials are faster now because one always strives to beat the fastest times, and super riders like Beryl are born rarely - she is in a class of her own. The traffic on the roads today helps speed, and the women can race among the men which pulls out that little extra.

I wish you every success on your book sales, it will I am sure, be a book that will open the eyes of other sporting people."

Sincerely Eileen Sheridan.

The second letter was a thin Air mail letter to Alan J Ray from Hubert Opperman at the Australian High Commission Office in Malta, dated **3rd November 1971**. I have picked out some relevant paragraphs from Hubert's letter to Alan.

"Dear Alan,

I received one of the most pleasant surprises of my life, when your comprehensive history of the 'Lands End to John o Groats' arrived.

First, I must say, the warmest of congratulations. You have linked most effectively, extremely valuable historic cycling data concerning this grand old event.

I can assure you I have read the vivid and illuminating accounts of the trials and tribulations, experienced by so many throughout the years of pedalling endeavour, with a great feeling of pride at having been one of their number. It represents a wonderful asset to cycling , to have record attempts registered in such sentimental and chronological detail.

Thank you for being so generous towards myself. I always felt a regret at having taken the record from that excellent sportsman, Jack Rossiter.

Having competed in France and been toughened mentally and physically, and with judgement sharpened by the essential close study of material, roads and opponents, I knew because of the contrast in his preparation and equipment, that the record must fall my way. It is therefore with respect and a salution, I read your tribute to his hours awheel. I always felt he was one of the last true amateurs, with his record lowered by the first of a new breed of professionals.

Although I have not as yet fully studied all of the attempts you describe, I am pleased to note the references to women riders. Their feats of stamina are really stupendous. I always had an extra degree of admiration for Marguerite Wilson. In addition to physical prowess, she had a photogenic personality, which added an extra touch of distinction to her remarkable returns of time and distance.

Currently, of course, the Burton girl is simply phenomenal. It used to be said of world sprinters, Frank Kramer and Bob Spears, that on their day they rose from class champions into a super standard of superiority. Beryl is just such a one.

I note your reference to black tights. These certainly astonished us, and Milliken and Stuart invariably referred to them as the 'undertakers outfit'. After being accustomed to what was by contrast continental flamboyance, we used to shrink away from the public gaze as rapidly as possible when in this sombre garb. Paradoxically enough, today the European riders in training, and even girls in street dress, wear tights, almost similar to the ones in which we felt so embarrassed.

Our greatest concern though, was for safety. At night (before 'Scotchlite') in a complete black outfit with a car, by regulation, one hundred yards in the rear, one was practically lost in the shadow of trees on narrow roads.

We compromised and created new rules from the old ones which stipulated being dressed from neck to ankle in a dark costume. I discarded the alpaca jacket (wind resisting with its pockets and buttoned front) and had special continental type rear pocket cashmere sweaters made. Then I wore a white cap with white socks peeping discreetly below the ankle.

The London to York attempt was held up for half an hour while these details were discussed and checked with the rule book. Finally it was accepted, at least the cars headlights could now pick up the lighter coloured cap and socks.

Thanks for the book with a shake hand across the years, and best wishes".

Yours sincerely 'Oppy'

Johnny Helms - Thoughts on an 'End to End' - 'Magical Memories'

Most people know 'Helms' for the famous cartoons that he has produced on a weekly basis for various cycling magazines and publications over a period of some 55 years at least. A lot of people know him equally as a clubman cyclist who has raced, toured, and observed on record attempts.

He has spoken at many club dinners over the years. His cartoons are always topical, thought invoking and comical. In the past I've enjoyed some of his characters, 'Baz' and 'Honk' being two favourites. His 'snarling chasing dog', Lynne, myself, and I am sure many other cyclists have experienced in the past. His experiences as a marshall, observer or 'pusher off' have shone through in many of his cartoons.

Living in Widnes which is close to Warrington, means he is virtually 'on course' to see the End to Enders through. John has seen most of the record breakers on this historic route since 1948. He jotted down a few random thoughts about his years of checking riders through Warrington.

Jim Letts on trike was his first in 1948 although it was unsuccessful. John recalls it was Saturday dinnertime when Letts arrived, in those days people worked a five and a half day week, finishing at Saturday midday. All the factories were shutting and thousands of workers were going home on their bikes. Jim Letts on his trike just couldn't get through, John reckons it took Jim about 10 minutes to cover just 200 yards at one point.

The main difference over the years is the time at which the riders reach Warrington. The records get faster and faster and whereas in the late 'forties' a rider would be due at Warrington at dawn, they can now be there at midnight or soon after. John said that years ago it was simple. The rider went straight through the centre of the town, but nowadays a by pass is used which requires a lot more marshalls and checkers. With dwindling numbers of club folk the town has become harder to marshall. A few years ago the checkers would ring up from home and find out from the telephone HQ as to the rider's progress and what time they were needed 'on duty'. John recalls being in position on quite a few occasions and waiting for hours, usually in the rain, only to find out that the rider had abandoned a few miles before reaching Warrington.

On all but the men's solo record there is leeway to be up to two hours or more behind schedule at Warrington and still get the record, and he recalls riding to work at 6am a number of times, after being out all night waiting for a rider to appear.

Drunks in the town centres are a problem on an operation like this, with Wolverhampton, Stafford, Stone, Congleton, and Warrington all being hotspots for both the marshalls and riders. John still thinks there are better ways through many of the towns and suburbs than are currently being used, and that record organisers are not putting local club folks knowledge of an area to good use. Despite all of this he still has 'magical memories' and as he said in an article in The Cycling Magazine in 1987 'If you get a chance to see a record bid, do not miss it' !

My thanks to Johnny Helms for this information and for his permission to use a few very relevant cartoons.

"I caught him loitering near the bank, and he told me some cock-and-bull story about waiting for somebody riding a tricycle from Land's End to John O'Groats!"

SECTION 14

"WILL WOMENS (OR MENS) 'END TO END' EVER BE BETTERED" ?

Extracts from an article by George Herbert Stancer (G.H.S) written in 'Cycling' July 22nd 1954 :

"The scintillating quality of the two End to End rides reported last week bears the strong suggestion that this chapter of cycling history, perhaps the most stirring and romantic of all, is approaching its close. It would be rash to say that we shall not see another woman to equal Eileen Sheridan. Many people felt like that about her great predecessor, Marguerite Wilson.

What must be taken into account however, is that the 'Groats' record will not only call for a woman of Mrs Sheridan's exceptional powers of endurance, but will need the same elaborate and well conceived organization, at least equally good weather conditions, and the financial backing, without which such a tremendous undertaking will in future be impossible. Hence the chances of another girl being given the opportunity of eclipsing Eileen's figures must be rated as rather remote.

Eileen Sheridan was the first to say that her triumph over the End to End and 1000 miles was a dual affair, with Frank Southall playing a major part in the success. Eileen had complete faith in the man who had designed her record breaking career. Before the start of her epic record, these were her instructions to Frank. "If I should cry or want to stop when I shouldn't you must make me go on. If I want an hours sleep and you think I should have only 15 minutes, waken me when the quarter hour has gone by and tell me I've had an hour."

Such delicate and touching words, but of course, GHS had reckoned without the determination of 'girls' such as Pauline Strong in 1990 and then Lynne Taylor in 2001 and again in 2002. How good the benefit of hindsight is. Certain records, I think can still be attainable by a racing fit, hard riding, club person. These records are all RRA Standards:

End to End Womens Trike	4 days 12 hours	Womens 1000 miles Trike	5 days
End to End Womens tandem	3 days 12 hours	Womens 1000 miles Tandem	4 days 12 hrs
End to End Womens tandem trike	4 days	Womens 1000 miles tandem trike	4 days 12 hrs
End to End mixed tandem trike	3 days 7 hrs	Mixed tandem trike 1000 miles	4 days
And finally -		Mixed tandem - 1000 miles	3 days 12 hrs

Knowing that Crimes and Arnold lost a lot of hours through illness on their End to End, I think it feasible for for two good 24 hr riders and End to Enders such as Gethin Butler and Andy Wilkinson, if they got similar weather to Albert and John, they would get the end to end on tandem trike. Another combination would be Ralph Dadswell and Dave Brabbin, but whether any of them would want to is the question.

Another record where time was lost through hospitalization is the Swinden and Withers End to End on tandem in 1966. If you take off the time lost it puts the record inside two days. The only problem is finding two riders of exceptional quality to do it. Crimes and Arnold and Swinden and Withers rode so compatibly together and both teams were the fastest at the time on the End to End route for the 24 hours with crimes and Arnold being the fastest on any machine at the time for the End to End and 1000 miles.

Knowing how Ralph Dadswell lost time from the borders onwards with sleep deprivation and loss of motivation, losing possibly 2 hours towards the end, I think there is room for someone to prune a few minutes off his End to End. The only problem is that there are no young trike riders to be seen riding the distance events any more, in fact, any events. In fact, the average age of the time trialling trikie is probably 55.

For the mixed tandem or tandem trike records it has to be Ralph Dadswell and Marina Bloom. For the womens tandem and tandem trike it has to be Marina and Lynne. After all this surmising, one still can't rule out Tracey Maund , also a Walsall Roads Ladies Team rider who has turned out some excellent rides, to clinch 3rd place in the BAR this year - 2004 - beating Lynne and Marina into 5th and 6th place.

All three of them could contest any of the vacant ladies End to End and 1000 mile titles on different machines. If you study the records and time trial results you will realise that apart from Christine Roberts in recent years, these three riders have consistently swept the board at 12 hrs and 24 hrs and have put up Competition Records at 100 miles, 12 hrs and 24 hrs, in years 2003 and 2004. One lady rider who excels at all distances including 100 miles is Ruth Eyles from the Beacon Roads CC who seems to get better, the farther she rides, so perhaps another contender for the 'Blue Riband'.

When you read through any of the reports, barring Gethins's, I think you will have realised that either through bad weather or adverse winds, illness, physical problems or tiredness, there is time to come off all of the records. But, as I mentioned in another part of the book, there's one Kevin Dawson, nine times 'BAR' winner, but he hasn't ridden a 24 hr yet. So come on Jim Turner, work your magic on him; offer him the best day out he's ever had in his life; get Doug Clark to send him an entry form for the Mersey RC 24 hr 2005.

Finally, a dedication to Margaret Hopper, a stalwart supporter of long distance riders. She boosted Lynne's spirits on many occasions. Margaret passed away in March 2005 after a short illness. We miss her.